DIVINING SLAVERY AND FREEDOM

Since its original 2008 publication in Brazil, *Divining Slavery and Freedom* has been extensively revised and updated in this first English translation, complete with new primary sources and an updated bibliography. It tells the story of Domingos Sodré, an African-born priest who was enslaved in Bahia, Brazil, in the nineteenth century. After obtaining his freedom, Sodré became a slave owner himself, and in 1862 he was arrested on suspicion of receiving stolen goods from slaves in exchange for supposed "witchcraft." Using this incident as a catalyst, this book discusses African religion and its place in a slave society, analyzing its double role as a refuge for blacks as well as a bridge between classes and ethnic groups (such as whites who attended African rituals and sought help from African diviners and medicine men). Ultimately, *Divining Slavery and Freedom* explores the fluidity and relativity of conditions such as slavery and freedom, African and local religions, and personal and collective experience and identities in the lives of Africans in the Brazilian diaspora.

João José Reis is a professor of history at the Universidade Federal da Bahia, Brazil. An award-winning historian and lifetime honorary foreign member of the American Historical Association, he has published extensively on the history of slavery in nineteenth-century Brazil.

H. Sabrina Gledhill is the author of many scholarly articles, essays, and book chapters on Afro-Brazilian history and culture and has translated more than thirty books.

NEW APPROACHES TO THE AMERICAS

Edited by Stuart Schwartz, Yale University

Also Published in the Series:

DIVINING SLAVERY AND FREEDOM

THE STORY OF DOMINGOS SODRÉ, AN AFRICAN PRIEST IN NINETEENTH-CENTURY BRAZIL

João José Reis

TRANSLATED BY
H. Sabrina Gledhill

CAMBRIDGE
UNIVERSITY PRESS

CAMBRIDGE
UNIVERSITY PRESS

32 Avenue of the Americas, New York, NY 10013-2473, USA

Cambridge University Press is part of the University of Cambridge.

It furthers the University's mission by disseminating knowledge in the pursuit of
education, learning, and research at the highest international levels of excellence.

www.cambridge.org
Information on this title: www.cambridge.org/9781107439092

First published in Portuguese as *Domingos Sodré, um sacerdote africano* 2008
First English edition published 2015

Printed in the United States of America

A catalog record for this publication is available from the British Library.

Library of Congress Cataloging in Publication Data
Reis, João José.
[Domingos Sodré, um sacerdote africano. English]
Divining slavery and freedom : the story of Domingos Sodré, an African priest in
nineteenth-century Brazil / João José Reis; translated by H. Sabrina Gledhill.
pages cm. – (New approaches to the Americas)
Includes bibliographical references and index.
ISBN 978-1-107-07977-9 (hbk) – ISBN 978-1-107-43909-2 (pbk.)
1. Sodré, Domingos, –1887. 2. Slaves – Brazil – Bahia (State) – Biography.
3. Freedmen – Brazil – Bahia (State) – Biography. 4. Slavery – Brazil – Bahia (State) –
History – 19th century. 5. Blacks – Brazil – Bahia (State) – Social conditions –
19th century. 6. Bahia (Brazil: State) – Social conditions – 19th century.
7. Candomblé (Religion) – Brazil – Bahia (State) – History – 19th century. I. Title.
HT869.S55R4513 2015
306.3'62092–dc23   2014047358

ISBN 978-1-107-07977-9 Hardback
ISBN 978-1-107-43909-2 Paperback

For Stuart Schwartz
and
Katia Mattoso, in memoriam

CONTENTS

Preface

At 4:30 P.M. on July 25, 1862, a Friday, an African freedman named Domingos Pereira Sodré was arrested in his home in Salvador, the capital of Bahia, then a province in northeastern Brazil. He had been personally reported to the chief of police by a customs officer who accused him of receiving goods that slaves had stolen from their masters as payment for his divining sessions and for "witchcraft." His accuser, whose charges were immediately investigated, was himself a slave owner and one of the alleged victims. *Candomblé* – the term that the police chief used to describe what was going on in the African's home – was already in vogue at the time to denote religious beliefs and practices of African origin, or purported to be, as well as the place of worship. I will use the same broader meaning of the term in this book. Candomblé, it should be said from the start, is a spirit possession religion primarily based in Bahia, but also found in different parts of Brazil. It ranks as one of the most popular Afro-Brazilian religions, which also include Umbanda, Batuque, and Xangô, terms that are sometimes also used to refer to Candomblé.

More than twenty years ago, I came across the first documents pertaining to Domingos Sodré's arrest, which consist of a number of official letters exchanged between the chief of police, Antônio de Araújo Freitas Henriques, and the *subdelegado* (deputy chief constable) for the parish of São Pedro, Pompílio Manoel de Castro, where Domingos Sodré lived. These sources led me to others that enabled me to broaden the focus on the incident that took place in 1862. I went after information regarding the African freedman accused of witchcraft and theft and unearthed a great deal. He was born in Lagos, in what is now Nigeria, and was captured and sold to transatlantic slave traders under

unknown circumstances. After arriving in Bahia, he became a slave
on the property of a major sugar planter in the Recôncavo, as the fertile lands that surround the Bay of All Saints are called, and there are
strong indications that he won his freedom upon his master's death.
I do not know when Domingos moved from the countryside to the City
of Bahia, as Salvador was known at the time, but I found him there for
the first time in the mid-1840s, in the baptismal records, standing godfather. By this time he was a freedman. Domingos prospered in the city,
apparently as a merchant, and became a slaveholder himself, which
I discovered in deeds of purchase and sale and letters of manumission
registered by several notaries in Salvador, who also registered the purchase and sale of two houses that he owned. Domingos got married in
a Catholic church, became a widower, and married again, according to
the parish records. I have found that on at least two occasions, he took
other African freedmen to court, one of whom he accused of murdering a friend of his. When he was near death, he dictated his last will
and testament, leaving his few earthly possessions to his wife, Maria
Delfina da Conceição. His probate records tell the story of his final
illness, death, and funeral rites.

The sheer volume of information found so far about Domingos
Sodré – and more is bound to appear – makes him an exception,
although not the only case, among Africans brought to Brazil as slaves.
However, while it has been possible to shed light on several aspects
of his life story, we are still in the dark about many others. Therefore,
our protagonist frequently leaves the center stage in this book to give
way to the world he lived in and to the other characters that peopled
it, through whom his story is largely told. This narrative method – call
it micro-historic – fits well in any biography, because everyone lives in
a certain context, whether immediate or broader, in which other individuals belong, with varying degrees of proximity. Naturally, the documents available to recount the history of the barons of slave society in
monarchical Brazil are, as a rule, more abundant than those for slaves
or freedpersons. The biographies of the latter are more fragmented, and
necessarily full of gaps. Nevertheless, in addition to illuminating many
aspects of specific life experiences, they serve as a guide that enables us
to get to know a time, a society, and particularly the men and women
who peopled this world, many of whom made up the social networks of
the subjects of those biographies, with their ethnic differences; social
and economic ranks; and institutional, social, political, and cultural
practices.

Sodré's life in Brazil covered most of the nineteenth century. The century is full of landmarks in that country's history. In 1808, the Portuguese court migrated to Brazil, fleeing Napoleon's troops, and stayed there until the return of King João VI in 1821, leaving his son Pedro as regent. Prince Pedro proclaimed independence from Portugal the following year and became Brazil's often despotic – although with the title of "constitutional" – emperor for almost ten years until, under popular pressure and amid political turmoil, he abdicated the crown on behalf of his infant son, Pedro II, in 1831. For the next ten years, under successive regents, a series of regional, federalist, and liberal revolts shook the country from north to south, until the mid-1840s. Pedro II's reign was long and generally peaceful, except for a five-year war against Paraguay (1864–1870) in alliance with Uruguay and Argentina. The monarchy was abolished in 1889, in part because the emperor had lost support from land and slave owners dissatisfied with the abolition of slavery the year before.

Slavery had reached its peak during the imperial regime, having been kept untouched after independence, despite isolated voices who recommended its reformation. Since the beginning of the nineteenth century the slave trade had intensified manifold to provide the workforce for the sugar plantations and cattle ranches in the northeast, the sugar and coffee plantations in the southeast, the salted meat industry in the extreme south, as well as cities, towns, and villages all over the country. But slavery was not just the domain of major planters and ranchers. All sectors of agriculture, including small and medium-sized farms dedicated to sugar, cotton, and tobacco for export and to food production for internal consumption, used slave labor. Slaves could be found everywhere in the labor structure. Besides toiling as field workers, they were employed as miners, metalworkers, domestics, artisans, porters, barber-surgeons, fishermen, sailors, and in every occupation in the "mechanics" and building trades, to name just a few. In the cities, the ownership of one, two, and three slaves by people of lesser means was widespread, especially until 1850, when the transatlantic slave trade was definitively banned, having resisted, through officially tolerated contraband, the first legal attempt to abolish it in 1831. After 1850, however, a vigorous internal slave trade persisted and transferred thousands of enslaved men and women primarily from the decadent sugar-planting northeast to the prosperous coffee-growing southeast. But the decline of the slave population was inevitable when the African traffic ended, and it intensified after the 1871 "Free Womb" law that freed children born to slaves.

Already at the beginning of the century, way before the end of the slave trade, a large and fast-growing free Afro-Brazilian population had been formed, which substantially outnumbered the slave population by mid-century. Partly because of manumission, a particularly widespread phenomenon in Brazil, free and freed people, including the African-born, would become especially vital to the economic, social, and cultural fabric of major cities like Rio de Janeiro, Recife, and Salvador, among others. Although patron-client relationships functioned as a powerful mechanism of social control, poor Africans and Afro-Brazilians would become a source of concern because of their potential or actual support and participation, often in positions of leadership, in the social and political conflicts of that time.

Domingos Sodré either witnessed or participated in several of the processes that stand as the foundation of modern Brazil. When he disembarked in Bahia around the mid to late 1810s, he found a region that was experiencing a period of prosperity strongly linked to its main source of wealth – sugar production. Sugarcane was grown and processed in the plantations of the Recôncavo, primarily by African-born slaves, whose numbers rose dramatically when the slave trade intensified to keep pace with the triumph of Bahia's plantation economy. Domingos was one of the numerous victims of that Atlantic boom. In the land that enslaved him, he saw dozens of slave rebellions rise and fall on the plantations of the Recôncavo and in Salvador and its surroundings in the first half of the 1800s. Between 1820 and 1840, Domingos also witnessed major transformations and recurring political crises, starting with the struggles for independence from Portugal, followed by anti-Portuguese riots, federalist and republican movements, military uprisings, and a revolt against the ban on church burials. In the following decades, he saw a general strike of African street workers and a food riot, at a time when the city of Bahia was reorganizing its urban landscape by building roads and plazas, diversifying its public transport system as the local population grew in direct proportion to the decline of its African counterpart. Domingos witnessed (and suffered from) the local elites' embrace of civilizing projects molded along European lines that combated African and Afro-Brazilian customs they considered uncivilized. Slavery grew, changed, and declined with the end of the Atlantic slave trade, and became virtually extinct during his lifetime in Bahia. Domingos died on the eve of the abolition of slavery.

Through Sodré's life, we enter the world of African freedpersons, thousands of men and women who had negotiated with their masters to

Figure 1. View of the city of Salvador, Bahia.

obtain their manumission, sometimes free of charge, but more often –
especially for African-born slaves – by purchasing their freedom. These
freedpersons, most of whom worked in the streets, played a key role in
the formation of Candomblé, a religion whose broad outlines developed
precisely when Domingos lived in Bahia. Many of the leading figures
in nineteenth-century Candomblé appear in this book, and their life
stories are intertwined with his. Called *feiticeiros* (witches or sorcerers)
in the official records and the press, these diviners, healers, and heads
of houses of worship were the target of systematic persecution by the
Bahian police, but the authorities did not always agree on the best way
to punish them, or even if they should be punished at all. The police
agenda often stressed the danger that these people represented to law
and order in a slave society because of their transactions with slaves
who went to them for help in confronting their masters. But the fact
that other free segments of the community were also Candomblé practitioners, including whites of some social standing, was not the least
of the concerns of those who combated the beliefs and ritual practices
that Africans brought to Brazil and transformed and re-created there.
Sodré's life unfolds as part of this cultural conflict and serves as a narrative thread when telling the history of Candomblé in the Bahia of
his time.

Abbreviations

ACMS	Arquivo da Cúria Metropolitana de Salvador
AI	Arquivo do Itamarati, Rio de Janeiro
AMS	Arquivo Municipal de Salvador
AN	Arquivo Nacional, Rio de Janeiro
APEB	Arquivo Público do Estado da Bahia
ASCMS	Arquivo da Santa Casa da Misericórdia de Salvador
BNA	British National Archives
BNRJ	Biblioteca Nacional, Rio de Janeiro
FHC	Family History Center, Church of Latter Day Saints, Salvador
FO	Foreign Office
LNT	*Livro de Notas do Tabelião*
LRT	*Livro de Registro de Testamentos*

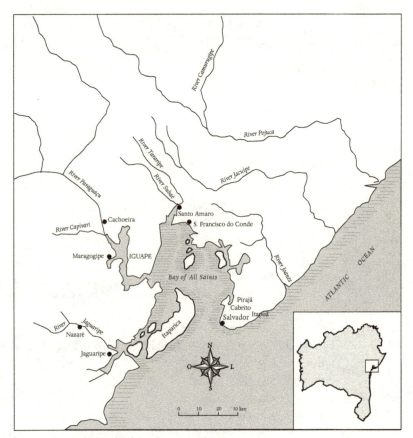

Map 1. Recôncavo of Bahia, the sugar plantation region.

Cops and Candomblé in Domingos
Sodré's Day

CANDOMBLÉ BETWEEN TOLERANCE AND REPRESSION

The day before Christmas Eve, 1858, a group of African freedpersons (i.e., ex-slaves) gathered for a *batuque,* the general expression then used for an African drumming session, in the Cruz do Cosme neighborhood on the outskirts of Salvador. Suddenly, the police surrounded and invaded the house, arresting people and seizing objects pertaining to Candomblé ceremonies. This raid caused a rift between the local subdelegado, or deputy chief constable, and the chief of police. In an official letter to his superior, subdelegado Manoel Nunes de Faria complained that he had not been informed of that police action. He later found out that the group of Africans had been arrested "for being found drumming." He questioned that charge, and protested:

> First, for your information, there was no such batuque, of which I am very well aware, and the Africans were at work, and this is nothing more than harassment, and if you perchance should pass by one afternoon and see the work of these Africans you would be amazed, and would even want to ensure that they stay in this parish, therefore it is precisely in light of this persecution that you should have them released and if you do so you will be doing them a great justice.[1]

He went on to state that the lieutenant commander of the urban police had acted "as if there were no subdelegado in the parish, which is highly

---

[1] Manoel Nunes de Faria to the chief of police, December 23, 1858, APEB, *Polícia. Subdelegados,* maço 6232.

astonishing"; and described the raid as typical "absolutism," indicating
a lack of confidence in his authority. If the chief of police did not trust
the subdelegado, "it would only be just to fire him," the aggrieved officer
concluded.[2]

To provide a better understanding of this controversial issue and
others that would arise later, I should say something about the structure of the police service in Bahia at the time. The provincial police
chief, whom the emperor appointed directly, was at the top of the chain
of command, and beneath him were *delegados* (chief constables), subdelegados, and the armed police force, which had its own hierarchy.
The posts of delegado and subdelegado were created by the 1841 police
reform act, and the president of the province chose their occupants
from a police chief's list of three candidates. They replaced most of the
police functions previously held by the justices of the peace, elected
officials who held a post created in the late 1820s.[3] Salvador had two
delegados, one for the urban parishes, the other for suburban and rural
parishes. But the police chief interacted directly with the subdelegados,
who were in charge of the day-to-day policing of each parish – or one
of two districts in larger parishes – with the help of a clerk, constables,
and, when necessary, bailiffs and urban guard officers. The urban guard
patrolled the city day and night, on the lookout for lawbreakers. The
post of subdelegado was unpaid but reflected and added to the power,
respectability, and prestige of the men who held that office. It was precisely in an effort to defend those attributes of his post that the subdelegado of Cruz do Cosme complained to the police chief about the raid
on the Africans' home.[4]

The Cruz do Cosme district was typical of what was then the rural
outskirts of Salvador. Located in the second district of the rather large
Santo Antônio Além do Carmo parish, it was home to a sizable number of African freedpersons who lived and farmed there, selling their
produce for a living, as its subdelegado accurately stated in his letter to

[2] Ibid.
[3] For justices of the peace, see Thomas Flory, *Judge and Jury in Imperial Brazil, 1808–
     1871: Social Control and Political Stability in the New State* (Austin: University of
     Texas Press, 1981).
[4] The rules governing police ranks and titles can be found in Araujo Filgueiras
     Junior, *Codigo do Processo do Imperio do Brasil* (Rio de Janeiro: Eduardo e
     Henrique Laemmert, 1874), particularly chaps. 2 and 3; and the "Regulamento"
     (Regulations) for the Urban Guard of May 18, 1857, Art. 6, followed by the
     "Instruções" (Instructions) of July 25, 1857, APEB, *Polícia*, maço 2946.

the chief of police. Following the food traditions of their homelands, these freedpersons, sometimes with the assistance of slaves, mainly planted yams for both their own consumption and the city's food supply.[5] This rural district was typical of the "black countryside" to which historian Flávio Gomes refers in his study of Rio de Janeiro, in which solidarity and negotiation, as well as competition and conflict, marked the daily lives of the communities that formed around small farms and businesses.[6]

Cruz do Cosme was frequently mentioned in police reports. In September 1859, subdelegado João de Azevedo Piapitinga (remember his name) reported that he had received frequent complaints from farm workers regarding "constantly occurring thefts." Three Africans were arrested for stealing yams from other Africans.[7] But produce theft was not the only problem. According to the subdelegado, there was a great deal of "disorder" in that area, particularly on weekends, when a large

[5]   The Yoruba people were the most numerous group among the Africans who arrived during that period in Bahia, where they were called nagôs, and yams always came first in descriptions of Yoruba agriculture. See, for example, Samuel Johnson, *The History of the Yorubas* (London: Routledge & Kegan Paul, 1966 [orig. 1897]), 109–110; Paul Lovejoy, *Transformations in Slavery: A History of Slavery in Africa* (Cambridge: Cambridge University Press, 1983), 174. Yam farming was widespread in the African forest zone while millet predominated in the savannah area, according to Robert July, *A History of the African People*, 2nd ed. (New York: Charles Scribner's Sons, 1974), 131–132. The tuber played an important role in the diet of slave ships, according to Robert Hall, "Savoring Africa in the New World," in *Seeds of Change*, ed. Herman J. Viola and Carolyn Margolis (Washington and London: Smithsonian Institute, 1991), 163–165; and Markus Rediker, *The Slave Ship: A Human History* (New York: Viking, 2007), 237, which indicates that yams were eaten aboard by slaves imported specifically from the bights of Benin (from where most slaves embarked for Bahia) and Biafra. Yams were served at the meal the Malês ate before the 1835 revolt, according to "Devassa do levante de escravos ocorrido em Salvador em 1835," *Anais do Arquivo do Estado da Bahia*, no. 38 (1968): 63. In other slaveholding cities such as São Paulo, freed Africans also settled in rural districts like Cruz do Cosme. See, for example, Maria Cristina Wissenbach, *Sonhos africanos, vivências ladinas: escravos e forros em São Paulo (1850–1880)* (São Paulo: Hucitec, 1998), esp. chap. 4.

[6]   Flávio dos Santos Gomes, *Histórias de quilombolas: mocambos e comunidades de senzalas no Rio de Janeiro, século XIX* (São Paulo: Companhia das Letras, 2006).

[7]   João de Azevedo Piapitinga to the chief of police, September 29, 1859, APEB, *Polícia*, maço 6232.

number of city residents passed through there.[8] In 1860, Piapitinga had requested police reinforcements to combat the "murderers, deserters, fugitive slaves, escaped convicts and gamblers" in his district.[9] Many of those people frequented the Candomblé sites established there, which many officials also considered part of the "disorder" in the outskirts of the city. This is where the Christmas 1858 raid on the African drumming session comes in.

In his account of this episode to the president of the province, the police chief reported that on December 23, among other measures, they arrested one man and twelve women – all African freedpersons – found "in dances and batuques, having seized several objects and garments used in those dances." He did not give any details about the confiscated objects and garments, but listed the names of the individuals arrested.[10] Also according to the chief of police, this time in response to subdelegado Faria's protest, the raid was due to "repeated complaints from neighbors regarding the rumpus that many blacks frequent[ly] made at the Candomblé in the house that was raided." And he went on to accuse the subdelegado of dereliction of duty, because that measure would have been unnecessary if "the police had been so vigilant and active" in that district that he, the police chief himself, would not have been obliged to take steps against those Africans. Finally, he said he was surprised at the "immoderate tone" of his subordinate's letter and concluded by threatening to remove him from office because he lacked the "serenity which is indispensable to anyone in any small position of authority."[11]

---

[8] João de Azevedo Piapitinga to the chief of police, June 5, 1858, APEB, Polícia, maço 6232.

[9] João de Azevedo Piapitinga to the chief of police, September 12, 1860, APEB, Polícia, maço 6233.

[10] A. M. de Aragão e Mello to the president of the province, December 23, 1858, APEB, Polícia. Correspondência, vol. 5730, fl. 58. The majority of this group was made up of women, which fits with what we know about the gender of the people arrested at nineteenth-century candomblés in Bahia. See João José Reis, "Sacerdotes, seguidores e clientes no candomblé da Bahia oitocentista," in Orixás e espíritos: o debate interdisciplinar na pesquisa contemporânea, ed. Artur César Isaia (Uberlândia: Editora da Universidade Federal de Uberlândia, 2006), 57–98.

[11] A. M. de Aragão e Mello to the subdelegado of the second district of Santo Antônio, December 24, 1958, APEB, Polícia. Correspondência, vol. 5732, fls. 9v–10v.

The subdelegado's response, dated December 27, was humble and conciliatory. He wrote that his first letter was an outburst in response to a raid that had undermined his authority, as it was carried out without his knowledge in his own district. Now that he knew that the order had come directly from the chief of police, he understood and accepted it. He concluded by promising to be "always ready to serve the public," leaving out of his thoughts the Africans whom he had previously defended as unjustly treated.[12]

But the Africans themselves, better yet, the women in the group, headed by Aniceta Rita Junqueira, put up a capable defense. The day after their arrest, they sent a petition to the police chief explaining that they were nothing more than honest washerwomen who went to the house the police raided to get some food and rest after a hard day's work. After that, they would go to the city, where they claimed to live, but "the house where they used to stay was surrounded by a police detachment, and then they were arrested and imprisoned in the Aljube," a religious jail dating from colonial times that was now used to house individuals, particularly slaves, accused of petty crimes. The African freedwomen claimed that "they were not in that house for illicit purposes," and asked to be set free. The chief of police released them that same day. They were in luck, because he did so before the dispute with the subdelegado began. Otherwise, he might have kept the African women in jail to avoid giving the impression that an insubordinate underling had pressured him to let them go.[13]

This episode is typical of what went on behind the scenes of the police repression of nineteenth-century Candomblé in Bahia. Police officials frequently disagreed about how to handle it. Referring to the colonial period, Nina Rodrigues observed that "the suppression or maintenance of the drumming sessions was an apple of heated discord."[14] Generally

---

[12] Manoel Nunes de Faria, December 27, 1858, APEB, *Polícia. Subdelegados*, maço 6234.

[13] Petition from Aniceta Rita Junqueira et al. to the chief of police, December 23, 1853, APEB, *Polícia*, maço 6322. Aniceta owned at least one slave, a woman named Esperança. APEB, *Índice de alforrias, 1861–1861*, maço 2882.

[14] Raimundo Nina Rodrigues, *Os africanos no Brasil*, 4th ed. (São Paulo: Editora Companhia Nacional, 1976), 155–156. Nina refers to the different repression policies of Count da Ponte and Count dos Arcos. For details, see João José Reis, *Rebelião escrava no Brasil: a história do levante dos malês em 1835* (São Paulo: Companhia das Letras, 2003), chap. 3; João José Reis and Renato da Silveira, "Violência repressiva e engenho político na Bahia do tempo dos escravos," *Comunicações do ISER*, 5, no 21 (1986): 61–66. Renato da Silveira has

speaking, the same can be said of the policy of repressing Candomblé in Domingos Sodré's time. During this period, police chiefs generally exerted stricter control of African cultural expressions, while many subdelegados – who had to deal with the problem firsthand on a daily basis – often opted for a policy of tolerance and negotiation, as the numerous complaints about candomblés and other drumming sessions that resounded from several parts of the city suggest. As historian Dale Graden has noted, some police officials "recognized the benefits to be gained from quiet diplomacy."[15] The press repeatedly accused the police and other authorities of colluding with the candomblés and African drumming sessions. In 1864, for example, the O Patriota newspaper published a satirical poem criticizing a judge for suspending a robbery investigation to protect the Candomblé community. A passage of the poem said, "the judge makes no justice/When there is a whiff of Candomblé."[16]

But no newspaper was as insistent as O Alabama in accusing police officers of protecting Africans, permitting them to engage in their practices and even taking part in Candomblé ceremonies. I have even found in the pages of this paper a complaint about a subdelegado who was said to be possessed by an African divinity. Self-styled by its mulatto editor as a "critical and jocular" publication – a common motto of such publications in nineteenth-century Brazil – the newspaper preached that these officers were holding back the march of progress and civilization – European civilization, that is – in that province, which was its main concern.[17]

conducted an extensive study of the dynamics of repression/tolerance by church and state, in which doctrine and political strategy converge. See Silveira, O candomblé da Barroquinha: processo de constituição do primeiro terreiro baiano de Keto (Salvador: Maianga, 2006), esp. chaps. 1–3.

[15] Dale Graden, From Slavery to Freedom in Brazil: Bahia, 1835–1900 (Albuquerque: University of New Mexico Press, 2006), 118.

[16] O Patriota, vol. 5, no 3, June 6, 1864, p. 4.

[17] Regarding O Alabama's coverage of Candomblé, see Dale Graden, "'So Much Superstition among These People!': Candomblé and the Dilemmas of Afro-Bahian Intellectuals," in Afro-Brazilian Culture and Politics: Bahia, 1790s to 1990s, ed. Hendrik Kraay (Armonk, NY/London: M. E. Sharpe, 1998), 57–73. See also Reis, "Sacerdotes, seguidores e clientes," 57–94; Nicolau Parés, A formação do candomblé: história e ritual da nação jeje na Bahia (Campinas: Editora da Unicamp, 2006), 141. At the end of the century, the press attacked black carnival groups and continued harassing Candomblé. See Rodrigues, Os africanos, 238–253; Peter Fry, Sérgio Carrara, and Ana Luiza Martins-Costa, "Negros e brancos no Carnaval da Velha República," in Escravidão e

The police were not the only authorities who were ambiguous about Candomblé practices. The courts and even politicians disagreed on how to deal with Candomblé and its followers and clients. Some members of the public complained about African healers and diviners, while others consulted, protected, or at least tolerated them – sometimes out of fear, as they had a reputation for wielding extraordinary powers, such as the ability to disseminate witchcraft. When Domingos Sodré was arrested, both Candomblé temples, or *terreiros*, and individual practices – such as divination – that were not based on an organized religious community could already be found throughout the city, although the temples were more often located on the outskirts of the city, places like Cruz do Cosme, far removed from the sensitive ears of city dwellers and the vigilance of the powers that be.[18] Nevertheless, I must stress that their success was due to patient negotiations of tolerance with society, because Candomblé was always on a knife edge, pressured by complaints from the great and the small, particularly the press, which more often than not led to police repression.

A Chief with a Style of His Own

In 1862, the year when the raid on Domingos Sodré's house took place, the head of the police in Bahia was forty-year-old Chief João Antônio de Araújo Freitas Henriques (Figure 2), who would play a leading role in even more heated disagreements on the same subject with his subdelegados than his predecessor's dispute with the subdelegado of Cruz do Cosme. João Henriques had enjoyed a brilliant career in the judiciary and served on high courts of the imperial government. He occupied

invenção da liberdade: estudos sobre o negro no Brasil, ed. João José Reis (São Paulo: Brasiliense, 1988), 232–263; and Wlamyra R. de Albuquqerque, *O jogo da dissimulação: abolição e cidadania negra no Brasil* (São Paulo: Companhia das Letras, 2009), chap. 5. In the first decades of the twentieth century, the press continued its campaign and accused the police of complicity with Candomblé. See Angela Lühning, "'Acabe com este santo, Pedrito vem aí...,'" *Revista USP*, 28 (1995–1996): 194–220.

[18] See, for example, Rachael E. Harding, *A Refuge in Thunder: Candomblé and Alternative Spaces of Blackness* (Bloomington: Indiana University Press, 2000); Nicolau Parés, *A formação do Candomblé*, 138–142, for instance; Silveira, *O candomblé da Barroquinha*, esp. chap. 8; and particularly Jocélio Teles dos Santos, "Candomblés e espaço urbano na Bahia do século XIX," *Estudos Afro-Asiáticos*, 27, no. 1–3 (2005): 205–226.

Figure 2. João Antônio de Araújo Freitas Henriques (1822–1903), the police chief who ordered Domingos Sodré's arrest.

the position of chief of police in several provinces (Maranhão, Paraíba, Pernambuco, Alagoas, and Bahia) and that of president of Ceará (1869–1870) and Bahia (1871–1872), among various public offices.[19] The son of a colonel in the National Guard, he had held conservative ideas since his youth. At one point, he published a subterfuge-filled defense of large rural landholdings, claiming that they were ideal for furthering economic progress. He praised Britain for the "maintenance of large farms," which "preserved an aristocracy of great repute that is strongly committed to national prosperity."[20] Apparently, for him, what

[19] Arnold Wildberger, *Os presidentes da província da Bahia, efectivos e interinos, 1824–1899* (Salvador: Typographia Beneditina, 1949), 591–598.
[20] J. A. de Freitas Henriques, "Se a Terra deve ser dividida em grandes ou pequenas propriedades e quaes são os seus resultados econômicos e políticos," *O Musaico*, 15 or 16 (?) (Sept.? or Oct.? 1846): 230, 246.

was good for Britain – if indeed it was – was good for Brazil. Henriques wrote that article when he was twenty-four. Now, sixteen years later, he was committed to his role of protecting Bahian aristocrats and commoners alike from the propagation of vibrant African cultural expressions that abounded in the province.

Since he had taken office in late November 1861, João Henriques had worked hard to eradicate candomblés, and more. Although I would like to focus on his crusade against that religion, I should at least mention his antipathy toward other African and creole customs – folk customs in general, in fact – that were widely popular in the province. For example, he prohibited Catholic devotees from collecting alms for the saints, a common activity among the members of black confraternities, which raised funds that way to take care of their altars and churches, organize their lavish and entertaining devotional feasts, and care for their poor brethren in life and death. According to Henriques' law, alms gatherers could only operate in the city with the official authorization of the archbishop. The "intent is to punish those who use the cloak of religion to profiteer, taking advantage of the public's credulity," the police chief explained in a bulletin to his subdelegados.[21] As we will soon see, he used similar terms against followers of Candomblé, and added even harsher words.

Outside the religious sphere, Henriques sought to repress lesser infractions and offenses by enslaved, freed, and free blacks, such as bouts of capoeira street fighting, the African-derived martial art. On June 18, 1862, he sent a circular letter to his subordinates ordering them to clamp down on capoeiras – in this case the practitioners of the martial art – in all parishes of the city. This is an interesting document for various reasons, and worth quoting in full:

Seeing that on previous Sunday afternoons a large number of scamps have gathered in Barbalho Field, who in organized gangs and from various places will go there to make it their stopping place, where, according to the press, on the afternoon of Sunday last there was a great outcry and noise, and some were wounded, I demand that you pay attention to this. As I have issued orders for them to be taken by surprise in that area, it is likely that they will seek another position to practice the fight and game of capoeira, a

[21] Circular letter from the police chief to the subdelegados of Salvador, May 31, 1862, APEB, *Polícia. Correspondência*, vol. 5754, fls. 146–146v.

business that should not be overlooked, in view of what goes on in the Court [of Rio de Janeiro], whose police, although surrounded by other means, have not been able to put an end to those turbulent "capoeiras."

In fact, based on the foregoing, I recommend that you be fully vigilant in your district, to prevent gatherings of such people, and I hope that you will take action in this regard with full energy and zeal.[22]

The following day, Cosme Firmino dos Santos, a creole (Brazilian-born black) freedman who worked as a tailor, was arrested "for capoeira" in Santana parish and sent to prison.[23]

This order to crack down on capoeira eloquently speaks for itself and is the first document to establish a clear relationship between capoeira as a martial art and a game. But the duality of being both a game and a fight was not the heart and soul of capoeira alone, and João Henriques did not seem to realize this when he proposed to eradicate cultural practices with African roots and hues in Bahia. But he was not alone. The press had issued constant warnings about the operations of candomblés since at least the beginning of February 1862, two months after Henriques became the highest police official in the province. At the time, the *Diário da Bahia* newspaper reported the presence of a "major batuque, and in due form, to which a few dozen Africans abandoned themselves in a backyard in Agony alley," not far from where Domingos Sodré lived. It was a celebration in honor of a recently deceased Candomblé dignitary, "solemn obsequies" as the paper ironically described it, although it was a perfectly accurate description: the candomblés marked the passing of the most important members of the African community with a solemn ceremony and even a feast, accompanied by the consumption of food and drink. However, the editors of the *Diário* were only interested in spreading the news that the celebration was accompanied by the "hubbub of shouting, the hellish din of instruments," and plenty of hard liquor. They concluded by appealing to the police

[22] Circular letter from the police chief to the subdelegados of Salvador, June 18, 1862, APEB, *Polícia. Correspondência*, vol. 5754, fl. 171v.

[23] Chart of the prisoners in the penitentiary, June 19, 1862, APEB, *Prisão. Relação de presos*, maço 6272. For capoeira in nineteenth-century Bahia, see Frederico José de Abreu, *Capoeiras: Bahia, século XIX* (Salvador: Instituto Jair Moura, 2005).

to combat, on behalf of civilization, those "brutal practices, children of the stupidest superstition."[24]

Throughout this book, you will read several excerpts from newspaper articles arguing in this vein. The Bahian press made a huge contribution to the police harassment of Candomblé in Salvador and the nearby rural districts, before and after Chief Henriques took office.[25] We have an example from the Recôncavo region, where the majority of the enslaved population was concentrated on the sugar plantations that drove the provincial economy. In October 1850, O Argos Cachoeirano, a newspaper published in the city of Cachoeira, featured a long and fantastic report on the "prodigies of the African blacks' saints," who had recently managed to drive five members of the same family insane "on the same day." A young girl had even cut her own throat, "and it was a horrific spectacle," of course; another family member was said to have been locked up in a dungeon because he posed a danger to society. The local subdelegado was called in to investigate this episode, but when he visited the Candomblé house and conducted his sober investigation, he found nothing out of order. Furthermore, he concluded that "he was not sure what he should investigate." However, the editors of the Cachoeira newspaper, who apparently were fervent believers in witchcraft, decided to teach the police how to do their job: "The suicide as well as the insanity is the result of crimes that are offenses to morality, to religion: the Candomblé houses are inside and all around the city! And there is nothing to investigate!!!" They rounded off by insisting: "And so the houses, the oracles of superstition, that give rise to these sad and horrible events should keep going? And there is nothing to investigate!!!"[26]

---

[24] Diário da Bahia, February 6, 1862. The word "form" is underlined in the original. For African funerals in Brazil, see João José Reis, A morte é uma festa: ritos fúnebres e revolta popular no Brasil do século XIX (São Paulo: Companhia das Letras, 1992), 159–162.

[25] The persecution of Afro-Brazilian religious customs in the name of civilization and science in the press was also common in other parts of the country. For São Paulo, see Lilia Moritz Schwarcz, Retrato em branco e negro: jornais, escravos e cidadãos em São Paulo no final do século XIX (São Paulo: Companhia das Letras, 1987), 125–128; and for Rio Grande do Sul between the late nineteenth and the early twentieth century, see Sandra Jatahy Pesavento, "Negros feitiços," in Orixás e espíritos: o debate interdisciplinar na pesquisa contemporânea ed. Artur César Isaia (Uberlândia: EDUFU, 2006), 129–152.

[26] O Argos Cachoeirano, October 26, 1850, p. 2.

The Bahian press tirelessly repeated the narrative that the police were not doing their duty in item after item. Some officials, whether fearing a public scandal or out of personal conviction, responded to their urgings. And they investigated. However, this does not seem to have been the case with law enforcement in Cachoeira in 1850, proof that some police officers acted cautiously and professionally in such matters.

However, Chief João Henriques was on the same page with the *Diário da Bahia* and *O Argos Cachoeirano*. In April 1862, he launched a fierce campaign against Candomblé houses in the provincial capital. His first target was the recently opened terreiro in the second district of Santo Antônio parish, the same general area where the Christmas 1858 episode occurred. History seemed to repeat itself. This time, Henriques wrote to the subdelegado for that district, João de Azevedo Piapitinga, and ordered him to join a police detachment he had sent to attack the candomblé located on the Pojavá Pequeno estate before dawn on the following day, a Monday. The chief gave his subordinate the following orders: "You will conduct a thorough search, sending all the people found [there] to me, as well as all suspicious items," which was certainly a reference to ritual objects.

Albeit a success, the raid did not produce satisfactory results for the police chief. He was angry with subdelegado Piapitinga because he suspected that, in the first place, he had authorized that large gathering, and on a very Catholic Easter Sunday at that, "numbers greater than 100, given up to all sorts of immoralities and the practice of superstitious acts that do such harm to the naive." Being "civilized," Henriques demanded an explanation from his careless subordinate and ordered the constable responsible for policing Pojavá, the specific site where the candomblé was located, to see him in person.[27]

Henriques had treated the subdelegado with suspicion since the beginning of that police action. In his letter advising him about the raid on Pojavá, he said that the detachment sent there for that purpose – headed by the lieutenant colonel who was the police commander – would not even stop outside the subdelegado's house so as not to raise the neighbors' suspicions about their mission, which had been kept secret thus far. As a result, the chief seems to have wanted

[27] Chief Henriques to the subdelegado of the second district of Santo Antônio, April 19 and 23, 1862, APEB, *Polícia. Correspondência*, vol. 5754, fls. 106, 110. See also Harding, *A Refuge in Thunder*, 142–143.

to take not only the Candomblé community but the subdelegado him-self by surprise, perhaps fearing that he would sound a warning about the imminent attack. At the very least, Piapitinga, like his alternate Manoel Faria four years earlier, had been sidelined from an important police operation in his own jurisdiction. As a result, he was too late to see the start of that Monday morning raid because he only received the letter from his boss at 7 A.M., when he went over to Pojavá and saw the police force leaving with prisoners, some carrying the seized ritual objects. It was an embarrassing situation for Piapitinga.[28]

But he would then be charged with a smaller mission. To name and shame the prisoners, Chief João Henriques ordered the subdelegado to "publish a list of all those arrested, their [skin] colors and trades." But that did not happen. The *Diário da Bahia* hailed the raid on the Pojavá candomblé, and recommended that a list of "the followers of such a mys-terious association" be published but did not print their names, proba-bly because Piapitinga did not provide them with any.[29] The newspaper merely published an article two days later stating that most of those arrested were creoles – twenty-two men and twenty-three women – as well as four *pardas* (brown, or light-skinned mulatto) women and three pardo men. There were just three Africans – two women and one man, all of them freedpersons – among the prisoners. The women's occupa-tions were not specified, but except for one farm worker, all the men had trades, and were therefore city dwellers.[30] Their occupations may better explain why the police chief wanted to intensify the hunt for the African religion's followers. No longer a belief system held exclusively by people considered "African savages," Candomblé was spreading fast among professional people born and raised in Brazil, particularly cre-oles, but also pardos and whites. Incidentally, the police chief men-tioned that there were more than 100 people there, although only about sixty were arrested. There were no whites among the prisoners, possibly because the police let them go on the pretext that they were just curious bystanders.[31]

---

[28] Subdelegado João de Azevedo Piapitinga to the chief of police, April 24, 1862, APEB, *Polícia. Subdelegados*, maço 6234.

[29] *Diário da Bahia*, April 23, 1862. For a more detailed discussion of the people arrested in Pojavá, see Reis, "Sacerdotes, devotos e clientes no candomblé da Bahia oitocentista," 81–83.

[30] *Diário da Bahia*, April 25, 1862.

[31] Since the 1830s, police officials had been amazed at the presence of creole women among Bahian candomblés. See João José Reis, "Nas malhas do poder escravista: a

The Pojavá incident sparked animosity between Chief João Henriques and subdelegado João Piapitinga, who had held his post for seven or eight years by 1862. Piapitinga, sixty-six, a respectable white citizen, a lieutenant colonel in the National Guard, and a clerk at the Naval Hospital, had just been called a liar by an arrogant police chief twenty-six years his junior but superior to him in rank in several ways. The subdelegado, who was also a slaveholder, did not appreciate the implication that he had been tolerant with the Candomblé houses within his jurisdiction. In two letters to Henriques, he angrily responded that he was not accustomed to "prevaricating," and claimed that, on the contrary, he harshly combated the candomblés in his district. In fact, he believed he had the Africans fully under control, the vast majority of whom were engaged in honest and successful work on their farms, mainly planting yams. Mind that his alternate used the same argument in 1858. Certainly, they had joined forces to carry out what they believed to have been a successful mission to civilize the Africans. Both, in fact, followed guidelines set down by the powerful head of the Conservative Party of Bahia, Francisco Gonçalves Martins, the Viscount of São Lourenço. When he governed Bahia from 1848 to 1850, Martins sought to prevent Africans from holding jobs in the city, because he wanted them laboring in the fields, preferably as docile serfs on the Recôncavo's sugar plantations. In his mind, urban jobs should be reserved for Brazilian-born workers, including whites, blacks, and mulattos. Piapitinga and his alternate apparently agreed with the viscount.

As for African festivals, Piapitinga claimed to tolerate those that were "decent" and properly supervised – those, in fact, that attracted upstanding city folk seeking an exciting but safe adventure on the outskirts of the capital. He invited the police chief to see for himself. The subdelegado explained that the existence of a Candomblé house in Pojavá was just as surprising to him as it was to his superior. He guaranteed that on the day of the drumming session, he had just replaced the acting subdelegado, Sinfrônio França, who had gone into town because his mother had just died. In other words, if there had been any

invasão do candomblé do Accú," in João Reis e Eduardo Silva, *Negociação e conflito: a resistência negra no Brasil escravista* (São Paulo: Companhia das Letras, 1989), 32–61. The process of creolization of Candomblé in nineteenth-century Bahia is discussed in Reis, "Sacerdotes, devotos e clientes."

complaints about the gathering in Pojavá, they would have been made, not to him, Piapitinga, but to the other subdelegado, who had not done anything about them because he had more urgent, funereal business to attend to. Piapitinga added that the site of the candomblé was a good distance from his home, so he could not hear the drums. Finally, he admitted that he had not been paying much attention to the behavior of the creoles because he had not suspected that they, too, were interested in that sort of "entertainment," which he felt was typical of the Africans – although that was not true of the Africans who lived in his district, of course, whom he had reformed through and for labor.[32]

When he said he did not know that creoles had adopted Candomblé, it may have slipped Piapitinga's mind that this was not the first time he had been accused of protecting Brazilian-born blacks who followed the African religion, or at least those who frequented terreiros in his district. Seven years earlier, a constable under his command had complained to another police chief that Piapitinga had failed to investigate an incident involving contempt of authority, which I will summarize as follows. It was 6 A.M. on October 21, 1855, when Constable Francisco de Moura Rosa reprimanded a member of a group of creole men and women coming from the city for uttering "the most dishonest and obscene words in loud voices." According to the constable, the group ran to "one of the houses of ill repute in this district called Candomblés." One Marcolino, a municipal police officer from the neighboring parish of Brotas, was said to have insulted the constable and threatened to hit him if he arrested any member of the group, backed up by an armed pardo man. The constable reported the incident to Piapitinga, and suggested sending a police detachment, because the place was "very popular among vagabonds because of those Candomblés, where sometimes over 200 people get together to engage in immoral acts." The idea that sexual promiscuity infested Candomblé ceremonies was widespread in the

---

[32] The dispute between the police chief and the subdelegado can be followed in Henriques to the subdelegado of the second district of Santo Antônio, May 3, 1862, APEB, Polícia. Correspondência, vol. 5754, fls. 119–119v; Piapitinga to the chief of police, April 26 and May 16, 1862, APEB, Polícia. Subdelegados, maço 6195. For the subdelegado's ownership of slaves, see APEB, Índice de alforrias 1860–1861, maço 2882 (Silvana, a slave woman, is listed in the alphabetical index); and for his work as a hospital clerk, see Almanak administrativo (1863), 291. For Martins' policy on African workers, see Manuela Carneiro da Cunha, Negros, estrangeiros: os escravos libertos e sua volta à África (São Paulo: Brasiliense, 1985). This subject will also be discussed in Chapter 2.

police and press reports of the time, presented as one of the strongest signs of its followers' un-Christian and therefore uncivilized lifestyle. In his complaint to the police chief, the constable, after stating that his immediate superior had "done nothing" about the case, despondently concluded, "finally, the said creole Marcolino has protectors who do their utmost to defend him." He was implying that the subdelegado had caved in to pressure from above – either that, or that Piapitinga himself was protecting the creole Candomblé practitioner.

Four days later, Piapitinga replied to the police chief that, contrary to his subordinate's accusation, the subdelegado had taken action and even discovered the full name of the subject of that complaint, Marcolino José Dias. He had not arrested him yet because that measure would depend on the results of an investigation by the subdelegado of the parish where the accused individual resided. Piapitinga did not seem to be very efficient.[33] These events transpired in late 1855. I don't know what caused the incident, but a few months later the same man would no longer be the head of that police district, although he returned there in 1862 in time to witness the raid on the Pojavá candomblé.

There is further evidence that Piapitinga may have been on good terms with Africans who were fond of Candomblé. In May 1860, he was a witness at the wedding of an African couple who lived in his district. That in itself is unremarkable. The bride and groom, however, were among the Africans arrested around Christmas 1858 and charged with practicing Candomblé, the incident with which this chapter began. João Costa, a freedman, was very ill when he got married, and may have taken that step because he wished to die on good terms with the Catholic Church. According to the vicar who married them, he and his bride had been living in "an illicit union" and already had two children named Simplício and Libania. It was all set down in the marriage registry of Santo Antônio parish. The same house that had shaken to the beat of Candomblé drums was now the backdrop of a Catholic ceremony presided by a parish priest and canon, and witnessed by a subdelegado and his constable, a pardo man by the way.[34] In short, there

33 Inspector Francisco de Moura Rosa to the subdelegado of the second district of Santo Antônio, October 21, 1855; Rosa to the chief of police, November 8, 1855, Piapitinga to the chief of police, November 12, 1855, APEB, *Polícia. Subdelegados*, maço 6231.
34 Arquivo da Cúria Metropolitana de Salvador (ACMS), *Livro de registro de casamentos da Freguesia de Santo Antônio, 1840–1863*, registry dated May 26, 1860.

are indications that João Henriques had good reason to suspect that Piapitinga was turning a blind eye to Candomblé celebrations in his jurisdiction.

Going back to April 1862, we find Chief João Henriques reading the *Jornal da Bahia* on the 22nd. One of the most important newspapers in Salvador, it reported that there was a "big drumming session by residents of some shacks near the Estrada Nova arch, where they take part in all sorts of immoral practices." Luckily for Piapitinga, the drumming was not done in his district. Henriques immediately ordered the local subdelegado to investigate and take all the appropriate measures.[35] He must have suspected that this subordinate was also overlooking such African vices. Better yet, he probably supposed that such tolerance was widespread and had decided to put the house in order. Two days after the *Jornal da Bahia* published that report, in the course of his exchange of barbed comments with João Piapitinga, the police chief distributed the following circular letter to all subdelegados of the City of Bahia:

> To the 18 Subdelegados of the City. As I have learned that in various parts of this city there are profiteers who, by way of divination, and promises of removing spells, make a living by extorting money from fools and imbuing them with superstitious beliefs, by which, in addition to financial benefits, they take advantage of them for vile ends, I demand that you provide me detailed information about this through thorough investigations conducted by your Constables, because I am also aware that even people of a certain status attend the gatherings these profiteers hold for such purposes. This is a very grave matter that merits serious attention due to the infiltration of such pernicious ideas in the public [mind] and must be fully addressed.[36]

Henriques was not the first to advise his subordinates how to combat candomblés in their districts, but his style and even his objective were different from those of his predecessors. Let us compare them. In January 1854, Chief of Police Araújo Góes also wrote a memo to his

---

Frutuoso Mendes's color (pardo) is stated in subdelegado Piapitinga's letter to the chief of police, March 10, 1858, APEB, *Polícia. Subdelegados*, maço 6232.

[35] Henriques to the subdelegado of the first district of Santo Antônio, April 22, 1862, APEB, *Polícia. Correspondência*, vol. 5754, fls. 108–108v.

[36] Circular letter from the chief of police to the subdelegados of Salvador, April 24, 1862, APEB, *Correspondência*, vol. 5754, fl. 111.

subdelegados demanding the "full prohibition of African gatherings, under any pretext whatsoever, whether for drumming sessions, or due to someone's death, which gives rise to practices and ceremonies that must not be tolerated."[37] Here, the police chief viewed the Africans' religion as limited to that group alone, and did not realize that it had extended to other segments of society. Furthermore, the decision to engage in religious intolerance had an implicit political aim, which was to prevent Africans from gathering and to keep the peace in the slave quarters and slums of the City of Bahia. In the middle of the previous year, persistent rumors had circulated about a Muslim conspiracy because Arabic writings had been found just like twenty years earlier in the wake of the Revolt of the Malês, in 1835, an event that traumatized the local free population. Therefore, it was natural for the authorities to fear the Africans' religion – those "ceremonies that must not be tolerated."[38]

Between the late 1850s and the early 1860s, Bahia had some police chiefs who, given the growing number of complaints received, took a hard line against Candomblé. These officials had nurtured a veritable psychology of fear, and João Henriques continued to do so. One of the methods of punishment they adopted was deporting African "sorcerers," a form of repression of Candomblé specialists that I will discuss in more detail in Chapter 4. For now, suffice it to say that the argument that the authorities repeatedly used when adopting that measure – deportation – was the difficulty to prove the crimes with which they were charged, including the poisoning deaths of other Africans, both slaves and freedpersons. During that period, fear of Muslim rebels had receded, and the police no longer considered Candomblé a danger to public order, but deleterious to the private economy, as well as a disruptive influence on morals and good behavior. They had also reached a consensus that Candomblé had transcended the bounds of the African and creole community and now contaminated other segments of society.

João Henriques was an exemplary follower of that doctrine. For him, Candomblé was nothing but a jumble of superstitious beliefs controlled by conmen who exploited the ignorants – particularly women – in many ways, even sexually, but now, the police chief believed, their victims also included worthy and well-educated citizens or, in his words, "people

---

[37] Circular letter from Chief M. de Araújo, January 31, 1854, APEB, *Polícia*, livro 5716, fl. 3–3v.

[38] I will discuss the 1853 conspiracy in Chapter 6.

of a certain status." Therefore, it was necessary to suppress "pernicious ideas" that led to allegedly pernicious practices, and prevent them from continuing to infiltrate the city's population from the bottom up. This represented a mind-set that, although it also defended the social system, gave priority to upholding a "civilized" way of life. In other words, we are faced with a clash between two conflicting world views.

A QUESTIONABLE COMPLAINT DURING WITCH-HUNT TIMES

Henriques' eagerness to crack down on the people accused of witchcraft seems to have found an echo in the public, as can be read in an anonymous letter to the police chief sent in early July 1862. The author, who must have read the police chief's circular letter to his subdelegados in the newspapers – which commonly published official correspondence – described him as "an educated man of strict, honest and upstanding character." This letter, which is so intriguing that I have quoted it in full in the following box, accuses one of the alternate subdelegados of the second district of Santo Antônio parish, Sinfrônio Pires da França, of complicity with the practices of quackery, divination, and other activities attributed to an alleged Candomblé priest named Libânio José de Almeida, described as a "light-skinned mulatto."

An Anonymous Complaint to the Chief of Police about an Alleged Witch Doctor

To Your Excellency, the Chief of Police of this Province, an educated man of strict, honest and upstanding character to whom the good citizens owe so much; the complaint is as follows. Libânio José de Almeida, a light-skinned mulatto, aged 24 to 26, a resident of Cruz do Cosme, without any trade or employment of any kind, but astute, has sought to seek his fortune as a witchdoctor and Father of Terreiro [Pai do Terreiro, Candomblé high priest], practicing that useful lifestyle in a house where he currently lives in the above site built at the expense of his flock; there they engage in practices that morality demands that we silence. And could the police possibly be unaware of this? Certainly not. Among the many bad acts that evil man has perpetrated, the worst is as follows. For about 5 years, there lived in this City an unfortunate young

woman, white, a comely widow, and the mother of four innocent
little children; it so happened that she fell ill with a disease that did
not give way to the efforts of the skilled Physician who treated her;
the Mother of that poor lady, ignorant and fanatical, was advised
by another of like mind who frequented her home to consult Pai
Libânio, because she said "your daughter's body is bewitched," and
in view of this advice, she went to Pai Libânio's house, and accompanied by his assistant named Salomão, a mulatto, blind in one
eye, who used to work at the Naval Arsenal, they artfully instilled
in her mind that her slave woman named Fa (the only one she
had) was killing [the young widow] with witchcraft, and so she had
to sell her to effect a cure, and celebrate the Saint – and so it was
said and done. What was the result of all this? The unhappy young
woman died, poisoned by the herbs that monster gave her; and
this villainy was only brought to light by someone who was concerned about the unfortunate young woman, but too late, because
her own Mother covered everything up: that scoundrel has been
involved in many other cases, even the murder of his own wife,
when he lived in Chinello alley in Santo Antônio Parish. I hope
Your Excellency, who has merited such high praise from men of
good standing for your wise administration, will not fail to punish
a thief who is so dangerous to society that he has taken by these
means 950$000 from four innocent creatures. Your Excellency is
our Father. Bahia July 3, 1862. I swear before God that everything
written here is the honest truth.
Source: APEB, Subdelegado, 1861–62, maço 6234

The reader may remember that Cruz do Cosme was subdelegado
Piapitinga's district, and that Sinfrônio França, now being accused of
leniency, was the same officer who received the complaint about the
Pojavá candomblé and had done nothing about it. In this case, however, the target of the complaint was neither an African nor a creole
but a "light-skinned mulatto," almost white, who had allegedly set up a
Candomblé temple with funds from his clients, who went there looking
for good luck and cures for their ailments. The whistle-blower charged
"Pai Libânio" with causing the death of his own wife, but focused on
the story of another of his alleged victims, a young widow and mother
of four children who had also died in his care. Deeply concerned about

her daughter's illness, the young woman's mother is said to have sought the advice of one of the witch doctor's "fanatical" followers and paid him to cure her daughter.

This accusation contains an unmistakable tone of patriarchal conde-scension. It seems to have been written by a man who sought to include the women involved in these practices among the "fools" who fell for these scams, as the police chief viewed them, because a daughter, a mother, and a female adviser are the main characters in this plot. One was the victim, and the other two were the witch doctor's accomplices. It was as if these events had transpired because the women were not only impressionable but lacked male protection. The younger woman was a widow, and apparently her father was dead, as he was not shown in the picture. In short, the family was vulnerable because there were no men to defend their womenfolk from other men, particularly "profi-teers" like Libânio.

There was also a fourth woman involved, the young widow's slave, whom the alleged Candomblé priest was said to have accused of bewitching her owner, whose illness was purportedly caused by magic spells. Pai Libânio was said to have advised them to sell the slave – a punishment in itself – and to use the money to "celebrate the Saint," namely a pagan spirit or deity, that would cure her unfortunate mistress. The slave was sold, Libânio got paid, but his "saint" did not cure the young woman. Instead, Libânio's herbs were said to have killed her. Yet another family had lost one of its members through the pernicious work of a Candomblé witch doctor.

Called in by Chief João Henriques, subdelegado Sinfrônio França, Piapitinga's substitute, investigated the complaint and concluded that it was unfounded. On July 5, two days after he was informed of the case, França interrogated Libânio, who denied everything, and narrated pas-sages of his life story. Libânio said he had worked as a painter until he married the daughter of a merchant from the city, and her dowry had enabled him to start his own business. To prove that he lived by trade, he presented a document signed by an established merchant who guar-anteed that he had lent Libânio the considerable sum of 1,250,053 reis, the equivalent of the average price of a prime male slave in 1860. Half that sum was said to have been delivered "in goods," which suggests that the business transaction involved food products with which Libânio now traded. The accused assured the subdelegado that his house was not "built at the expense of his clients" – members of his so-called temple – as the whistle-blower had alleged, but purchased with the profits from his sales. He also said that he grew sugar cane and vegetables in a nearby parish, through a partnership formed two years earlier with the scion of a powerful Bahian family, the Rocha Pitta clan, which he attested with a copy of a contract the two associates had signed. To convince the subdelegado that the charges of quackery were false, Libânio also declared that all illnesses in his family, including that of his late wife, were treated by medical professionals and not by him, which he proved with a letter from a certified physician, confirming that he was the family doctor. Finally, according to the subdelegado, a search of Libânio's house found no signs of "his being a witchdoctor." The case was closed and the subdelegado reported the results of the investigation to the chief of police in a letter dated July 24, 1862, the day before Domingos Sodré's arrest.[39]

The case may have been closed at the police station, but not in the pages of *O Alabama*. Two years after Libânio was cleared, the newspaper would rehash the complaint as follows:

> The Subdelegado of the 2nd district of Santo Antônio should keep a vigilant eye on one Libânio, a well-known figure who lives in Cruz do Cosme, to ensure that he does not continue working as a witchdoctor, exorcist of demons and more besides … whom morality demands that we silence, given that some time ago said witchdoctor sent an unfortunate mother to eternity, it is said, after extorting 800$000 from the wretch, the value of a slave that she had sold; the intermediary in this knavery was Josefa So-and-So, a resident of Pilar, one of the worthy priestesses at the temple of that high priest.[40]

Despite the suggestion that Libânio continued to work as a healer, and that his terreiro was still active, the story added little to the complaint of 1862, except for Josefa's first name, which was not mentioned in the anonymous letter, as well as the amount – a smaller one – that Libânio was said to have extorted from the young widow. Even the expression "morality demands that we silence" also appeared in the anonymous letter sent to the chief of police. Because his complaint to law enforcement had gone nowhere, the author had apparently sought out the editor of

---

[39] Letter from Sinfrônio Pires da França, alternate subdelegado of the second district of Santo Antônio, to the chief of police, July 24, 1862, APEB, *Subdelegados, 1861–62*, maço 6234.
[40] *O Alabama*, April 13, 1864.

the newspaper to tell him the same story, which indicates that he was still doing his best to incriminate Libânio. Perhaps because he thought it was excessive, the editor preferred not to publish the charge that Libânio had also murdered his own wife.

The wife in question was Maria Chaves do Sacramento, who had died shortly after marrying Libânio. They were wed in October 1857 and had a daughter, Bárbara, born in September 1858, but only christened in September 1862 (the baptismal records state that she was white).[41] By 1862 Maria Chaves was dead already, and Libânio was living with Virginia Paula de Almeida, his second wife, whom he had "kidnapped" from a family that lived in Cruz do Cosme. This most likely means that the young woman had run away from home to elope with Libânio of her own free will. This was a common family transgression at the time, and to a certain extent, it was serious. The Church had punished the eloping pair with excommunication. But it was not long before the moral and religious offense was forgiven and the "kidnapping" followed by marriage. On September 30, 1862 – three months after the accusation of quackery and ten days after Bárbara was christened – they married in front of a domestic oratory in Libânio's home after being "absolved of excommunication, which they had incurred due to the kidnapping of the bride," as the presiding parish priest noted in the wedding registry for Santo Antônio parish.[42] That book also states that Libânio was born out of wedlock, but Virginia was not.

Virginia must have been heavily pregnant when she got married, because a week after the Catholic marriage ceremony, she gave birth to a daughter named Julia, who was registered as white. Another daughter, Damiana, was born two years later, and she had a twin brother, Cosme, who apparently died. Both were registered as pardos. A third child, Pedro, was also born in 1878. His color was not stated in the birth records. Libânio died that same year, at the age of forty. His work as a

---

[41] ACMS, *Livro de registro de casamentos. Santo Antonio Além do Carmo, 1840–1863*, fl. 152v; ACMS, *Livro de registro de batismos. Santo Antonio Além do Carmo, 1851–1866*, fl. 166v. It was not unusual for years to go by before a person was baptized. Among many others, this baptismal registry shows three people baptized in 1852, one born in 1833 (fl. 139), one born in 1840 (fl. 140), and another born in 1842 (fl. 170).

[42] ACMS, *Livro de registro de casamentos, freguesia de Santo Antônio Além do Carmo, 1840–1863*, fl. 186v.

painter before he became a merchant may have actually been harmful
to his health, as he had claimed in the 1862 interrogation. If he really
was a healer, he had not managed to heal himself.

None of this information provides a clue as to Libânio's possible
involvement with traditional medicine and divination, much less suggests that he had set up a Candomblé terreiro. However, his large bal-
conied house on Cruz do Cosme road may have sheltered more than
just his nuclear family, as it contained six rooms, parlors and dining
rooms, and a kitchen in the backyard. I have not been able to ascertain
whether slaves or other household members lived with him. He did not
own any slaves when he died, and "other household members" could
represent the community activity typical of a terreiro.

At his death, Libânio owned two other, smaller houses in the same
district. Neither those nor the big house were valuable properties,
because they were located in a remote, semi-rural district full of small
farms and populated by black freedpersons. When they were auctioned
off after the death of his widow in 1882, the three houses, initially valued at 800,000 reis, only sold for a little more than 500,000 reis the following year, which was not even half the purchase price of a good slave.
If Libânio actually had taken nearly a million reis from that young
widow twenty years earlier, he had not invested it wisely. Even his legitimate business had not prospered, possibly damaged by the scandal of
the anonymous complaint. He died penniless.[43]

It is entirely possible that Libânio the "light-skinned mulatto" –
although the records for his first marriage show him as "white" – may
have mobilized a vast and powerful network of protectors, clients, and
patients, including subdelegado Sinfrônio, to defend himself from the
charge of quackery in 1862. The speed with which he managed to
gather evidence in his defense and the high status of the people who
backed up his statements are impressive. They included a respected
physician, a wholesaler, and a rural landowner with a family name that
was above suspicion – Rocha Pitta, his partner in the farming enterprise. In fact, six decades earlier, Libânio's partner's father had dealings
with Domingos Sodré's master, who had leased a famous sugar plantation, named Freguesia, from him.[44] As I have suggested, people of the

[43] APEB, *Judiciária. Inventários*, 04/1405/1874/06.
[44] Cristóvão da Rocha Pitta, the father, was born illegitimate, but was recognized
and made the heir of the captain-general of the same name, the owner of the
Freguesia plantation studied by Wanderley Pinho, *História de um engenho do*

same social standing as these witnesses could have been involved in traditional medicine, divination, and Candomblé, but I have not found stronger evidence in Libânio's story to confirm that.

Therefore, it seems that although the author of the anonymous letter swore by God, the complaint was nothing but "slander," as Libânio had called it. It is possible that the charge of "quackery" and Virginia's elopement may have been connected, given the coincidence of dates. If the marriage took place in September, by early July, when the subdelegado received that anonymous letter, the "kidnapping" was a fait accompli, and the young woman's belly was growing. The accuser may have been a disgruntled relative who felt their family had been dishonored, or even one of Virginia's disappointed suitors.

In any event, Libânio's secret enemy, who must have lived in the same district, was probably inspired by recent events in the neighborhood – namely, the raid on the Candomblé in Pojavá – when he wrote that incriminating letter. In that case, he must have paid close attention to the clash between Chief João Henriques and subdelegado Piapitinga a few months earlier, because things of this sort leaked from official police channels to chats in bars and pubs, workshops, and barbershops, as well as the doors, windows, and parlors of private homes. The author of the complaint may even have witnessed the raid on the Pojavá Candomblé. He must also have read Henriques' bulletin in the newspapers, in which the chief ordered his subordinates to crack down on the Candomblé practices. In short, these episodes probably inspired him to concoct that tirade against Libânio. In any case, and this is the point I want to underscore, the anonymous accuser had taken advantage of the atmosphere of religious repression that the police chief exacerbated in the city in order to embarrass his rival, at the very least, and perhaps not just him, as the letter also implicated subdelegado Sinfrônio, charging him with favoring Candomblé in his district, just as two police chiefs had done in regard to local subdelegados Faria and Piapitinga. It could be that the poison pen had invented the story from whole cloth, or just adapted it with different characters.

Recôncavo, 2nd ed. (São Paulo: Companhia Editora Nacional; Brasília, Instituto Nacional do Livro, 1982), esp. 177–183. Domingos Sodré's master, whom we will meet in the following chapter, leased the Freguesia plantation in 1829. See "Escriptura de arrendamento que faz Christovão da Rocha Pita...ao Coronel Francisco Maria Sodré Pereira ...," June 10, 1829, APEB, *LNT*, vol. 236, fls. 29–29v.

A charge like that, even when unfounded, did nothing to bolster Chief João Henriques' confidence in his auxiliaries. But he did not think the police were just lenient toward Bahian candomblés. In his view, this issue led to another matter: the masters' failure to control their slaves. According to the police chief, uncontrolled slaves helped grease the works of African "sorcerers," as well as posing a threat to law and order in Salvador. Therefore, on April 23, 1862, the day before he issued his communiqué to the subdelegados, Henriques published a notice in the newspapers ordering slaveholders to keep a close eye on their slaves' behavior, making them return home before curfew and stay there, forbidding them from wandering the city streets in defiance of city laws that banned them from "uttering obscenities, [engaging in] drumming sessions, uproar, roughhousing and gatherings for various purposes."[45] Now the chief of police was interfering directly in private negotiations between masters and slaves, which often resulted in less oppression and more autonomy for the enslaved, as long as the slaveholders' economy was not affected. These negotiations enabled many slaves to escape the day-to-day control of their masters and work, eat, sleep, and live on their own. They were known as *negros de ganho*, slave earners or slaves for hire. Many of these men and women would only meet up with their masters on Saturdays to "pay for the week," meaning that they gave them a contracted portion of the products of their labor. Slaves for hire lived off what was left over and, with luck and hard work, some managed to build up enough savings to invest in their own manumission. These informal agreements between masters and slaves were typical of urban slavery. Masters and district officials often formed a paternalistic network that exerted negotiated control over bondmen and women, unlike the control required by a police chief who was disturbed by African drumming sessions that, in his belief, hindered the flourishing of civilization in Bahia.[46]

[45] Communiqué by the chief of police, April 21, 1862, *Diário da Bahia*, April 23, 1862.

[46] For the urban slaves' living arrangements in nineteenth-century Bahia, see Reis, *Rebelião escrava*, chap. 12, and particularly Ana de Lourdes Costa, "*Ekabó!*: Trabalho escravo e condições de moradia e reordenamento urbano em Salvador no século XIX," MA thesis, UNIVERSIDADE FEDERAL DA BAHIA School of Architecture, 1989. For Rio de Janeiro, see Ynaê Lopes dos Santos, *Além da Senzala. Arranjos escravos de moradia no Rio de Janeiro (1808–1850)* (São Paulo: HUCITEC, 2010).

A Trustworthy Subdelegado

I have no idea what masters and slaves thought of Chief João Henriques' communiqué to his subdelegados. As for the latter, generally speaking they did not respond enthusiastically to his orders on Candomblé. I have found a letter from the police chief to the subdelegado of the small parish of Rua do Passo, in which he commented on "your amiable response to my bulletin." Here, too, Henriques complained that superstitious practices to "bring good fortune and remove spells" reflected "poorly on our civilization" as well as giving rise to unspecified "crimes and misfortunes." He wrote that he was counting on the subdelegado for Passo and his inspectors to stay on the alert to combat that "criminal enterprise."[47]

Another subdelegado who aptly met Henriques' expectations was in charge of São Pedro parish – the same officer who would be responsible for Domingos Sodré's arrest a few months later. He had replaced the former subdelegado, a lawyer named Antônio José Pereira de Albuquerque, who had recently resigned for health reasons.[48]

A resident of Ladeira de São Bento (Figure 3), not far from Domingos' home, Pompílio Manoel de Castro was forty-two in 1862, and married. He was not a lawyer, because he is never given the title of *doutor*, a perquisite of people with law or medical degrees. However, he was a denizen of the world of parochial arts and letters in the provincial capital. He served as the director of the Philosophical Society in the mid-1840s, and in 1862 he was the president of Bahia's Philharmonic Society. At the same time, he occupied the position of second secretary of the Drama Conservatory, the agency responsible for censoring plays in the province. He was also a founding member of the Historical Institute of Bahia and attended its opening session on May 5, 1856. On that occasion he found himself among authorities such as the president of the province and the militia commander, as well as figures from Bahia's intelligentsia, including English art collector and medical school professor Jonathas Abott, educator Abílio César Borges, poet Agrário de Meneses, and others.

[47] Chief of police to the subdelegado of Rua do Passo, May 1, 1862, APEB, *Correspondência*, vol. 5754, fl. 115v.

[48] For Albuquerque's sick leave, see his letter to the chief of police, J. R. Barros de Lacerda, January 17, 1863, APEB, *Correspondência*, maço 5754, fl. 350; for Pompílio's appointment as second alternate in 1860, see his letter to the chief of police dated March 1, 1860, APEB, *Subdelegados*, maço 6233.

Figure 3. Ladeira de São Bento (ca. 1870), the address of subdelegado Pompílio Manoel de Castro, who arrested Domingos Sodré. The African freedman lived just a few feet away.

Pompílio served as second secretary of the Historical Institute for many years, under the supervision of its president, Archbishop Primate Romualdo Seixas. In the 1873 *Almanak*, a register of all public employees and professionals in Bahia, the subdelegado's name appears as third vice president of that institution, as well as vice president of the general assembly of the Montepio da Bahia charity, which had more than 200 members and considerable capital – 39 million reis. Finally, he was an alternate member of the Voter Qualification Board of São Pedro parish, a strategic position in the city's politics. In the time left over from so many activities, Pompílio earned his living as section chief of the Imperial Treasury, a post that made him the fourth-highest person in the ranks of an agency made up of nearly 200 civil servants. In short, Domingos' arresting officer was no small fry.[49]

---

49 For information about Pompílio: *Almanak ... de 1863*, 234, 299, 304, 305; *Almanak...de 1873*, 106, 113, 165; *Periódico do Instituto Histórico da Bahia*, 1 (1863): 17; *O Musaico*, 17 (November 1846): 273; Arquivo Municipal de

In addition to his salary, Pompílio probably lived off the earnings of his slaves. He owned at least two African slave women, Leopoldina and Henriqueta, and Henriqueta's three daughters, Feliscicima (whose name ironically means "Overjoyed"), Aniceta, and Maria. I am convinced that the young Crioula called Feliscicima got her name – which is ridiculous for someone born into slavery – because she had come into the world on July 2, 1854, the ever-festive anniversary of Bahia's independence from Portugal. Pompílio wanted to play the patriot by giving the poor slave girl that name. Other masters preferred to free their slaves as proof of their patriotism.[50]

It is already clear that Pompílio was a provincial intellectual capable of producing gems like this:

> True education can never harmonize with the character of so-called philosophers, who, little content with renouncing all Religious feeling, even struggle and strive to suffocate them [sic] in their fellows, showing even more commitment when it begins to sprout in the nascent spirits of unsuspecting youth.... Forward! O beautiful and hopeful youth, full of knowledge.... I have therefore asked Providence that you should always tread the path of learned and religious men.[51]

In this speech, given in the presence of an assembly of unsuspecting youths at the Educational Society of Bahia, the subdelegado demonstrated that his beef was not just with the African religion but extended to the European Enlightenment as well. He believed, as he would say, in the "true enlightenment of the Catholic Faith," and that was the predominant mind-set in

Salvador (AMS), *Livro de qualificação de votantes. São Pedro, 1863*, vol. 596, fl. 9v (age and marital status). For delegados and subdelegados, see Flory, *Judge and Jury*, esp. chap. 9; and Richard Graham, *Patronage and Politics in Nineteenth-Century Brazil* (Stanford, CA: Stanford University Press, 1990), 55–64 and passim.

50 Pompílio's slave women appear in baptismal records for 1854, 1855, 1856, and 1863. See *Livro de registro de batismo. Freguesia de São Pedro, 1853–1851*, fls. 59, 105, and 142v; and ACMS, *Livro de registro de batismos. Freguesia de São Pedro, 1861–1865*, fl. 109v.

51 "Allocução recitada pelo orador da Comissão Philosophica Pompílio Manoel de Castro por ocasião do convite que lhe fez a Sociedade Instrutiva afim de ser presente à mesma Sociedade a sua sessão geral, em o dia 24 de março de 1845," *O Musaico*, 17 (November 1846): 273.

the intellectual environments in which Pompílio moved, including the Historical Institute headed by Archbishop Romualdo.[52]

The chief of police had found in this subdelegado the ideal soldier for his war on Bahian Candomblé.

Two days after issuing the April 24 communiqué, Henriques ordered Pompílio to investigate reports of a powerful drumming session. It was located on a busy street, Rua de Baixo de São Bento (now Carlos Gomes), on the corner of Ladeira de Santa Tereza, where Domingos lived. Pompílio acted quickly, and the following day he wrote to Henriques that the tenant of the house cited in the complaint should be punished. She was a slave who had long been devoted to the "trade" of African beliefs, one of those slave women who, sometimes with the help of certain esoteric knowledge, lived far outside their masters' ken. But the chief wanted to delve even deeper, and asked his subordinate to find the person responsible for renting out that house and have them "sign a promise of good behavior through which they undertake to follow an honest livelihood that is not offensive to morality and respectable customs, seeing that I am aware that in addition to those superstitious acts, other heinous events take place in that house that excite the neighbors' imaginations." These heinous events were, undoubtedly, the same "vile acts" the police chief had mentioned in his communiqué to the subdelegados – that is, veritable sexual orgies were said to take place behind the scenes of Candomblé. Of course, generally speaking, this was nothing more than the product of the neighbors' fevered imaginations, and the police chief's as well. He decided to put the blame on the constable, Francisco Januário Cordeiro, whom he deemed another advocate of tolerance, as well as a follower of African customs, particularly the "vile" part.[53]

The police chief accused Cordeiro, poor lamb, of colluding with the candomblé on Rua de Baixo (literally Lower Street), an area within the constable's jurisdiction, which explained how that activity could have gone on "for many months, if not years" without being disturbed. João Henriques was probably right. Unfortunately, I have not been able to find the constable's response to that charge, just the reply from the

52 See, for example, "Memória lida no Instituto Histórico da Bahia na sessão de 14 de junho de 1857 pelo 1º secretário dessa sociedade, Manoel Correa Garcia," *Periódico do Instituto Histórico da Bahia*, 6 (1864): 84–100.

53 Chief Henriques to the subdelegado of São Pedro, April 26 and May 2, 1862, APEB, *Polícia. Correspondência*, vol. 5754, fls. 113 and 117.

obedient subdelegado Pompílio, sent a week later, stating that he had forced the owner of the house to sign the agreement. Pompílio had also recommended that the constable "not consent to immoral acts, for which he would answer, if he allowed them to continue, as they were against the law and respectable customs," and thus repeated the sound words of his enlightened superior.[54]

Domingos' arrest took place at a time of tremendous tension for leaders, followers, and clients of Candomblé and other religious practices associated with the Africans. The police authorities, although not always sure how best to combat them, did not take a clear stance in their defense. That was not how the game was played. Tolerance was a discreet movement among the people involved in Candomblé and the authorities directly responsible for policing the city's various districts, whether they were subdelegados or inspectors. To survive and function, Candomblé houses also depended on their neighbors, who could either complain or keep quiet about what they saw and heard from their homes, the more or less strict vigilance of the press, and varying degrees of pressure from political authorities and high-ranking police officers. Given so many variables, the lives of those who engaged in or sought out Candomblé were risky, even more so when orthodox figures like João Antônio de Araújo Freitas Henriques and Pompílio Manoel de Castro joined forces. Either one of them would have been a worthy adversary for Domingos Sodré, but the diviner was faced with both.

In the next chapter, we will learn a bit more about this African. After all, he is the protagonist in this story, and our guide through the world of nineteenth-century Bahian Candomblé.

[54] Chief Henriques to the subdelegado of São Pedro, May 2, 1862, APEB, *Polícia. Correspondência*, vol. 5754, fl. 117; Pompílio Manoel de Castro to the chief of police, May 9, 1862, APEB, *Polícia. Subdelegados*, maço 6234.

CHAPTER TWO

From an African in Onim to a
Slave in Bahia

Domingos' African Background

We know very little about Domingos' African background. Once he was in Bahia, he was identified as a Nagô, one of the many African "nations" or ethnic terms that, in this case, designated the Yoruba-speaking people. In 1882, Domingos stated in his last will and testament that he was born in the Yoruba kingdom of Onim, and I estimate his birth to be in the late eighteenth century. He also declared that he was the "legitimate child" of African parents, Porfírio Araújo de Argolo and "Bárbara de tal," or "surname unknown."[1]

I can think of two possible narratives for this African family's enslavement. One is that Domingos and his parents were sold and shipped to Bahia together, because he mentioned Christian names for both of them as well as his father's Brazilian surname, neither of which sufficed to find them in the local archives.[2] Their names also indicate that both parents managed to achieve manumission, because slaves rarely carried surnames. They also suggest that each member of the family belonged

---

[1] Domingos Sodré's last will and testament is reproduced in full in Appendix 1.

[2] Maria Inês Côrtes de Oliveira, "Viver e morrer no meio dos seus: nações e comunidades africanas na Bahia do século XIX," *Revista USP*, no. 28 (1995–1996): 177–179, identifies members of African families brought to Bahia together on the same ship or who were reunited in nineteenth-century Bahia after arriving on different vessels. See also the case of the African woman named Francisca da Silva, a Candomblé high priestess whose two sons were sentenced for participation in the 1835 rebellion: Lisa Earl Castillo and Luís Nicolau Parés, "Marcelina da Silva: A Nineteenth-Century Candomblé Priestess in Bahia." *Slavery & Abolition*, no. 31 (2010):1–27.

to a different master, at least at the time when they were freed. The son's surname was Sodré, the father's was Araújo de Argolo, an aristocratic family name in Bahia, and the mother's was unknown: by the time he dictated his will in his old age, Domingos could no longer remember it.

Another, less likely, possibility is that Domingos' parents were freed-persons who had returned to Africa from Bahia, and that is why he referred to them by their Christian names, which returnees usually retained. Most of the former slaves known to have embarked on that return journey did so at a later time, particularly after the Revolt of the Malês in 1835, when many were deported from Brazil and others decided to leave Brazil after relentless government harassment. The returnees formed veritable colonies of "Brazilians" – also called *agudás* – in several ports in the Bight of Benin during that period, but there are records of Africans who returned from slavery in the eighteenth century. Domingos' parents might have been among them. In this case, our protagonist would presumably have been born into a family that had left Brazil and settled in Onim.[3]

The place where Domingos stated he was born, and from where he was eventually deported as a slave, was Onim, the term used at the time by Europeans to refer to the kingdom of Lagos, now a very large metropolis in Nigeria. Travelers from Portugal and Brazil called it Onim and, less frequently, Lagos, while its indigenous name was and still is Èkó.

---

[3] For communities of returnees in the Bight of Benin, see, among many other titles, Pierre Verger, *Flux et reflux de la traite des nègres entre le golfe de Benin et Bahia de Todos os Santos* (Paris: Mouton, 1968), chap. XVI; Michael J. Turner, "*Les Brésiliens*: The Impact of Former Brazilian Slaves upon Dahomey," PhD dissertation, Boston University, 1975; Cunha, *Negros, estrangeiros*; Milton Guran, *Agudás: os "brasileiros" do Benim* (Rio de Janeiro: Nova Fronteira, 2000); Linda Lindsay, "'To Return to the Bosom of Their Fatherland': Brazilian Immigrants in Nineteenth-Century Lagos," *Slavery & Abolition* 15, no. 1 (1994): 22–50; Alberto da Costa e Silva, *Francisco Félix de Souza, mercador de escravos* (Rio de Janeiro: Nova Fronteira, 2004); Robin Law and Kristin Mann, "West Africa in the Atlantic Community: The Case of the Slave Coast," *The William and Mary Quarterly* 56, no. 2 (1999): 307–334; Robin Law, "A comunidade brasileira de Uidá e os últimos anos do tráfico atlântico de escravos, 1850–66." *Afro-Ásia*, 27 (2002): 41–77; Silke Strickrodt, "'Afro-Brazilians' of the Western Slave Coast in the Nineteenth Century," in *Enslaving Connections: Changing Cultures of Africa and Brazil during the Era of the Slave Trade*, ed. José C. Curto and Paul E. Lovejoy (Amherst, NY: Humanity Books, 2004), 213–244; and Alcione Meira Amos, *Os que voltaram: a história dos retornados afro-brasileiros na África Ocidental no século XIX* (Belo Horizonte: Tradição Planalto, 2007).

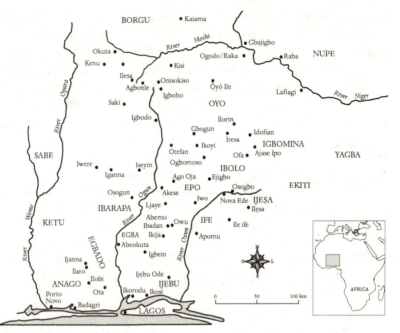

Map 2. Map of Yorubaland.

British diplomat, explorer, and scholar Richard Burton, who visited Onim a year before Domingos' arrest in Bahia, wrote that "The town is known to its population and throughout Yoruba as Eko."[4]

The Yoruba people were not a politically unified group in Domingos' Africa. They occupied a vast territory in the southwest of what is now Nigeria, and part of the east of the present-day Republic of Benin, an area that ranged from the powerful kingdom of Ọ̀yọ́ in the north to Lagos near the Atlantic in the far south.[5] Domingos' birthplace was a small kingdom

[4] Richard F. Burton, *Wanderings in West Africa* (New York: Dover, 1991 [orig. 1863]), 2 vols., ii: 231. The name Lagos appears in the documentary records for the first time in the mid-1850s, and from that time forward it would gradually replace the name Onim, according to A. B. Aderibigbe, "Early History of Lagos to about 1850," in *Lagos: The Development of an African City*, ed. A. B. Aderibigbe (Lagos: Longman Nigeria, 1975), 15.

[5] I will sometimes use the term *Yoruba* here, but I should explain that it was not in use at the time when Domingos embarked for Bahia as a term of ethnic self-identification or a language identified by that name. It came into use gradually in Africa over the course of the second half of the nineteenth century. In Domingos' time, Oyo's northern non-Yoruba neighbors used Yoruba, Yarriba, and other, similar terms when referring to the people of Oyo. See John Peel, "The

located in marshlands at the tip of a peninsula that lay between the ocean and the complex of lakes and lagoons on the Slave Coast, the region in the Bight of Benin that got its name because of its importance as a slave-trade entrepôt. Roughly the same coastal region was known to the Portuguese and Brazilians as the Mina Coast, or Costa da Mina, a term derived from the fifteenth-century fort of São Jorge of Elmina in present-day Ghana. There were several famous slave ports on that coast, including Little Popo (or Anécho), Grand-Popo, Ouidah (or Ajudá), Jakin, Porto Novo (or Ajase), Badagry, and Lagos. Domingos' native land began to attain growing importance in the Atlantic trade circuit in the late eighteenth century and became the busiest port of slave embarkation in the last three decades of the slave trade with Bahia, between 1820 and 1850. In 1823, for example, the British seized the ship of one of the most powerful Bahian slave traders of that time, José de Cerqueira Lima, near Lagos. That kingdom was then at war with the neighboring kingdom of Badagry, its rival in the human trafficking business, a situation that always attracted traders eager to snatch up prisoners of war.[6]

The 1823 conflict was probably an outcome of the struggle for the succession to the throne of Lagos that began at the turn of the century – when Domingos was still a child – between two half-brothers, Osinlokun and Adele. According to local tradition, Osinlokun was a wealthy slave trader and the eldest brother, and therefore the presumed heir to the throne. However, he was passed over in favor of Adele, who was younger but more adept at politics. Also according to local tradition, Adele obtained the backing of the traditional chiefs and king makers, perhaps

Cultural Work of Yoruba Ethnogenesis," in *History and Ethnicity*, ed. E. Tonkin, E. M. McDonald, and M. Chapman (London and New York: Routledge & Kegan Paul, 1989), 198–215. For a brief introduction to the history of the kingdom of Onim/Lagos, see Robert S. Smith, *Kingdoms of the Yoruba* (London: Methuen, 1969), esp. 89–94; and for a recent authoritative study, Kristin Mann, *Slavery and the Birth of an African City: Lagos, 1760–1900* (Bloomington: University of Indiana Press, 2007).

6 Report from José Maurício Fernandes Pereira de Barros to the minister of foreign affairs, September 21, 1867, Arquivo Histórico do Itamarati (AHI), *Comissão Mista*, lata 64, pasta 1, maço 3. For Lagos's rise as a slave-trading entrepôt in the late eighteenth century, see Robin Law, "Trade and Politics behind the Slave Coast: The Lagoon Traffic and the Rise of Lagos, 1500–1800," *Journal of African History*, vol. 24 (1983): 321–348. See also Law and Mann, "West Africa and the Atlantic Community"; and Mann, *Slavery and the Birth of an African City*, chap. 1. For the slave trader Cerqueira Lima, see Verger, *Flux et reflux*, 449–451, for instance.

swaying them with gifts. Oṣinlokun was said to have accepted their choice of Adele at first, and some sources say that he even supported his half-brother, possibly because he realized he had no chance of defeating him. But he later regretted that decision when Adele began to threaten his commercial interests, and war broke out between their supporters. Vanquished in Lagos, Adele went into exile to Badagry, his mother's birthplace, where he was crowned king and set up a major slave trade base with the help of and investments from the famous Brazilian slave trader Francisco Felix de Souza, also known as Chachá, whose main base of operation was Whydah, and his son Isidoro. Human trafficking flourished significantly in Badagry during that period. In the course of his political and trade war with Lagos, Adele occasionally attacked his former kingdom while making war on the other powers in the region, such as Porto Novo, which were also his business rivals. Oṣinlokun died around 1829, and his son Idewu Ojulari succeeded him, reigning until about 1835. After waging yet another series of military campaigns against his nephew, Adele regained the throne of Lagos and transferred most of his slave trade business to that kingdom.[7]

According to historian Kristin Mann, the conflict between the two half-brothers began sometime between 1811 and 1820, during Adele's first reign, which is the most likely period when Domingos was taken to Bahia, probably closer to the first than to the last date. In the middle of the century, a British consul assessed that, in Lagos, a "constant succession of civil wars" had reduced "a great portion of its inhabitants" to slavery.[8] Therefore, there is a very good chance that Domingos became one of the victims of the first waves of that fratricidal war, and as such, was sold to Bahian slave traders. It is less likely that Domingos was kidnapped or sold as punishment for a crime that he or a family member had committed. Theft, adultery, gambling, and unpaid debts were some of the offenses punishable with being sold to the transatlantic slave

[7] For these conflicts and the sale of their victims to the slave trade, see Robin Law, "The Career of Adele at Lagos and Badagry, c. 1807 – c. 1837," *Journal of the Historical Society of Nigeria*, no. 2 (1978): 35–59; Robin Law, "Francisco Felix de Souza in West Africa, 1820–1849," in *Enslaving Connections*, 200; Kristin Mann, "The World the Slave Traders Made: Lagos, c. 1760–1850," in *Identifying Enslaved Africans: Proceeding of the UNESCO/SSHRCC Summer Institute*, ed. Paul E. Lovejoy (Toronto: York University, 1997), 201–204, 207; and Mann, *Slavery and the Birth of an African City*, esp. 45–47.

[8] Mann, *Slavery and the Birth of an African City*, 47, 52, regarding the beginnings of the conflict in the region and the British consul's assessment, respectively.

trade. No matter which of these mechanisms transformed him into a commodity, when Domingos fell into the slave traders' net, he would have been between fifteen and twenty years old.

When Domingos was enslaved in Africa, wars were a constant fact of life in Yorubaland, from north to south, and both Lagos and Badagry were involved in these conflicts. Thousands of people were shipped across the Atlantic between the late 1810s and 1850, the victims of wars of Islamic expansion and successive clashes in the interior of Yorubaland that would lead to the decline and fall of the once-powerful empire of Ọ̀yọ́, followed by struggles for political hegemony among the various Yoruba states. Richard Lander and John Lander, two brothers who visited the region as emissaries of the British government in the early 1830s, witnessed the heavy toll these conflicts exacted from the perspective of the political elite: "It is somewhat strange that the chief or governor of almost every town through which we have passed since leaving Badagry, who was alive and well on my return to the coast three years ago, has been either killed in war, or has died from natural causes."[9]

Bahia was the most likely destination for prisoners of the Yoruba wars. In fact, during Domingos' time there, emissaries of the king of Lagos visited that part of Brazil on several occasions, and the reason for their missions was none other than the slave trade. One of those envoys is said to have been a black man named Manoel Alves (or Alvares) Lima, who happened to be in Bahia during the war for independence in

---

[9] Richard Lander and John Lander, *Journal of an Expedition to Explore the Course and Termination of the Niger* (New York: Harper & Brother, 1837), 126. There is an extensive bibliography on the rise and fall of Ọ̀yọ́ and the ensuing strife in that region. See, among others, Robin Law, *The Oyo Empire, c. 1600 – c. 1836: A West African Imperialism in the Era of the Atlantic Slave Trade* (Oxford: Oxford University Press, 1977); Robin Law, "The Chronology of the Yoruba Wars of the Early Nineteenth Century: A Reconsideration," *Journal of the Historical Society of Nigeria*, no. 2 (1970): 211–222; and Toyin Falola and G. O. Oguntomisin, *Yoruba Warlords of the Nineteenth Century* (Trenton, NJ: Africa World Press, 2001). For the connection between the conflicts in the interior and the slave trade, see also Peter Morton-Williams, "The Oyo Yoruba and the Atlantic Trade, 1670–1830," *Journal of the Historical Society of Nigeria* 3, no. 1 (1964): 25–45; Paul Lovejoy, "The Central Sudan and the Atlantic Slave Trade," in *Paths Toward the Past: African Historical Essays in Honor of Jan Vansina*, ed. Robert W. Harms et al. (Atlanta, GA: African Studies Association, 1994), 345–370; and especially Olatunji Ojo, "The Organization of the Atlantic Slave Trade in Yorubaland, ca. 1777 to ca. 1856," *The International Journal of African Historical Studies*, 41, no. 1 (2008): 77–100.

1823, when he wrote several letters to the prince regent, later Emperor Pedro I, to report on the ups and downs of the campaign against the Portuguese. The same person entered and left the province of Bahia in the following years. In 1825, he lived in Rio de Janeiro at the expense of the imperial government, but he wanted to return to Bahia. We know that he gave Pedro I an African "cane walking stick which according to his account is the badge of dignity conferred by African monarchs upon their representatives," according to a report from the British consul general in Rio de Janeiro, Henry Chamberlain, who was referring to a *recade* (not a "walking stick"), a baton that he correctly defined as a symbol of the Oba of Onim´s authority given to his envoys. That same year, the consul informed London that Manoel Alves Lima had introduced himself as the "Ambassador of the Emperor of Benin" and had spent twelve years in Bahia. Perhaps as a result of Lima's efforts, but particularly because of the commercial interests linking Lagos and Bahia, Oba Oṣinlokun was probably the first foreign leader to recognize Brazil's independence from Portugal in 1822, although that gesture meant nothing to the Europeanized Brazilian political elites of the day.[10]

David Eltis calculates that between 1801 and 1825, about 114,200 slaves, almost all of them prisoners of war from Yorubaland, passed through Lagos, of the total of 236,600 embarked from all the ports in the Bight of Benin to various parts of the Americas. During that same period, the number of Yoruba speakers specifically deported to Bahia through the ports on the Slave Coast totaled about 175,200. Over the course of the first half of the nineteenth century, nearly four out of five slaves who left the Bight of Benin disembarked in Bahia. An estimate made for 1846 found that 72.6 percent of the 9,403 slaves imported by Bahia had embarked in Lagos.[11]

[10] Verger, *Flux et reflux*, 270–273, 276–277; Alberto da Costa e Silva, "Cartas de um embaixador de Onim," *Cadernos do CHDD* 4, no. 6, (2005): 195–205; H. Chamberlain, consul general, to George Canning, Rio de Janeiro, January 29, 1825, British National Archives, Foreign Office, 13/8, fls. 109–110. I thank Hendrik Kraay for providing a copy of this document, which he also uses in "Muralhas da independência e liberdade do Brasil: a participação popular nas lutas políticas (Bahia, 1820–25)," in A *Independência brasileira: novas dimensões*, ed. Jurandir Malerba (Rio de Janeiro: Editora FGV, 2006), 303–304.

[11] David Eltis, "The Diaspora of Yoruba Speakers, 1650–1865: Dimensions and Implications," in *The Yoruba Diaspora in the Atlantic World*, ed. Toyin Falola and Matt D. Childs (Bloomington and Indianapolis: Indiana University Press, 2004), 24, 31, 38. Regarding slaves imported in 1846, see Ubiratan Castro de

Domingos was among that impressive number of people deported to Brazil during this era, and possibly his parents as well, but they came from a Yoruba kingdom that had few representatives among the Africans in Bahia. According to Nina Rodrigues, most Nagôs disembarked in Bahia in the first half of the nineteenth century came from Ọ̀yọ́, Ileṣa, and Egba, in that order, which coincides with what we now know about the progress of the wars in Yorubaland. "Those from Lagos, Ketu and Ibadan are fewer in number," wrote the professor of medicine in the late nineteenth century.[12] However, Lagos would become an important cultural and political reference for the Africans who lived in Bahia after the slave trade ended in the 1850s, as a result of three main and combined factors: the trade between that kingdom and Bahia, which increased its imports of West African products, principally red palm oil, textiles (pano-da-costa), and Candomblé ritual objects; the communities of returnees that had formed in Lagos; and the fact that Africans and their children who lived in Bahia frequently traveled there, often for both secular education and training in Yoruba religion.[13]

DOMINGOS' MASTER

When Domingos arrived in Bahia sometime in the mid to late 1810s, the sugar trade was booming. He was a victim of Bahia's renewed progress, beginning in the late eighteenth century, bolstered by the slave revolution in Haiti (1791–1804), which had destroyed plantation slavery on the island and removed the world's leading sugar supplier from the market. The international demand for sugar boosted Bahia's production, along with that of the sugar-planting colonies in the Caribbean,

Araújo, "1846: um ano na rota Bahia-Lagos. Negócios, negociantes e outros parceiros," Afro-Ásia, 21/22 (1998–1999): 90.

[12] Rodrigues, Os africanos no Brasil, 104.

[13] For these voyages, see J. Lorand Matory, Black Atlantic Religion: Tradition, Transnationalism, and Matriarchy in the Afro-Brazilian Candomblé (Princeton, NJ and Oxford: Princeton University Press, 2005), esp. chap. 1. For detailed archival research on the subject, see Lisa Earl Castillo, "Between Memory, Myth and History: Transatlantic Voyagers of the Casa Branca Temple," in Paths of the Atlantic Slave Trade: Interactions, Identities, and Images, ed. Ana Lúcia Araújo (Amherst, NY: Cambria Press, 2011), 203–238; idem, "Vida e viagens de Bamboxê Obitikô," in Minha vida é orixá, ed. Air José Souza de Jesus and Vilson Caetano de Souza Jr. (São Paulo: Editora Ifá, 2011), 55–86; and Castillo and Parés, "Marcelina da Silva".

increased the number of sugar plantations, expanded the cane fields, and consequently fueled the traffic in forced African labor. Bahia's thriving sugar economy would only fizzle temporarily during the struggles for independence in 1822 and 1823. Domingos' master was one of the fortunate individuals who benefited from these developments.[14]

In the numerous documents I have consulted, the African priest's name appears as Domingos Sodré, Domingos Sodré Pereira, and even Domingos Pereira Sodré. Sodré is often spelled Sudré in these sources.[15] The freedman had a prestigious surname that belonged to the heir of an entailed estate, founded in 1711 by wealthy field commander Jerônimo Sodré Pereira. When Domingos arrived in Bahia as a slave, the estate was headed by militia colonel Francisco Maria Sodré Pereira. In addition to owning the family's property in Portugal, the colonel was a major landowner in the Recôncavo, the region of Bahia where sugar plantations were concentrated.[16] Domingos began his life as a slave in Brazil on one of those plantations.

In 1882, Domingos stated in his will that he had been christened on the Engenho (or sugar plantation) Trindade in Santo Amaro da

---

[14] For the sugar economy in Bahia during this period, see Stuart Schwartz, *Sugar Plantations in the Formation of Brazilian Society: Bahia, 1535–1835* (Cambridge: Cambridge University Press, 1985), chap. 15; and B. J. Barickman, *A Bahian Counterpoint: Sugar, Tobacco, Cassava, and Slavery in the Recôncavo, 1780–1860* (Stanford, CA: Stanford University Press, 1998), chap. 2.

[15] I have decided to use the more modern spelling of Sodré. For the social reasoning behind naming slaves and freedpersons in Bahia at that time, see Jean Hébrard, "Esclavage et dénomination: imposition et appropriation d'un nom chez les esclaves de la Bahia au xixᵉ siècle," *Cahiers du Brésil Contemporain*, no. 53–54 (2003): 31–92.

[16] For the colonel's interests in Portugal, see "Procuração bastante que faz o coronel Francisco Maria Sodré Pereira," June 23, 1825, APEB, *LNT*, vol. 214, fls. 134–134v. Regarding *morgados*, or entailed estates, Kátia Mattoso writes: "they are estates of limited ownership. They are perpetually in the hands of a specific family and can never be shared or sold because, once created, an entailed estate is indivisible and inalienable. Therefore, the main objective of this system is to maintain a family's prestige and protect its fortune. The institution of entailed estates was very rare in Bahia: there were just ten or so throughout the entire colonial period." Mattoso, *Família e sociedade na Bahia no século XIX* (Salvador: Corrupio, 1988), 53. For the Sodré family, see Mario Torres, "Os Sodrés," *Revista do Instituto Genealógico da Bahia*, no. 7 (1952): 89–148; Mario Torres, "Os morgados do Sodré," *Revista do Instituto Genealógico da Bahia*, no. 5 (1951): 9–34; and Dain Borges, *The Family in Bahia, Brazil, 1870–1944* (Stanford, CA: Stanford University Press, 1992), 60, 123, 249–251.

Purificação, where Colonel Francisco Sodré owned and leased land. In 1807, the Trindade plantation, located on the Acupe River in São Domingos de Saubara parish, was registered as the property of Thereza Maria de França Corte Real. I have not yet found any record of Francisco Sodré's having purchased that property, but the deed of a loan he took out mentions that he owned the Trindade plantation – as well as the Engenho Novo – in August 1816. The collateral for the 4,600,000-reis loan contracted with João Baptista de Araújo Braga, a merchant, was a building on Ladeira de Santa Tereza street, where Domingos would eventually come to live, as well as the income from both plantations, Trindade and Novo.[17] That same year, 1816, perhaps shortly after Domingos arrived at the Trindade plantation, 18,266 slaves lived in Santo Amaro and the adjacent town of São Francisco do Conde. Most of those working on plantations (83 percent) were grouped in communities of forty slaves or more. Domingos' master must have owned more than 100 slaves, figuring among the top 10 percent of the wealthiest landowners in that region, who altogether held 54 percent of the slaves in Santo Amaro.[18]

An extraordinary document written by a former slave from the Trindade plantation (or by someone else at his request) casts doubt on Colonel Francisco Sodré's fair dealings with bondmen and women under his control. It is a letter from Florêncio, a freedman, published in the *Correio Mercantil* newspaper in January 1839. That document is quoted in full in the following box. Florêncio declared that in 1822 he registered his letter of manumission, which his former mistress, Thereza Maria Corte Real, had granted some time before, when she still owned the Trindade plantation – therefore, prior to 1816. It seems that, as was common practice, his manumission was conditional on the slave's continued service to his mistress during her lifetime. It is very likely that Colonel Sodré had purchased the plantation, along with its slaves,

---

[17] "Ecriptura de debito, obrigação, e hipoteca que faz o coronel Francisco Maria Sodré Pereira, ao comerciante João Baptista de Araújo Braga da quantia de 4:600$000 reis," APEB, *LNT*, vol. 188, fls. 61–63.

[18] For the demographics of plantations in the Recôncavo, see Schwartz, *Sugar Plantations*, 441; and Barickman, *A Bahian Counterpoint*, 129, 144–146. These authors' figures do not always agree. The location of the Trindade on the Acupe River is shown in the map that is partially reproduced in Figures 4 and 5, as well as in the *Carta do Recôncavo da Bahia* produced by engineer Theodoro Sampaio in 1899. This source has been published in Museu AfroBrasil, *Theodoro Sampaio, o sábio negro entre os brancos* (São Paulo: Museu AfroBrasil, 2008), 187.

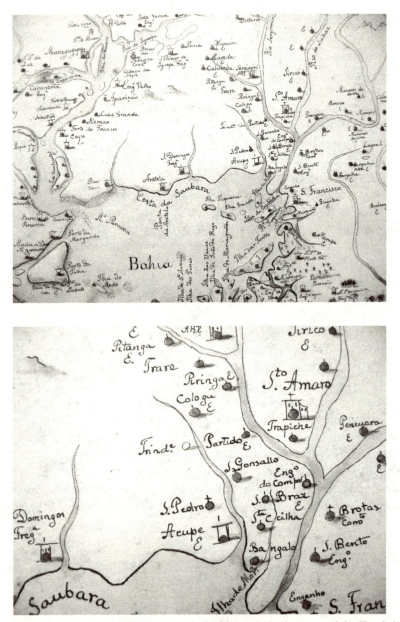

Figures 4 and 5. Detail of the ground plan showing the location of the Trindade plantation in São Domingos de Saubara parish, Santo Amaro, 1816.

from her heirs after Thereza Maria's death. However, the colonel did not recognize Florêncio's right to freedom, although his letter of manumission could be found among the legal documents of the property he had acquired. So Florêncio remained a slave on the Trindade plantation, from where he was later transferred to the colonel's Engenho Novo plantation.

Florêncio's letter also states that Colonel Sodré had sold or leased Engenho Novo and its slaves to a Mr. Pedroso, probably the powerful Antonio Pedroso de Albuquerque, a major landowner in the Recôncavo and a well-known slave trader.[19] In October 1838, while working for this man, Florêncio decided to flee and sue for his manumission in court to obtain legal recognition of his status as a freedman. Why he took so long to do so is a mystery, but it was certainly not because he accepted his life as a slave. He stated that while he was illegally enslaved, "I never forgot my freedom." The announcement of his manumission in the press, while expressing a sense of subordination to legitimate and illegitimate masters, is at the same time a poignant protest made "so the respectable public will learn of the years I worked as a slave while being a freedman." They totaled at least twenty-two years, between 1816 – when the colonel still owned the Trindade plantation – and 1838, when Florêncio escaped from Pedroso and decided to publicize his story.

Letter by Florêncio, an Illegally Enslaved Freedman

On August 20, 1822, registry book no. 25 pg. 119 of the Almeida notary's office in the City of Santo Amaro, showed my letter of manumission, which was granted to me by my mistress Dona Thereza Maria da França Corte Real, and upon her death, with me still in her company on the Trinity Plantation, this came to belong to Senhor Francisco Maria Sudré, who became my owner, despite having some knowledge of my letter of manumission, which was among the documents pertaining to that household, and the aforementioned Senhor Sudré was in possession of them, and thence I was transferred as a slave to the Engenho Novo, which was transferred to my Master Pedroso, by lease or sale. At that time, never forgetting about my

---

[19] Verger, *Flux et reflux*, 451–452.

freedom, I managed to obtain a certificate, and with it sued for a warrant of legal possession [of freedom] dated October 31, 1838, and because of that I am enjoying my freedom, and providing transportation services at the Engenho Passagem, in the same city of Santo Amaro, to earn my livelihood, and in order for my Master Pedroso to take me under his protection, and not view me as a runaway, I am publishing this announcement, as well as to make the respectable public aware of the years I served as a slave, being a freedman from the date of the death of my Mistress to the present date of the above warrant.

I am the Editor's most obliged servant.

The slave Florêncio, now a freedman

Source: Correio Mercantil, no. 18, January 22, 1839

Florêncio's story is interesting, and not just because it attests to Colonel Francisco Maria Sodré's character – or the lack thereof. The letter was written by a slave (or freedman) who most certainly knew Domingos during his servitude on the Trindade plantation, someone whose personal drama must have been well known to other slaves, his workmates, as well. Florêncio's statement sheds light on the world in which Domingos spent at least part of his years in slavery. We know the names of other men and women, some of whom, at least, also shared the slave quarters of the Trindade plantation with Domingos. Their life stories may have been as harrowing as Florêncio's, or even more so.

The Trindade plantation became the property of Maria Adelaide Sodré Pereira, Colonel Francisco Maria Sodré's eldest daughter, when he died in 1835. That year, she married José Lino Coutinho, a physician, poet, and prominent liberal politician. Their marriage lasted less than a year, because Coutinho died in 1836. At the time, an inventory of the couple's estate was conducted, and the probate records included the Trindade plantation and a list of its 118 slaves, valued at more than 33 million reis, a considerable fortune at the time. The couple owned another eleven slaves in their sizeable home in Salvador, on Rua da Quitanda Velha, in São Pedro, the same parish where Domingos lived when he was arrested in 1862. Lino Coutinho's interest in slavery was not limited to owning slaves as domestics and field hands; he also seems to have invested – albeit modestly – in the slave trade. The British Navy seized a ship on the west coast of Africa for illegal slave trafficking in which Coutinho held "a small interest," according to a document attached to his probate records.[20]

Domingos did not work on just any plantation. The number of slaves at Engenho Trindade, 118, was higher than the average for plantations in the sugar-planting region of the Recôncavo, which ranged from fifty to 100. In nearby Iguape, one of the richest regions of the Recôncavo, in 1835 the average slave contingent per plantation was 123, which is therefore close to the number found on Trindade.[21] In 1836, it stood as one of the few plantations in the region with steam-driven sugar mills, using a six-horsepower engine valued at 6 million reis, enough to purchase thirteen young, healthy slaves. The entire property – slaves, cattle, land, tools, machines (including the steam engine), the big house, slave quarters, chapel, chaplain's house, and so forth – was valued at more than 100 million reis, of which the price of the slaves was no more than 30 percent.

Domingos' name does not figure on the list of plantation slaves inventoried in 1836. He may have left Trindade the previous year, after the old colonel died and his estate was divided, as I will explain further on. Domingos, however, may have known and worked with most of the slaves listed that year as part of the plantation estate. The *senzalas* (slave quarters) of Trindade in 1836 housed eighty-one slaves from Africa and thirty-seven born in Brazil. Thus, Africans formed nearly 68.6 percent of that plantation's enslaved workforce, which was much higher than the average for the region. In Iguape, for example, Africans represented 58 percent of plantation slaves in 1835.[22] Trindade's slaves were mostly young, as 59 percent of them were vaguely described as "youths" (*moços*) – somewhere between fifteen and twenty-five years of age – and nearly all were born in Africa.[23] At the time, Domingos would

[20] Probate records for Lino Coutinho (1836), APEB, *Judiciária. Inventários*, no. 01/105/157/04, passim. The confiscation of the slave ship is mentioned in fl. 55v.

[21] Barickman, *A Bahian Counterpoint*, 146.

[22] Ibid., 156.

[23] The percentage of "moços" and "moças" on the Trindade plantation was much larger than what I found in my study of 635 slaves, mostly rural, listed in Bahian probate records between 1813 and 1826, where they represent just 45.2 percent. See João José Reis, "População e rebelião: notas sobre a população escrava na Bahia na primeira metade do século xix," *Revista das Ciências Humanas*, no. 1 (1980): 148–149.

have been about forty, so he did not belong to that younger group of Africans. Slaves on Trindade, for the most part, belonged to the same African nation as Domingos, the Nagôs, who made up 42.5 percent of all enslaved workers on the plantation, and 61.7 percent of those imported from Africa. However, Domingos had an opportunity to live and work alongside members of the other eleven nations represented there, particularly the numerous Cabindas, as well as Brazilian-born Crioulos. More than half of the Crioulos on the Trindade plantation were still children born to African slave women. Aged twelve and under, they represented 19 percent of the slave contingent, a percentage that was generally lower than that found in other parts of Brazil.[24]

Keeping pace with the booming sugar trade in the 1830s, the Trindade plantation was going full steam ahead, judging by its owner's ability to renew the enslaved workforce, particularly through the transatlantic slave trade, and more modestly through natural reproduction. Benedita, a young creole woman, had five children with ages ranging from a "nursling" to a ten-year-old; Esmenia, a young Nagô woman, had already given birth to seven. However, the ratio of children to women of childbearing age – those listed in the probate records as "moça" (young woman) and "meia idade" (middle aged) – was less than one to one. It was an extremely low birth rate, which also indicated a high child mortality situation. This was the norm for Recôncavo plantations. Like its counterparts in the region, Trindade's proportion of creole slaves was not larger because of the high male-female ratio (187 men per 100 women), which is also higher than

---

[24] In rural Rio de Janeiro, between 1826 and 1830, the proportion was much higher – 26.1 percent (for properties with up to nine slaves), and 30.2 percent (for properties with more than twenty slaves), but in the newborn to 14-year-old age group. Manolo Florentino and José Roberto Góes, A paz nas senzalas: famílias escravas e tráfico atlântico, c. 1790 – c. 1850 (Rio de Janeiro: Civilização Brasileira, 1997), 66. For that same age group, José Flávio Motta, Corpos escravos, vontades livres: posse de cativos e família escrava em Bananal (1801–1829) (São Paulo: Annablume/Fapesp, 1999), 297–298, has found a percentage that is closer to the one on Trindade – 21.1 percent in Bananal, in the Paraíba Valley, São Paulo, in 1829. None of the slaves on the Trindade plantation was aged thirteen or fourteen. In Campos dos Goitacases, Rio de Janeiro province, over the course of the eighteenth century, the percentage was higher, between 24.9 percent (for properties with up to fifteen slaves), and 26.2 percent (for properties with more than fifteen slaves), including children aged twelve and under, as I have found in the case of the Trindade plantation. See Sheila de Castro Faria, A colônia em movimento: fortuna e família no cotidiano colonial (Rio de Janeiro: Nova Fronteira, 1998), 299.

Slaves on the Trindade plantation, 1836

Origin	Men	Women	Total
AFRICA			
Nagô	32	18	50
Cabinda	8	8	16
Mina	1	3	4
Tapa	2	–	2
Hausa	2	–	2
Cape Verde	1	1	2
Calabar	–	1	1
São Tomé	–	1	1
Congo	1	–	1
Modumbi	–	1	1
Mozambique	–	1	1
Total (68.6%)	47	34	81
BRAZIL			
Crioulo*	9	9	18
Cabra*	1	5	6
Pardo*	–	1	1
Mulatto	1	–	1
Unknown	6	5	11
Total (31.4%)	17	20	37
TOTAL	64	54	118

Source: APEB, Judiciária, no 01/105/157/04
* Crioulo was a Brazilian-born black person; Cabra stood
  for a dark-skinned mulatto; and pardo for a light-skinned
  mulatto.

the ratio found on plantations in Iguape (155 men per 100 women), but a bit lower than that for plantations in another sugar-producing municipality, Cachoeira (189 men per 100 women).[25] Unfortunately, I do not know if Domingos formed a relationship with any of the slave women on Trindade. If he did, they did not bear any children who survived him; at least he does not mention any in his will, written several decades later.

There were also some older slaves on Trindade in 1836. At least a few of them were probably there when Domingos arrived, and one or two were in his age group and may have endured the Middle Passage along with him. Therefore they would have been his *malungos*, a term for "big canoe," but also fellow travelers in several Bantu languages, here meaning shipmates. Mostly Nagôs, like the younger ones, they were

[25] Barickman, A Bahian Counterpoint, 156.

described in the plantation inventory as "of age," "old," or "elderly," such as Hércules, Afonso, Bruno, and Rafael. The descriptions of the last three also reflected the damage that slavery had inflicted on their bodies because they were "injured in the groin" (hernia) or simply "broken," which I suppose to mean that they were physically incapacitated, perhaps crippled. Hércules lived up to his slave name because, although he was identified as elderly, he did not display any diseases or physical handicaps. In addition to his ethnic kin, the Nagôs, Domingos spent many years in the company of older slaves who came from several parts of Africa, such as Lino, from the Cabinda nation, in northern Angola, described as "of age with bad feet"; Pantalião, a Hausa, "elderly, injured in the groin"; Balthazar, a Congo, a "broken old man"; José, a Benguela, an Angolan port of trade south of Luanda, a cobbler who worked in the cane fields despite being old and having a trade; and Liborio, a Tapa, from Nupe, a kingdom adjoining Yorubaland but far from Lagos, who was "now old and sick."[26]

As a member of a community of slaves who were predominantly from his own nation, Domingos managed to avoid the isolation that he might have suffered if he had had to work on a small sugar, tobacco, or cassava farm, where the slaves were generally younger and Brazilian born, and where the master's influence was more strongly felt.[27] In a large slave quarters, he must have had more leeway for his independent personality to blossom, including, perhaps, more room for the expression of ritual abilities brought with him from Africa. As he grew older among the numerous Nagôs on Trindade in the mid-1830s, he may have been able to exert his influence and authority over them.

The Trindade slaves were housed in two groups of slave quarters. One of them was described as a "house divided into twelve *senzalas*, and two living quarters for the head overseer and the clerk, with seventeen outside piers and columns in the center, roofed with tiles, walled with bricks and clay." This arrangement enabled the overseer to keep a close eye on the slaves, even during their rest periods. The other

---

[26] Probate records for Lino Coutinho (1836), APEB, *Judiciária. Inventários*, no. 01/105/157/04, fls. 69v–76v (list of slaves on the Trindade plantation). On *malungo*, see Robert Slenes, "'*Malungu n'goma* vem!': África coberta e descoberta no Brasil," *Revista USP*, no. 12 (1991–1992): 48–67.

[27] Barickman, *A Bahian Counterpoint*, chap. 6. For an earlier period, see Luis Nicolau Parés, "O processo de crioulização no Recôncavo baiano (1750–1800)," *Afro-Ásia*, no. 33 (2005): 87–132.

Figure 6. Thatched senzalas similar to those found on the Trindade plantation, 1865.

quarters were much simpler, but numerous, described as "25 senzalas of mangrove wood, thatched," meaning that they were individual
cabins set apart from the collective housing or slave quarters proper.
Unfortunately, we do not know how the slaves were distributed in those
two types of accommodations. The cabins could have housed families
or older people – in short, the more tractable slaves who required less
vigilance than the young, unattached, and potentially rebellious Nagôs
who occupied the other buildings. At the age of about forty, and therefore a mature man, if Domingos was still living on the plantation when
the colonel died, he would probably have occupied one of the thatched
cabins, or even a room in the big house.

Although it was an excellent plantation, Trindade did not boast
an opulent big house. The inventory shows a home that was part of a
complex described as the "plantation house" and valued at 16 million
reis, about 16 percent of the estate's value. Located on a river, surely
the Acupe, it was built on stone and lime-mortar foundation piers and
subdivided into boiler rooms, purging rooms, and "a residential division of a parlor and two bedrooms situated in the southern part."[28] This

[28] Probate records for Lino Coutinho, fl. 79.

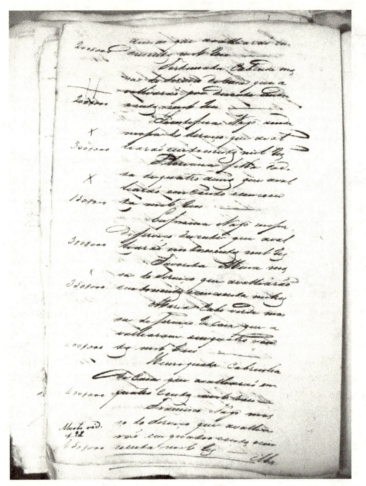

Figure 7. Page of the inventory of slaves on the Trindade plantation, 1836.

arrangement, in which the big house and factory appear to be under the same roof, represented a trend in the organization of communal space on nineteenth-century Recôncavo sugar plantations that was introduced in the second half of the previous century. Architectural historian Esterzilda Berenstein de Azevedo observes that "the conjunction of the two buildings gave the master direct control over production activities."[29] In this type of panoptic big house, slaves who worked

[29] Esterzilda Berenstein de Azevedo, "Açúcar amargo: a construção de engenhos na Bahia oitocentista," PhD dissertation, Universidade de São Paulo, 1996, 118.

in the sugar mill could be supervised more effectively. Better yet, the master or his administrator could keep a close watch on them from a convenient position – his modest residence on the Trindade plantation. Three slaves are listed as domestics: Fortunata, a young Cabinda woman; Maria, a young Cape Verde woman; and Henriqueta, a dark-skinned mulatto girl, or *cabrinha*. Furthermore, the probate records describe the big house's furnishings: twelve chairs and a couch made of Brazilian rosewood, twenty-four chairs of "wood from the North," six of conduru wood, and two armchairs. That many chairs – and good ones at that – must have been used for large social gatherings.[30]

Because Colonel Sodré owned other properties, his main country house may have been located elsewhere, and there were plenty of sites to choose from. He also owned homes in Salvador, one of them in the Bonfim district, on the scenic Itapagipe peninsula, where he may have liked to stay when he was in town. It had several rooms and fruit trees in the yard. His successors on Trindade, his daughter Maria Adelaide and son-in-law Lino Coutinho, do not appear to have lived there together. Soon after they were married, they went to Paris, and returned from there to occupy the large home where they lived in Salvador, waited on by eleven slaves: Francisco, Saul, Isac, and Tomiras, their litter bearers, all young Nagô men; Militão, a cabra house slave, about fifteen years old; Joaquim, a nine-year-old cabra boy, who already worked as a house slave; Bernardo, a young pardo butler; Juliana, a young Nagô washerwoman; Mariana, a young ironing woman, of the Jeje nation (a Gbe speaker from Dahomey or one of its neighbors); Anastácia, a cabra seamstress; and Clara, a creole girl, age twelve, who was an apprentice seamstress. In the 1840s, however, Maria Adelaide now remarried to Antonio Muniz de Aragão, and their two children, lived on the Trindade plantation. By then, the big house may have been more comfortable, expanded, or recently built to accommodate the large contingent of house slaves to which she was accustomed in the city.[31]

In 1836, the Trindade chapel, probably the same one where Domingos was baptized, was not at all modest – unlike the big house – being valued at 3,200,000 reis, the equivalent of the price of seven prime slaves from the same plantation. There was a chaplain living on the property, in a house made of stone and lime mortar, with a tiled

[30] Probate records for Lino Coutinho, fls. 25–25v.
[31] Torres, "Os Sodrés," 106. The accounts for the couple's trip to Paris can be found in Lino Coutinho's probate records.

roof. A stable and an infirmary were attached to it, standing side by side.
While the chaplain tended to the slaves' spiritual health, so that they
could better adjust to enslavement as good Christians, a British physician, Dr. George E. Fairbanks, who was probably not a resident on the
plantation, cared for their physical well-being so they would not miss a
day's work in the sugar mill and cane fields. Both the priest and the physician would have been Domingos Sodré's competitors if he was already
practicing his trades as a diviner, healer, and herbalist when he lived on
Trindade, which he very likely did, perhaps in secret.[32]

Colonel Francisco Sodré's slaves, like Florêncio, the freedman who
complained of his illegal enslavement in the press, may have circulated
between Engenho Trindade and other farms and plantations the colonel owned or leased. Florêncio stated that he had been transferred from
Trindade to one of the colonel's other properties, Engenho Novo. In
addition to Trindade and Engenho Novo, the colonel owned the Pé
de Serra farm in Santo Amaro and the São João plantation in Matoim
parish, where he also leased land, and the famous Engenho Freguesia,
owned by Cristóvão da Rocha Pita, the father of Libânio Almeida's
business partner, as we have seen in the previous chapter. Between 1827
and 1834, Colonel Sodré leased the small Britos plantation in Santo
Amaro, which had thirty slaves, owned by Maria Ana Rita de Meneses.
Domingos' master also owned the Cassucá plantation, which was registered in his name in 1830. It was located in São Tiago do Iguape,
next to Engenho Novo, at the edge of town in Cachoeira. During that
period, however, Cassucá and its slaves were leased to Maria Rita, the
owner of the Britos plantation. Maria Rita was a woman with a fiery
personality. That year, 1830, she got involved in a serious quarrel with
Captain Thomé Pereira de Araújo, the owner of the neighboring Cruz
plantation, because, to drive his watermill, he had attempted to build
an aqueduct across Cassucá's land against her wishes. That fine lady
marshaled Colonel Sodré's slaves – more than 100 strong – as well as
overseers and servants, who set out with sickles in hand to confront the
slaves who were building the conduit for Captain Araújo.[33]

---

32 APEB, *Judiciária. Inventários*, no. 01/105/157/04, fls. 76v–81 (cattle, buildings,
    equipment, etc. on the Trindade plantation). Dr. Fairbanks opened a clinic
    (Casa de Saúde) in Salvador in 1835, according to the *Almanak para o anno de
    1845* (Bahia: Typ. De M. A. da S. Serva, 1844), 208.

33 "Escriptura de venda, paga, e quitação que faz o Pe. José Rodrigues da Gama
    ao coronel Francisco Maria Sodré Pereira de uma sorte de terras denominadas
    Codumbó pelo preço e quantia de Rs 800$000," May 27, 1829, and "Escriptura de

Maria Ana Rita, a woman from an elite Bahian slaveholding family, the daughter of the captain major of Cachoeira, Antonio Brandão Pereira Marinho Falcão, played many roles – lessor, lessee, and lover of Colonel Francisco Sodré, who also had a wife, Maria José Lodi Sodré. Maria Rita's married life had been turbulent, as she was not one to take things lying down. She was first married to her cousin and uncle Colonel Gonçalo Marinho Falcão as a child bride, aged twelve or thirteen, which was not unusual for Brazilian elite families at the time – neither her age nor the degree of inbreeding.[34] For these and other reasons, including the young woman's rebellious nature, the marriage did not last. Maria Rita sued her husband for divorce, claiming, among other things, that "the same day she went to live in the home of the respondent [Gonçalo] he slept in [the married couple's] bedroom with two slave women ... who, for that reason, became insolent." Her patience ran out when one of those slave women physically assaulted her. She begged her husband to punish her assailant, but he revealed on the spot that he had already freed her, "showing her [Maria Rita] the letter [of manumission] he had given her [the slave woman]," and reading it aloud "as if on the trading floor." This humiliation drove the lady to ask the Church authorities for divorce at a time when remarriage was forbidden.[35]

Maria Rita had probably managed to separate from her husband and was now living as the mistress of a married man with whom she had complex kinship and business relations. Their union produced an illegitimate son, Francisco Pereira Sodré, who married Cora Cezar Coutinho, the illegitimate daughter of Lino Coutinho, who, in turn had married the colonel's eldest daughter, the heiress to the Trindade plantation! In other words, the colonel was the father-in-law of both the father and daughter, Lino and Cora. In 1834, Colonel Sodré wound up whatever business dealings he may have contracted with his mistress. In March, Maria Rita settled a debt of more than 1,862,000 reis that she owed to Sodré. In May, she canceled the lease and other transactions

arrendamento que faz Christovão da Rocha Pita ... ao Coronel Francisco Maria Sodré Pereira ...," June 10, 1829, APEB, *LNT*, vol. 236, fls. 27, 29–29v; APEB, *Matrícula dos engenhos*, vol. 632, entries 424 (Trindade) and 643 (Cassuca). For the conflict between Maria Rita and Captain Araújo, see Schwartz, *Sugar Plantations*, 180–181; and Barickman, *A Bahian Counterpoint*, 103–104; regarding Cassucá's location next to the Novo plantation in Iguape parish, see p. 115.

34 See Mattoso, *Família e sociedade*, 139–158.
35 APEB, *Cartas do governo*, vol. 143, fls. 265–265v.

related to the Britos plantation. That same year, shortly after Francisco and Cora were married, Maria Rita sold the plantation to her son and daughter-in-law.

A true patriarch of Bahia's plantation world as he proved to have been, Colonel Sodré engaged in bold financial transactions simultaneously involving his wife and mistress. For example, in 1832, the married couple jointly borrowed 12: 626$477 (12,626,477 reis) from Commander Manoel José de Mello, mortgaging as collateral "the property of the fine homes in Bonfim in Itapagipe and all the other land they own there." The same mortgage deed also stated that the colonel had paid the commander "5:556$504 reis for three claims, one against himself and two against D. Maria Anna Rita de Menezes," his mistress. These are just some aspects of the financial and sentimental life of the interesting slaveholding family that owned Domingos.[36]

We know something about Colonel Sodré's public life as well. He was a high-ranking militia officer. Like other Recôncavo potentates, he became involved in Bahia's war for Brazil's independence from Portugal. He was the commander of the Honorary Imperial Army Infantry Battalion, which the interim government of Bahia created during the conflict in January 1823. Sodré contributed a young son, his firstborn, Jerônimo, and a company that he personally financed to that battalion, which played a leading role in the defense of Itaparica, an island off the city of Bahia in the Bay of All Saints. Previously, Colonel Sodré had also participated in important aspects of the anti-Portuguese campaign in Santo Amaro. In January 1822, he helped set up the local war chest,

---

[36] "Escritura de paga, e quitação que faz o Coronel Francisco Maria Sodré Pereira a Donna Maria Anna Rita de Meses da quantia de Rs. 1:862$149," and "Escritura de declaração de destrato ... de todas as contas, débito e obrigação, que fazem Francisco Maria Sodré Pereira e Donna Maria Anna Rita de Meneses," May 13, 1834, APEB, LNT, vol. 244, fls. 154v, 168v–169v; "Escritura de contrato ante nupcias que fazem Francisco Maria Sodré Pereira e Dona Cora Cezar Coutinho," APEB, LNT, vol. 243, fl. 59; "Escritura de compra, venda, paga, debito e obrigação que fazem como vendedora Dona Maria Anna Rita de Menezes, e como compradores Francisco Pereira Sodré, e sua consorte Dona Cora Cezar Coutinho Sodré do Engenho denominado dos Britos," APEB, LNT, vol. 240, fls. 298–301v; "Escritura de debito e obrigação que fazem o coronel Francisco Maria Sodré Pereira e sua mulher Maria José Lodi Sudré ao apotecario o Comendador Manoel José de Mello da quantia de 12: 626$477," APEB, LNT, vol. 237, fls. 162–163. For Cora and her father, Lino Coutinho, see Adriana Dantas Reis, Cora: lições de comportamento feminino na Bahia do século XIX (Salvador: Centro de Estudos Baianos da UFBa, 2000).

together with other important sugar planters. In mid-June, the Santo Amaro City Council proposed to create a national government headed by Prince Pedro – who would soon become Brazil's first emperor – with an army, navy, national treasury, supreme court, and free trade, among other measures. This proposal, which Colonel Sodré supported, was not quite a declaration of independence but close to it. At the end of that month, he signed the minutes of the extraordinary session of the Santo Amaro City Council that proclaimed Pedro the "Royal Prince and Constitutional Regent, Perpetual Protector and Defender of the Kingdom of Brazil."[37] In August, his name appeared on the manifesto that insisted on creating a general government in the province of Bahia as an alternative to the provisional council that was based in Salvador, a city now controlled by Portuguese troops. In September of that year, he signed a document that swore allegiance to Pedro and the interim government established in his name in the Recôncavo. At this point Pedro had already proclaimed Brazil's independence from Portugal, on September 7, 1822, an act that would be followed by the creation of a monarchical regime, the Empire of Brazil, unique in Latin America. However, the political developments in the south were not enough to make the Portuguese troops desist from occupying the capital of Bahia. There, the war intensified, and so did Domingos' master role in it. Underscoring the colonel's prestige among the leaders of the sugar planters that had led the war against the Portuguese, the Interim Governing Council in late March 1823 appointed him to present the emperor with a protest against the French General Pedro Labatut, commander of the army, a famous episode in Bahia's struggle for independence.[38]

[37] Braz do Amaral, *História da Independência na Bahia*, 2nd ed. (Salvador: Progresso, 1957), 202–203; Wanderley de Pinho, "Discurso proferido pelo Dr. Wanderley de Araújo Pinho na sessão solemne realisada no Conselho Municipal de Santo Amaro, a 14 de junho de 1922, para solemnisar o início da participação da Villa de S. Amaro na campanha da Independência," *Revista do Instituto Geográfico e Histórico da Bahia*, no. 48 (1923): 1–60.

[38] Amaral, *História da Independência na Bahia*, 207–208; Ignácio Accioli de Cerqueira e Silva, *Memórias históricas e políticas da Província da Bahia*, annotated by Braz do Amaral (Salvador: Imprensa Oficial do Estado, 1931), 5 vols., iii: 377–383, 442; Pinho, "Discurso proferido," esp. 21, 28, 58. Regarding the events in Santo Amaro, see also Luís Henrique Dias Tavares, *Independência do Brasil na Bahia* (Salvador: EDUFBa, 2005), 93–96; "Acta em 29 de março de 1823. O conselho delibera enviar a Corte o Coronel Francisco Maria Sodré Pereira sobre a nomeação do General Labatut," *Revista do Instituto Histórico e Geográfico da Bahia*, 4, no. 12 (1897): 180–182.

Figure 8. Santo Amaro da Purificação.

It is worth noting that one reason the lords and masters of the Recôncavo joined the cause of independence in increasing numbers was their fear that the free poor and the enslaved population would take advantage of the schism among powerful whites to rebel. For example, according to the city councilmen, recognizing Pedro's authority in Santo Amaro was necessary to "prevent any ill-intentioned spirit from driving the people to engage in anarchistic excesses or deviate from the Constitutional Monarchy System."[39] The Recôncavo slaveholders had risen up against the Portuguese to defend a type of society that worked for them. One reason for the conflict between those slaveholders and General Labatut was precisely his insistence on recruiting freed slaves into the Brazilian army. The Santo Amaro City Council vehemently opposed that proposal in April 1823, arguing that "those freedmen would later become dangerous, possibly joining forces with other slaves with whom some maintained ties of kinship and partnership."[40]

Slaves, however, did join the rather improvised Liberating Army, hoping that they would be freed if they fought against the Portuguese. Domingos himself did just that. He joined the Companhia de Libertos do Imperador (Company of the Emperor's Freedmen), also known by the more pompous name of Batalhão dos Libertos Constitucionais e Independentes do Imperador (Battalion of the Emperor's Constitutional and Independent Freedmen), which was formed by General Labatut

[39] Amaral, *História da Independência na Bahia*, 202.
[40] In Pinho, "Discurso proferido," 15.

in late 1822. Despite its name, many slaves were recruited by Labatut to serve in this battalion, particularly those confiscated from loyalist Portuguese proprietors, but other slaves joined in response to rumors – which were nothing but – that they would be freed upon enlisting. In these cases, slaves literally fled their owners to join the army. It seems, however, that some masters let their slaves take up arms; others allowed them to serve only as assistants in nonmilitary tasks, usually menial work fit to slaves. We still do not know precisely how Domingos ended up in the ranks of the Batalhão de Libertos. Because his master and his son were directly involved in the war, it is possible that Colonel Sodré allowed Domingos to serve in the army, although without any promise of freedom. The diviner not only enlisted, but, according to an affidavit he prepared twenty years later, proved that he had been wounded, "with a sword-cut by the enemy," on March 1, 1823, and taken to hospital, from where he was only discharged on the 23rd of that month. In this same suit he declared that he used the surname Sudré for the first time when he enlisted, but we do not know if he did so with or without his master's permission. This information, on the other hand, suggests that he may have pretended that he was already a freedman, in which case he may have fled from the colonel. It is a fact, in any case, that he was not freed after the war, unlike many other slaves.[41]

Slave Rebellions in the Recôncavo

The masters of the Recôncavo had good reason to mistrust their slaves. Numerous slave revolts and conspiracies had sown fear in the Recôncavo, Salvador, and the outlying region throughout the first half of the nineteenth century. In Santo Amaro itself, where Domingos lived as a field slave, and in neighboring São Francisco do Conde, another important sugar-producing hub, there were significant revolts in 1816 and 1827, and two in 1828. The uprising of February 12, 1816 was the most serious of them all, and directly ignited the region where Domingos lived. The spark was an all-night drumming celebration,

---

[41] See Domingos' affidavit of 1853 in APEB, *Policia*, maço 6315. I would like to thank Lisa Earl Castillo for providing me with a copy of this document. On the recruitment of slaves during the war of independence in Bahia, see Hendrik Kraay, "'Em outra coisa não falavam os pardos, cabras, e crioulos': o 'recrutamento de escravos na guerra da independência na Bahia,'" *Revista Brasileira de História* 22, no. 43 (2002): 109–128.

probably one with religious connotations, involving slaves from several plantations, Lagoa, Crauassú, Itatinga, Guaíba, Cassarondongo, and Quibaca, among others. There are indications that slaves from Salvador were in on the conspiracy that led to the uprising. The rebels fought for four days, burning several plantations, attacking homes and people in Santo Amaro, and killing an unknown number of whites as well as slaves who refused to join the rebellion. They were defeated by militias and loyal slaves, headed by Militia Colonel Jerônimo Fiúza Barreto, the owner of the Quibaca plantation. At least thirty slaves were arrested and sent to Salvador.

Given the extent of that movement, local planters tried to convince the governor of Bahia, Count dos Arcos, a Portuguese nobleman influenced by the European Enlightenment, that his slave control policy was disastrous and one of the reasons for that and other rebellions. In fact, dos Arcos believed that the slaves were rebelling because their masters mistreated them, and if they were not given an outlet, they would inevitably rise up en masse. Enabling them an escape valve from slavery was certainly the reason the governor permitted public gatherings of slaves at batuques and other entertainments. At the same time, the count believed that allowing the replication in Bahia of the rituals and customs of their own nations – their religions included – would divide the Africans politically, thus avoiding a Haitian-style confrontation with the whites.[42]

The planters, however, believed that the solution was tighter control over their slaves, and it was in that spirit that they gathered in São Francisco do Conde on February 27, 1816. In a petition sent to the government in Rio de Janeiro – to where the Portuguese court, led by Prince Regent João VI, had fled from Napoleon's troops in 1808 – they proposed drastic measures to block the wave of slave rebellions, such as deporting suspicious freedpersons back to Africa and hanging rebellious slaves without trial. Suggestions like these were not popular with most planters because, in addition to being unacceptable to the governor, they were not in the slaveholders' best interests – particularly slave executions that meant the destruction of property. Unlike other slave societies in the Americas, in Brazil masters were not compensated when their rebellious slaves were executed. Bahian planters therefore decided to send a petition to the count proposing less drastic solutions. One

[42] Reis, *Rebelião escrava no Brasil*, 89–93.

suggested that no black person should ever be permitted to sit down in the presence of a white person to mark out their unequal positions in society on a racial basis. Another decision obliged masters to punish with 150 lashes any slave found in the streets or highways without written permission from his owner. To make the punishment even more humiliating, it had to be meted out in the presence of the deviant slave's family if he or she had one. Furthermore, it recommended the creation of a force of 320 armed men "to police the blacks" in the Recôncavo region. In practice, all of these measures could have directly affected the lives of Domingos and his enslaved coworkers at Engenho Trindade.[43]

Aside from these measures, the planters suggested that the government immediately encourage the immigration of "one hundred white families of artisans and farm workers" to reduce the population imbalance that favored blacks in the Recôncavo. A letter from the planters' representative to Dom João, the Portuguese prince regent in Rio de Janeiro, set forth a detailed plan for the immigration of white settlers – a venture that slaveholders accustomed to treating people as a commodity labeled "the importation of foreigners." The missive even suggested where the money for the project could come from: a property tax on slaves, a unique case of self-taxation, reflecting the Bahian slaveholders' desperation about the repeated rebellions in their own backyard. The letter to His Royal Highness ended on an optimistic note: "in a few years the White Settlement will grow to the point that there will be no longer the slightest fear of new insurrections from the blacks." This may have been one of the first statements from Brazil's dominant class in favor of whitening the population through immigration, explained by their fear of being in the minority amid a growing and increasingly rebellious African community. Referring to the entire captaincy of Bahia, the letter estimated that the total population came to 411,190, of whom precisely 89,004 (21.6 percent) were white, and "all the rest pardos and ignorant or savage blacks."[44] The dangerous segment of the population was even larger in the Recôncavo. Historian B. J.

[43] Petition signed by Recôncavo landowners, February 24, 1816, Biblioteca Nacional, Rio de Janeiro (BNRJ), Manuscripts Division, C 9, 5, docs. 3 and 6.

[44] Alexandre Gomes Ferrão Castelo Branco to the Marquis Aguiar, March 14, 1816, and March 15, 1817 (the latter contains a detailed plan to encourage white immigration to the Recôncavo), BNRJ, Manuscripts Division, C 9, 5, docs. 4 and 1, respectively. The quotations are from the second document.

Barickman suggests that "perhaps less than one-fifth" of the inhabitants of that region were white, and the rest were black and mixed race, including slaves, freedpersons, and free people. About 90,000 of those nonwhites were enslaved in 1817.[45]

Domingos found himself in the Recôncavo after the region had plunged into a state of war, but his master's family did not seem to have been deeply involved in that conflict. There is no record of any slave rebellions on their plantations. The petition to Prince João's government was signed by more than 130 Recôncavo planters, including men with resounding family names, such as Bettancourt Aragão, Gomes Ferrão, Teive Argolo, Calmon de Almeida, Fiúza Barreto, Sá Barreto, Borges de Barro, Gomes de Sá, Araújo Pinho, Vilasboas, Freire de Carvalho, Costa Pinto, Carvalho de Menezes, Amaral Gurgel, Siqueira Bulcão, and Dantas Maciel, among others that made up the sugar aristocracy of the Recôncavo. The signatories also included smaller landowners, sugar cane farmers, merchants, and artisans, a sign that the sugar barons wished to inform the Crown that they had a following among less prominent subjects. Curiously enough, unlike what would occur later during the war against the Portuguese, the powerful Colonel Francisco Maria Sodré Pereira's signature is nowhere to be found on this document, nor do we find the signature of any other member of the Sodré clan. Could it be that they were so loyal to Count dos Arcos that they refused to participate in what amounted to a serious criticism of his administration? Or were the Sodrés satisfied with the efficiency of their perhaps paternalistic rule, which in their minds would explain why their slaves did not rebel?

In the 1820s, slave rebellions continued in the Recôncavo. In fact, there was an upsurge, keeping pace with the considerable increase in the slave trade in the five years prior to its prohibition in 1831, when slave imports increased more than 60 percent, from 6,037 in 1825 to 16,297 in 1829. The most serious uprising occurred in April 1827, involving at least ten plantations in São Francisco do Conde. In March of the following year, there was another revolt on plantations near Salvador, and in April, two more were reported in Cachoeira. In mid-April 1828, for example, the acting president, Nuno Eugênio, recommended to the local military commander that the troops based in Santo Amaro keep a closer watch on the roads. The aim was to prevent

[45] Barickman, A Bahian Counterpoint, 15–16. See also Schwartz, Sugar Plantations, 439–440.

slaves working on different plantations from communicating with each other, arresting all those who left home without express written permission from their masters, another measure that must have directly impacted Domingos' life.[46]

Control methods like these did not prevent fresh uprisings from breaking out that same year in the rich Iguape region and Santo Amaro. In September 1828, a revolt exploded on Engenho Novo, which had once belonged to Domingos' master and was now owned by Colonel Rodrigo Antônio Falcão. The rebels burned down the slave quarters, invaded and looted the big house. They went on to join the slaves on the neighboring Acutinga, Campina, and da Cruz plantations. They killed slaves and freedpersons, mostly Crioulos, who refused to support them on those and several other plantations. Troops sent from Cachoeira put down the uprising, and the soldiers spread out onto plantations and farms in the region to prevent further incidents, but peace was short-lived.

After days of terrifying rumors of an imminent revolt, at 11 P.M. on November 30, 1828, African slaves on the Tanque plantation in Santo Amaro killed their overseer and several creole slaves and set out to attack the big house. The rebels assaulted the overseer's wife, but she and the mistress managed to escape to a neighboring plantation with the help of loyal slaves, probably Crioulos. Part of the plantation was set ablaze, but the flames did not spread because it was raining heavily. The itinerant magistrate of Santo Amaro immediately sent soldiers to the site, where they met with fierce resistance. The final tally was a few slaves killed and one soldier wounded. The same magistrate ended his report on that incident with a complaint about the lack of sufficient men, weapons, and ammunition "to defend the property of the sugar plantations, and the same town threatened with an invasion of desperate savages in slavery, who have friends and relatives inside our own homes."[47] His words reflected the fear of an alliance between house and field slaves, which the recent revolts did not seem to justify. The slaves

---

[46] Dom Nuno Eugênio de Assis e Seilbiz to the military commander, Salvador, April 18, 1828, copy in the Archives du Ministère des Affaires Étrangére (France), *Mémoires et Documents. Brésil*, vol. 5, fls. 159–159v. The numbers of the slave trade in this paragraph comes from the Slave Voyages Database at www.slavevoyages.org.

[47] Manoel M. Branco to the Viscount de Camamu, Santo Amaro, December 1, 1828, APEB, *Juízes. Cachoeira*, maço 2580.

working in the big houses were mostly Crioulos who generally had little sympathy for the African rebels, most of whom had recently crossed the Atlantic. The slaves on the Trindade plantation, both Africans and Crioulos, do not appear to have taken part in any of these episodes, but the November rebellion came very close to one of Colonel Sodré's other properties, specifically the Cassucá plantation, which was right next to the Novo plantation.

In the following decade, the revolts moved to the capital. One took place in 1830, in an important commercial area of Salvador. A small group of rebels attempted to mobilize slaves who had recently arrived from Africa and were being held in a slave traders' warehouse, awaiting sale. The uprising was quickly crushed, followed by a veritable massacre of the rebels – more than fifty died.

The most important rebellion during that period took place in Salvador, in the early hours of January 25, 1835. Known as the Revolt of the Malês, it terrorized the city's residents for the few hours it lasted. Nearly seventy African combatants lost their lives. The rebels had connections with the Recôncavo, particularly Santo Amaro, from where some had come to fight in the capital city. Domingos may have known some of the people from that region who were involved. In the days following the defeat, the African community in Salvador was subjected to a brutal crackdown led by the police and armed citizens. The violence was as intense as the fear that had taken hold of the residents because they thought African slaves and freedpersons would attempt a fresh uprising at any moment.

I do not know if Domingos had already moved to Salvador from the Recôncavo by this time, but presumably he had not. He probably moved there after Colonel Sodré's death the following year. If that was so, he would have encountered growing intolerance toward African freedpersons, which included harsh laws restricting their mobility, housing, and employment, as well as taxes specifically targeted at that segment of the city's population. At that time, African freedmen and -women represented 7 percent of Salvador's estimated 65,500 inhabitants.[48] Two years later, in 1837, by which time he was probably living in Salvador, Domingos witnessed and perhaps supported, actively or

---

[48] Reis, *Rebelião escrava no Brasil*, 24 (regarding the percentage of African freed-persons in Salvador's population), and all of Part IV (on repressive measures following the Revolt of the Malês).

discreetly, a liberal revolt called the Sabinada, which most of the capital's black population – enslaved, freed, and free – either applauded or effectively joined.[49]

Except for the Sabinada, which was a revolt of free Brazilians, the Nagôs, Domingos' people, played a prominent – make that dominant – role in the cycle of slave uprisings, particularly those that occurred in the 1820s and 1830s. In 1835, for example, Muslim (or Malê) Nagôs were chiefly responsible for organizing and launching the revolt, although non-Muslim Nagôs also took part. However, it cannot be said that Muslims were always the masterminds and makers of African rebellions in Bahia. The drumming session that preceded the 1816 uprising in Santo Amaro was characteristic of a pagan religious ritual, if religion was in any way involved; according to an early student of this movement, the slaves, "after dancing all Sunday night, set off in droves to the sound of trumpets and drums, some armed with bows and arrows, some with machetes and some with rifles."[50] Unfortunately, I have not found documentary evidence about this narrative of the 1816 uprising. Ten years later, in 1826, the Urubu quilombo revolt on the outskirts of Salvador seems to have been headed, or at least supported, by Orișa worshippers like Domingos, according to indications pointing to the presence of a Candomblé house inside that maroon community.

I have not been able to determine how our protagonist behaved in relation to these and other revolts. In the affidavit I mentioned before, he swore he had always been a well-behaved African, specifically denying participation in any African insurrection ever. His manumission suggests that he generally behaved like a loyal and hardworking slave, even if, understandably, he may not have always toed the line (hinted by his possible flight to enlist in the army during the war for independence from Portugal). This does not mean he was content with his life

---

[49] For slave rebellions in Bahia in general, see Reis, *Rebelião escrava no Brasil*, and for the Sabinada, see Paulo César Souza, *A Sabinada: a revolta separatista da Bahia* (São Paulo: Brasiliense, 1987); Hendrik Kraay, "'As Terrifying as Unexpected': The Bahian Sabinada, 1837–1838," *Hispanic American Historical Review*, 72, no. 4 (1992): 501–527; Douglas G. Leite, *Sabinos e diversos: emergências políticas e projetos de poder na revolta baiana de 1837* (Salvador: EGBA/Fundação Pedro Calmon, 2007); and Juliana Sezerdello Crespim Lopes, "Identidades políticas e raciais na Sabinada (Bahia, 1837–1838)," MA thesis, Universidade de São Paulo, 2008.

[50] Eduardo de Caldas Britto, "Levantes de pretos na Bahia," *Revista do Instituto Geográfico e Histórico da Bahia*, 10, no. 29 (1903): 84.

as a slave, just that he had chosen to overcome his condition by other means than open, armed, and collective slave rebellion. Domingos would invest his energy in the politics of manumission, the traditional formula for negotiated individual emancipation in the Brazilian slaveocracy – and one of the masters' control strategies, for a slave's good behavior was the first step toward, although not a guarantee for, obtaining freedom.[51]

MANUMISSION

Domingos began his life as a slave in Brazil in the cane fields, where most of the recent arrivals worked, but he must have been promoted to more prestigious posts on the plantation or even in the big house itself. His later career suggests that he managed to get closer and gain his master's trust and even his esteem. To achieve that, loyalty alone was not enough. He had to be clever and show that he had certain skills, such as the ability to understand and appropriate the seigniorial culture to manipulate it in pursuit of more breathing room in order to rise to the more rewarding positions in the slave labor structure. His ritual skills may also have been useful – to him and possibly the master and his family as well – helping him gain more upward mobility within slavery and eventually to leave it altogether. In short, if he had been just another ordinary slave, he would have stayed on the plantation and lived and died in bondage, which was the fate of most. His was very different.[52]

According to the subdelegado who arrested him in 1862, Domingos gained his freedom in 1836 "from the late Sodré," certainly a reference to Colonel Francisco Maria Sodré, who had died of natural causes in 1835, the year of the Revolt of the Malês. But the African only received his letter of manumission in 1844, for which he paid 550,000 reis to the colonel's eldest son, Jerônimo Pereira Sodré, the heir to the entailed estate.[53] This finding confirms the African's statement in his 1882 will,

---

[51] However, the attainment of manumission by such means did not necessarily mean a passport for security. Many of the people involved in the Revolt of the Malês were freedpersons. Reis, *Rebelião escrava no Brasil*, esp. chap. 11.

[52] Regarding an African freedman, Tito Camargo, who was also a religious leader in Campinas, São Paulo and had a similar story to the one suggested here, see Regina Célia Lima Xavier, *Religiosidade e escravidão, século XIX: Mestre Tito* (Porto Alegre: Editora da UFRGS, 2008), esp. chap. 3.

[53] Domingos' manumission letter was written October 15, 1844, and registered two days later. APEB, *LNT*, vol. 282, fl. 19. See Appendix 2.

in which he refers to his "former master Jerônimo Sudré."[54] This declaration suggests that, when he was manumitted, Domingos belonged to Jerônimo Sodré himself, or, alternately, to the entailed property he inherited. It is possible that Jerônimo's father put a value on his slave when he wrote his will, which I have not been able to locate so far, and that it took almost ten years for Domingos to amass enough money to buy his freedom. That would explain why the subdelegado declared that the African had obtained his manumission from the "late Sodré," and not from his son.[55]

There is, however, another possibility that could explain how and from whom Domingos obtained his freedom: he had become Jerônimo's slave at the time of the colonel's death as part of a legacy. The value the slave paid for his freedom, besides its timing, is more in line with 1840s manumission prices (average 528,000 reis) than with 1830s prices (average 347,000), meaning that the colonel did not set the price of his freedom in his will after all.[56] To explain the impression that Domingos' arresting officer had that he received his freedom when "the late Sodré" passed away, I would suggest that although our character was still a slave in the early 1840s, he lived on his own as a freedman, most likely in Salvador – where he was well known to the subdelegado who arrested him since the time of his owner's death – while his young master lived on his sugar plantation in the Recôncavo. In the aforementioned 1853 affidavit, he declared that he had been living in Salvador for "many years." If this was the case, Domingos probably paid Jerônimo part of what he earned in the city. They may also have reached an agreement that allowed the slave to keep everything he earned to save up for his freedom. Yet again, if a deal was reached, it had perhaps been arranged by the deceased colonel. As for the source of the money Domingos

---

54 Will of Domingos Sodré, APEB, *Judiciária. Testamentos*, no. 07/3257/01.
55 Jerônimo Sodré Pereira had a nephew of the same name, a doctor, professor of physiology at the Bahia School of Medicine, and a politician who, in 1852, while still a student, got together with his classmates to found the short-lived 2nd of July Abolitionist Society, and would preach the gospel of Abolitionism as a congressman. Regarding this other Jerônimo Sodré, see Jailton Lima Brito, *A abolição na Bahia, 1870–1888* (Salvador: Centro de Estudos Baianos/EDUFBa, 2003), 106–107.
56 On price of manummission, see Katia Mattoso, Herbert S. Klein, and Stanley L. Engerman, "Notas sobre as tendências e padrões dos preços de alforrias na Bahia, 1819–1888", in *Escravidão e invenção da liberdade: estudos sobre o negro no Brasil*, ed. João José Reis (São Paulo: Brasiliense, 1988), 60–72.

used to purchase his manumission, it must have come from some sort of business – in the 1853 affidavit the subdelegado of his district wrote that he was "employed in business" ("*empregado em negócio*") – and presumably from payments for his services as a Candomblé expert. We will see more about this in later chapters.[57]

The man who signed Domingos' freedom paper was a truly original character. Jerônimo Pereira Sodré went to school in England, and was a lesser nobleman of the Brazilian Imperial House, a knight of the Order of Christ, and a major in the National Guard. He served as a lieutenant alongside his father in the war of independence in Bahia. In 1872, he had a home in Salvador, then a city of about 130,000, but he preferred to live on the São João plantation in Matoim, a rural parish with a population of less than 2,500, a few more than 1,000 of whom were enslaved.[58] A bachelor, he lived there with slave mistresses who bore him three daughters and five sons. He gave them his family name and officially declared them legitimate in the notary's office. This led to a tremendous feud over the heir's estate involving the major's siblings and nieces and nephews when he died in 1881. At the time, his fortune was valued at roughly 100 million reis in urban real estate, including the Francês and Paris hotels, which stood a few yards from Domingos' home, as well as rural properties, including the São João plantation. Soon after the major's death, his mixed-race children occupied that plantation, taking up arms to defend what they believed to be their rightful inheritance. But they were quickly evicted by force, and lost the legal battle for their inheritance five years later, although their descendants continued to pursue those claims until at least 1928.

Antonio Ferrão Moniz, Jerônimo's brother-in-law, remarked on the latter's mixed-race children's occupation of the São João plantation in his diary on November 2, 1881, a week after the last heir to the entailed estate had died:

We are now taken up with claims. Jerônimo Sodré, who was the last administrator of the entailed "Sodré" estate, died last month (October 24) and recognized the children of his slaves and married one of the daughters to a *marotinho*.

[57] Domingos' affidavit of 1853 in APEB, *Policia*, maço 6315.
[58] The figures are from Manoel Jesuíno Ferreira, *A Província da Bahia: apontamentos* (Rio de Janeiro: Typographia Nacional, 1875), 32.

Figure 9. Hotel Paris, on the corner of Ladeira de São Bento, the property of Domingos Sodré's young master.

These individuals have got it in their heads that they can inherit the estate, and therefore are engaging in unruly behavior to seize the plantation that is part of it, and in fact they have seized it by force and are there, bearing arms, so it is necessary to drive them out by force.[59]

The Bahian aristocrat's arrogant and bigoted tone seeps through in every word, and not even the major's Portuguese-born son-in-law, Antonio Rodrigues Môcho, the little *maroto* (or *marotinho*), escapes. *Maroto*, which meant "plebeian, unpolished and discourteous young person," was a pejorative term that Brazilians used for people born in Portugal no matter what their social rank. When he was writing that entry in his diary, Antônio Muniz apparently did not know that Jerônimo's nephew João Vaz de Carvalho had already seized the São João plantation from his uncle's children.[60]

I have found manumission records for some of Jerônimo Sodré's female slaves. The first received her freedom unconditionally, graciously granted in January 1841. Her name was Thereza and she was

---

[59] Quoted by Torres, "Os morgados do Sodré," 23.

[60] Probate records of Jerônimo Sodré Pereira, APEB, *Judiciária. Inventários*, 09/4064/10. The family quarrel can be followed in these records, and is also reported by Torres in "Os morgados do Sodré," 22–26. However, this author is a descendant of the "legitimate" Sodré family and not at all impartial on this subject. On maroto, see Antonio de Moraes Silva, *Diccionario da lingua portugueza* (Lisbon: Typographia Lacerdina, 1813), 2 vols., ii: 272.

a light-skinned mulatto. In December 1843, he freed Aniceta, a Nagô woman, for 400,000 reis, although he would only register her manumission papers in 1856. On the first day of that same year, the major freed Henriqueta, a cabra, free of charge, "on account of her good services ... and the freedwoman is obliged to accompany me throughout my lifetime." Henriqueta was probably the same slave listed with that name in 1836 in the inventory of the Trindade plantation, where she is described as a "*cabrinha*," a young cabra, engaged in "domestic service" and valued at 400,000 reis. Lest we forget, the colonel had bequeathed the Trindade plantation to Jerônimo's sister, and Henriqueta's experience illustrates how ownership of slaves could be transferred from one member of their master's family to another.

Jerônimo Sodré also granted manumission to other slaves. In 1859, the major freed Carlota, a creole woman, also for good services and under the same conditions imposed on Henriqueta. I have found another letter of manumission that he signed several years later, in May 1880, for Cosma, again a creole woman. This time, he stated that her freedom was "full" and granted without payment, "on account of good services." By then, Jerônimo was nearing the end of his life. All of these letters of manumission were granted to women, and only those born in Brazil were freed without payment, although even in this case two manumissions were conditional. It is possible that the "good services" these freedwomen provided included sexual favors, and that they were the mothers of Jerônimo's children.[61]

Jerônimo Sodré was definitely not inclined toward freeing male slaves, which bolsters the hypothesis that the manumission letter he signed for Domingos was granted by his father. Although I say it was granted, manumissions in general were given with the slaves' active participation, and therefore resulted from sometimes arduous negotiations between the two parties involved. Studies of manumissions have indicated that most were conditional and/or paid for by the freedperson. Furthermore, Brazilian-born female slaves were more likely to

---

[61] The manumission letters granted by Jerônimo Sodré can be found in the following sources: APEB, *LNT*, vol. 269, fl. 98 (Thereza); vol. 325, fl. 116v (Aniceta); vol. 356, fl. 11 (Henriqueta); vol. 403, fl. 44 (Carlota); vol. 653, fl. 49v (Cosma). An African named Eduardo was freed in return for payment of 1,300,000 reis in 1875 by one Jerônimo Sodré Pereira, but I am inclined to believe that his master was the nephew of the same name. See APEB, *LNT*, vol. 474, fl. 3v. Domingos' young master may have granted other manumissions that I have been unable to locate.

benefit from this practice than those born in Africa, as was the case with Jerônimo Sodré's bond people.[62]

LIFE AS A FREEDMAN

Africans forcibly brought to Brazil as slaves, like Domingos, officially became foreigners in the country when they obtained their freedom. They did not have any of the rights of a Brazilian citizen, not even those conceded to Brazilian-born freedpersons, who enjoyed civil and most political rights, except standing for elected office – but they could vote in primaries, for instance. The Imperial Constitution of 1824 did not allow freed Africans to participate in the political life of the nation in any way. They could not vote or be elected to public office, or become civil servants at any level. As historian Sidney Chalhoub suggests, being a freedperson in nineteenth-century Brazil was "a burden."[63] And a heavier burden still if the freedperson was born in Africa.

In Bahia, furthermore, African freed men and -women were subjected to a variety of humiliating limitations that increased exponentially after the Revolt of the Malês in 1835. Three decades after that uprising, measures introduced at the time to confront African unrest were still in place and even tightened. One example was a law in effect at the time of Domingos' arrest in 1862, which broadly restricted the Africans' freedom of movement between the provinces and counties at any time, and even in the city streets at night. Article 70 of the Procedural Code of the Brazilian Empire obliged African freedpersons, like slaves in general, always to carry their passport with them when traveling, even when accompanied by their "masters and patrons," the latter expression being a term that identified an ex-master. As for the municipal laws, take edict no. 86 of 1859, which punished with a 1,000-reis fine or four days in jail any "African slave" found in the streets at night without a note signed by

[62] For manumissions in Bahia, see Kátia Mattoso, "A Propósito de cartas de alforria," *Anais de História*, no. 4 (1972): 23–52; Stuart Schwartz, "The Manumission of Slaves in Colonial Brazil: Bahia, 1684–1745," *The Hispanic American Historical Review* 54, no. 4 (1974): 603–635; Mieko Nishida, "Manumission and Ethnicity in Urban Slavery: Salvador, Brazil, 1808–1888," *The Hispanic American Historical Review* 73, no. 3 (1993): 361–391; and Katia Lorena Novaes Almeida, *Alforrias em Rio de Contas – Bahia, século xix*, Salvador EDUFBA, 2012.

[63] Sidney Chalhoub, "The Politics of Silence: Race and Citizenship in Nineteenth-Century Brazil," *Slavery & Abolition* 27, no. 1 (2006): 73–87. Regarding the precarious legal and political status of African freedpersons in Imperial Brazil, see also Cunha, *Negros, estrangeiros*, 68–81.

their master or mistress, "stating where they are going, their name and place of residence"; the same edict penalized with a fine of 3,000 reis or eight days in jail "African freedpersons" found out and about after dark "without a note from a Brazilian Citizen."[64] This and similar edicts would have directly affected Domingos Sodré. As a freedman, in many ways he would still be treated like a slave because he happened to be born on the other side of the Atlantic. In order to get about in the city without a master, Domingos would have had to engage in a relationship of patronage with a free citizen who trusted him enough to write him a document that amounted to a safe-conduct.

Not only were the movements of African-born freedpersons restricted but they were also denied access to certain sectors of the labor market in Bahia. Between 1849 and 1850, for instance, both enslaved and freed Africans – but not Crioulos – were banned from working on the *saveiros*, the dhow-like sailboats that ferried merchandise from ships, many arriving from West Africa, to the docks in the port of Salvador.[65] That prohibition was still in effect in the early 1860s. In July 1861, the president of the province ordered the harbor master to revoke the registration of an African freedman who had signed up as a hoy rower. The president learned about his illegal registration from a group of Brazilian rowers, most of whom were certainly as black as the African they were trying to bar from working on the saveiros. The harbor master observed in a letter to the president that, on consulting the law, he had found that "Indeed Africans in general are prohibited from rowing saveiros [to and] from the docks of this city."[66]

Among the municipal edicts issued in 1857, number 14 stated that it was "absolutely forbidden for African freemen, freedmen or slaves to trade in staples, food and small items ... whether on their own account

[64] Araújo Filqueiras Junior, *Codigo do Processo do Imperio do Brasil* (Rio de Janeiro: Eduardo & Henrique Laemmert, 1874), 33; "Ultima redação das Posturas da Câmara Municipal da Capital [1850]," APEB, *Legislativa. Posturas, 1835–1884*, maço 853; *Posturas da Câmara Municipal da Cidade de S. Salvador, capital da Província da Bahia* (Bahia: Typ. de Manoel Agostinho Cruz Mello, 1860), 20. Tax laws and other discriminatory regulations affecting African freedpersons are listed in *Legislação da Província da Bahia sobre o negro, 1835–1888* (Salvador: Fundação Cultural do Estado da Bahia/Direção de Bibliotecas Públicas, 1996).
[65] Cunha, *Negros, estrangeiros*, 74–100.
[66] Harbor master Augusto Wenceslau da Silva to the president of the province, July 18, 1861, APEB, *Polícia do porto*, maço 3155.

or for their masters in the granaries and public markets." The punishment for disobeying this edict was a fine of 30,000 reis, which doubled if
the infraction was repeated.[67] Freedpersons who sold their wares in glass
boxes, on trays, or in wooden bowls, as well as those who carried sedan
chairs or rowed boats outside the port, paid an additional tax of 10,000
reis per year. The fine for late payment of those taxes reached 50,000
reis in 1848, and their goods and other objects of trade could be confiscated if city inspectors caught them without the proper permits. Sedan
chairs and perishable items were daily seized and sold at auction. "For
lack of a permit and payment of taxes," a freedwoman named Domingas
saw her goods – in this case farm produce or food products – confiscated and auctioned off. A more specific announcement published in
the papers by the manager of the provincial board of revenue advertised the auction of "2 chicken coops and 262 yams seized from the
Africans Tiburcio Ferreira and Caetano Dundas, for want of permits,
which items are impounded in the warehouse of that same board."[68]
Auctioning off confiscated chickens and yams – that is how far the government's despoilment of African freedpeople could go!

The taxes Africans paid to the province for the right to engage in
commerce would double to 20,000 reis in 1856. They also had to pay
2,000 reis to the Salvador City Council. That same year, a tax of 10,000
reis was levied on African freedpersons and slaves who engaged in any
kind of trade or craft. The tax did not include those who worked in fac-
tories and mills, but it did fall on Africans who worked independently
in workshops or in their own homes. This discriminatory fiscal policy
was obviously not a means to supply the public coffers, given that the
return did not amount to much, but it functioned as a strategy to drive
Africans out of commerce, the workshops, crafts, in short, any kind of
small independent productive activity, making work on export-oriented
plantations or on vegetable gardens to feed the city the only occupation
left open to them. It is therefore not surprising that so many of them
worked as farmhands in the outskirts of Salvador in places like Cruz do
Cosme, as we have seen in the previous chapter.[69]

---

[67] APEB, *Câmara de Salvador*, maço 1404.

[68] See *Correio Mercantil*, July 1, August 12, 1848, and January 24, 1849 (second
quotation), March 5, 1849, May 16, 1849 (first quotation).

[69] See Budgetary Law no. 607, chap. 2, art. 2, par. 27; and Budgetary Law no. 608,
both from 1856, in *Legislação da província da Bahia*, 53–55. See also Cunha,
Negros, estrangeiros, 74–100; and Ricardo Tadeu Caires Silva, "Caminhos

The pressure on African workers led to an original collective response in 1857. In June of that year, blacks who worked for hire held a ten-day general strike in response to a municipal ordinance that not only charged them a tax for doing their jobs but required freedmen to present a document signed by an "upstanding citizen" that guaranteed their good behavior. These black workers, Africans in their vast majority, also protested against having to wear a metal plate around their necks stamped with the registration number assigned them by the City Council. The 1857 strike, the first in Brazil to halt an entire sector of the urban labor force, was yet another movement that Domingos might have joined, if he worked for hire. Even if he did not, he must have known Africans who did.[70]

When they were allowed to work, African freedpersons were subjected to a veritable fiscal persecution that intentionally made their lives more difficult, with the aim of pressuring them into giving up on life in Bahia and "spontaneously" returning to Africa. In fact, Law no. 9 of May 1835, issued in the wake of the repression of the Revolt of the Malês, stipulated just that, even though it did not work in the long run. The same law obliged Africans to pay an annual head tax of 10,000 reis to continue living in Salvador. They were also forbidden to acquire real estate, such as houses and land. Partly for this reason, many enterprising Africans chose to invest their money in slaves whenever possible, and when they bought real estate they would register it in the name of a Brazilian-born relative – a son, daughter, nephew, or niece.[71]

The discriminatory laws against Africans covered many aspects of life. They were not allowed to get together for drumming sessions or sambas or to organize parties to celebrate baptisms, weddings, funerals, or other festive occasions – yes, following traditions brought from

---

e descaminhos da abolição: escravos, senhores e direitos nas últimas décadas da escravidão (Bahia, 1850–1888)," PhD dissertation, Universidade Federal do Paraná, 2007, chap. 2; and Richard Graham, *Feeding the City: From Street Market to Liberal Reform in Salvador, Brazil, 1780–1860* (Austin: University of Texas Press, 2010).

[70] João José Reis, "'The Revolution of the Ganhadores': Urban Labour, Ethnicity, and the African Strike of 1857 in Bahia, Brazil," *Journal of Latin American History* 29, no. 2 (1997): 355–393.

[71] Law no. 9 is published in *Colleção de Leis e Resoluções da Assembléia Legislativa da Bahia sancionadas e publicadas nos annos de 1835 a 1838* (Bahia: Typ. de Antonio O. da França Guerra, 1862), i: 22–27, and discussed in Reis, *Rebelião escrava no Brasil*, 498–503.

overseas, funerals were festive occasions for them. Fortunately, as we have seen in the previous chapter, some officials turned a blind eye to infringements of these ordinances. To enjoy their festivities in peace, African freedpersons had to rely on paternalist gestures, which were few and far between. For example, the African freedwoman Rita Maria Antonia was refused permission from the chief of police to "put on a dancing entertainment" in the Engenho Velho neighborhood between June 24 and 27, 1857, starting with the celebration of St. John's Day, which was also a time for Candomblé ceremonies. The police chief advised the subdelegado to observe the "strictest ban on drumming sessions" or *batuques*.[72]

Not only were their own amusements forbidden but Africans were also barred from entering some officially sanctioned places of entertainment. The imposing São João Theater (Figure 10), where abolitionist plays and poetry were often presented, located in what is now Castro Alves Plaza, then the most important theater in Bahia, did not admit slaves of any color or background or Africans of any social status. Discrimination was not based on race, but on ethnicity or origin. Brazilian-born free and freed blacks and mulattoes could enter the theater, but Africans of the same status could not. Because of this rule, Domingos Sodré probably never set foot in that theater as a freedman, although he lived a short distance away.[73]

When it came to Africans, a tenuous line divided their status as slaves and freedpersons. The daily lives of freedmen and -women born in Africa were circumscribed in many ways, and not only because their beliefs and customs were different from those of most whites. The eloquent words we read in manumission letters, which state that the freedpersons, whether African or not, would thenceforth be "as free as if born from a free womb," did not reflect reality. It is therefore not surprising that Africans sought the protection of their former masters, now treated as "patrons," a common expression in slaveholding Brazil, and even a legally binding relationship. Although it was rare, a freedperson's letter of manumission could be revoked and the individual re-enslaved if he or she did not show loyalty to the person who had "sponsored" their

---

[72] Police Chief Francisco S. de Mattos to the subdelegado of the second district of Santo Antônio, June 23, 1857, APEB, *Polícia*, vol. 5722, fl. 153v.

[73] For the São João Theater's regulations, see *Correio Mercantil* (Rio de Janeiro), October 12, 1854.

Figure 10. The São João Theater, located in Domingos' neighborhood. The theater caught fire in 1922 and was demolished. What was once Theater Square is now called Castro Alves Plaza.

freedom. Symbolically cementing these bonds of dependence, freedpersons generally adopted their patrons' family names. Domingos Pereira Sodré was among them. Nevertheless, like other freedpersons of his time, Domingos would overcome legal obstacles, side-step the machinery of domination, and negotiate some room for autonomy in the white man's land, for despite all the obstacles, Bahian society was not absolutely impermeable to the advancement of savvy Africans.

CHAPTER THREE

Domingos Sodré, Diviner

Domingos' Home, Parish, and City

The police chief, João Antônio de Araújo Freitas Henriques, took the complaint from customs official José Egídio Nabuco against Domingos Sodré's candomblé very seriously. Chief Henriques ordered a raid headed by Pompílio Manoel de Castro, the acting subdelegado of São Pedro Velho parish, where Domingos lived. The subdelegado was accompanied by two constables, José Thomas Muniz Barreto, a small jeweler, and Adriano Pinto, whose occupation I have been unable to ascertain. He was a neighbor of the African freedman. In addition to these men, the officials present during the search included Lieutenant Colonel Domingos José Freire de Carvalho, none other than the commander of the police, which would supply the physical force for the operation – each officer would be armed with a rifle and a pistol – as the subdelegados, as a rule, did not have any armed police under their command. The entire operation reflects how seriously the chief of police had taken the complaint.[1]

---

[1] The documents regarding the complaint and the measures that the chief of police and his subordinates took as a result include: João Henriques to the subdelegado of São Pedro Velho parish, July 25, 1862, APEB, *Polícia. Correspondência expedida, 1862*, vol. 5754, fls. 214v–215; Pompílio Manoel de Castro to the chief of police, July 26 and 27, 1862, APEB, *Subdelegados, 1862–63*, maço 6234. These sources were also used by Harding, *A Refuge in Thunder*, 50–51, 93–96, and 196–204, to discuss the incident. For the occupations and addresses of the constables, see *Almanak administrativo, mercantil e industrial da Bahia para o anno de 1863, organizado por Camilo de Lelis Masson* (Bahia: Typographia de Camillo de Lelis Masson e Co., 1863), 254, 372.

The complainant had sent Chief João Henriques detailed information about where to find Domingos Sodré. He lived in a two-story townhouse on 7 Ladeira de Santa Tereza, a narrow, sloping street connecting Rua de Baixo de São Bento (now Rua Carlos Gomes) and Rua do Sodré, which was named after Domingos' master's family. From the corner of Ladeira de Santa Tereza and Rua do Sodré, the freedman could have seen the eighteenth-century manor that once had belonged to the Sodré family and was now the home of the famous abolitionist poet Antonio de Castro Alves's family. It was just a short distance away, which means that the poet and the freedman were neighbors. Even if they were unaware of each other's existence, the slaves in the abolitionist's household – namely two litter bearers, Augusto and Pedro, a cook, Martinha, and a maid, Vitória, all of whom were African, and a creole washerwoman, Lucrecia – probably knew Domingos and heard about his arrest in 1862. They may even have witnessed the commotion that the incident must have caused.[2]

The building where Domingos lived may have been the same one that his former master, Colonel Francisco Maria Sodré Pereira, owned in 1816 and used as collateral for a loan. At that time, the resident – probably a tenant – was one Francisco Faura.[3] I do not know exactly when Domingos moved to Ladeira de Santa Tereza, but baptismal records in which he appears as a godfather state that he had lived in São Pedro parish since at least 1845. It is therefore highly possible that Domingos had been living at that address for seventeen years when he was arrested there in 1862. In any case, he had been living there "for many years" when a constable registered his residence in 1853 – all freed Africans were obliged to undergo such a registration every year since the 1835 revolt – also declaring that the building belonged to Dona Maria de Saldanha, a lady with a resounding family name, and had been rented to the freedman.[4]

2   "Inventário do Dr. Antonio José Alves," *Anais do APEBa*, vol. 30 (1947): 56–57 (the probate records for Antonio José Alves, who died on January 23, 1866); and Waldemar Mattos, "A Bahia de Castro Alves," ibid., 278, where the author describes the Sodré manor, including "two *lojas* (basements) at the entrance and several rooms for slaves."

3   "Escriptura de débito, obrigação e hipoteca que faz o coronel Francisco Maria Sodré Pereira, ao commerciante João Baptista de Araujo Braga da quantia de 4: 600$000 rs. como abaixo se declara," August 16, 1816, APEB, *LNT*, 188, fl. 61v.

4   See ACMS, *Livro de registro de batismos. Freguesia da Conceição da Praia, 1844–1889*, fl. 11v and fl. 12; Domingo's residence registration, signed by Constable Tito Nicolau Capinam, May 14, 1853, APEB, *Polícia*, maço 6315.

Domingos' home was just a few yards from the Convent of St. Theresa and the attached archdiocesan seminary, where the Catholic Church trained its priests, both on Rua do Sodré. The seminary was conceived with the mission to rehabilitate the lax behavior of the Bahian clergy and actually did impose strict discipline on the bodies and minds of its pupils, characterized by controlling their living space, time, and movements both inside and outside the institution through dedication to systematic study and severe punishment for infractions. Historian Cândido da Costa e Silva describes the spirit of the seminary as "closed, outside the pale, reducing communication with the world to a minimum, building walls against the contagion and corruption that seeped in from all sides." Although the strict Lazarite priests who ran the seminary had recently been removed, their methods of teaching and indoctrination were deeply ingrained.[5] It is ironic that Domingos Sodré practiced Candomblé, a religion with little dogma, so close to an institution created to tighten the reins of Catholic orthodoxy. And it is surprising that the vigilant priests at the seminary were unaware of what was going on in the arena of religious "corruption" on the other side of the street.

The chief of police of Bahia seemed to be a stricter Catholic than the dean of the seminary. But to make the target of the raid more precise, João Henriques informed subdelegado Pompílio Manoel de Castro that the townhouse where Domingos lived had just four windows, "where there are flowerpots, and in the rear it is connected to the houses in Rua de Baixo [de São Bento], facing the sea."[6] The newspaper report in *Diário da Bahia* stated that the freedman only occupied the *loja* of the building, which was a kind of basement common to houses of that period, with small square or oval windows called oculi that were generally grated and looked out on the sidewalk at street level. Lojas were typical housing for slaves and freedpersons in Salvador at the time.[7] However, I do not think the police authorities would have failed to mention that Domingos was only living in that part of the building. Therefore, I believe that the

---

5   For the seminary, see Cândido da Costa e Silva, *Os segadores e a messe: o clero oitocentista na Bahia* (Salvador: EDUFBa, 2000), 168–177. The original quotation is on p. 173.

6   Chefe João Antonio de Araújo Freitas Henriques to the subdelegado of São Pedro, July 25, 1862, APEB, *Polícia. Correspondência expedida, 1862*, vol. 5754, fl. 214v.

7   *Diário da Bahia*, July 28, 1862. For this sort of low-income housing, see Costa, "Ekabó!"

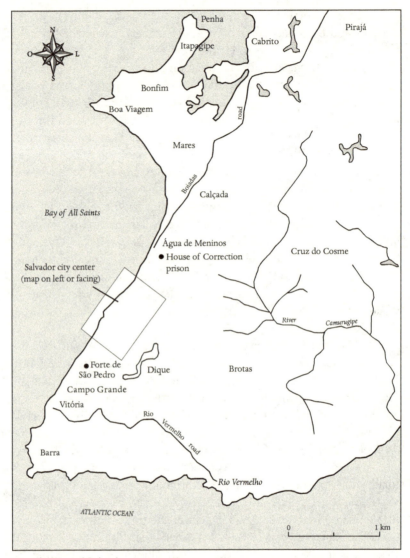

Map 3. Map of Salvador.

African freedman actually did occupy the entire house, for it was just a small, two-story building with four windows facing the street.

The townhouse on Ladeira de Santa Tereza was probably no different from the rest of the neighborhood, where Africans lived in buildings converted into tenements as they did in several other parts of the

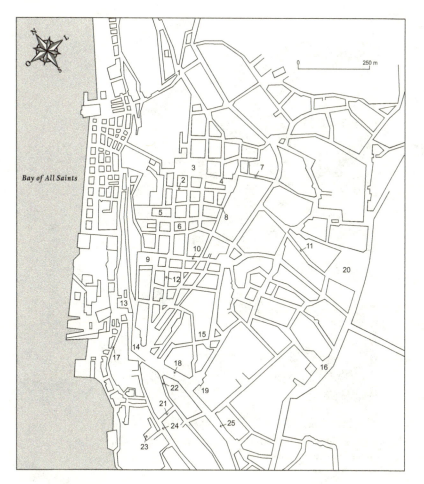

LOCAIS MENCIONADOS NO TEXTO

1. Baixa dos Sapateiros
2. Rua do Bispo
3. Terreiro de Jesus
4. Cruzeiro de S. Francisco
5. Sé church
6. Aljube jail
7. Ladeira da O. T. de S. Francisco
8. Rua São Francisco
9. Praça do Palácio
10. Ladeira da Praça
11. Rua do Tingui
12. Rua da Ajuda
13. Conceição da Praia
14. Largo do Teatro
15. Barroquinha
16. Rua da Lapa
17. Ladeira da Preguiça
18. Ladeira de S. Bento
19. São Bento monastery
20. Campo da Pólvora
21. Ladeira de S. Tereza
22. Rua de Baixo de S. Bento
23. Santa Tereza convent
24. Rua do Sodré
25. Rua de São Pedro

Map 4. Map of the center of Salvador.

Figure 11. Ladeira de Santa Tereza, the street where Domingos Sodré lived, with the convent in the background.

city. In 1869, *O Alabama* published the following complaint about the goings-on on Rua do Sodré, in Domingos´ neighborhood:

> It is old news, but it takes on larger proportions every day. I want to talk about a multitude of houses, located on that street [Sodré], which, being occupied only by Africans of both sexes, are veritable *quilombos* [runaway slave settlements]. The owners of these houses, concerned only about the prompt receipt of rents, care little that their properties are ruined, and that the neighborhood is disturbed. An African rents a house, and is preferred to any Brazilian applicant; he reduces the rooms, bedrooms and kitchen into small cubicles, divided by boards, mats, and even blankets, and overnight all these hovels are occupied. The black man who

Figure 12. In the top right of the photo, the Convent of St. Theresa, with the seminary (now demolished) to its left, ca. 1860.

Figure 13. Domingos Sodré's neighborhood, showing the seminary in the foreground, to the right. The two white townhouses on the left stood on Ladeira de Santa Tereza.

Figure 14. Sodré manor, which once belonged to the family of Domingos' master, and later on to the family of Castro Alves. The freedman could see the manor from the corner of Ladeira de Santa Tereza.

rents the house, in addition to receiving a one hundred percent profit from this speculation, is the head of the *quilombo*.[8]

The use of the term *quilombo* to describe these tenements suggests a contemporary understanding of their role as a place of African resistance, similar to rural runaway slave communities.[9] This was not a

8   *O Alabama*, May 6, 1869.
9   Other newspapers also called quilombos venues where black people held noisy gatherings. One 1851 example, from the *A verdadeira marmota* newspaper, can be found in Abreu, *Capoeiras*, 74. In Rio de Janeiro, this kind of urban

recent invention. During the investigation of the Malê revolt in 1835, the rebels' homes were sometimes called quilombos. The tenements reported by *O Alabama* represented a collective African alternative to the bourgeois concept of urban organization advocated by educated men in Bahia who considered themselves the bastions of civilization. This concept underscored as a desirable model for Brazil the nuclear family living in a spacious, well-planned, ventilated house, although it also had to accommodate "uncivilized" slaves under the same roof, as the family could not and would not do without their services.

Domingos Sodré lived in the city of Bahia at a time when important changes to the urban landscape were in progress, inspired by the European concept of social hygiene and the modern occupation of public space. Although goods and people were transported on the backs of Africans until the eve of abolition in 1888, donkey-drawn vehicles, including passenger trams that ran on rails, began transforming urban transportation. The streets near Domingos' home benefited from these innovations and were even paved, as can be seen in photographs from that period. In the early 1870s, the Conceição parish hydraulic elevator appeared, the precursor to the present-day Lacerda Elevator, linking the Lower and Upper Cities. Gradually, gas lighting appeared in the streets and a water supply system functioned through standpipes with taps controlled by Companhia do Queimado (the city's water utility), whose customers would come to include Domingos himself. Jails, hospitals, poorhouses, sanitariums, and cemeteries were built or came to occupy existing buildings outside the city, with a view to isolating the undesirable groups on the margins of society: the physically and mentally ill, convicts, beggars, and the dead. According to the reformers of the day, the city had to embrace the values of modernity with full force, engage in the process of civilization, clean up its houses and streets, and

---

housing was called a *casa de quilombo* (quilombo house). See Carlos Eugênio Líbano Soares, *Zungú: rumor de muitas vozes* (Rio de Janeiro: Arquivo Público do Estado do Rio de Janeiro, 1998), 56–58. Even for rural areas, the concept of the quilombo has broadened in recent studies. See chapters of João José Reis and Flávio dos Santos Gomes (eds.), *Liberdade por um fio: história dos quilombos no Brasil* (São Paulo: Companhia das Letras, 1999), as well as several studies by Flávio Gomes, such as *Histórias de quilombolas*, and *A Hidra e os pântanos: mocambos, quilombos e comunidades de fugitivos no Brasil (séculos XVII-XIX)* (São Paulo: Editora da UNESP, 2005), besides *Experiências atlânticas: ensaios e pesquisas sobre a escravidão e o pós-emancipação no Brasil* (Passo Fundo: Editora da Universidade de Passo Fundo, 2003).

Figure 15. Sidewalks, paved streets, tram rails, water sellers, and black women selling goods from trays: the old and the new side by side on Rua de São Pedro (ca.
1885), the main street in the parish where Domingos Sodré lived.

refine its artistic sensibilities according to the European fashion. But
the Africans and their customs were getting in the way of progress, or
so the reformers thought.[10]

However, it should be said that Bahians did not uniformly con-
demn the African presence, particularly its urban "quilombos." The
less enlightened owners of those buildings, for example, were pleased
to see that their African tenants paid their rent on time, and even the
anti-African *O Alabama* conceded that Brazilian tenants could not
always be relied on to do the same. Africans lived together there or
elsewhere, as a collective self-protection measure, in part because of discrimination against African-born persons by people who thought like
that newspaper's editors.

This does not mean that Africans lived in an ethnic or racial ghetto.
Salvador was almost entirely integrated, socially speaking, because of
slavery itself, which forced enslaved and free people to live together in
the same households. Black Africans and Brazilians could be found all

[10] Consuelo Novaes Sampaio, *50 anos de urbanização: Salvador no século XIX* (Rio
de Janeiro: Versal, 2005); Reis, *A morte é uma festa*; Walter Fraga Filho, *Mendigos,
moleques e vadios na Bahia do século XIX* (São Paulo: Hucitec; Salvador, EDUFBA,
1996); and Venétia Durando Braga Rios, "O Asylo de São João de Deos – as
faces da loucura," PhD dissertation, Pontifícia Universidade de São Paulo, 2006.

Figure 16. The Conceição Elevator, inaugurated in 1873, was a symbol of progress in Bahia.

over the city, which was steadily growing and changing. Unfortunately, we do not know the exact size of Salvador's population at the time of Domingos' arrest. British visitors John Candler and Wilson Burgess estimated that there were 125,000 souls in the city in 1853, and German physician Robert Avé-Lallemant pointed to 180,000 in 1859, although both figures are probably exaggerated. The first national census, conducted in 1872, when the population should have been larger, reported that 129,109 people lived in Salvador and its outskirts, 108,138 in the urban parishes alone. This last estimate included an enslaved contingent of 12,501 people, the equivalent of 11.5 percent of Salvador's population. By that time, Africans represented just 15 percent of the slaves, but there were certainly many more ten years earlier. Together with

Figure 17. Logo of Salvador's water company, whose customers included Domingos Sodré, 1887.

the local black people, they gave foreign visitors the impression that they were in an African city. Candler and Burgess mentioned an "overflowing" black population, which they believed to consist entirely of slaves, and Avé-Lallemant observed about Salvador: "Everything seems black: blacks on the beach, blacks in the city, blacks in the lower city, blacks in the upper districts." And he added: "Everything that runs, shouts, works, everything that fetches and carries is black." A few pages further, the German traveler would describe the city of Bahia as a "black metropolis."[11]

Little is left of a census conducted in 1855, although it is still possible to put together demographics for the parish where Domingos lived. São Pedro Velho was basically residential, 40 percent white, 25 percent African, and the remainder Crioulos, pardos, and cabras. Its residents

[11]   John Candler and Wilson Burgess, *Narrative of a Recent Visit to Brazil* (London: Edward Marsh, Friends' Books, 1853), 49; Robert Avé-Lallemand, *Viagens pelas províncias da Bahia, Pernambuco, Alagoas e Sergipe (1859)* (Belo Horizonte: Itatiaia/São Paulo: Edusp, 1980), 22, 31. For the estimate based on the 1872 census, I used data from the CD-ROM organized by Pedro Puntoni, *Os recenseamentos gerais do Brasil no século XIX: 1872 e 1890* (São Paulo: CEBRAP – Centro Brasileiro de Análise e Planejamento, n.d). My estimates do not always concur with those of Kátia Mattoso, *A cidade de Salvador e seu mercado no século XIX* (São Paulo: Hucitec, 1978), 131, 133–136.

included public servants and professionals, such as doctors and lawyers, as well as artisans. Just 13 percent of its population was enslaved.[12]

The 1872 census is more reliable. It indicates that the slave population was larger, making up 16 percent of residents, or 2,346 people. Just 25.7 percent of them were born in Africa – precisely 601 enslaved men and women. They probably formed the main potential clientele for Domingos Sodré's candomblé. I have not been able to determine the number of African freedpersons, but the parish's population was divided by color (including the free and enslaved) as follows: 3,722 whites, 5,878 pardos, 3,314 blacks, and eighty-two caboclos. Those listed as whites were the minority – just 28.6 percent.

Domingos Sodré lived in a socially, racially, and ethnically varied neighborhood. In addition to the constable and jeweler José Muniz Barreto, I have managed to identify other residents of Ladeira de Santa Tereza: canon and Latin teacher Manoel dos Santos Pereira; Treasury Department official Tito José Cardoso Rangel, 33, married; customs warehouse officer Cincinato Luzia Botelho Damásio, 21, single; musicians Porfírio Lima da Silva e Mello, 30, a bachelor, and Euclides José de Souza; tailors Galdino "so-and-so" and Luiz da França; Rita "so-and-so," a creole woman; African freedman Antão Teixeira; a Portuguese sales clerk whose name I was unable to find and worked for a baker on the corner of Ladeira de Santa Tereza and Rua de Baixo de São Bento.[13] These people, most of whom were probably white or mixed race and included a priest – not to mention the clerics in the nearby seminary – were not responsible for the complaint against the African freedman, although they must have suspected what was going on inside his home. This is noteworthy.

Was Domingos Sodré the head of an urban quilombo, an African collective residence like the one described in O Alabama? At the time of his arrest, Domingos suggested that other people lived in his house besides himself, and, at the very least, a slave woman he owned. The

---

[12] Maria Amélia Vieira Nascimento, *Dez freguesias da cidade do Salvador* (Salvador: Fundação Cultural do Estado da Bahia, 1986), 83.

[13] *Almanak ... de 1863*, 335; *Almanak ... de 1873*, 64, 66, 167, 169, part 4, p. 30; João Henriques to the subdelegado of São Pedro parish, April 28, 1862, APEB, *Polícia. Correspondência*, vol. 5754, fl. 114v. I was able to identify the ages and marital status of two of the residents thanks to AMS, *Livro de qualificação de votantes. Freguesia de São Pedro, 1863–1865*, fls. 103v, 169v; AMS, *Livro de qualificação de votantes. Freguesia de São Pedro, 1870–1875*, fl. 133.

chief of police did not use the term *quilombo* to describe the freedman's house, but he did call it a "den," which sounded no less dangerous than a refuge for runaway slaves. The order to attack did not lack something of military strategy and crowd control methods, because he ordered his subdelegado "to watch the backyards to ensure that the operation is successful in arresting the people found in the said house, who must be immediately taken to jail before a multitude gathers, as tends to occur on these occasions." Henriques said he was aware that the Candomblé gatherings over which Domingos presided were usually held on Tuesdays and Fridays, and he wrote his orders on a Friday, so the timing of the raid was not arbitrary. Subdelegado Pompílio Manoel de Castro, the same aficionado of the arts and literature, would carry out the raid competently that same day.[14]

DOMINGOS' CANDOMBLÉ

According to Subdelegado Pompílio Manoel de Castro's report to the chief of police, they found "miscellaneous objects of witchcraft, made of metal and wood, in an extraordinary quantity" in Domingos' home, along with personal items and jewelry, which the official presumed to be stolen. Four other adult Africans and a "black lad" were arrested along with Domingos.[15] A summarized report of the police rounds that day confirmed that "several objects of witchcraft and dances of blacks" were seized, as well as "the slaves João, a Crioulo, [and] Elesbão, Elisia, Teresa and Delfina, Africans."[16]

These words reflect a cultural battle, which of course was also social. In the pejorative sense always used in police documents, witchcraft (*feitiçaria*) involved doing evil, and was therefore the Other's religion. In this case, the staunchly Catholic Pompílio preliminarily defined Candomblé as witchcraft, something characteristic of Africans and, to a lesser extent, their Brazilian-born children. The subdelegado had forgotten – although he was well aware – that Catholics, including whites, also relied on the manipulation of certain symbolic, material, and ritual resources to control or attack others, defend themselves, make people

---

[14] Chief João Antonio de Araújo Freitas Henriques to the subdelegado of São Pedro, July 25, 1862, fls. 214v, 215.

[15] Pompílio Manuel de Castro to the chief of police, July 26, 1862, APEB, *Polícia. Subdelegados, 1862–63*, maço 6234.

[16] Police Reports (Partes de Polícia), July 26, 1862, APEB, *Polícia*, maço 1023.

sick, or cure them. Most of the "miscellaneous objects" found in the home of Domingos Sodré can be identified as objects of worship, religious items, and not ingredients specifically used in witchcraft or traditional healing, although the freedman was familiar with those as well, and certainly owned them. Africans also believed in and performed witchcraft, which was severely punished in their homelands, and there were probably sanctions against it in the African communities throughout Brazil as well. As will be seen in the following chapter, Domingos cast spells and prepared concoctions to keep slave owners under control. But he did not need to do that to be deemed a sorcerer in Bahia. After all, Candomblé was the equivalent of witchcraft in the mindset and hegemonic mentality of the time, and men and women – the vast majority black and African – were often arrested for that practice.

João, the young creole slave arrested in Domingos' home, was the same "black lad" (moleque) that Subdelegado Pompílio mentioned in his report. Teresa and Elesbão were African-born slaves.[17] As for Elisia, her real name was Ignez, and later on she declared that she was a freedwoman. This African woman introduced a problem of personal identity. On the date he was arrested, Domingos owned a slave woman purchased three years earlier who answered to Ignez, as well as other names. But she appears in the purchase documents as Maria, Maria Archangela, and twice as Maria Ignez, including her registration for tax purpose. Although Ignez was a very common name, the coincidence raises the suspicion that the woman arrested that day was Domingo's slave Maria Ignez. If she was, this would explain why she initially stated that she was a slave, but not why she gave the false name of Elisia. Her muddled identity, after all, was not just inscribed in property documents and may have reflected the instability of many Africans' status in Bahian society.[18]

Regarding Delfina, she was very probably the same Maria Delfina da Conceição whom Domingos married in a Catholic ceremony nine years later, in 1871, after they had lived together as common-law partners for many years.[19] I believe that Delfina was not yet a freedwoman

[17] João Henriques to the jailer at the House of Correction, July 31, 1862, APEB, Polícia. Correspondência expedida, 1862, vol. 5756, fl. 149.
[18] The documents pertaining to the purchase of Maria Ignez (or Archanja) are registered in AMS, Escritura de escravos. Freguesia da Conceição da Praia, 1855–1859, no. 66.7, fls. 105–107.
[19] ACMS, Livro de registro de casamentos. São Pedro Velho, 1844–1910, fl. 128v.

when she was arrested in 1862. In his orders to the subdelegado to raid
Domingos' house, the police chief stated that the African freedman was
working "in conjunction with two African women, also freedpersons,
who sell boxes," meaning that they were street vendors who sold their
wares from glass-sided boxes (see Figures 20–21).[20] Presumably, one of
the two women accused of being Domingo's accomplices was Delfina,
and I will discuss this further later on. The only Delfina registered as an
inmate of the prison at the time of this incident was listed as the slave
of one Domingos Joaquim Alves.[21] This Delfina, whom I believe to be
Domingos Sodré's affective partner and future wife, would have been
one of the women who earned her living as a hire-out slave. This category of slave often did not live with their masters, but paid them for
"the week," that is, they gave them a previously negotiated weekly sum
and kept the rest. For this reason, the police and their informants could
have mistakenly identified Delfina as a freedwoman at first.[22]

The police searched Domingos' house until nightfall that Friday,
June 25, 1862, when the operation was interrupted because it could not
be successfully done by candle- or torchlight. A more thorough examination would have to wait until the following day, when the subdelegado expected to find numerous stolen items, as well as objects related
to ritual practices. As he wrote in an enthusiastic missive to the chief
of police:

> There are chests and trunks for which he [Domingos Sodré]
> says he does not have the keys, or that their owners were not at
> home, which makes me presume that they must contain some
> stolen items. I am convinced that it will be necessary, in view
> of the large quantity of vile objects of his superstitious trade,
> that you will have to furnish me with people to carry them or
> authorize the burning of the same, although it is true that some
> are made of metal, including rattles, short swords in the form of

---

[20] João Henriques to the subdelegado of São Pedro, July 25, 1862, fl. 214v.
[21] João Henriques to the jailer at the House of Correction, July 26, 1862, APEB,
    Polícia. Correspondência expedida, 1862, vol. 5756, fl. 142.
[22] Regarding female hire-out slaves in Bahia at the time, see Cecilia Moreira Soares,
    "As ganhadeiras: mulher e resistência negra em Salvador no Século XIX," *Afro-
    Ásia*, no. 17 (1996): 57–71, also published in Cecília Moreira Soares, *Mulher
    negra na Bahia no século XIX* (Salvador: Editora da Universidade Estadual da
    Bahia, 2007), chap. 2.

cutlasses and other trinkets that the Africans generally use in their orgies.[23]

This report bolsters the thesis that Domingos was the head of an urban quilombo where other Africans lived or at least spent a great deal of their time, and that they were the owners of some of the chests and trunks found on the premises. Even when they did not live outside their masters' households, slaves frequently left their belongings with freed persons for safekeeping. Domingos could have kept his tenants' chests without having the keys to them, which their masters would probably not allow. But it is equally possible that the freedman was just trying to obstruct the police investigation; he also claimed that he could not find the key to the front door, which incidentally stayed open after the authorities had left with their prisoners. Therefore, three policemen were posted outside Domingo's house until the following day, when the subdelegado vowed to conduct another search. If more Africans lived in that house, or were just storing their belongings there, the police presence would probably have kept them, and potential thieves, far away that night. The theater of power had been assembled to define once again the proper place African freedpersons should have in Bahian society.

The prisoners were taken to the jail in Fort Santo Antônio, in the parish of the same name, where the House of Correction had been installed some years before. While Domingos was on his way to jail, some of the ritual objects confiscated in his house were sent to police headquarters. João Henriques praised Subdelegado Pompílio's work, sending orders to bring Domingos before him immediately and to conduct the promised search the following day. He went even further, saying that "all objects that are apparently stolen as well as clothing" should be collected "so that their owners can identify them." He also said that "all objects used for witchcraft that are not made of metal or valuables" should be destroyed. He concluded his orders by having Pompílio publish the names of the arrested slaves in the press so their masters could reclaim them.[24]

---

[23] Pompílio Manuel de Castro to the chief of police of the province of Bahia, July 26, 1862.
[24] Reply from the police chief to the letter from Subdelegado Pompílio, July 26, 1862.

The next day, Saturday, July 26, Subdelegado Pompílio returned to
Domingos Sodré's house, and his clerk wrote a "Search and Findings
Report" that listed the items confiscated there. Brought back from
prison, the freedman was present during the search, but there is no
record of how he behaved or felt on that occasion. Pompílio, who
only seemed to have visited poor Africans' homes, was impressed by
what he had seen there. To him, Domingos seemed like a suspiciously
prosperous freedman. The evidence included a Brazilian rosewood
bureau, which was not a common piece of furniture in impoverished
homes. At one point, Pompílio mentioned the furnishings in the
house. Although he did not describe them at the time, they must
have included a sofa and chairs, which were listed in the African's
probate records years later. "Two valuable wall clocks" also piqued
the subdelegado's interest.[25]

Items Found in Domingos Sodré's Home
on June 26, 1862

COPY OF THE SEARCH AND FINDINGS REPORT

On the twenty-fifth day of July in the Year of Our Lord Jesus Christ,
eighteen hundred and sixty-two, in this Loyal and valiant City of
São Salvador Bahia de Todos os Santos and the Parish of São Pedro
Velho, at No. 7 Ladeira de Santa Tereza, the home of the African
Freedman Domingos Sodré, where the Alternate Subdelegado, the
Citizen Pompílio Manoel de Castro, with myself, a scribe from his
office, the undersigned, Constables Adriano José Pinheiro, José
Thomas Muniz Barreto, being there in the presence of the subdelegado the owner of the house, the said Domingos Sodré, the search
was carried out, opening drawers, chests and cabinets, finding the
following objects: four metal rattles; a box with several wooden
figures and other objects like beads and shells, and a blunt brass
cutlass without a tip; an iron rod with shells and a wooden sword;

---

[25] Pompílio Manoel de Castro to the chief of police, July 26, 1862. If he was familiar
with the lives of African freedpersons, the subdelegado would have known that
some were very prosperous. See Chapter 6 and Maria Inês Côrtes de Oliveira, *O
liberto: seu mundo e os outros* (São Paulo: Corrupio, 1988), esp. 35–51.

two wall clocks; a rosewood bureau with a great deal of clothing with the initials D.S. D.C; several paintings of saints on the walls; a white strap with shells; bloomers; a box of used women's clothing; a trunk containing the same, a silver chain with miscellaneous objects; fourteen pieces of clothing [decorated] with shells; four caps; a bowl of West African chalk and several mystical objects; a lacquered box containing his last will and testament; a gold Rosary with a crucifix also of gold, containing eighty-nine large beads; a gold necklace with six loops and a Cross of the same [metal]; a pair of gold cuff links, two pairs of hoop earrings, one silver-gilt, and one gold; a necklace with nineteen coral beads and thirteen gold beads, another with eighty-five coral beads and twenty-two gold beads; a rod of silver chain, regular, four silver rings, a silver key ring, two broken gold rings, a silver knob, and two small coral figas [mano fico amulets].

Five boxes were forced open, containing black people's clothing, some used and some in good condition, including one with a few pieces of new cloth belonging to a vendor´s box, and the box of cloth itself. Except for the furniture in the house, I say, all the other objects mentioned herein remained in the same house, except the wood Saints and objects pertaining to Candomblé, which were then sent to the Police department. They were held in custody, with the above-stated gold objects, a will by Domingos Sudré recognized by Notary Lopes da Costa. And there being nothing else, the subdelegado had me write this report, which is signed by the same subdelegado and myself, José Joaquim de Meirelles, who made, wrote and signed it, with the witnesses José Thomas Muniz Barreto, José Pinheiro de Campos Lima, Francisco Alves da Palma, José Joaquim de Meirelles.

In compliance with the law.

The Scribe José Joaquim de Meirelles

I hereby declare that the original is signed by the deputy, and by the witnesses. Meirelles.

Source: APEB, Polícia. Subdelegados, 1862–63, maço 6234.
Note: although this document is dated July 25, 1862, the search and listing of items found were only concluded the following day, according to Subdelegado Pompílio's report to the chief of police of Bahia, dated July 27, 1862.

The gold and coral necklaces, chains, and silver rings, including what seems to be a *balangandã* (cluster of silver charms), probably belonged to Delfina and the other women who worked as hire-out slaves and either lived in or frequented Domingos' home, including at least one of the freedman's slave women, Maria Ignez. Contemporary foreign travelers commented on the fact that black freedwomen and female slaves owned this kind of jewelry in Bahia. Some even went out to sell their wares bedecked in jewels, as this announcement in the *Argos Cachoeirano* newspaper, published in 1851, suggests:

> The undersigned advises the public that on the 25th of this month, this year, when his slave woman of the Jeje nation, by the name of Luiza, went out to sell pasties and sweets, she lost or had stolen from her neck thick chains weighing 17 eighths of gold and a gold heart, anyone who provides the author of this announcement with information about its whereabouts will be well rewarded when the abovementioned items are recovered.[26]

In this case, the slave owner himself may have paid for the lost necklace in order to attract more customers to buy his hire-out female slave's wares. This happened in a village in the sugar district of Cachoeira. Something of the sort was probably also true in the more competitive market in Salvador. Those adornments, which black women were banned from wearing in colonial times, were a sign of prosperity, a large clientele, and therefore advertised that the hire-out slave's wares or food were of the finest kind. But in addition to being decorative, jewelry could also be used as amulets – the balangandã, and particularly the two small mano fico amulets that were found in Domingos' house confirm that – and this method of building up a nest egg may have been considered safer than hoarding money.[27]

---

[26] *Argos Cachoeirano*, no. 30, January 15, 1851.

[27] See, for example, James Wetherell, *Brazil: Stray Notes from Bahia* (Liverpool: Webb & Hunt, 1860), 72–74; see also Candler and Burgess, *Narrative*, 53; Rodrigues, *Os africanos*, 119; Eduardo França Paiva, "Celebrando a alforria: amuletos e práticas culturais entre as mulheres negras e mestiças do Brasil," in *Festa: cultura e sociabilidade na América portuguesa*, ed. Ístvan Jancsó and Íris Kantor (São Paulo: Hucitec/Edusp/Imprensa Oficial/Fapesp, 2001), 505–518; Silvia Hunold Lara, "Sedas, panos e balangandãs: o traje de senhoras e escravas nas cidades do Rio de Janeiro e de Salvador (século XVIII)," in *Brasil: colonização e escravidão*, ed. Maria Beatriz Nizza da Silva (Rio de Janeiro: Nova Fronteira, 2000), 177–191; Simone Trindade Silva, "Referencialidade e representação: um

The search report confirms that Delfina made her living as a street vendor. We can see that the police found "pieces of new cloth belonging to the box" and "a vendor's box of cloth." These were certainly *panos-da-costa*, hand-woven shawls imported from West Africa through the same ports that had once supplied the slave ships. The African population of Salvador and the Recôncavo was the main market for these products. African women wore panos-da-costa draped over their shoulders or wrapped around their waists. Many of these shawls were still stiff when they arrived and were softened and sometimes even dyed in Bahia, as black scholar Manuel Querino documented at the turn of the twentieth century. The cloth in general was sold in Africa by the Ijebu, a Yoruba group, to merchants in Lagos, who exported them to Bahia. Captain John Adams, who published his memoirs of a voyage to West Africa in 1823, wrote the following about that subject: "It is these people [the Ijebu] who send so much cloth to Lagos and Ardrah [Allada], which the Portuguese traders for the Brazils purchase for that market, and which is held there in much estimation by the black population; probably, not only on account of its durability, but because it is manufactured in a country which gave many of them, or their parents, birth, as the Portuguese have always carried on an extremely active trade in slaves at Wydah, Ardrah and Lagos."[28] Besides being part of their attire, the cloth worked toward retaining memories of a world the Africans had to a large extent lost in Bahia.

Other items of "new clothing worn by blacks" that the police found may also have been intended for sale. This and other findings suggest that Delfina lived in that house with Domingos. Various signs confirm

---

resgate do modo de construção de sentidos nas pencas de balangandãs a partir da coleção do Museu Carlos Costa Pinto," MA thesis, Universidade Federal da Bahia, 2005. Gomes de Oliveira Neto distinguishes between the *balangandã* – which he spells *barangandan* – from the *penca* or cluster, stating – unlike other authors – that clusters were worn at the waist and balangandãs around the neck. Oliveira Neto in Braz do Amaral, *Fatos da vida do Brasil* (Salvador: Tipografia Naval, 1941), 121–123. Photos of women wearing balangandãs, necklaces, etc. can be seen in Christiane Silva de Vasconcelos, "O circuito social da fotografia da gente negra, Salvador, 1860–1916," MA thesis, Universidade Federal da Bahia, 2006.

[28] Manuel Querino, *A raça africana e os seus costumes* (Salvador: Progresso, 1955 [orig. 1916]), 88; Oliveira Neto, in Amaral, *Fatos da vida do Brasil*, 120; Captain John Adams, *Remarks on the Country Extending from Cape Palmas to the River Congo* (London: Frank Casss, 1966 [orig. 1823]), 97.

Figures 18 and 19. Black women wearing bead necklaces and balangandãs.

this and also indicate that the African couple had already formed a committed relationship. The indications among the personal items the police listed that suggest they were already an established couple include the clothing monogrammed with the initials D. S. (Domingos Sodré) and D. C. (Delfina Conceição) found in the rosewood bureau. We can therefore discard the *Diário da Bahia*'s fanciful interpretation that the ransacked house contained a great deal of "clothing with cabalistic initials and letters."[29]

It was the custom among Bahian families to put the owners' initials on items of clothing to prevent them from being lost or stolen

[29] *Diário da Bahia*, no. 170, July 28, 1862.

Figures 18 and 19. (*continued*)

when they were sent to the laundry in fountains around the city. In the case of the African couple, they may have initialed their clothes for the same reason, as well as to prevent them from being mixed up with those of the other people who lived in or frequented the house on Ladeira de Santa Tereza. Also, if clothes were mislaid, it gave their owners a better chance of recovering them. No matter what the reason for these initials, they clearly showed the demarcation of property and say something about a personal relationship and concept of privacy that is rarely set down in the documents regarding Africans' way of life in Bahia at the time. It was much more common to see wills like Domingos' stored in a lacquered wood box, a document that certainly, among other things, contained dispositions about his property,

Figures 20 and 21. Black street vendors with glass-sided boxes similar to those found in Domingos' home.

including some of the same goods now being searched and confiscated by the police. Unfortunately, a copy of this will was not attached to the police report.[30]

---

[30] I have not been able to find the will confiscated in 1862, but I have found the one written twenty years later and registered after Domingos' death. Studies based on the probate records of freedpersons in Bahia include Kátia M. de Queirós Mattoso, *Testamentos de escravos libertos na Bahia no século XIX: uma fonte para o estudo de mentalidades* (Salvador: Centro de Estudos Baianos da UFBa, 1979), also published in Mattoso, *Da revolução dos alfaiates à riqueza dos baianos no século XIX* (Salvador: Corrupio, 2004), 225–260; and Oliveira, *O liberto*.

Figures 20 and 21. (*continued*)

Religious Items

I have not been able to identify the religious items precisely and even less the ideas and meanings associated with them and their use in specific ritual contexts. Ideally, we would like to have Domingos' own explanation of what they represented in his world view. Because his authoritative voice is lacking, all we can do is speculate, imagine possibilities, and try to understand his "forest of symbols."[31]

[31] This problem also affects studies of "magic" practices in Europe. See, for example, Keith Thomas, *Religion and the Decline of Magic* (Harmondsworth: Penguin, 1973), 219.

Not all of the ritual artifacts were included in the subdelegado's list. The search and seizure report lists four metal rattles, "wood saints," a "blunt" brass cutlass, and a wooden sword; an iron bar, a white strap, and fourteen pieces of clothing, all decorated with sea shells; a large number of loose shells and a gourd bowl of chalk; and other "mystical" ingredients. The shells, arranged in various decorative patterns, represented wealth, power, and prestige in Domingos' African culture. A large quantity was always seized in the many of the candomblés subjected to police searches since the first half of the nineteenth century. In 1829, a justice of the peace from Brotas parish, in the outskirts of Salvador, confiscated "a Doll all trimmed with ribbons and shells, and a large African calabash full of Shells ... and gourd bowls trimmed with shells," among other ritual objects at a Candomblé house.[32] These shells, like those found in Domingos' home, were certainly cowries, a type of shell found in the Zanzibar and especially the Maldive archipelagos in the Indian Ocean that was used as currency in West Africa, where it also had a ritual dimension in offerings and divination, as will be seen further on. Cowries were also found on the beaches of Caravelas in southern Bahia. Called *zimbo* or *jimbo*, they had been part of the slave trade with West Central Africa (the kingdoms of Kongo and the broad present-day Angola region) since the sixteenth century. But this use for Bahian cowries did not stop there. They were also employed in the trade with the Bight of Benin, although they were not as renowned as those from the Indian Ocean. These Bahian cowries must have been the contents of 160 barrels of shells shipped in 1846 by a major Bahia slave trader, Joaquim Pereira Marinho, to his agent in Porto Novo, the powerful Domingos José Martins.[33]

---

[32] Reis, "Nas malhas do poder escravista," 36.
[33] Marion Johnson, "The Cowrie Currencies of West Africa," Part I, *The Journal of African History*, 11, no. 1 (1970): 17–49 (for origin, transportation, introduction, and expansion of cowrie money in West Africa); Part II, *The Journal of African History*, 11, no. 3 (1970): 331–353 (for equivalence to gold, silver dollar, inflation in the Bight of Benin as a result of introduction of Zanzibar cowries in the mid-nineteenth century). See also Alberto da Costa e Silva, *A manilha e o libambo: a África e a escravidão de 1500 a 1700* (Rio de Janeiro: Nova Fronteira, 2002), 313; Luiz Felipe de Alencastro, *O trato dos viventes: formação do Brasil no Atlântico sul* (São Paulo: Companhia das Letras, 2000), 256–259; Araújo, "1846: um ano na rota Bahia-Lagos," 86. Cowries continued to be important to calculate bride-price into the colonial period in Nigeria. See J. Lorand Matory, *Sex and the Empire that Never Was: Gender and the Politics of Metaphor in Ọ̀yọ́ Yoruba Religion* (New York and Oxford: Berghahn Books, 1994), 46–49.

Precisely because they represented wealth, cowries were also used in offerings to the divinities, and in Brazil, they could be accompanied by the national currency. In the Brotas candomblé mentioned earlier, "some copper money mixed with the offerings" was also found among the cowries.[34] Attached to other objects, cowries could turn artifacts into a form of protection, into amulets. The iron rod decorated with them would have been a strong candidate for a household charm.[35]

If the other items found in Domingos Sodré's home were used by initiates when they were possessed or "mounted" by their patron divinities, particularly the swords and decorated clothing, this would confirm Domingos' connection to established Candomblé temples – and there were many in Salvador – where ceremonies of that kind were held all year long, generally according to a specific calendar. Some of these items could have belonged to Domingos, his partner, Delfina, and other African associates – or else to the gods of their devotion.

The numerous beads made from glass and other materials, as well as the coral, either loose or strung in necklaces, sometimes intermingled with gold beads, perhaps should also be considered of ritual, and not just decorative, use. When he visited Bahia in 1860, Prince Maximilian of Habsburg, later the ill-fated emperor of Mexico, gave a delighted description of the elegant black women he saw in the city streets, observing that "glass beads with profane amulets hang in long strands on their bosoms." British vice-consul James Wetherell saw coral beads decorating and protecting the bodies of black children in the streets of Salvador. He also observed that black people wore bead bracelets made of opaque glass of several colors as amulets. Even if they were originally produced in Europe and often used as objects of exchange in the slave trade, the beads seen in Bahia were imported from West Africa, possibly because their wearers believed them to be a more powerful form of protection if they came from there.[36] In West Africa, beads adorned

[34] Reis, "Nas malhas do poder escravista," 36.
[35] Regarding the role of cowry shells in the material and symbolic cultures of the Yoruba, see Akinwumi Ogundiran, "Of Small Things Remembered: Beads, Cowries, and Cultural Translations of the Atlantic Experience in Yorubaland," *International Journal of African Historical Studies*, 35, no. 2–3 (2002): 445–455. Their ritual use extended to their Dahomean neighbors. See, for example, A. Le Herissé, *L'Ancien Royaume du Dahomey: moeurs, religion, histoire* (Paris: Émile Larose Libraire-Editeur, 1911), 149, 150.
[36] Maximiliano de Habsburgo, *Bahia 1860: esboços de viagem* (Rio de Janeiro: Tempo Brasileiro; Salvador: Fundação Cultural do Estado da Bahia, 1982), 82; Wetherell, *Brazil*, 30, 114.

representations of divinities, and among humans, they were worn by
kings and other powerful figures during the period of the transatlantic slave trade. The list John Adams provides of ideal products from
Europe to be traded with the Africans included beads, as "some of them
are considered an expensive article of merchandise; but they cannot
be dispensed with."[37] During a visit to the Ibo people, neighbors of the
Yorubas, William Allen and T. R. H. Thomson, two emissaries of the
British crown, in 1841 saw what they described as a local "idol," a "rude
representation of a human being, carved in wood" with "beads round
the neck." The gifts the queen of England sent to convince an Ibo chief
to put an end to the slave trade included thirty-six necklaces made of
various kinds of beads. Further north of the Niger Valley, in predominantly Muslim Hausa country, travelers found that beads were even
more popular. Young women wore strands of beads and shells around
their waists, and adults wore them as earrings.[38]

Beaded crowns adorned the heads and cascaded down over the faces
of Obas, or Yoruba chiefs, and on certain occasions, could be worn
only by them. In 1825, while en route to the Yoruba region, Hugh
Clapperton described one that covered the head of a local chief as "a
cap made of small glass beads of various colours, surrounded by tassels of
small gold-coloured beads, and three large coral ones in front," which
stood out as the most striking adornment in his raiment. The handle of
what the traveler defined as the chief's fly whisk, a symbol of his authority, was also adorned with beads. A few months later, Clapperton visited
the Alafin of Ọ̀yọ́, who was wearing "round his neck some three strings
of large blue cut-glass beads." Not even his highest-ranking subjects
were allowed to wear showy garments or glass and coral beads in the
king's presence. In short, beads meant power under the circumstances,
and "no ... grandeur of any kind must appear, but on the king alone."[39]
The Lander brothers described the crown worn by the Alafin, with
whom they had an audience on May 13, 1830, as "profusely decorated
with rows of coral beads."[40]

---

[37] Adams, *Remarks*, 264.
[38] William Allen and T. R. H. Thomson, *Narrative of the Expedition sent by Her
Majesty's Government to the River Niger in 1841* (London: Richard Bentley,
1848), I: 232 (quote), 257, 396, 405, etc.
[39] Hugh Clapperton, *Journal of a Second Expedition into the Interior of Africa from
the Bight of Benin to Soccatoo* (London: Frank Cass, 1966 [orig. 1829]), 3, 37, 47.
[40] Lander and Lander, *Journal*, I: 165.

These beads were not just ornamental. They were considered suffused with mystical power, Yoruba *aṣe*, and therefore were an essential component of the divine powers of the Oba. It is noteworthy that Olokun, the divinity of the sea, who was very popular in Domingos' hometown, Lagos, was specifically identified by his mythical and mystical relations with the use of beads and shells. One of his praise names is precisely "owner of the beads." On the divination tray, beads represent wealth among the Yoruba. Beads also decorate and add power to the objects used in divination, such as the *opele*, or divining chain. In Bahia, during the era of slavery, beads seem to have been widely used among Africans and their descendants. As Maximilian's and Wetherell's observations suggest, Candomblé practitioners already wore bead necklaces in the colors of their patron gods, those to whom they were especially devoted and to whom they often "belonged" for having been initiated to serve them. In a ceremony described in 1870 in *O Alabama*, one of the officiating priests was "decorated with *gés*," the term for beads in the Fon language, one of the languages spoken by the Jeje nation in Bahia.[41] Therefore, it was probably not for strictly decorative purposes that Domingos had such a large quantity of beads in his care. The specialist in the sacred added mystical value to these objects. Perhaps for that reason, the loose beads found in a box were mixed with shells and carved wooden representations of divinities, labeled "wood figures" by the clerk who wrote the report on the search conducted in the freedman's home.[42]

These "wood figures," which the police also described as "wood saints," drew the attention of the press. They must have been wooden sculptures, including naked women with exposed breasts, which were common in Nagô religious statuettes. The *Diário da Bahia* mentioned the confiscation of "lascivious figures that could appear in the temple

---

[41] Quoted in Parés, *A formação do Candomblé*, 149. Gés = beads, according to this author.

[42] Regarding the ritual use of beads in Yoruba culture, see Ogundiran, "Of Small Things Remembered," 427–457; Suzanne Preston Blier, *The Royal Arts of Africa: The Majesty of Form* (New York: Harry N. Abrahams, Inc., 1998), 79–83; Henry John Drewal and John Mason, *Beads, Body, and Soul: Art and Light in the Yoruba Universe* (Los Angeles: University of California Fowler Museum of Cultural History, 1998); Wande Abimbola, *Ifá: An Exposition of Ifá Literary Corpus* (Ibadan: Oxford University Press Nigeria, 1976), 4–5, note to Figure 1. Regarding the circulation of coral and glass beads in Africa, and their origins and descriptions, see Silva, *A manilha e o libambo*, 200–201.

Figure 22. Crown believed to have belonged to Glele (1858–1889), the king of Dahomey, adorned with beads in the style of Yoruba Obas.

of the God Pan or Priapus," which, if the informant was being literal, could have been referring to a common representation of Èṣù with an erect penis. These figures may also have included an "iron Devil" the police chief mentioned in one of his many memos about the case. Since at least the mid-eighteenth century, in both Africa and Brazil, Europeans associated the Yoruba Èṣù (or Exu) and Dahomean Legba, unpredictable trickster and messenger divinities, with the Devil of the Christian tradition. The crux of this association was their heightened sexuality. The presence of rampant sexuality was a constant theme in police and journalistic narratives on what went on in Candomblé gatherings. In the minds of the police and journalists, these "lascivious

Figure 23. Crown of Olokun, a divinity particularly venerated in Lagos, also decorated with beads.

figures" confirmed that stereotypical depiction of Candomblé rituals
and mores.[43]

---

[43] *Diário da Bahia*, no. 170, July 28, 1862; João Henriques to the director of
the War Arsenal, July 26, 1862, APEB, *Polícia. Correspondência expedida,
1862*, vol. 5750, fl. 326v. Pierre Verger, *Notes sur le culte des Orisa et Vodun
à Bahia, la Baie de Tous les Saints, au Brésil, et l'ancienne Côte des Esclaves en
Afrique* (Dakar: Institut Fondamental de l'Afrique Noir, 1957), 120–122, contains excerpts from writings by foreign travelers in Africa who associated Eşu,
Elegbara, or Legba (the term used in Dahomey) with the devil. One of them,
Pruneau de Pommegorge, who lived in Ouidah from 1743 to 1765, described
Legba in the same style as the Bahian newspaper – as a "Priapic god ... with his

(a)   (b)

Fig. 9 — Trono ou banco esculpido do culto de Iemanjá (de frente)

Figures 24 (a, b). The "wood saints" the police confiscated in Domingos' house were probably sculptures like these photographed in the late nineteenth century, possibly at the Gantois temple.

No animal remains, votive foods, or other offerings were found, nor is there any indication of the presence of an altar or *peji* in the raided home, although there must have been one somewhere; representations of divinities – or rather of spirit-possessed devotees – were found. According to Candomblé beliefs, they could have been mystically present in the items contained in jars, bowls, and other recipients

main attribute, which is enormous and exaggerated compared with the rest of the body" (p. 120). American Baptist missionary Thomas Bowen wrote in 1857 that "the Yorubas worship Satan himself, under the name of *Eshu.*" Thomas J. Bowen, *Adventures and Missionary Labours in Several Countries in the Interior of Africa from 1849 to 1856* (London/Edinburgh: Frank Cass, 1968 [orig. 1857]), 317. Regarding Minas Gerais, Brazil, see Antonio da Costa Peixoto, *Obra nova da língua geral de mina* (Lisbon: Agência Geral das Colônias, 1943–1944 [orig. 1741]), 32, in which the author identifies "Leba" (Legba) with the "Devil." Nina Rodrigues, a contemporary of Domingos Sodré, wrote about Jeje-Yoruba sculptures in Bahia and photographed and described several religious items in *Os africanos*, 160–171, from where Figures 24 (a, b) were taken.

(c)
(d)

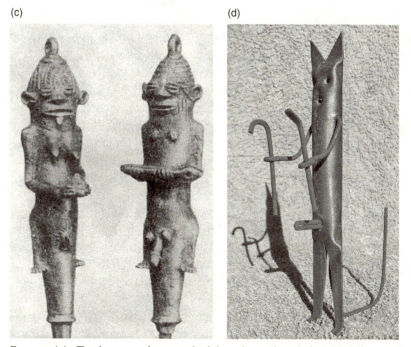

Figure 24(c). Two bronze sculptures, which have been identified as ritual objects of the Yoruba Ogboni society.

Figure 24(d). "Iron Devil" now sold at São Joaquim market in Salvador.

mentioned in the police reports. It is also possible that there actually was a peji in Domingos' house, but it went unnoticed. An Ifá altar, for example, could have been nothing more than an unobtrusive mound of earth in his back yard. If the altar was inside the house, Domingos may have had time to dismantle it and stow most of its components away in drawers, chests, or trunks, where they were found by the police.

The African freedman may have been keeping the emblems and rit-ual clothing, some trimmed with cowries, to be used mainly at ceremo-nies held elsewhere, but not in his home, where, according to the police, he merely received his clients and acolytes for divination sessions and other consultations held twice a week on Tuesdays and Fridays. If there is one, I have not managed to find a ritual explanation for the choice of those specific days of the week. The four days between one session and another suggest a Yoruba week, but only the first day would have been devoted to the oracle.

Fortune Teller

The large amount of ritual objects found in Domingos Sodré's home – "in an extraordinary quantity," according to the subdelegado – suggests that the freedman was not a common-or-garden diviner or healer. There are indications that Domingos was a babalawo, a priest of Ifá, the god of divination, owner of fate and wisdom, also known as Òrúnmìlà, one of the most important members of the Yoruba pantheon. Thomas Bowen and William Clarke, two American Baptist missionaries who visited Yorubaland between 1849 and 1858, commented on the popularity of Ifa. "[T]he great and universal [sic] honored Ifa, the revealer of secrets, and the guardian of marriage and child-birth," wrote Bowen, emphasizing the role of the god as protector of the family wellbeing. "The worship of Ifa is one of the principal branches" of the Yoruba religion, observed Clarke more generally.[44] Ifá, or its Dahomean counterpart, Fa,[45] was well known in Bahia, according to verses published in O Alabama in 1867. They tell the story of a Bahian police chief who engaged the services of an African diviner named Arabonam to find a criminal. Arabonam was a real person and a contemporary of Domingos, who died two years before him.[46]

The blunt cutlass found among the objects confiscated in Domingos' home could very well have represented the sword of Ifá (adá Òòsa), one of the divinity's emblems. But there were more swords, possibly related to other divinities, which could have been Ogun, Sàngó, Yansan, Òsun, or Osaguian, because they all carry them, besides other metal instruments. Other objects seized were commonly used in divination rituals, among others, such as the cowries, the rattle, and the West African chalk. The latter, for example, when scattered on the Ifá tray, was used to draw the symbols of the divination session under way.

Oil palm nuts may have been found and listed in the report among what the police described as "insignificant objects," although they were

---

[44] Bowen, Adventures and Missionary Labours, 317; William W. Clarke, Travels and Explorations in Yorubaland, 1854–1858 (Ibadan: Ibadan University Press, 1972), 279.

[45] The Dahomean divination called Fa was imported from the Yoruba, probably during the time of King Agaja, who reigned from 1708 to 1732. See Le Herissé, L'Ancien Royaume du Dahomey, 146–147.

[46] O Alabama, September 3, 1867, p. 7. Arabonam is the subject of another study of the Candomblé of Bahia in which I am presently engaged.

highly significant for the diviner. Sixteen of those nuts are used in the Ifá divination system. Similarly, the object described as a "silver chain with miscellaneous objects" is reminiscent of the ọ̀pẹ̀lẹ̀, known in Brazil as the Ifá rosary, and considered a lesser tool of divination compared with the palm nuts, although more frequently used by babalawos to see the future in Brazil. The ọ̀pẹ̀lẹ̀ consists of a string of eight halves of palm nuts equally separated from each other. At each end of the chain, the Ifá priest, according to Wande Abimbọla, "ties a number of objects such as small beads, coins and cowries."[47] The palm nuts are also associated with a legend in which they are given to Ifá by Èṣù as divination instruments – which would put the "iron Devil" found with Domingos in a specific ritual context. According to William Bascom, the many names of Èṣù are pronounced several times during the initial invocations of a divination session, and Èṣù is the main beneficiary of the sacrifices required to facilitate communication with the other divinities. When an animal is sacrificed, for example, its head always belongs to Èṣù, the owner of the crossroads.[48]

The same verses published in *O Alabama* suggest that the Ifá method of divination was used in Bahia during Domingos' time. They portray Fa as the instrument of divination, because the priest was said to have arrived at police headquarters "Equipped with his Fa and other preparations." Further on, it is said that he "sowed" the Fa, which leads us to suppose that he conducted the Ifá divination session with the sacred palm nuts or other seeds that may have replaced them in his Bahian exile.

In the 1890s, shortly after Domingos' death, Nina Rodrigues described a divining chain he had seen in Bahia: "That [process of divination] that is attributed to Ifa in these parts involves a metal chain in which half a dried mango pit is inserted in each space. The wizard picks up the chain at a certain point and tosses it in a special manner. The

[47] Abimbọla, *Ifá*, 11 (see illustrations and explanations on pp. 4–5, 8–12). Abimbola observes that metal plates could sometimes have replaced nuts in the opele. Regarding objects babalawos used in divination, see also William Bascom, *Ifa Divination: Communication between Gods and Men in West África* (Bloomington and London: Indiana University Press, 1969), 26–39.

[48] The oil palm tree and nut are sacred in many Ifá myths, including those mentioned by Bowen and Clarke. Rodrigues, *Os africanos*, 227, cites Alfred Ellis's version of a myth that associates Ifá with Èṣù. Regarding the strategic position of Èṣù in Ifá divination, see Bascom, *Ifá Divination*, 38, 60, 65, 83, for example.

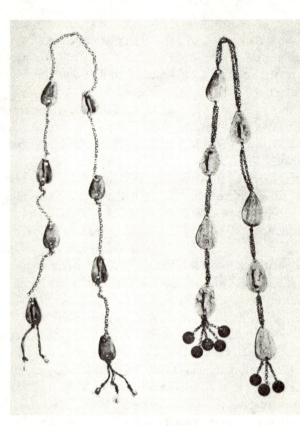

Figures 25, 26, 27. Òpèlè, the divining chain used in Ifá, Ifá rattles, and the sword of Ifá. These are Yoruba items that merely suggest how the objects found in Domingos Sodré's home may have looked.

omen or prediction is deduced from the position of the mango pits."[49] The sacred aspect of and mythic narratives about the palm nut did not prevent it from being replaced with the pit of another fruit, without detriment to its main ritual function as a tool of divination. And there

[49] Rodrigues, Os africanos, 228. See also Rodrigues, O animismo fetichista, 55. Also, according to Querino, palm nuts were replaced with dried mango pits when making the Yoruba divining chains in Bahia. Querino, A raça africana, 57. It is worth investigating why mango pits were used the same way in Cuba. See Alejo Carpentier, Écue-Yamba-Ó (Madrid: Alianza Editorial, 2002 [orig. 1927]), 83. In Rio de Janeiro, tortoiseshell was used, according to João do Rio, As religiões no Rio (Rio de Janeiro: Nova Aguilar, 1976 [orig. 1904]), 24.

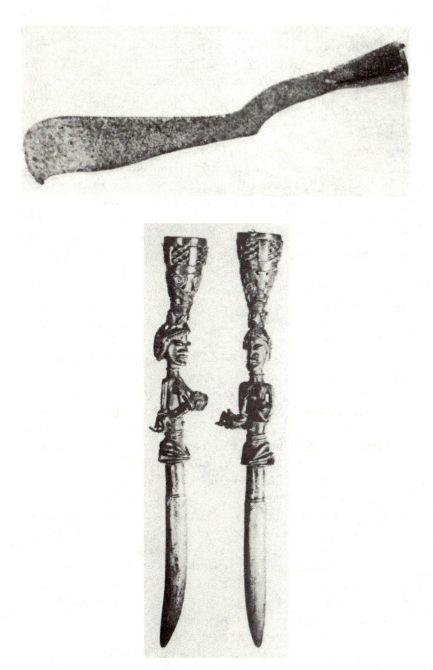

Figures 25, 26, 27. (*continued*)

is no record of the invention of consecrated mango trees to accompany
the switch, while red oil palms, and particularly *dendê*, the oil derived
from them, remained a common ritual element in Candomblé, an indispensable ingredient in the foods of many divinities. But if the symbolic
dimension shared by the material culture and the rite was lost, the ritual
foundation of divination was not, guaranteed as it was by the meanings
of the divining chain tossed by the priest. Meaning is, after all, what
counts most in culture making. At the time of Domingos' arrest, however, the replacement of palm nuts with mango pits may not have been
widespread, if it had occurred at all. Had this been the case with the
chain the police found in 1862, we would probably have been informed
of it by the police because of their likely familiarity with mango pits.
Instead, the report listed "miscellaneous objects," as if the author did
not know where they belonged, culturally speaking. Therefore, I pre-
sume that Domingos' divining chain – if that is what it was – was made
from palm nuts that were probably imported from West Africa. It is also
unlikely that it was one of Delfina's necklaces, because the silver and
gold objects were listed in detail for further investigation to determine
whether they were stolen.

The reader has already met some Candomblé priests in these
pages and will come across a few more, but the police authorities did
not ascribe the same status to them as they did to Domingos Sodré.
Subdelegado Pompílio Manoel de Castro seems to have made inquiries about Domingos – either that or he already knew of his reputation before the incident in 1862 – because he accused him of being
"number one in the congregation of sortilege and spells" in Salvador.
By *sortilege* (*sortilégio*) in the subdelegado's words, he meant the art of
operating divination tools. Pompílio was probably repeating the *vox
populi*, which he had the duty to hear and investigate to better perform his work as a police authority. To amplify the voice of the people,
the *Diário da Bahia* repeated the subdelegado's words with few altera-
tions and published a statement that the freedman was "reputed to be
the venerable master of sortilege and spells." We must not overlook
the terms with which Domingos' ritual position was described as the
leader of a "congregation," that is, a group, an organization, a confraternity of diviners and wizards. And it is also important to note the
insistence on his oracular powers. Regarding the objects confiscated
from his home, Subdelegado Pompílio said that they "pertained to or
were used for evildoing and fortunetelling, which this African used to

perform for people who ... went there to know their future."[50] This indicates the subdelegado was not entirely unaware of the meaning of what he had seen.

The use of the term evildoing (malefício) denotes a police mentality that was still firmly rooted in the principles of the Catholic Inquisition, which used that term to designate the diabolical arts practiced by so-called witches and sorcerers, and their capacity to do harm by occult means, such as herbs, prayers, incantations, the evil eye, and imprecations. In fact, the inquisitors reduced all forms of paganism and magical practices, even if they were harmless or even beneficial – including traditional medicine – to the category of maleficium.[51] This also included the practice of fortunetelling, as the subdelegado called the art of divination – and as it was commonly known at the time. This arcane art also fell within the purview of witches and sorcerers.

Also according to Pompílio, "this African is known by [the name of] papai Domingos, and he has established himself as a diviner and fortuneteller."[52] Holding the title of papai (literally "daddy"), as well as pai (father), in Afro-Bahia at the time meant that the holder enjoyed ritual seniority and a leadership role in the world of Candomblé. This detail bolsters the hypothesis that he was a babalawo, which in Yoruba means father (baba) of the secret or mystery (awo). Another term used to designate the occupants of that post was baba onifa, father of those who have the Ifá.[53] I have ruled out that Domingos might have been a typical babalorişa, or high priest in an Orişa temple, unless he was about to found one when he was arrested in 1862. However, the term papai could be used in both cases – for diviners and high priests – as well as to designate any individual with a reputation for wizardry in Bahia at that time. Among the Yoruba, baba means that and much more, including – in addition to biological father and patriarch – "connotations of priority, dominance, leadership, or superior efficacy in any sphere, human

[50] Pompílio Manuel de Castro to the chief of police, July 27, 1862, APEB, Polícia. Subdelegados, 1862–63, maço 6234; Diário da Bahia, no. 170, July 28, 1862.

[51] Regarding maleficium in the European tradition, see Thomas, Religion and the Decline of Magic, 519ff; Norman Cohn, Europe's Inner Demons (Frogmore: Paladin, 1976), chap. 9.

[52] Pompílio Manuel de Castro to the chief of police, July 27, 1862.

[53] Michka Sachnine, Dictionaire usuel yorùbá-français (Paris/Ibadan: Karthala/IFRA, 1997), 69 and 73. Regarding baba onifa, see Bascom, Ifa Divination, 81.

or otherwise."[54] This also goes along with the celebrated principle of seniority that is such a prominent part of the ideology of Candomblé, as Vivaldo da Costa Lima has emphasized. Just as in his homeland, within the African community in Bahia, when he was about sixty-five, Domingos Sodré's years certainly added to his prestige and strengthened people's confidence in his gifts as a diviner.[55]

Babalawos belonged to an all-male priesthood that was considered the most important of its kind for the administration of daily life and the formulation of life plans among the Yoruba in Africa. Their prestige, which was social and even political, resided for the most part in the Yoruba custom of consulting them not only to determine their patron divinities and how to please them, which was essential to the devotee's good fortune, but also when making any and all important decisions in life. In 1851, in the vicinity of Abeokuta, Bowen saw a babalawo in activity: "Under the shed was a man consulting his Ifa, the Orisha which foretells future events." As for the answers to the consultations, "the natives believe in them as sincerely as an Irishman does in St. Patrick," wrote the Protestant minister, without missing the chance to take a swipe at Catholics as well.[56] During the same period, Clarke observed that the people of that part of Africa sought out a babalawo to consult him about all kinds of current problems and future plans, including curing diseases and ensuring success in marriage.[57] There were no limits to what Ifá could see and bring about, as E. Bolaji Idowu, a scholar of the Yoruba religion, observes regarding more recent times:

> It seems absolutely impossible for a Yoruba whose soul is still fettered to his traditional belief to attempt anything at all without consulting the oracle by *Ifá*. It has always been throughout

---

[54] J. D. Y. Peel, *Religious Encounter and the Making of the Yoruba* (Bloomington and Indianapolis: Indiana University Press, 2000), 72. The expressions *papai* and *mamãe de terreiro* and, less frequently, *pai-de-santo* (I have not found *mãe-de-santo*) were already used in Bahia in the second half of the nineteenth century. The first two appear in several issues of *O Alabama*. I have only found *pai-de-santo* once in that newspaper and nowhere else. For the oldest use of that term that I know of, see *O Alabama*, July 28, 1868.

[55] See Vivaldo da Costa Lima, *A família de santo nos candomblés jejes-nagôs da Bahia* (Salvador: Corrupio, 2003), 77–79, for instance. Brothers Richard and John Lander also observed "profound respect and reverence" for elders in Badagri in the early 1830s, during Adele's time, *Journal*, i: 77.

[56] Bowen, *Adventures and Missionary Labours*, 135.

[57] Clarke, *Travels and Explorations*, 280.

the history of the Yoruba a *sine qua non* to life. Before engage-
ment betrothal, before a marriage, before a child is born, at the
birth of a child, at successive stages in man's life, before a king is
appointed, before a chief is made, before anyone is appointed to
a civic office, before a journey is made, in times of crisis, in times
of sickness, at any and all times, *Ifá* is consulted for guidance and
assurance.[58]

This ancient Yoruba custom, which used to be a veritable life-guiding
principle for an entire people, accompanied those who arrived in Bahia
to endure the harsh life of slavery. We can clearly see the importance
of diviners, and not just babalawos, for the vast Nagô population,
the Yoruba folk who lived there in Domingos' time. This also suggests why the "fortunetellers" were so successful among Africans in
nineteenth-century Bahia, most of whom were Nagôs.

Papai Domingos may never have become the head diviner of the
Nagôs in Bahia, a title that probably did not even exist, except in the
creative minds of the police authorities. But the sources' insistence that
he was a renowned fortuneteller means something, even if he was not
a specialist in Ifá specifically. It would also be wise to consider that
he may only have been familiar with the simpler form of divination,
using sixteen cowries – the *erindinlogun*, associated with the goddess
Òṣun. Equally used in traditional Yoruba divination, it is practiced by
the *awoloriṣa*, literally "owner of the secret of the Oriṣa" or "diviner
of the Oriṣa's devotees." As we have seen, the objects confiscated
from Domingos included loose shells, which may have been used in
this method of divination. This method was well known in Bahia in
the mid-1800s. In December 1858, three creole men were arrested – a
slave, a freedman, and another who "calls himself a freedman" – along
with an African freedman "for being found engaged in cowry divination," according to the subdelegado of Pilar parish.[59] And a similar
story published in *O Alabama* in January 1864 tells about a woman
who fell ill and consulted a diviner (perhaps Domingos) who "cast his
cowries and informed her that the lady was bewitched, and that [her]
slave woman had cast the spell, and that it would be deadly if it were

[58] E. Bolaji Idowu, *Olódùmarè: God in Yoruba Belief* (London: Longmans, 1962),
77–78. Something similar is said about the Fa of the Dahomeans: Le Herissé,
L'Ancien Rouaume du Dahomey, 140.
[59] Antonio de Góes Tourinho to the chief of police, December 20, 1858, APEB,
Polícia, maço 6264.

not circumvented without delay."[60] In short, both Ifá and sixteen-cowry
method were well-known divination procedures in nineteenth-century
Bahia, and consulted not only by slaves but by their masters as well.
Later on, in the 1940s, anthropologist Edison Carneiro would refer to
the use of "eight or sixteen cowries arranged in a rosary or loose, cast
by the diviner."[61] In other words, they used an òpèlè made with cowries instead of oil palm nuts – a "perfect" hybrid, possibly conceived
in Bahia.

Unfortunately, I cannot tell how much training Domingos Sodré
received to practice divination, a complex and prestigious activity of
the Yoruba priesthood. Preparation for the office of diviner, particularly
a babalawo, required steady training during many years of practice to
memorize and interpret the signs, or *odus*, that make up the divinatory
system, and are indicated by the pattern the palm nuts or cowries form
on a tray. The odus refer to a literary corpus formed of verses that tell of
the problems confronted and solutions found by mythical figures, who
may have been divinities or mortals, or anthropomorphized animals or
plants. To perform Ifá divination according to the classical standards,
according to Bascom, one would have to learn "well over a thousand
of those verses."[62] The same author recalls that divination with sixteen cowries also requires memorizing a significant number of verses,
and he underscores this and various other similarities between the two
oracular systems. To accentuate the importance of erindinlogun and its
patron divinity Òșun, Abimbola suggests that the lesser complexity of
this method may have been a sign of greater antiquity compared with
Ifá, which he seeks to demonstrate through an analysis of some verses.[63]

[60] *O Alabama*, January 12, 1864.
[61] Edison Carneiro, *Candomblés da Bahia*, 7th ed. (Rio de Janeiro: Civilização
     Brasileira, 1986 [orig. 1948]), 26.
[62] William R. Bascom, "The Sanctions of Ifa Divination," *The Journal of the Royal
     Anthropological Institute*, 71, no. 1/2 (1941): 43.
[63] Several authors mention Òșun as the patron divinity of sixteen-cowry divina-
     tion, which is said to have resulted from her incomplete knowledge of the Ifá
     method. See Wande Abimbola, "The Bag of Wisdom: Òșun and the Origins of
     Ifá Divination," in *Òșun across the Waters: A Yoruba Goddess in Africa and the
     Americas*, ed. Joseph M. Murphy and Mei-Mei Sanford (Bloomington: Indiana
     University Press, 2001), 141–154, in which the author also values the impor-
     tance of Òșun in the development of both Yoruba divinatory systems. Regarding
     similarities and differences between the two, see William Bascom, *Sixteen
     Cowries: Yoruba Divination from África to the New World* (Bloomington and
     London: Indiana University Press, 1980), esp. 5–31.

The subdelegado's report stressed that Domingos worked at home as a diviner and sorcerer. In other words, in addition to divination, he performed other services involving the monitoring and manipulation of the spiritual universe and earthly materials, especially plants. One activity was closely related to the other, because those who divine a problem must also be able to divine its solution. According to an Ifá myth, Setilu, of Nupe origin, was believed to have introduced this oracle in Yorubaland, and over the years he "began to practice witchcraft and medicine."[64] Setilu is believed to have bequeathed this knowledge to his followers and successors, or so the myth establishes. And it is through divination – by whatever means – that the will of the divinities is interpreted and the rites and offerings they require from their devotees are determined. "The babalawos are as much herbalists as diviners," writes Bascom, "although divining is their primary function."[65] Domingos operated in this ritual register, which the police viewed as witchcraft. In short, aside from divining – and through divination – he knew which offerings were suitable to satisfy the divinities and probably prepared them for his clients. In his role as a traditional healer, a manipulator of the herbal world, he also made potions for his clients (or whomever he designated) to drink. Therefore, divination was just one part of a broader, more complex ritual system.

It is possible that Domingos only received partial training as a diviner in his native land. Lagos did not have as rich a religious life as other Yoruba kingdoms, with their popular, elaborate, and festive public rites and numerous Orişas. But through its inclusion in the Atlantic world – meaning the slave trade – and the ensuing prosperity, particularly the enrichment of its king, "Lagos became a divine Yoruba monarchy, then gradually adopted forms, rituals, institutions and accoutrements of the Yoruba kingdoms" (including the introduction of beads as a mark of royal power), writes historian P. D. Cole. There was an important elite group in Lagos made up of veritable "spiritual chiefs," the Ogalade, who specialized in various branches of local medicine. Specialists in divination systems enjoyed tremendous popularity and social status. Diviners could achieve prominence in the political life of the kingdom of Lagos.

[64] Samuel Johnson, *The History of the Yorubas* (London: Routledge & Kegan Paul, 1966 [orig. 1897]), 33.
[65] Bascom, *Ifa Divination*, 61. See also Pierre Verger, *Ewé: o uso das plantas na sociedade iorubá* (São Paulo: Companhia das Letras, 1995), chap. 1.

According to historian A. B. Aderibigbe, the Ifá oracle was "the most important piece in the king-making machine," and accusations of witchcraft confirmed by a babalawo could easily ruin a powerful individual's reputation. Diviners were very close to the inner circle of power and the king used their services regularly. Ologun Kutere, the father of Adele and Oṣinlokun, was the son of Alagba, an important babalawo, and Erelu Kuti, a sister of the Obá of Lagos. Adele himself was said to have a talent for witchcraft, perhaps inherited from his grandfather.[66] Simply put, a war between the grandsons of a powerful African diviner may have been responsible for the Bahian slavery of Domingos Sodré the diviner, who came into this world and grew up in a place where divination played a highly significant role in society and politics. He may have been groomed as a child – or have begun training – to play that role before he was captured and sent to Brazil as a slave.

I do not know exactly when Domingos arrived in Bahia, but if my surmise is correct – between the middle of the second and the beginning of the next decade of the nineteenth century – he would have been in his early twenties when he disembarked from a slave ship in Brazil. If so, he could have been well advanced in his Ifá apprenticeship if he began his training as a child, which Abimbola says was common practice in Africa half a century ago, and may also have been so in the Africa of the slave trade.[67]

But we must not stick too closely to the idea that Domingos underwent every step of his training in Africa and reproduced a thorough knowledge of the secrets of Ifá or another divinatory art in Brazil. After all, internecine wars in Yorubaland, the slave trade, and slavery itself had thrown community and family ties, social standards, and political and religious hierarchies into disarray, which must also have helped soften the rigid orthodoxy of many priestly practices. We should also consider the probable loss of part of the memory of divinatory verses due to their less frequent and more repressed use by those in bondage in Brazil. That

---

[66] P. D. Cole, "Lagos Society in the Nineteenth Century," in *Lagos*, ed. Aderibigbe, 30 (quotation), 36, 37; Aderibigbe, "Early History of Lagos to about 1850," in idem, 8, 16–17 (quotation); G. O. Gabadamosi, "Patterns and Developments in Lagos Religious History," in idem, 174; Mann, "The World the Slave Traders Made," 203; Law, "The Career of Adele," 44.

[67] Abimbola, *Ifá*, 18. Regarding the hierarchy of babalawos in Ife – an important ritual center, considered a sacred city and the mythical birthplace of the Yoruba people – see Bascom, *Ifa Divination*, 81–82.

which is not practiced is forgotten, at least in part. Anthropologist and babaloriṣa Julio Braga recalls that babalawos required "constant practice of divinatory knowledge [to bring about] the continual cultural revitalization of the knowledge involved, which is only possible within the socio-cultural dynamics of their society of origin." This is the anthropologist's explanation for the gradual disappearance of babalawos in Brazil. He even suggests a process of cultural realignment that he believes enabled hybrid divinatory practices to flourish, Ifá divination simplified and/or combined with the sixteen cowries or other, even less orthodox, perhaps made in Brazil methods.[68] It is possible that it was this hybrid method that Papai Domingos used. At a Jeje candomblé denounced in verse by O Alabama, there are indications that such a mixture already existed in Bahia at the time:

They asked papai Dothé
To go and consult Fa;
But when he threw the cowries
There was nothing he could see.[69]

In other words, in Bahia in 1867, cowry divination was viewed as being within the jurisdiction of Ifá, perhaps because the latter was considered virtually synonymous with divination, and the guide of individual destinies, no matter which oracular methods based on the West African tradition were utilized. It is at the same time perhaps relevant that Ifá refused to respond to the cowries thrown by Papai Dothé, as if the deity did not recognize them as efficacious to a divination session performed in his name.

Another sign of the transformations that took place on the other side of the Atlantic was the role of Oriṣa priests as diviners, trespassing on the babalawos' exclusive turf in Yoruba ritual. For example, Arabonam, whom we met a few pages earlier – the priest recruited by the chief

[68] Julio Braga, O jogo de búzios: um estudo da adivinhação no candomblé (São Paulo: Brasiliense, 1988), 33 (quotation), and 78–79. See also Roger Bastide and Pierre Verger, "Contribuição ao estudo da adivinhação em Salvador (Bahia)," in Olóòrìsà: escritos sobre a religião dos orixás, ed. Carlos Eugênio M. de Moura (São Paulo: Ágora, 1981), 57–85. Regarding the importance of the babalawo to the Candomblés of "yesteryear," see Carneiro, Candomblés da Bahia, 119–120. For a contemporary report, see Rodrigues, Os africanos, 236.

[69] O Alabama, February 2, 1867. The Jeje identity of that Candomblé temple is suggested in Parés, A formação do Candomblé, 154–155. As he explains, "dote is a title in the Fon hierarchy" (p. 155).

of police to solve a crime – seems to have actually been a priest of
Ṣàngó, the Yoruba thunder god and patron deity of Ọ̀yọ́. According to
O Alabama, while performing the divination for the police, the African

> Wiped his forehead with his hand, deep in thought,
> Invoked Sango;
> Placed two obis in the chief's hand
> And there sowed the seeds of Fa.[70]

In verses that describe typical moves in an Ifá session, such as placing two kola nuts "in the client's hand," Ṣàngó is transformed into an
assistant of the god of divination. The name of the diviner, Arabonam,
should not go unnoticed: it must have been derived from Airá Igbonan,
or Àrá-gbigbóná (or "hot" Àrá), a specific thunder deity worshipped in
the kingdom of Ketu and believed to have originated in neighboring
Savé. In Africa, Àrá and Ṣàngó are parallel but different thunder deities; in Bahia the first became a "quality" of the second, and this phenomenon is signified in the combination of Arabonam's name and the
way he features in the O Alabama narrative as a priest of Ṣàngó. Besides,
although the priest was particularly consecrated to a thunder god and
not to Ifá, he clearly practiced divination.[71]

While innovations and adaptations inevitably existed, it is unlikely
that the sacred rules of divination were relaxed completely, allowing
just anyone to practice it. Therefore, Domingos could not have become
a papai in Bahia by chance. It would have been difficult for him to lay
legitimate claim to the art of divination and "witchcraft" without having his skills tested and his knowledge evaluated by the many Nagô
priests who lived there, and were to a varying extent familiar with
Yoruba divination protocols. Domingos would also have been tested
by his own clients, particularly if they were Nagôs, accustomed as they
were to consulting diviners all the time in their homelands. Bascom
stressed the active participation of the client in divinatory sessions,

[70] O Alabama, September 3, 1867, p. 7.
[71] Regarding Airá Igbonan/Àrá-gbigbóná, see Verger, Notes sur le culte des Orisa
      et Vodun, 314–315, 445; and Marc Schiltz, "Yorùbá Thunder Deities and
      Sovereignty: Àrá versus Ṣàngó," in Ṣàngó in Africa and the African Diaspora,
      ed. Joel E. Tishke, Toyin Falola, and Akíntúndé Akínyemí (Bloomington and
      Indianapolis: Indiana University Press, 2009), 78–108. The cult of this quality
      of Ṣàngó and the other Airás is still present in Bahian Candomblé. See Silveira,
      O candomblé da Barroquinha, 380–384.

both Ifá and sixteen-cowry divination, because the client indicates, for example, which parts of the verses the diviner recites are pertinent to his or her particular case.[72] At any rate, as George Park suggests in relation to any kind of diviner: "by skilful diagnosis he must establish his own extraordinary powers ... and that would give to his cures their value."[73] Whether he was a babalawo, an owoloriṣa, or something else – because he could also have used kola nuts, water, and so forth as divination tools – Domingos seems to have established his credentials in mid-nineteenth-century Bahia.

I do not know if Delfina, then Domingos' conjugal partner, and Maria Ignez, his slave, also had ritual responsibilities in Domingos' house, as the police chief alleged, based on the complaint he had received. He would accuse the two freedwomen of having "become diviners and fortune tellers" along with Domingos, a charge echoed by the *Diário da Bahia*.[74] Could they have been *apetebi*, devotees of Òṣun whose ritual aid the babalawos customarily enjoyed?[75] It is hard to say, and this may be a moot point in light of the possibility of important shifts in Yoruba divinatory practices in Bahia. If – as the evidence suggests – they lived in Domingos' home, however, Delfina and Maria Ignez probably had ritual duties to perform, even if they did not involve divination.

Furthermore, although the babalawo's position was exclusive to men, women – and not just apetebis – could use divination methods other than Ifá. Some clearly did so in nineteenth-century Bahia. In 1857, for example, the *Jornal da Bahia* accused an "old black woman" who lived in the same parish as Domingos of "fortunetelling for those who seek her [out for her] reputation." In the next chapter, I will introduce the reader to a freedwoman named Constança do Nascimento who was active in the sugar-planting region of the Recôncavo in 1861. Three years later, *O Alabama* accused a certain Mãe Maria das Neves of telling fortunes

---

[72] Bascom, "The Sanctions of Ifa Divination," 48–50; Bascom, *Sixteen Cowries*, 5.

[73] George K. Park, "Divination and Its Social Contexts," *The Journal of the Royal Anthropological Institute*, no. 93, part. 2 (1963): 202.

[74] João Henriques to the subdelegado of São Pedro parish, July 25, 1862; *Diário da Bahia*, July 28, 1862. The newspaper reported that Domingos and "two African women ... touted themselves as diviners and fortunetellers."

[75] Bastide and Verger, "Contribuição ao estudo da adivinhação," 66–67; Roger Bastide, *O candomblé da Bahia: rito nagô* (São Paulo: Companhia das Letras, 2001), 117–118.

in her home in the center of Salvador. However, nothing is mentioned about which method of divination these women employed.[76]

Following African tradition, the people who appear in the records as diviners were mostly men who, in fact, formed the majority of those charged with witchcraft and similar ritual practices over the course of the nineteenth century. Through language denoting ritual author- ity and descriptions of their activities in the archival sources, I have identified – not without some doubts here and there – eighty-six reli- gious specialists, including fifty-four men and just thirty-two women. However, women appear in larger numbers – particularly in the second half of the nineteenth century – among those who were initiated into the religion as priests of their patron divinities.[77]

There are even more indications that Domingos Sodré was no small fry in that world. If there was just one Papai Domingos in Bahia at that time, which I believe to be the case, O *Alabama* confirmed the accused man's fame. His name appeared in this newspaper in 1864 as the African who presided over Candomblé ceremonies at a "farm" in the semi-rural Brotas parish. In the style of a formal communication to the local sub- delegado, O *Alabama* charged that, "in the place called Becco do Acú, large numbers of women gathered on the farm of a certain Mistress Marocas, under the direction of an African named Domingos, to prac- tice vile, immoral and scandalous acts that go against not only morals but our holy religion, and this very Sunday, among other practices, they skinned an ox alive."[78] According to the taste of the time, the reporter painted Domingos as a depraved and cruel enemy of Brazil's dominant religion, and a spiritual leader of Candomblé.

Again, in 1865, a Pai Domingos appears in satirical verses in O *Alabama* that state: "He agreed with Pae Domingos / To leave him the old wood donkey saddles / And of the corn eaten there / To have him bring the husks."[79] The donkey driver was a character created by the author of this rhyme – and appears in a few issues of the newspaper – to portray a citizen above suspicion who is involved in corruption and protected by the priest's magic spells in exchange for a pittance. This is not a real story, of course, but a caricature of a plausible situation in the

[76] *Jornal da Bahia*, January 4, 1857; O *Alabama*, January 14, 1864.
[77] Reis, "Sacerdotes, seguidores e clientes," 65–66. See also Parés, A *formação do Candomblé*, 136.
[78] O *Alabama*, September 14, 1864.
[79] O *Alabama*, August 12, 1865.

cultural context of Bahia at the time, involving characters who were not clearly identified but supposed to exist in local society, including Domingos Sodré, and possibly inspired by him.

Finally, in 1870, O *Alabama* accused "Papai Domingos," along with Mãe Mariquinhas Velludinho – another name that frequently appeared in that paper – of conducting ceremonies for the soul of another famous African priest, Chico Papai, who had died "over five years ago."[80] The diviner's job in this case may have included discovering which sacrifices were required to perform the seven-year funeral rites for that important high priest, or to use divination to determine whether the dead man had adjusted himself to the afterlife and was happy with his position in it.

These reports may confirm what I have surmised before, that Domingos did not carry out major Candomblé ceremonies in his own home, but instead in established Orișa temples, some of which were headed by women. As he lived in densely populated urban area, Domingos preferred to avoid rituals that would attract attention, such as those that involved drumming. No drums were found in his home, and they are essential instruments in numerous celebrations in which initiates are possessed by the divinities. As I have suggested, Domingos seemed to restrict his activities in his own home to giving consultations and preparing ritual offerings and medicine that would not leave much evidence behind. In the terminology of Luís Nicolau Parés, his activities at home remained in the sphere of the "diviner-healer" complex, which Parés contrasts with the ecclesiastical complex of the Candomblé temples, made up of groups of initiates devoted to the systematic worship of the divinities. He also suggests that, in nineteenth-century Bahia, "one religious specialist could alternately function individually and as part of a broader congregation."[81] I believe this was the case with Domingos. Although he was not the leader of a specific temple, there are indications – including the emblems and clothing of Orișas found in his home, as well as the newspaper reports cited earlier – that he placed his divination skills in the service of organized candomblés. There were many of them in Bahia during his time, each with its own set hierarchy and initiation group, calendar of public festivals with drumming and hymns, dances, and rites of possession. Toward the end of the century Nina Rodrigues observed that while some ceremonies could involve priests from different temples who belonged to the cult of the Orișas being

[80] O *Alabama*, June 23, 1870.
[81] Parés, *A formação do Candomblé*, esp. chaps. 3 and 4. The quotation is from 119.

honored, the babalawos were most in demand on those occasions, usually elderly Africans brought in from "great distances, sometimes jour-
neys that were very difficult for those little old men to make."[82] They
probably came to perform divination to guarantee the successful com-
pletion of the ritual processes activated during those festive occasions.

Diviners like Domingos would have been particularly respected and
popular among the heads of Candomblé houses because, through their
consultations, they propitiated ceremonies, gave advice on rituals, and
presided over the succession of the high priests and priestesses, among
other tasks involved in their profession. They could also send their clients to a given Candomblé temple or priest to worship a certain divinity
because divination had so advised.[83] As a result, specific temples and
devotions depended to some extent on having respected diviners to
help them bring in more followers, who would contribute funds, prestige, and power to the recommended priests, and offerings for the deities and temples chosen. By increasing the number of their devotees,
the Orişas had for centuries blossomed, flourished, and gained strength
among the Yoruba, just as, in a mirror image, the more dependents a
local chief had among his following, the more power he possessed.[84]

If my guess is correct, Domingos' position as a priest was comparable to that of the famous Bahian-born babalawo Martiniano Eliseu
do Bonfim (1859–1943), who was a contemporary of Domingos in
Martiniano's youth. American sociologist E. Franklin Frazier, who
interviewed Martiniano in the late 1930s, by which time he said he
had retired from Candomblé, wrote: "In former times, the babalao was
a male connected with the Candomblés who practiced divination and
sorcery."[85] Presumably Domingos, like Martiniano, frequented different

---

[82] Rodrigues, Os africanos, 236.
[83] Here I was inspired by Bascom, "The Sanctions of Ifa Divination," 44.
[84] See Karin Barber, "How Man Makes God in West Africa: Yoruba Attitudes
towards the Orişa," Africa 51, no. 3 (1981): 724–745. Obviously, having a
large number of dependents was not a base of power in Yorubaland alone. It
was also true in Brazil, for example. As Richard Graham writes, "The measure
of a man was the size of his clientele," particularly, but not exclusively, in rural
Brazil. Graham, Patronage and Politics in Nineteenth-Century Brazil (Stanford,
CA: Stanford University Press, 1990), 22. See also Silveira, O candomblé da
Barroquinha, chap. 7, in which he discusses Portuguese, African, and Brazilian
traditions of patronage and clientelism.
[85] E. Franklin Frazier, "The Negro Family in Bahia, Brazil," American Sociological
Review, 7, no. 4 (1942): 475. Regarding Martiniano, see also Vivaldo da

Candomblé temples where he practiced divination and may have performed other ritual tasks. However, it was for his private practice of divination and antislavery sorcery, particularly what he earned from it, that the police put Domingos behind bars.

Costa Lima, "O candomblé da Bahia na década de 30," in *Cartas de Édison Carneiro a Artur Ramos*, ed. Waldir Freitas Oliveira and Vivaldo da Costa Lima (Salvador: Corrupio, 1987), 37–73; Braga, *Na gamela do feitiço*, chap. 2; Matory, *Black Atlantic Religion*, chap. 3; Lisa Earl Castillo, *Entre a oralidade e a escrita: a etnografia dos candomblés da Bahia* (Salvador: Editora da UFBA, 2010), 101–144; and idem, "Between Memory, Myth, and History." The itinerancy of babalawos in Yorubaland is also indicated by Abimbola, *Ifá*, 25.

CHAPTER FOUR

WITCHCRAFT AND SLAVERY

WHAT SORT OF CRIME IS WITCHCRAFT?

The attorney defending Agostinho José Pereira asked a similar question in Recife in 1846: a black Brazilian, or creole/crioulo, Pereira headed a Christian cult similar to Protestantism in its rejection of images in worship and its devotion to individual reading and interpretation of the Bible. For this reason, historian Marcus Carvalho called him a pastor, but in his time, Agostinho was known as Divine Teacher, and ended up being imprisoned for preaching revolt and threatening to do in Brazil what slaves had done in Haiti, among other charges. His attorney believed his arrest was all about religious persecution and asked the court: "What sort of crime is being a schismatic?"[1] After all, religious schism was not a crime at all. Article no. 5 of Brazil's 1824 constitution stated that, although the "Roman Catholic Apostolic Religion" was the country's official faith, "all others" were permitted as long as they were limited to "domestic or private worship in houses used for that purpose, without having the external shape of a Church."[2] Lawmakers,

[1] Marcus J. M. de Carvalho, "'Que crime é ser cismático?' As transgressões de um pastor negro no Recife patriarcal," *Estudos Afro-Asiáticos*, no. 36 (1999): 97–121; and idem, "'É fácil serem sujeitos de quem já foram senhores': o ABC do Divino Mestre," *Afro-Ásia*, no. 31 (2004): 327–334.
[2] *Constituição Política do Império do Brasil* (Rio de Janeiro: Typ. de Silva Porto, 1824), 5. There is also article 179, paragraph v, but I have not seen it invoked in any of the cases I have found. It states that "No one may be persecuted for reasons of Religion, as long as it respects the State and does not offend public Morals" (idem, p. 60). Article 179 deals with the rights of citizens, including the right to property, which guaranteed the continuation of slavery in independent Brazil.

126

however, had not intended to extend freedom of religion to "schismatic" cults headed by blacks like Agostinho Pereira, much less to devotees of Candomblé or Islam, which were typically African faiths in nineteenth-century Bahia. If the letter of the law stated that religions would be tolerated, the spirit of the law was intent at protecting religious freedom among white Protestant foreigners who resided in Brazil, such as Anglican British merchants. Religious freedom or tolerance was conceived with them in mind.

During Brazil's imperial period, religious practices of African origin existed in a kind of legal limbo. The authorities did not consider them a religion, and therefore worthy of toleration under constitutional law. The dominant parlance – among civil and religious authorities and the press, for example – called them a superstition or simply "witchcraft." But these ways of seeing and experiencing the world also fell outside the definition of a crime according to the Imperial Criminal Code, unlike the former Portuguese colony of Brazil, which was governed by the rules of the Inquisition and other ecclesiastical and even civil laws. The Imperial Code contained a chapter that punished "offenses against religion and morality" (but only "in public places"), and another that banned "illicit gatherings," although it did not explicitly state that religious ceremonies of any kind were offensive to Catholicism or illicit, much less individual consultations with diviners and healers and other private rituals. The penalties were up to forty days in jail and a fine. In fact, I have not found anyone charged under the terms of that code for engaging in Candomblé gatherings in Bahia.[3] Therefore, when the authorities labeled African priests as sorcerers and promoters of superstitions, this charge did not have direct legal consequences. It was the hegemonic discourse of social, cultural, and ethnic disqualification, although it did have dire consequences for those who were thus disqualified. There was no lack of ways to punish black people who deviated from the official religion and conventional morality, particularly means of harassing the leaders of religions like Candomblé.

Throughout the first half of the nineteenth century, African *batuques* (drumming sessions) were banned because police officials and municipal

[3] The Criminal Code articles in question are 280 and 285 to 294. See *Código Criminal do Império do Brazil, annotado com os actos dos Poderes Legislativo, Executivo e Judiciário etc* by Araújo Filgueiras Junior (Rio de Janeiro: Eduardo & Henrique Laemmert, 1876), 300, 302–306. See also Silveira, *O candomblé da Barroquinha*, 250–252, and passim.

lawmakers believed they presaged slave revolt. Along with these concerns, municipal ordinances, resolutions, and police edicts justified the
ban because drumming disturbed the residents of cities and towns, as
well as supposedly encouraging indecent behavior, drunkenness, and
disorder and distracting slaves from their work. In the second half of
the century, once fears of slave revolts had subsided – along with the
revolts themselves – these other motives gained more ground in the
reasoning behind the repression of Candomblé. But as I have already
pointed out in Chapter 1, a more general argument was used against
African batuque and Candomblé in particular, which was portrayed as a
powerful obstacle to the advance of European civilization, in the bosom
of which the educated elites desired to include Brazil. In these terms,
repression also lacked a clear legal basis, but even so, it was usually
carried out through local regulations. In Salvador, there was a ban on
lundus (an Afro-Brazilian rhythm and dance), batuques, and any other
nocturnal "entertainments" that could disturb the peace. In 1860, a
couple of years before Domingos' arrest, Municipal Ordinance no. 59
stated: "batuques, dances and gatherings of slaves are banned in any
place and at any time," under penalty of eight days in jail. These laws
were insistently reissued, with variations, until the early 1880s at the
very least. Although it was not explicitly mentioned, the prohibition
included Candomblé drum-driven and possession dance ceremonies.[4]

The legal reasoning embedded in these edicts was often subject to the
free interpretation of the authorities, which at least created loopholes
for negotiating tolerance. This is clear in an episode that took place in

[4] See *Posturas da Câmara Municipal da Cidade de S. Salvador* [1859], 15. The laws
issued in this regard during the colonial and independent periods can be fol-
lowed in *Repertório de fontes sobre escravidão existentes no Arquivo Municipal
de Salvador: as posturas (1631/1889)* (Salvador: Fundação Gregório de Mattos/
Prefeitura Municipal do Salvador, 1988); and *Legislação da Província da
Bahia sobre o negro*. Regarding the repression of batuques, see João José Reis,
"Tambores e tremores: a festa negra na Bahia na primeira metade do século
XIX," in *Carnavais e outras f(r)estas: ensaios de história social da cultura*, ed. Maria
Clementina Pereira Cunha (Campinas: Editora da Unicamp, 2002), 101–155;
and Jocélio Teles dos Santos, "Divertimentos estrondosos: batuques e sambas
no século XIX," in *Ritmos em trânsito: socioantropoolgia da música baiana*, ed.
Livio Sansone and Jocélio T. dos Santos (Salvador: Projeto A Cor da Bahia,
1997), 15–38. Traditional healing and witchcraft were banned and criminal-
ized by the Republican criminal code of 1890, articles 156, 157, and 158. See
Yvonne Maggie, *Medo do feitiço: relações entre magia e poder no Brasil* (Rio de
Janeiro: Arquivo Nacional, 1992), 22–23.

December 1860. When he was heading an investigation of a complaint made to the chief of police, subdelegado Miguel de Souza Requião, from the first district of Santo Antônio parish, raided a house where "there were forbidden dances." Along with the person who lived there, an African freedwoman named Maria Benedita, he arrested another freedwoman and five slave women, and took them all to jail, which was close by.[5] At the attacked house, Requião found "objects pertaining to the same dances" that he confiscated and sent to the chief of police. In a letter sent the same day regarding the subdelegado's report, his superior wrote: "since there are no facts that would lead to criminal proceedings, after twenty-four hours, have them set free with a warning that they must stop disturbing the peace."[6] They did not spend even the eight days in jail stipulated by law.

The police edicts and city ordinances did not even distinguish religious batuques from house or street lundus and samba gatherings. However, Domingos Sodré did not fit the description of a disturber of the peace because he did not hold any kind of drumming, singing, or possession dance ceremonies in his home, as far as we know. He would have to be investigated and punished for some other infraction, and suspicion of receiving stolen objects, or larceny, was the crime with which African priests were generally charged when the authorities decided to remove them from circulation.[7] Certainly, police and political authorities might disagree on what action to take. The police chief cited earlier punished his Candomblé prisoners with just twenty-four hours in jail

[5] Regarding the jails mentioned throughout this book, see Claudia Moraes Trindade, "A reforma prisional na Bahia oitocentista," *Revista de História*, no. 158 (2008): 157–198.

[6] Miguel de Souza Requião, subdelegado of the first district of Santo Antônio, to the chief of police, September 22, 1860, APEB, *Polícia. Subdelegados*, maço 6233; José Pereira Moraes to the subdelegado of Paço, September 24, 1860, APEB, *Polícia. Correspondência*, vol. 5741, fl. 162v.

[7] See the case of Juca Rosa in Gabriela dos Reis Sampaio, *Juca Rosa, um pai-de-santo na Corte imperial* (Rio de Janeiro: Arquivo Nacional, 2009); and that of Pai Gavião, in Luiz Couceiro, "Acusações de feitiçaria e insurreições escravas no Sudeste do Império do Brasil," *Afro-Ásia*, no. 38 (2008): 211–244. Even for the mid-twentieth century, there are examples of similar charges in Bahia. See Julio Braga, *A cadeira de ogã e outros ensaios* (Rio de Janeiro: Pallas, 1999), 111–148. During the imperial period, an article of the Criminal Code regarding serious physical offenses was also used. See *Pajelança do Maranhão no século XIX: o processo de Amelia Rosa*, ed. Mundicarmo Ferreti (São Luís:CMF/FAPEMA, 2004).

for disturbing the peace. Chief Henriques, on the other hand, considered all Candomblé leaders "profiteers" who were harmful to the public economy. And it was for that offense that he initially intended to bring charges against Domingos.

The police were particularly interested in the two wall clocks and jewelry found in the house on Ladeira de Santa Tereza. Why would an African freedman be so interested in telling the time? In theory, he could not or should not own wall clocks, at least not honestly. There was something wrong with an African being interested in an object that was so closely associated with modernity. Once again, I will turn to the words of Subdelegado Pompílio:

> [I]t appears to me that many African women and men were induced to take objects stolen from their masters to the same [Domingos] as offerings to obtain their freedom, and even obtain drinks and concoctions to tame their masters, among other nonsense that impresses such stupid people; and so these profiteers take advantage of the credulity of the unwary, and contribute to the loss of many Africans who are now useless, as their owners can no longer rely on their services.[8]

Like a loyal flunkey, the subdelegado was merely confirming in almost identical words the suspicions Chief João Antonio Henriques had communicated to him – that the priest's clients were slaves who exchanged stolen objects for an easier life in or a definitive break from bondage. José Egídio Nabuco, the customs official, had denounced Domingos Sodré precisely because one of his slave women, Theodolinda, a member of the Nagô nation like the diviner, had "taken to that den immense [numbers of] valuables, as well as money," according to the police chief's report. Nabuco lived on Rua da Lapa, which was also in Domingo's parish, no more than a ten-minute walk from the diviner's residence. Also according to Chief Henriques, Domingos and his minions had other clients, aside from Theodolinda. The freedman's crew was always "enticing slaves to steal everything they can carry from their masters' homes and take them to him to obtain their freedom through witchcraft."[9] Added

---

[8] Pompílio Manuel de Castro to the chief of police of the province of Bahia, July 27, 1862.

[9] João Henriques to the subdelegado of São Pedro, July 25, 1862, APEB, *Polícia. Correspondência expedida, 1862*, vol. 5754, fl. 214v; *Almanak ... 1863*, 189 (for Nabuco's address).

to the offense of helping make the master easier to handle and the slave useless for work was the crime of obtaining manumissions without the master's full control of the process, a dangerous move in a society where freedom should be a master's decision alone and one that would only favor loyal, obedient, and hardworking slaves – this was a golden rule of the prevailing paternalist ideology of slave control.[10]

The police chief had an intuitive idea about the political economy of witchcraft, but Henriques may have needed to know a little more about it, for example, that consultations and ritual offerings could be costly to avoid a poor result or total failure in negotiations with the gods and ancestors. African priesthood was, by cultural consensus, a paid occupation based on individual services rendered. Some of this came from Africa, where the culture of divination and ritual offerings was widespread at the time. Even more money probably circulated in this context on the other side of the Atlantic. J. D. Y. Peel observes that, during the nineteenth century, payment for divination and healing sessions was one of the most important sources of debt among the Yoruba.[11]

Of course, there were priests and diviners in Bahia who overcharged, so to speak, demanding sums and offerings that were much larger than those suggested by the deities in divination sessions. Like a consumer protection agency, the police received complaints in this regard, including from Africans who felt they had been cheated. In 1856, Maria Romana de Santa Rosa, a Jeje freedwoman, claimed that she had lost everything she owned, including a house, to an African healer. She argued that he had promised to cure her husband but killed him instead.[12] Chief Henriques believed that all members of the African religious community belonged to that ilk. He was convinced that Salvador was teeming with "profiteers" like Domingos and promised to fight them to "keep the property of others safe and prevent unfortunate consequences." When writing this, he certainly had in mind the interests of slaveholders like the customs official José Egídio Nabuco and even bigger slave owners, not African freedpersons like Maria Romana.

---

[10] On paternalism as a strategy of class control in nineteenth-century Brazil, see Sidney Chalhoub, *Machado de Assis historiador* (São Paulo: Companhia das Letras, 2003).

[11] The others were loans for business, ransoming relatives from slavery, paying taxes to local chiefs, and funeral expenses. Peel, *Religious Encounter*, 60.

[12] Reis, "Sacerdotes, seguidores e clientes," 72–74. Romana was able to get back some of her belongings, but I will save the details for another work in progress.

That is what was meant by the "unfortunate consequences" that had to be avoided. The threat Candomblé posed to the smooth functioning of slavery largely explained its repression in this and other cases. The chief of police was adamant when he communicated to the subdelegado his commitment to eradicating "similar superstitions, all the more noxious in a country where a large part of its wealth is invested in slaves."[13]

THE ART OF TAMING MASTERS

It was a commonly held opinion in Bahia at the time that Candomblé and slavery were a bad combination. Similar accusations abound in police documents and the press. The subdelegado who arrested an African named Cipriano José Pinto in 1853 (which I will discuss in detail in Chapter 6) considered him dangerous because the area where he had set up his Candomblé house, the Recôncavo, contained numerous sugar plantations and was hence a place where "a large number of Africans" lived. Therefore, precautions should be taken to prevent "the bad outcome of similar clubs arising."[14] This official was worried that the African's candomblé might become a seditious organization, a "club" that could actively organize slave revolts.

However, the relationship between Candomblé and slave resistance primarily took different paths, which they had actually followed since colonial times. The idea of using ritual means to control the slaveholders' power, to "tame the master," for example, was nothing new, as demonstrated in studies of the colonial period. One such case occurred in 1646, in the capital of Bahia, involving another Domingos, this time the freedman Domingos Umbata, who was therefore of Mbata origin, in territory located in Angola today. To protect his clients (two slave women) from their bad-tempered mistresses, he recommended bathing with an infusion of certain macerated leaves, a rattle, and a jaguar tooth. Later on, in 1702, a Jesuit reported that Angolan slaves in the Recôncavo of Bahia were using mystical concoctions to soften their masters' hearts. In the mid-eighteenth century, in Minas Gerais, two slave women, both named Joana, were accused of using witchcraft to

[13] João Henriques to the subdelegado of São Pedro parish, July 25, 1862, fl. 215.
[14] Gustavo Balbino de Moura e Camira, substitute subdelegado of Monte parish, to the delegado of São Francisco do Conde, March 15, 1853, in Cecília Moreira Soares, "Resistência negra e religião: a repressão ao candomblé de Paramerim, 1853," *Estudos Afro-Asiáticos*, no. 23 (1992): 139.

"soften and tame their mistress so that she would not punish them," as reported in a study by historian André Nogueira. Throughout the Portuguese Atlantic world, slaves were employing different means toward healing slavery. Some used wheat roots or shavings from the soles of the master's shoes to prepare mollifying potions; others used powder made from human skulls. The same year Domingos Umbata was casting spells on the slave women's mistresses, a Bahian mulatto woman named Beatriz filled her mistress's pillow with small amulets made from bits of bird feathers and beaks and sea shells so that she would treat her slave well and even "love her." In addition to making masters easier to live with, slaves in colonial Brazil also used those means to get rid of them through manumission. To thank him for helping with his escape route, a slave named Manoel de Barros gave another slave, João da Silva, an amulet to help him gain his manumission from his master. This took place in Jacobina, in the Bahian hinterland, in 1742.[15]

James Sweet argues these were methods of combat that slaves brought from Africa, while Laura de Mello e Souza suggests that spells for taming masters as well as those for obtaining manumission were not exclusively of African origin, but often mixed up with or recast as European magical traditions used by the powerless, and not just by slaves, against the powerful.[16] The popularity of colonial spells like those mentioned earlier continued in nineteenth-century Brazil and were part of the repertoire of services Domingos Sodré provided to slaves. In his case, however, although we do not have any details, the ritual paraphernalia the police found in his home points to a stronger African component, but it is not possible to establish whether, where, why, and what among its aspects

[15] Sweet, *Recreating África*, 164–165, 166–167, 185; Souza, *O Diabo*, 206–209, 265; André Nogueira, "Doenças, feitiços e curas: africanos e seus descendentes em ação nas Minas do século XVIII," in *Doenças e escravidão: sistema de saúde e práticas terapêuticas*, ed. Ângela Porto, (Rio de Janeiro: Casa Oswaldo Cruz/Fiocruz, 2008), available on CD-ROM. See also Laura de Mello e Souza, "Revisitando o calundu," in *Ensaios sobre a intolerância – inquisição, marronismo e anti-semitismo*, ed. Lina Gorenstein and Maria Luiza Tucci Carneiro, (São Paulo: Humanitas, 2002), 293–317. Similar ritual resources were used by slaves against masters in Portugal. See Daniela Buono Calainho, *Metrópole das mandingas: religiosidade negra e inquisição portuguesa no antigo regime* (Rio de Janeiro: Garamond/FAPERJ, 2008), 105–111.
[16] Sweet, *Recreating África*; idem, *Domingos Álvares, African Healing, and the Intellectual History of the Atlantic World* (Chapel Hill: University of North Carolina Press, 2011); Souza, *O Diabo*.

suffered discontinuities (or not) when transported from the eastern to the western shores of the Atlantic. Again we have lost the precise meanings of most of Domingo´s ritual paraphernalia and procedures. Nevertheless, we do know a great deal about their intended uses.

Masters being mollified by their slaves during the imperial period became part of what Flora Süssekind termed the "imaginary of fear" in her study of abolitionist writer Joaquim Manuel de Macedo's *Vítimas-algozes* (*Victims-Executioners*), published in 1869. In Macedo's work, the poisoning of a slaveholder is the central theme of the episode entitled "Pai Raiol – the wizard."[17] Stories such as this one were not entirely baseless, as the novelist had observed in Rio de Janeiro, a city and a province that concentrated a substantial slave population. Keeping to his aim of nurturing the perceived fears of slaves to better convince his readers of the advantages of abolishing slavery, Macedo wrote about the wide variety of effects of the concoctions prepared by the "black herbalist, the practical botanist who knows the properties and infallible actions of roots, leaves and fruits." These, among other results, "weaken the physical and moral strength of men and [achieve] what they call *taming* the master."[18] Note that the novelist states that the slaves themselves coined the expression *amansar senhor* ("master-taming"). This phenomenon and even the vocabulary of slave resistance witchcraft – aimed at mollifying masters – became known throughout Brazil. However, it never reached the epidemic proportions of prerevolutionary Haiti, for instance. There, in addition to the outbreaks of poisoning deaths of slaves and masters that preceded the revolution, in the everyday routine of resistance slaves tried to tame their masters with homeopathic doses of poison, sometimes administered for months on end. "If the master's cruelty persisted," writes Carolyn Fick, "the doses could be increased and finally induce death."[19] In Brazil there is at least one known case in which an attempt to tame masters was connected to an 1882 slave revolt in Campinas, São Paulo. Methods

[17] Flora Süssekind, "As *vítimas-algozes* e o imaginário do medo," in Joaquim Manuel de Macedo, *As vítimas-algozes*, 3rd ed. (Rio de Janeiro: Scipione/Casa de Rui Barbosa, 1991 [orig. 1869]), xxi–xxxviii.

[18] See in particular the first pages of "Pai Raiol – o feiticeiro," in Macedo, *As vítimas-algozes*, 71–78.

[19] Carolyn Fick, *The Making of Haiti: The Saint Domingue Revolution from Below* (Knoxville: University of Tennessee Press, 1990), chap. 2, and p. 71 for the quotation.

to "break masters and overseers and make them weak and sickly" were reported in an inquiry set up to investigate the episode, a vast conspiracy led by men who said they held the spiritual "secret or power."[20]

In nineteenth-century Salvador, Domingos was not the only one in the business of controlling the masters' wrath and of promoting manumission. In 1848, for example, a subdelegado reported that free Africans from the Nagô nation who worked at the Navy Arsenal were trying to induce enslaved Africans "to cast spells and thus obtain their freedom."[21] By law, their employer, in this case the Navy, was supposed to aid, cure, baptize, and instill Christian doctrine into its wards, who had been seized as contraband after the slave trade was banned in 1831. The Navy did not seem to be fulfilling its obligations, at least that of Christianizing its African workers. The "free" Africans themselves must have had an interest in the spell they recommended to their enslaved peers, because they were themselves systematically treated as slaves. At the Arsenal they were "subjected to an overseer who reviewed them and locked them up at night," according to a Navy quartermaster.[22]

Five years later, on Itaparica Island, an African slave woman accused of trying to poison her master and his entire family declared that all she had done was mix cowry powder and lime juice into their coffee, "which she had done because she had been taught that it was a good

---

[20] Maria Helena Machado, *O plano e o pânico: os movimentos sociais na década da abolição* (São Paulo: EDUSP, 1994), 116.

[21] APEB, *Polícia*, maço 3113. Free Africans: this was the term used to describe slaves confiscated as contraband after the slave trade was officially banned, particularly by the 1831 law, and they were either put to work in public and philanthropic institutions or their services were hired out to private parties. Regarding Bahia, see Afonso Bandeira Florence, "Nem escravos, nem libertos: os 'africanos livres' na Bahia," *Cadernos do CEAS*, no. 121 (1989): 58–69, and by the same author, "Entre o cativeiro e a emancipação: a liberdade dos africanos livres no Brasil (1818–1864)," MA Thesis, Universidade Federal da Bahia, 2002. The free Africans accused of witchcraft mentioned in this paragraph may have been the same ones who were transferred to Rio de Janeiro that same year. See Beatriz Galotti Mamigonian, "Do que o 'preto mina' é capaz: etnia e resistência entre africanos livres," *Afro-Ásia*, no. 24 (2000): 78–79. The most complete, country-wide study of the subject is Mamigonian's forthcoming book, "Africanos livres: tráfico, trabalho e direito no Brasil oitocentista" (2014).

[22] José Joaquim Raposo, Navy quartermaster, to the president of the province, November 5, 1848, APEB, *Intendência da Marinha*, maço 3254.

way to tame masters."[23] Besides trusting her healer, this African woman
must have known that cowries were not just a form of currency on the
west coast of Africa but, perhaps for that very reason, played important
ritual roles – they adorned representations of the divinities and were
used in divination, for example – and therefore could also be useful in
achieving her stated objectives.

Cases of masters poisoned by their slaves – as well as slaves who
poisoned other slaves and even animals – appear time and again in
the police records, although they rarely report which ingredient was
administered. Herbs and roots known to African medicine were often
used, as well as other poisons purchased or stolen from apothecaries and
innkeepers – arsenic sulfide was the substance most commonly mentioned. According to the chief of police, the contents of the potion the
slave woman had served to her master and his family on Itaparica, for
example, was analyzed by physicians from Bahia's School of Medicine,
who concluded that it was "white arsenic acid or realgar."[24] Certainly,
the vomiting and dizziness suffered by those who drank that coffee would
not have been caused by cowry powder alone, but the slave woman may
have been misinformed by the healer, who had furnished her with realgar or some other kind of poison. In this case, a new material basis was
adapted to a known cultural universe through whose principles the efficacy of the ritual gesture was explained.

The sale of "poisonous drugs" to slaves was, of course, strictly forbidden, according to a municipal ordinance issued in Cachoeira in 1847.
In 1859, a Salvador municipal ordinance banned the sale of "poisonous and suspicious substances" by apothecary shops and other establishments without a "prescription or note from a duly authorized Professor
stating the quality and quantity, the name of the persons who intend
to purchase it and to what end." The penalty for violating this ordinance was a 30,000-reis fine – roughly a month's earnings for a hired-out
slave – or eight days in prison.[25] However, the use of plants could not be

[23] "Relatório dos sucessos, violências, e crimes que tiveram lugar na Província
durante o mez de Setembro de 1853," APEB, Polícia. Relatórios para a Presidência,
1849–54, livro no. 5689, fl. 344v.
[24] "Relatório dos sucessos, violências, e crimes que tiveram lugar na Província
durante o mez de Setembro de 1853," fl. 344v. Silva, "Caminhos e descaminhos
da abolição," 121–122, relates the case of a slave woman who killed her mistress
by putting ant poison in her food in revenge for mistreatment.
[25] Repertório de fontes, 67; Posturas da Câmara Municipal da Cidade de S. Salvador
[1859], 26.

controlled. There are indications that this was the method used in 1860 in the district of Brotas, on the outskirts of Salvador, by a slave named Manuel, a creole bricklayer, to poison his master, Constantino Nunes Mucugê, and two of his slave women, Felizarda and Maria, probably collateral victims who sampled the master's leftovers. Mucugê and Felizarda survived, but Maria died. Manuel was prosecuted under an 1835 law for which capital punishment was imposed on slaves who attempted to murder their masters.[26] Closer to Domingos, on the neighboring street of Areal de Cima, in 1879, a certain Senhorinha, last name unknown, was poisoned by her slave Elias, who patiently introduced, day after day, certain leaves into her habitual glass of wine. It is possible that the slave had administered an overdose to a mistress he had only intended to tame.[27]

It has crossed my mind that Domingos could have supplied the herbs Elias used, but even if he did not, in the broader sense, his work involved practices and beliefs like those described earlier. The African priest promised the slaves that he would work to help them get their freedom, or at least to ease the sufferings of slavery by taming their masters with medicinal formulas. The African pharmacopeia is very rich in herbs that can be used for attack and protection, to help and do harm, and their use always had to be accompanied by incantations pronounced by the babalawo. The healer's garden included guinea weed or guinea hen weed (petiveria alliacea), for example, which is also known as amansa-senhor in good Portuguese, a term one can find in conventional Brazilian dictionaries. It has anti-spasmodic properties, so it would be ideal for relaxing seigniorial muscles. Historian Maria Cristina Wissenbach observes that guinea weed, used by slaves against their masters, "was characterized by insidious and slow action, causing states of lethargy leading to death."[28] Botanist Roberto Martins Rodrigues gives more details on the effects of this plant: "fractionated powder from its roots causes hyper excitation, insomnia and hallucinations, followed by lethargy and even imbecility, and softening of the brain, tetanus-like convulsions, paralysis of the larynx and death within approximately one year, depending on the doses ingested."[29] Here we find guinea weed

[26] José Teixeira Bahia, subdelegado of Brotas, to the chief of police, November 8 and December 1, 1860, APEB, Polícia. Subdelegados, maço 6233.

[27] Tribuna, 4, no. 67, October 18, 1979, p. 3.

[28] Maria Cristina Cortez Wissenbach, "A mercantilização da magia na urbanização de São Paulo, 1910–1940," Revista de História, no. 150 (2004): 31.

[29] In José Flavio Pessoa de Barros and Eduardo Napoleão, Ewé Òrìsà: uso litúrgico e terapêutico dos vegetais nas casas de candomblé jêje-nagô, 3rd ed. (Rio de Janeiro: Bertrand Brasil, 2007), 197.

as a powerful instrument of attack. In the Yoruba medicinal ideology, according to Pierre Verger, guinea weed serves as a means of defense: "to avert someone's aggression" – the master's, for example. To that end, the babalawo explains how to prepare it by mixing it with goat weed (*ageratum conyzoides*): "Burn it. Draw the odu [divining verse/design] in the mixture. Make an incision in the head and rub in the preparation."[30] Of course, there is no guarantee that slaves used this recipe in Bahia, as Verger states that it was collected in Africa and therefore outside the Brazilian context. But it may have been created here and taken there, most likely by Nagô returnees, just as the plant itself was taken to Yorubaland in today's Nigeria, also according to Verger.[31]

Slaves used other kinds of plants to protect themselves from their masters' violence, which therefore became known as *amansa-senhor* as well. This was the case with *mulungu* or coral shrub (*erythrina speciosa*), which, conveniently, has soporific properties.[32] But the list goes on. Wissenbach cites the director of the National Museum in Rio de Janeiro, João Baptista Lacerda, who wrote in 1909 about the black herbalists he had interviewed: "Despite all my inquiries, they could never tell me from exactly which plants slaves obtained the poison they used on their masters: they indicated *anamu*, sweet acacia, jimson weed, nightshade, taro and wild caladium bicolor – all narcotic, irritating and paralyzing plants."[33] The herbs used to tame masters were, therefore, probably part of a medicinal complex that was not just limited to one or two types, and produced a variety of mollifying effects.

I do not know if Domingos used any of these or other herbs, and if he did use them, whether he learned about their properties in Brazil or in Africa. The term *guinea weed* suggests a long-term presence in Brazil, from the time when all Africans were called blacks or gentiles from Guinea. In the case of Bahia, I am particularly referring to the period between the sixteenth and mid-eighteenth centuries.[34] Therefore, it is difficult to determine this plant's specific African origins. However,

---

[30] Verger, *Ewé*, 367, 434–435, 707.

[31] Ibid., 40–41.

[32] The word *amansa-senhor* is found in the Houaiss Portuguese dictionary, for example, which associates it with both guinea weed and the coral shrub.

[33] Cristina Wissenbach, "Ritos de magia e de sobrevivência. Sociabilidades e práticas mágico-religiosas no Brasil (1890–1940)," PhD dissertation, Universidade de São Paulo, 1997, 172–173.

[34] See Maria Inês Côrtes de Oliveira, "Quem eram os 'negros da Guiné'? A origem dos africanos na Bahia," *Afro-Ásia*, no. 19/20 (1997): 37–73.

the term *mulungu* is obviously of Bantu derivation, and not only refers to a varied range of plants from the genus *Erythrina* but is the name of a kind of drum that is "long and narrow with a resonant sound," according to Yeda Castro.[35] If traditional Nagô healers in Bahia prescribed mulungo, they were utilizing pharmacological resources assimilated from Africans of different backgrounds. As Lacerda observed, in addition to mulungu and guinea weed, many other plants were part of the slaves' resistance efforts and fueled the techniques of master taming.

In addition to plants, many other elements of nature were certainly included in this medicine chest, as were minerals and animals such as snails, snakes, lizards, and toads – alive or dead, cooked or toasted, powdered or whole – cold-blooded creatures, many of them venomous, which were often confiscated by the Bahian police when searching the homes of traditional healers. In short, the master-taming arsenal was vast and complex and probably varied according to the enemy in question, depending on their social standing and skin color, whether they were Brazilian or African, a man or a woman. Their effectiveness also depended on the competence and creativity of the sorcerer, healer, priest, or whatever name was given to the master breaker.

By its very nature, slavery is a violent system of domination, but many masters went too far, and often had to be kept in line when their rage spiraled out of control. Masters like Colonel João Alves Pitombo, for example. In 1857, the police sent his slave women Gabriela and Ignez to the Charity Hospital of the Santa Casa da Misericórdia because "they were badly abused." Mistreating slaves seemed to be a habit for the Pitombo family. Five years later, the colonel's wife, Maria Rosa Alves Pitombo, slapped Gabriela until she bled. The slave woman complained to the police, who sent her back to her mistress because they considered the assault within the permissible legal limits allowed slave owners to control their bond people. But this slave rebelled against the law and refused to remain in Mrs. Pitombo's company, an offense for which Gabriela was arrested. At least, as long as she was behind bars, her mistress could not slap her around.[36]

---

[35] Yeda Pessoa de Castro, *Falares africanos na Bahia: um vocabulário afro-brasileiro*, 2nd ed. (Rio de Janeiro: Topbooks, 2005), 292.

[36] Francisco Bento de Paula, jailer at the prison, to the chief of police, May 26, 1857, APEB, *Polícia*, maço 6271; Lazaro José Jambeiro, subdelegado of the first district of Santo Antônio, to the chief of police, May 15, 1862, APEB, *Polícia. Subdelegado*, maço 6234.

The police often had to intervene on behalf of severely abused slaves. The Italian José Macina treated his slaves along the same lines as the Pitombos. After receiving a complaint that Macina was beating his slave woman (always a woman!), Subdelegado Miguel de Souza Requião went to his home and found him drunk in the dining room, while his slave was lying in the backyard, "badly mistreated by him." She had to be admitted to the charity hospital for treatment. The intoxicated Italian was married, and his wife and young children had managed to escape his fury by sheltering in a neighbor's house. The slave woman had borne the brunt of his brutality.

Many other slave women are known to have been abused by their masters, which adds an indisputable gender dimension to this subject. In September 1857, the chief of police protected an African woman named Emilia, whose master "she accused of mistreating her," and on another occasion the authority returned the slave woman Maria Antonio to her master, with a warning that he "could only punish his female slave moderately." Three months later, the police chief obliged Veríssimo Joaquim da Silva to sign a writ of responsibility obliging him "to treat his creole slave woman Maximiana well from then on, and not punish her as he was accustomed to doing."[37] There were even masters who specialized in breaking slaves through violence. During an inquiry in 1887 to investigate the death of a slave brutally beaten by his master, a witness stated that he was "extraordinarily inhumane and brutal with slaves, so much so that those who owned bold and bad slaves sent them to him to teach and tame them."[38] Slave-taming techniques needed not be subtle.

African-born slave owners could also show extreme cruelty. Such was the case involving a freedwoman named Maria Joaquina de Santana, of the Jeje nation, and her slave woman Rosa, a Nagô, in 1832. Claiming that her slave frequently escaped, the mistress punished her brutally. Their neighbors in the fishing village of Rio Vermelho, on the outskirts of Salvador, were horrified to witness the torture sessions. Once Maria Joaquina chained her slave to a log and took Rosa (carrying the log on her head) outside the village so she could punish her far from the

---

[37] Miguel de Souza Requião, subdelegado of the first district of Santo Antônio, to the chief of police, December 19, 1860, APEB, Polícia.Subdelegado, maço 6234; J. Madureira to the jailer at the Aljube prison, September 29, 1857, APEB, Polícia. Portarias e registros, vol. 5628, fls. 42v, 44; "Termo de responsabilidade," 3 de dezembro de 1857, APEB, Polícia, vol. 5649, fl. 143.

[38] Quoted in Silva, "Caminhos e descaminhos da abolição," 287.

Figure 28. The quiet fishing village of Rio Vermelho (ca. 1860), where the violent episodes involving the freedwoman Maria Joaquina and her slave Rosa took place.

reproachful eyes of the local residents. But on her way to the whipping session, Rosa managed to escape and sought sanctuary in a church, from where her mistress tried to remove her by force. A soldier intervened and took the victim before the justice of the peace. A forensic examination found old and new scars all over Rosa's body – buttocks, back, arms, legs – from whippings, and "furthermore there was the great defect of the loss of half of the upper lip to the left, exposing four teeth, which gives her a hideous aspect." Maria Joaquina, the mistress, spent twenty-five days in jail and was forced to sell Rosa. In more than three decades of research in the Bahian archives, I have not found a single case where a master was sued or much less punished for mistreating his or her slaves, except for fruitless inquiries when they died. As Teles dos Santos suggests, had Maria Joaquina been a white slaveholder, she probably would not have been punished at all.[39]

---

[39] Jocélio Teles dos Santos, *Ex-escrava proprietária de escrava (um caso de sevícia na Bahia do século XIX)* (Salvador: Programa de Estudos do Negro na Bahia – PENBA/FFCH da UFBa, 1991), quote on p. 23. Regarding slaveholders' violence, see the study by Silvia Hunold Lara, *Campos da violência: escravos e senhores na capitania do Rio de Janeiro* (Rio de Janeiro: Paz e Terra, 1988), part I, where she documents lawsuits brought against masters who beat their slaves to death or drove them to take their own lives.

All these cases of seigniorial violence occurred in Domingos' Bahia, and with the exception of the last episode, most were close to the time of his arrest. Often found in the police archives, they explain why slaves needed the help of healers to tame their masters, particularly when the police could not or would not help them. In a way, Domingos Sodré was competing with the chief of police to see who would do a better job protecting abused slaves, one with the help of his agents and the force of law, the other with the help of his gods and the power of traditional or invented medicine, amulets, and concoctions. The slaves could use one or the other, or both, in their efforts to control the masters' brutality.

Slaves who sought out Domingos were at the very least expressing a personal desire to disobey their masters and lighten their work loads, thereby making themselves "useless," as Subdelegado Pompílio would say. Flight was an implicit part of this. Often, a slave's escape was related to the fulfillment of specific religious rituals. Herein, perhaps, lies an important difference between Calundu in colonial times and Candomblé in the 1800s. In the nineteenth century, particularly the second half, slaves, mostly women, often slipped away to take part in celebrations related to the liturgical calendar that had been established over the course of the century in the Bahian terreiros; or they absconded so they could be confined for weeks and even months while undergoing initiation and other rites, or "precepts," which they had to observe or otherwise be punished by priests and divinities, both of whom also had to be duly tamed.[40] After all, the slaves were not at all stupid, as Subdelegado Pompílio and Chief Henriques believed them to be. When it came to serving their masters or their gods, many chose the latter, who promised to protect them against the abuse of the former and other evils derived or not from life under slavery.

---

[40] João José Reis, "Candomblé and Slave Resistance," in *Witchcraft in the Luso-Atlantic World*, ed. Roger Sansi and Luis Nicolau Parés (Chicago: University of Chicago Press, 2011), 55–74; Harding, *Refuge in Thunder*, 94; and Alexandra Kelly Brown, "'On the Vanguard of Civilization': Slavery, the Police, and Conflict between Public and Private Power in Salvador da Bahia, Brazil, 1835–1888," PhD dissertation, University of Texas, 1998, 127–128. Also in Rio de Janeiro, African houses of worship were suspected of harboring escaped slaves, according to Juliana B. Farias, Flávio Gomes, and Carlos Eugênio L. Soares, *No labirinto das nações: africanos e identidades no Rio de Janeiro, século XIX* (Rio de Janeiro: Arquivo Nacional, 2005), 44. Regarding the use of the term *preceito* (precept) for a religious rite or duty in Candomblé, see *O Alabama*, November 18, 1864, p. 5.

Slaves could also make themselves useless for work by ingesting substances prepared by African healers, which often mimicked the symptoms of nonexistent illnesses. For that very reason, Carlota Leopoldina
de Mello asked the chief of police in 1858 to punish Guilhermina, her
hire-out slave woman. As de Mello explained:

> Having left yesterday to sell bread, as she does every day, her slave
> Guilhermina, of the Nagô nation, stayed out in the streets until
> her arrest today, and now finds herself in the Aljube prison....
> There was no reason for such behavior except for vagrancy by
> the black woman, who, ill-advised by evil blacks, takes medicine
> administered by those same blacks, obliging the Supplicant to go
> to extraordinary expense, as she did a few days ago when she had
> Dr. Cabral treat that same slave, who is almost lost from taking
> drugs (for what purpose, I do not know) in such a way that she was
> disfigured by swelling, and if it were not for Dr. Cabral's care, she
> certainly would have been lost.[41]

De Mello went on to ask the chief of police to have her slave punished.
Here we find a conflict between mistress and slave, and a fierce competition between European and African medicine. The mistress had no
idea why her slave Guilhermina took African medicines, but they certainly left her unable to work, making her "useless." Like most members
of her class, de Mello could not perceive – without condemning her
own world view – "the infinite spectrum of human reactions to forms
of domination," as Michel-Rolph Trouillot pointedly writes regarding
similar perplexity among Haitian slaveholders.[42] One can imagine, in
this case, that the slave woman took drugs to simulate the symptoms of
diseases, such as swelling, as an excuse for not working, or to receive a
lighter workload, or as a way to lower her value in a manumission bid or
sale to a possibly gentler master. It was, in other words, a "strategic illness," one of the weapons of slave resistance.[43] Or, perhaps Guilhermina
had undergone a ritual procedure that involved ingesting medicine that

---

[41] Dona Carlota Leopoldina de Mello to the chief of police, March 13, 1857,
APEB, Polícia, maço 6322.
[42] Michel-Rolph Trouillot, Silencing the Past: Power and the Production of History
(Boston, MA: Beacon Press, 1995), 84.
[43] On strategic (feigning) illness, see Sharla M. Fett, Working Cures: Healing, Health,
and Power on Southern Slave Plantations (Chapel Hill and London: University of
North Carolina Press, 2002), chap. 7.

produced those symptoms as side effects. In any case, this was not about using master-taming drugs, but something else. The possibilities are many. However, we do know the outcome.

Two days later, in another petition to the chief of police, the same mistress alleged that her "slave woman was very saucy, to the point of not heeding" the complainant, "and failing to perform the duties that are her obligations."[44] The slave Guilhermina was swollen with rage and revolt. De Mello once again asked the police to punish and release her so she could return to work – hopefully a reformed woman. The chief of police sent out official replies to both petitions on the same day: in the first, he established the punishment of being feruled two dozen times; in the second, given the mistress's greater distress, he decided to increase the punishment to three dozen. This time, actually most of the time, the police protected the masters' interests, not the physical integrity of their slaves.[45]

Domingos Sodré was accused of taming masters, not inciting slaves. But one thing leads to the other. He was also charged with working to obtain his clients' manumission, and this may have been one reason for Guilhermina's swelling, as I have suggested. It is hard to think why Domingos would not have prepared bottles of concoctions for his enslaved clients to drink to help them obtain their freedom peacefully or increase their will to resist the masters' control by other means, such as slacking or escaping.

CRIME AND PUNISHMENT

To protect the institution of slavery, exemplary punishments were required for Candomblé practitioners like Domingos Sodré and his following. At the orders of the chief of police the subdelegado burned some of the sacred objects confiscated from Domingos. At the same time, Chief João Henriques instructed his subordinate to send him all the "objects of witchcraft" that were made of metal. As soon as he received them on July 26, Henriques sent them on to the commander of the War Arsenal to "give them an appropriate end." He listed them as three short swords and six metal rattles, twenty-eight rings of brass and

---

[44] Dona Carlota Leopoldina de Mello to the chief of police, March 15, 1857, APEB, *Polícia*, maço 6322.

[45] Regarding the role of the police in punishing slaves at the masters' behest, see Brown, "'On the Vanguard of Civilization,'" chap. 5.

seven of lead – possibly items once used as barter for slaves in Africa, just like cowries – an iron imp, and fifteen "miscellaneous objects of no significance."[46] It was appropriate that these items be sent to the War Arsenal, where they would meet the same end the subdelegado had given to other ritual objects: they were melted down in the Arsenal's furnaces, possibly to be transformed into other, non-ritual weapons, this time with cutting edges. In the end, it made perfect sense: the repression against Candomblé was, after all, a kind of war.

The prisoners of that war were subjected to humiliating treatment. Taken from the house on Ladeira de Santa Tereza, Domingos and five other black people were paraded to prison in the late afternoon of July 25, 1862. It was a roughly forty-minute walk, uphill and down through the busy city center, passing in front of the Paris Hotel (which belonged to his master), the São João Theater, the provincial president's palace, the City Council House, Santa Casa da Misericórdia church, the cathedral, the churches of the Jesuit College, the Our Lady of the Rosary Black Brotherhood in Pelourinho plaza, the Carmelite Convent, Our Lady of Boqueirão, a mulatto brotherhood, and finally, the parish church of Santo Antônio, located in the same square where the Correction House prison stood in Fort Santo Antônio. This prison had replaced the Aljube jail as the facility that housed people arrested during the daily police rounds in the city.

The following day, a slave named Elesbão, who was about fifty, received as punishment a dozen blows of the ferule at the request of his master, the physician Felipe da Silva Baraúna, who lived in Barbers Alley in São Pedro parish. Baraúna was an urban slaveholder connected to the sugar planters of the Recôncavo. In 1854, he had served as the agent of the owner of the Caboto plantation in the purchase of a Nagô field slave named Jorge. The buyer was the doctor's own father, João da Silva Baraúna, an accountant in the provincial treasury of Bahia. His cousin Elpídio had been the subdelegado of São Pedro parish in the early 1850s, and in 1840 he had witnessed the purchase deed for a slave named Francisca when she was bought by Domingos' first wife.[47] The freedman importuned important people whom he may have known personally.

---

[46] João Henriques to the director of the War Arsenal, July 26, 1862, APEB, *Polícia. Correspondência expedida, 1862*, vol. 5750, fl. 326v.

[47] "Escriptura de venda, paga e quitação que faz Antonio Felix da Cunha Brito por seu procurador bastante o Doutor Felippe da Silva Baraúna, a João da Silva

Figure 29. On the left, the entrance to Rua de Baixo de São Bento (ca. 1880). Following the tracks uphill, we soon arrive at the corner of Ladeira de Santa Tereza, where Domingos Sodré lived. The Convent of Santa Tereza stands behind the "Café Suisso."

Two days after Elesbão was beaten with a ferule, a young creole slave named João, age fifteen, received the same punishment. Unlike Elesbão, he was punished without the authorization of his master, the wealthy African freedman Manoel Joaquim Ricardo, a friend of Domingos whom the reader will meet again in Chapter 6. Ricardo had no reason to punish his slave, who was probably at the house on Ladeira de Santa Tereza with his consent, possibly to be cured of a chest ailment. Elesbão and João were released immediately after their beating.

The records are silent about what happened to Tereza, but she must have suffered the same punishment meted out to the other slaves in the group. Delfina, the African female slave of the blacksmith Domingos

Baraúna, de um seu escravo de nome Jorge, Nagô, do serviço da lavoura, pela quantia de Réis 600$000," APEB, *LNT*, vol. 316, fls. 103–105; and "Escriptura de venda, paga e quitação que faz Joaquim José Florence a Maria das Mercês de uma escrava nação nagô por nome Francisca por quatrocentos e sessenta mil reis," AMS, *Escrituras. S. Pedro*, vol. 1, fls. 132–133. Regarding Elpídio as subdelegado de São Pedro, see Brown, " 'On the Vanguard of Civilization,' " 91.

Figure 30. The provincial government palace (ca. 1860), on Domingos Sodré's route to prison.

Figure 31. The House of Correction where Domingos Sodré was jailed.

José Alves, also received twelve blows of a ferrule on the 26th. The blacksmith lived on Rua da Preguiça, not far from Domingos Sodré's house – going down Ladeira de Santa Tereza, turning right and then left, you will find yourself in Preguiça, where there was at the time a busy open-air market beside the bay. Finally there was Ignez, who may have been one of Domingos' slaves. To protect him and herself, she said she was a freedwoman and was treated as such by the police. She was not beaten, but had to endure six hard nights in jail. The slave may

Figure 32. Preguiça Market, near the address of Delfina's master.

have arranged with her master to hide her identity to escape the humiliation of the ferule.[48]

As for Domingos Sodré, the day after his arrest he was summoned to police headquarters in the city center, installed in a stately townhouse on Rua do Bispo, rented by the government from jurist Antônio Pereira Rebouças, a member of the General Assembly, imperial councilor, small slave owner, and father of the renowned abolitionist André Rebouças.[49]

[48] Regarding these punishments, see several letters from the police chief to the warden of the Correction House dated July 26 to 31, 1862, APEB, *Polícia. Correspondência expedida, 1862,* vol. 5756, fls. 140v–149. On July 28, an announcement was recorded in that same book, probably written two days earlier, to advertise the arrest of the slaves Tereza and Delfina, both older than thirty-five, João, a creole, age fifteen, and Elesbão, an African who was "nearly 50 years old." It advised those who had ownership rights over them to reclaim or have them reclaimed. Regarding the occupations and addresses of Elesbão's and Delfina's owners, see *Almanak . . . 1863,* 332 and 405. Regarding the slave João's chest ailment, see Chapter 6 of this book.

[49] Rebouças moved from Bahia to Rio de Janeiro in 1846, when he became a representative of the province of Alagoas at the General Legislative Assembly of the Empire. He took his family with him (André was eight years old at the time), as well as African, creole, and cabra slaves and dependents. See his undated request for a passport to the president of the province of Bahia in APEB, *Polícia. Passaportes,* maço 2896. Regarding the house where the police

There Chief João Henriques interrogated the freedman, but I have found no record of the questioning. Domingos was then sent back to jail. For the next three days, the police had enough time to determine whether he was actually receiving goods that slaves had stolen from their masters. All indications are that they failed to prove anything against the priest – either that or he managed to convince the police that he did not know the items and money he received from his enslaved clients had been stolen.

On July 30, after five nights in jail, Domingos was once again standing before Chief Henriques. Now we know exactly what went on, because at the end of that meeting the African was forced to forswear the life of "Candomblé and witchcraft," according to the document read out to him:

STATEMENT OF OBLIGATION

On July 30 of eighteen hundred and sixty two, in this Department of the Bahia Police, coming from the House of Correction prison where he had been held, African freedman Domingos Sudré, a resident of Ladeira de Santa Tereza, where he was arrested, after many objects of Candomblé and witchcraft were found in his home, and standing before the Chief of Police of the Province, undertook according to this document to follow an honest way of life, no longer enticing slaves [to steal] and as a diviner making them grand promises of freedom, inducing them to do harm to others. And as he has undertaken this and has been released on condition of spontaneously leaving for the Coast of Africa if he violates this statement, signed on his behalf by Manoel de Abreu Contreiras along with the Chief of Police. Written by me, Candido Silveira de Faria

M. Abreu Contreiras[50]

chief had his office, rented for 60,000 reis per month in 1854, see the letter from Chief of Police André Chichorro da Gama to the president of the province, January 24, 1854, APEB, *Polícia*, maço 5714. Regarding the life, political, and juridical activities of Antonio Pereira Rebouças, see Keila Grinberg, O fiador dos brasileiros: cidadania, escravidão e direito civil no tempo de Antonio Pereira Rebouças (Rio de Janeiro: Civilização Brasileira, 2002).

[50] APEB, *Polícia. Termos de fiança*, 1862–67, vol. 5651, fl. 88v.

After that, Domingos was released. The priest was apparently a first offender, which must have helped his case. I have not found any evidence that he had been tried or officially investigated before that. There is, however, a record of his arrest in late May 1853, when there were persistent rumors of an African conspiracy in Salvador. At the time, Domingos was detained by a patrol to help with "police inquiries," according to a letter from the chief of police. Five other Africans were arrested the same day, but those arrests do not seem to have been related to his. There are no indications that he spent much time behind bars. The fact that he was not deported when many others were that year suggests he was not seen as a person of interest, although his arrest indicates that the police initially saw him as a suspect, probably because of his leadership role among other Africans – at that time he was the head of a manumission society and perhaps already a renowned diviner. Even so, his name was not sullied by a criminal record on that occasion, probably because they were looking for conspirators against the slaveocracy and not against Christian customs. Besides, on that occasion Domingos presented documents proving that he was a veteran of Bahia's war of independence, and a declaration from his parish police officials that he was a peace-loving, law-abiding, well-behaved, and hard-working African freedman, all of which counted in his favor.[51]

Domingos had another run-in with the police a few months before his arrest. At about 9 P.M. on April 13, 1862, there was a considerable commotion when a police patrol headed by the brother of a constable surrounded a house on his street. They were after a Crioulo named Bráulio for reasons I have been unable to ascertain. He lived in the basement of the house and his landlady had made a futile attempt to obstruct the police raid in order to protect him. When he tried to escape through the back door, Bráulio fell into a ravine, broke his leg, and was arrested and dragged off by his persecutors. He died of tetanus a few days later in the Santa Casa charity hospital because of the injuries sustained in his fall and his delicate handling by the police. Domingos was called in as a witness in the investigation of that incident, ordered by the police chief – a witness to how black people were treated in the capital of Bahia, even a man who was born in Brazil and protected by

---

[51] See two letters from Chief André Chichorro da Gama to the president of the province, May 27, 1853, APEB, *Polícia. Correspondência*, vol. 5712, fls. 194 and 195.

whites. I have not been able to find the proceedings of this investigation containing Domingos' statement.[52]

When he was arrested four months later for practicing Candomblé, Domingos had a clean record, and that must have helped him. His age may also have been an advantage, because even a hard-liner like Chief of Police João Henriques must have thought it harsh to subject an older man of about sixty-five to more humiliation. I also suspect that a white person extended protection on his behalf. The help may have come from Dr. Antonio José Pereira de Albuquerque, none other than the subdelegado of São Pedro parish (lest we forget, Domingos was arrested by his alternate, Pompílio Manuel de Castro). I have reached that conclusion because that same year, 1862, Albuquerque was the freedman's attorney in a case that had been dragging on for nearly two years. Albuquerque, a fifty-five-year-old bachelor who lived at No. 7, Rua de São Pedro, was an eminent citizen, the justice of the peace with the largest number of votes, and president of the Voter Qualification Board in his parish, where Domingos also lived. If he did intercede on the freedman's behalf, it was all done under the table, and none of it went into the police record. However, this was not a classic case of clientelism in which the freedman was a hapless dependent. After all, the subdelegado was Domingos' lawyer at the time, and even if Albuquerque had not been hired to defend him from the charge of witchcraft and receiving stolen goods, one case may have led to the other, unofficially at least.[53]

There is also Manoel de Abreu Contreiras to consider. He may just have signed Domingos Sodré's statement of obligation because he was within convenient reach of the police chief and his prisoner that day, but it is also possible that he was there at Albuquerque's request. Contreiras was connected to the subdelegado's family. In 1871, Albuquerque's brother, Francisco Pereira de Albuquerque, wrote Contreiras's will when he was too sick to do it himself. Contreiras was a civil servant, probably a clerk, who was sixty-two in 1862. A married man, he had no children and few possessions when he died in 1873, at which point all he owned was a run-down, two-bedroom house with a tiled roof and no ceilings in the Barra district. He lived there with a slave woman named Benedita.

---

[52] João Henriques to the subdelegado of São Pedro, April 28, 1862, APEB, *Polícia. Correspondência*, vol. 5754, fls. 114–114v.

[53] Albuquerque's age, marital status, and position in the qualification board are recorded in AMS, *Livro de qualificação de votantes. São Pedro*, 1863, vol. 596, fls. 1, 9v.

However, he was better off when he signed Domingos' "obligation," given the number of slave women he owned at the time: Laura, a new-born parda girl freed free of charge in 1868; her mother, Sisislanda (date and terms of manumission unknown); and Isidora, a twenty-year-old Crioula woman freed in 1870 for the price of 300,000 reis.[54]

DEPORTING AFRICANS

In the statement of obligation Domingos was forced to make, he was threatened with deportation. It was not unusual for Africans involved in Candomblé to be deported. However, they were also frequently protected by influential figures and managed to remain in Brazil. Take the case of Rufo, an African freedman who was active in the populous Sé parish, the very heart of secular and religious power in the capital city. In November 1855, the subdelegado of Sé sent a complaint to the police chief stating that Rufo was one of the leading figures in Candomblé in his jurisdiction, and for that very reason he had once been "arrested for deportation but was not because of the great efforts that were made" against it.[55] He did not specify whose efforts, but certainly one or more individuals with enough social prestige and political clout to pressure the government. Perhaps because he felt that he had immunity from police harassment, Rufo took it up a notch. Because of a police operation unleashed by fresh rumors of a slave revolt, the homes of many African Candomblé followers were raided and searched. During the raids, the police did not find any threats to public safety, but they did arrest a few people and "seized several objects of their religious beliefs, such as statuettes, symbols, dead dried toads, rattles, tambourines and some clothing, which items I intend to have burned," wrote the subdelegado.[56]

Rufo was accused of inciting other Africans to resist arrest and protest against the anti-Candomblé operation, which he considered an abuse of authority, and was once again wanted by the police for his audacity. Under pressure, Rufo decided to disappear, so he slept in different places every night, mostly the homes of Africans who belonged

[54] Probate records of Manoel de Abreu Contreiras, APEB, *Judiciária*, no. 05/2194/2663/26.

[55] Joaquim Antonio Moutinho to the chief of police, November 4, 1855, APEB, *Polícia*, maço 6231.

[56] Ibid.

to his network of friends and clients. The freedman seems to have lost his protection among the great and the good because he had gone too far, but he was still protected by the lower ranks of Bahian society.

Like Domingos, Rufo had a clientele of slaves, which worried the police chief at that time as much as it did João Henriques in 1862. The chief of police in 1855 sent the following orders to the subdelegado: "Take note of the African Rufo to inform me of the names of the slaves who seek him out."[57] This story illustrates that, no matter how much support they had, Candomblé leaders always walked a tightrope. They could be protected one day and pursued the next. Domingos knew that the threat of deportation was serious, as since 1835 he had seen other Africans deported en masse – possibly even Rufo himself. João Henriques' threat to deport him was not based on a recent policy.[58]

Could Domingos have known Grato, the African freedman? When he was about fifty years old, Grato had moved from the semirural Cabula district to escape the persecution of João de Azevedo Piapitinga, the subdelegado of the second district of Santo Antônio whom I introduced in Chapter 1 and now returns to the central stage. As we have seen, Piapitinga claimed that he had eliminated the candomblés in the district under his jurisdiction, but he was also suspected of covering for some of them. It would be more accurate to say that he protected some Candomblé devotees and persecuted others. He protected his clientele, which did not include Grato. The African continued practicing his old trade in his new home near the city center, but still in Piapitinga's territory. To do so, he had managed to find shelter in a room in the backyard of a mulatto woman named Carlota. Grato was arrested there for divining for two young creole women, according to Piapitinga's report. In fact, two Crioulas and a mulatto girl, probably his clients, were found there: Maria dos Passos, age twenty, Luiza da França, age thirty, and Maria Eufemia, who was just eleven years old. The investigation conducted on May 31, 1859, was completed by the subdelegado of the first district of Santo Antônio, following the police chief's orders.[59]

---

[57] Ibid.

[58] Regarding the deportation of African freedpersons after the 1835 revolt, see Reis, *Rebeliãoescrava no Brasil*, chap. 15.

[59] João de Azevedo Piapitinga to the chief of police, April 26, 1862, APEB, *Polícia. Subdelegados*, maço 6195; Miguel de Souza Requião to the chief of police, June 1, 1859, APEB, *Polícia*, maço 6232; A. L. de Figueiredo Rocha to the vice president of the province, June 1, 1859, APEB, *Polícia. Correspondência, 1859*, vol. 5730,

An article published in the *Jornal da Bahia* stated that Grato had
been arrested "in the middle of his fortune telling laboratory." It is an
interesting image and possibly accurate. The chief of police produced
a detailed report of the materials found there, and better yet, provided
information about Grato's lab experiments and what they were used
for: "In this hideout several drugs were also found, pots where roots,
leaves, reptiles etc. were cooked. Large lizards, bred and tame, among
the clothing in a chest; and others dead, cooked and reduced to concoctions which they say he sold to slaves to tame their masters and to the
ignorant so they could be lucky in business and love, making the biggest
profits he could pluck from the former and the latter."[60] These few words
provide abundant information. Grato was working in the same line of
activity as Domingos, which included divining and taming masters, but
also helped a broader clientele with their financial ventures and roman-
tic mishaps. Unfortunately, I have not found such a detailed description
of Domingos' practices. Despite the bigoted views of the police, it gives
us a glimpse of what was going on in Grato's workplace. However, we
are once again in the dark about the specific meanings of this cultural
universe, populated with poisonous and repulsive creatures, according
to the civilized sensibilities of the police officer, and we will repeatedly
find the same animals in the pots and pans of other people charged
with sorcery. Because they appear repeatedly in the records, along with
roots and leaves, I believe that these animals were a firmly established
element of an African culture of witchcraft-based resistance in Bahia
during that time.[61]

fl. 225; A. L. de Figueiredo Rocha to the vice president of the province, June 4,
1859, APEB, *Polícia. Correspondência, 1859*, vol. 5734, fl. 20v.

[60] A. L. de Figueiredo Rocha to the vice president of the province, June 4, 1859,
APEB, *Polícia. Correspondência expedida, 1859*, vol. 5734, fl. 20v.

[61] In Yoruba tradition, the chameleon is a sacred animal, Agemo, the messenger
sent by Olorun to see whether Obatalá had successfully created the world, but
I would not go so far as to use that myth to understand Grato's lizards, even
if he was Nagô. Regarding Agemo, see Harold Courlander, *Tales of Yoruba
Gods and Heroes* (New York: Crown Publishers, 1973), 19; Idowu, *Olodumare*,
19; G. J. Afolabi Ojo, *Yoruba Culture: A Geographical Analysis* (Ile Ife and
London: University of Ife and University of London Press, 1966), 194–195. The
Ifá verses selected by Abimbola that mention animals do not include Grato's
menagerie but do include the lion, monkey, dog, pigeon, vulture, and other
birds and insects. See Abimbola, *Ifá*, 195–231. The toad is also not included,
which is another animal frequently found in the establishments of African healers in Bahia. I will discuss the use of certain animals by Africans, supposedly

Just as with the Nagô Domingos later on, Grato's house was also found
to contain religious objects that are listed in the box below exactly as
they appeared in the original document. These items included artifacts
adorned with cowry shells and beads, which were also found loose or as
adornments for clothing and other ritual objects in Domingos' home.
Grato's clay jars, full of "mystical things," could well have been part of
the African divinities' shrines. And could the "plumes of hair" have
been tufts of the hair of a person for (or against) whom Grato was preparing a spell? Or was it a kind of fly whisk made from the tail hairs of
horses or other animals, the symbol of ritual power as well as an accou-
trement and emblem of hunter divinities like Oṣoosi?

Another house Grato owned in Cabula – which he had abandoned
to escape Piapitinga – was also searched and there "other objects of
witchcraft were seized," according to the chief of police, whose list
I have been unable to discover.[62]

Objects Found in the House of Grato in 1859

List of objects that were found in the room of the African Freedman
named Grato during the search, which are being taken to the Police
along with things of witchcraft in two large baskets

5 Straw beams [caps?]
3 Three gourds adorned with cowries
1 One belt of small sticks ... trimmed with cowries and coral
1 One large sack adorned [sic] with several things inside

---

as ingredients in magic spells, on another occasion. What place would the
toad have occupied, for example, in African belief systems? Or had Africans
learned to use the animal in healing processes in Bahia? Toads were part of
an Iberian tradition of "death spells," according to Francisco Bethencourt, *O
imaginário da magia: feiticeiras, adivinhos e curandeiros em Portugal no século XVI*
(São Paulo: Companhia das Letras, 2004), 126; see also, for the use of toads by
Africans and their descendants in Portugal, Calainho, *Metrópole das mandingas*,
103. In colonial Brazil, toads, snakes, lizards, and other animals were said to be
removed from the bodies of the sick during healing rituals and used as ingredients in magic potions. See Souza, *O Diabo*, 173–176, 239, for example.

[62] Miguel de Souza Requião to the chief of police, June 1, 1859, APEB, *Polícia*,
maço 6232; A. L. de Figueiredo Rocha to the vice president of the province,
June 1, 1859, APEB, *Polícia. Correspondência, 1859*, vol. 5730, fl. 225v.

1 One sheet of tin plate covered with an ox bladder, adorned with cowries
1 One sheet with several pieces of broken pots and plates
2 Two small bags with miscellaneous items
1 One iron rod decorated like a sunhat
1 One larger gourd covered with cowries
Several clay jars with mystical things inside some of them
1 One sugar bowl with large lizards inside the same
A large number of small trinkets adorned with cowries and beads
Several plumes of hair and other numerous small items
1 One chest of clothes belonging to the same black man, Grato

Bahia, 1st District of ... Santo Antonio Além do Carmo Parish, June 1, 1859. Miguel de Souza Requião

Subdelegado

Source: APEB, Polícia, maço 6232

In a letter to the interim president of the province, appellate court judge Messias de Leão, Chief of Police Figueiredo Rocha claimed that the more lenient approach to controlling Candomblé, with shorter detentions and verbal warnings, had not been an effective means of eradicating "certain superstition that has progressed on a large scale and whose results are not easily predicted." Like Henriques three years later, he accused people like Grato of taking advantage of his clients, as well as fueling "libidinous passions." And he added: "This is a very serious business and it is high time to use other methods, unlike those milder ones employed in vain so far." He concluded his missive by suggesting a forceful solution: "Therefore, this African freedman has been jailed and because his presence among the population of this city, which contains many slaves, is becoming highly pernicious, and many people tend to believe in these things, I ask Your Excellency, as a necessary measure, to deport him through the competent means."[63]

[63] Agostinho Luis de Figueiredo Rocha to the vice president of the province, June 4, 1859, APEB, Polícia. Correspondência expedida, 1859, vol. 5734, fls. 20v–21. Regarding Gonçalo's arrest, A. L. da Gama to the president of the province, December 24, 1859, APEB, Polícia. Correspondência expedida, vol. 5735, fl. 40.

Vice President Messias de Leão agreed with the police chief's idea and authorized the deportation two days later. The proceedings were brief. Five days after his imprisonment, Grato's fate had been decided. On July 11, 1859, a little more than a month after the raid on his house and his arrest by the police, the healer was deported to West Africa aboard the *D. Francisca*, a ship flying the Portuguese flag. The news made the pages of the *Jornal da Bahia*, perhaps the most important newspaper in circulation at the time. The factor of the *D. Francisca* was a well-known slave trader – possibly retired at that point – and a wealthy philanthropist named Joaquim Pereira Marinho. The government paid him 50,000 reis to transport the African freedman across the Atlantic. It would have been ironic if Grato had arrived in Bahia as a slave aboard one of Marinho's ships.[64]

Just when it seemed that a hard-line policy was in place, a discordant voice was heard in the presidential palace. If Messias de Leão had readily agreed to Grato's expulsion from the country, a year later the same measure would not be well received by the new president of the province, Antonio da Costa Pinto, a native of Minas Gerais, in another case recommended by his chief of police, Agostinho Luís da Gama. Using arguments similar to those employed against Grato, Chief Gama wanted to deport Gonçalo Paraíso, an African freedman, more than forty years old, arrested in Paço parish on Christmas Eve 1859. According to the police chief, in the African's possession

there were found various ingredients and concoctions that he gave to ignorant people who sought him out as a healer, and whom he abused, making them suffer when they did not accede to his lustful demands, and not having a safe base, and proof to bring about an official suit against such a dangerous African, whom the *vox*

[64] Manoel Messias de Leão to the chief of police, June 6, 1859, APEB, *Polícia. Correspondência recebida da presidência da província*, maço 6152; Agostinho Luis de Figueiredo Rocha, to the vice president of the province, July 12, 1859, APEB, *Polícia. Correspondência expedida, 1859*, vol. 5734, fl. 37v; A. L. da Gama to the president of the province, December 31, 1859, APEB, *Polícia*, maço 3139-18; *Jornal da Bahia* cited in Verger, *Flux et reflux*, 536. Verger probably noted down the wrong date for the news report: January 17 (when it should have been July) 1859. Regarding the slave trader who took Grato back to Africa, see Cristiana F. Lyrio Ximenes, "Joaquim Pereira Marinho: perfil de um contrabandista de escravos na Bahia, 1828–1887," MA thesis, Universidade Federal da Bahia, 1999.

populi also accuses of using those medicines to take some people to
the grave, I will ask Your Excellency for the proper authorization
to deport him to one of the ports in the Coast of Africa.[65]

To Agostinho Luis da Gama's surprise, President Antonio da Costa
Pinto – a man with a solid legal background who had risen to the post
of judge in the Court of Appeals of Rio de Janeiro – replied to his letter
as follows, and somewhat curtly at that: "it has already been verbally
decided that the response is that [according to] art. 1 of Law no. 9 [of
May 13, 1835] deportation can only be used in cases of insurrection."[66]
Costa Pinto was referring to the law passed in the wake of the Revolt
of the Malês, which called for the expulsion of African freedpersons
suspected of involvement in slave insurrections. At least three Africans
were deported on the basis of that law in 1854 as a result of the slave
revolt scare of the previous year. But like Grato, the freedman Gonçalo
Paraíso was not rebelling against society. Actually, Grato's deportation
had been highly irregular, according to the president and former judge's
reasoning. Besides Grato and Rufo, whose stories we have just seen,
other Africans involved in Candomblé had already been deported, but
I have not yet been able to identify them.[67]

However, the president of the province failed to enforce his objec-
tion to Gonçalo Paraíso's banishment. Chief Agostinho Luis da Gama

[65] Agostinho Luis da Gama to the president of the province, July 20, 1860, APEB,
Polícia, maço 2961.

[66] Ibid. The president's letter is dated August 10, 1860. The argument about the
difficulty with prosecuting crimes that could not be proven, such as poisoning, as
well as the deportation of "sorcerers" suspected of committing such crimes, were
old stories dating from at least the seventeenth century. In 1671, the Salvador
City Council wrote to the king in Portugal that, because of the frequent poisoning of slaves in the Recôncavo, individuals who were publicly known as sorcerers should be exiled. See Salvador City Council to the king of Portugal, August
14, 1671, in Carlos Ott, *Formação étnica da cidade do Salvador* (Salvador: Manú,
1955), II, 102–103.

[67] According to Law no. 9, "Art 1. The Government is authorized to remove from
the Province, as soon as possible, and even at the cost of the Public Treasury,
any freed Africans of either sex who are suspected of fomenting in some fashion
a slave insurrection; and their imprisonment may be ordered until they can be
re-exported." See *Colleção de Leis e Resoluções da Assembléia Legislativa da Bahia
sancionadas e publicadas nos annos de 1835 a 1838*, vol. 1, p. 22. The use of the
verb *re-export* indicates that freed Africans were still treated or at least represented as slaves. Regarding Costa Pinto's career, see Wildberger, *Os presidentes*,
421–428.

resigned five days after the president issued his decision, claiming that a serious illness prevented him from being exposed to sunlight, dew, and humidity, requiring "complete repose."[68] Of course, the gullible might suppose that Gonçalo Paraíso had cast a spell on the chief of police. However, his replacement, José Pereira da Silva Moraes, was even more committed to the idea of banishing African witchdoctors. He seems to have devised a formula for getting around the law as the president recalled it. Moraes made sure that the decision about Paraíso's deportation was removed from the province's jurisdiction to that of the imperial government, specifically the ministry of justice. The police chief of Bahia wrote to Minister João Lustosa Paranaguá, providing a detailed account of Gonçalo Paraíso's case one month after he had replaced the former chief.

Most of Moraes' missive to Paranaguá was a copy of his predecessor's letter to the interim president of the province requesting authorization to deport Grato. The freedman Gonçalo Paraíso was accused of abusing the good faith of his clients, who in exchange for large sums of money were promised "health, mettle, a sound mind and life itself." He wrote that Paraíso had been arrested with "strange and suspicious objects ... various liquids and medications which by their state of fermentation were becoming poisonous, according to the doctors," and that it was "public knowledge" that the African was a sorcerer who had "destroyed some victims with his ambition, lust," and so on. The police chief was concerned about Bahia's image, because, according to him, the activities of people like this were "an indictment against our civilization" – which was well represented by the physicians who had analyzed Paraíso's medicines – and suggested the harshest means of punishment "ever employed here." He concluded by requesting the healer's expulsion to a West African port.[69]

Minister Paranaguá approved Chief Moraes' suggestion and signed an order to deport Paraíso in October 1860. On February 23 of the following year, we find Moraes writing to the harbor master, asking him

---

[68] A. L. da Gama to the president of the province, August 15, 1860, and José Pereira da Silva Moraes to the president of the province, August 21, 1860, APEB, *Polícia. Correspondência expedida*, vol. 5739, fls. 344–344v, 355, respectively.

[69] João Lustosa de C. Paranaguá to the president of the province, Rio de Janeiro, October 22, 1860, APEB, *Correspondência recebida*, maço 899; José Pereira da Silva Moraes to the minister of justice, September 20, 1860, APEB, *Polícia. Correspondência expedida*, vol. 5738, fls. 380v–381.

to provide a longboat to put Gonçalo Paraíso aboard the Portuguese two-masted tender *Paquete Africano*, which would take him back to Africa "as authorized by the Imperial Government," the police chief wrote triumphantly. The government paid 80,000 reis to deport the African healer, 60 percent more than the cost of Grato's voyage.[70]

This episode created a legal precedent. With the involvement of the imperial government, local authorities who wanted to take a hard line against so-called African witchcraft in Bahia had now found a new, safe strategy. From that time on, the cogs of power set up to deport Gonçalo Paraíso would be used against other African freedmen and -women accused of sorcery. The proceedings took more time, but they were politically and judicially sound – the punishment of witchcraft was elevated to a national dimension. In Paraíso's case, more than a year had elapsed between his arrest on Christmas Eve, 1859, and his deportation in early 1861. In the meantime, because he could not ply his trade in prison, Gonçalo Paraíso had to free one of his slaves, Isabel, of the Nagô nation, for the price of 500,000 reis, without failing to claim that this gesture was due to her good services.[71]

President Antonio da Costa Pinto, a member of the Liberal Party, governed the province between late April 1860 and early June 1861, and left his post after a conservative cabinet was formed in Rio de Janeiro that changed the distribution of provincial power in Brazil. In his last months in office, the Liberal politician had to deal with another request for deportation that he viewed with considerable unease. The victim in this case was to be a freedwoman, Constança do Nascimento, again of the Nagô nation, and the request for her deportation came from a powerful planter in the Recôncavo, João de Araújo Argollo Gomes Ferrão. In a letter that he sent from his plantation, Engenho de Baixo, to the chief of police, José Pereira da Silva Moraes, he claimed that Constança, "using candomblés and all of the means which those idolaters employ," had already caused the deaths of several people in that region, including "his sugar master and slave of high price and merit." Other slaves of less value and esteem had also been killed or "rendered useless" in mind and body once Constança cast her spells. She was accused of poisoning her

[70] José Pereira da Silva Moraes to the harbor master, February 23, 1861, APEB, *Polícia. Correspondência expedida*, vol. 5742, fl. 168; José Pereira da Silva Moraes to the president of the province, July 5, 1861, APEB, *Polícia. Correspondência expedida*, vol. 5747, fls. 101–101v.
[71] "Alforria de Isabel, Nagô," APEB, *LNT*, vol. 351, fl. 82v.

own husband, another slave of Argollo Ferrão, so she could more freely indulge her "excessive lust." "Enormous toads which she treated like inseparable companions, objects of sorcery, [and] liquids, which well denote their origin from poisonous herbs," were found in her home. Once again, along with the deadly arsenal of sorcery, the police narrative pushes the healer toward the animal kingdom, stressing, besides an uncontrolled sex drive, her close relationship with creatures that were apparently a trademark for African healers. Argollo Ferrão concluded by demanding that an "effective measure such as deportation" be taken against her, because her presence, "in addition to demoralizing the slaves [was] a constant danger for those who incur her hatred and dangerous instincts."[72] These words probably reflect the master's concern for his own health, as well as the loss of his property and the corruption of his slaves. Of course, there was no way to prove any of these accusations. Nor was Constança a social rebel who could be charged under the anti-insurrectionary law of 1835.

Costa Pinto seems to have been put in a tough spot by this complaint, made by a member of the Argollo Ferrão family, who not only wrote to the chief of police of the province but sought him out in person to underscore his accusations against Constança and requested – possibly demanded – her deportation. The president was informed of all this and asked the police chief for a more detailed explanation. José Pereira Moraes replied in a letter whose preliminary arguments again could have been a copy of his predecessor's justification for expelling Grato from the country. Then, Moraes cited the version of the case presented to him by Argollo Ferrão, whom he described as a "wealthy citizen, honest, reputable, and who served for many years as the subdelegado

[72] João de Araújo Argollo Ferrão to the chief of police, January 31, 1861, APEB, *Polícia (1860–1861)*, maço 6328. Cases of slaves being poisoned by other enslaved or freed "sorcerers" had been frequent in Brazil since colonial times. See, for example, Nogueira, "Doenças, feitiços e curas"; and Couceiro, "Acusações de feitiçaria." I have mentioned that Costa Pinto belonged to the Liberal Party, but there is no indication that political affiliation had any influence on the policy of repression or tolerance of Candomblé, with the possible exception of Francisco Gonçalves Martins, the Viscount de São Lourenço, a major conservative leader and twice president of the province of Bahia (1848–1852 and 1868–1871), who was known for his anti-African measures on several fronts. See Silveira, *O candomblé da Barroquinha*, 269–270. In fact, *O Alabama*, which was a liberal publication, accused the conservatives of an alliance with Candomblé, a charge that merits more careful investigation.

of the 2nd District of this City." The chief of police, a native of Bahia, wanted to make the president from Minas Gerais understand the local social pecking order, of which he seemed to be unaware. Chief Moraes attached a letter the planter had sent him about the freedwoman.

President Costa Pinto may have taken offense, not liking to be pressured, and three days later he ordered the police chief to investigate the complaint further to find evidence against Constança. The reply he received was that it was precisely because the charges could not be proven in court that the chief had recommended the "extraordinary measure" of deportation. A clearly vexed Costa Pinto sent the request for the African woman's deportation to the ministry of justice in Rio de Janeiro on February 21. Having washed his hands of the matter, he merely wrote to the minister that "taking into consideration the above mentioned correspondence [from the chief of police], please [resolve] this as you think best."[73]

A few days later, the police chief had to explain the situation to the man who deported Grato, Messias de Leão, who was now the president of the Court of Appeals in Bahia, because Constança had submitted a petition of *habeas corpus*. Moraes repeated Argollo Ferrão's story once again, this time to Leão, and took the opportunity to add that the impunity of "those people" who practiced Candomblé resulted from the "misguided protection raised in their favor." He seemed to be referring to his subordinate, the subdelegado of Conceição da Praia parish, who had forwarded the African woman's *habeas corpus* petition to the court. But he may also have had someone else in mind, his superior, President Costa Pinto himself.[74]

Given the barriers raised against her in Bahia, the undaunted Constança decided to appeal directly to the minister of justice, who asked Costa Pinto to give his opinion on her alleged innocence. I have not yet found the freedwoman's petition, but there are indications

[73] José Pereira da Silva Moraes to the president of the province, February 11 and 15, 1861, APEB, *Polícia. Correspondência*, vol. 5744, fls. 270–271, 279v–280v; Antonio da Costa Pinto to the chief of police, February 14, 1861, APEB, *Presidente da província. Registro de correspondência expedida*, vol. 1808, fl. 178v; Antonio da Costa Pinto to the minister of justice, February 21, 1861, APEB, *Presidente da província. Registro de correspondência expedida*, vol. 699, fl. 98–98v.

[74] José Pereira da Silva Moraes to the subdelegado of Conceição da Praia parish, March 2, 1861, APEB, *Polícia. Correspondência*, vol. 5741, fl. 246v; José Pereira da Silva Moraes to the president of the Court of Appeals, March 4, 1861, APEB, *Polícia. Correspondência*, vol. 5742, fls. 179v–180v.

that she accused Argollo Ferrão of lying and seems to have had some help with her defense from the subdelegado of Conceição da Praia. This is clear in yet another letter from the police chief to the president, who had sent him the minister's letter. Moraes replied that "what the African woman Constança alleges is a web of falsehood and slander against the serious and circumspect character of said Gentleman [Argollo Ferrão], whose victim she claims to be in order to delude the police and go unpunished for her crimes, which are always difficult to prove due to the methods she and those of her ilk nearly always commit them." The chief of police also said he had dressed down the subdelegado who helped her, as he had overstepped his authority in a matter "that was already within my jurisdiction." Liberal Party member Costa Pinto finally stopped insisting on a less extreme legal alternative and sent the "true facts" to Rio de Janeiro according to the police chief's version. The imperial government sent back the final deportation order, signed by Justice Minister Francisco Sayão Lobato, on May 25, 1861.[75]

The hard-line doctrine against Candomblé did not sit easy with the highest ranks of power in the province of Bahia, but in the cases of Gonçalo Paraíso and Constança Nascimento, it prevailed nonetheless. Sometimes, the stance toward Candomblé did not just vary from one authority to another, but the same authority was inconsistent in the measures taken. Police Chief José Pereira Moraes himself would take a tougher stand as time went on. Going back to the beginning of this chapter, the reader may recall that he released two African freedwomen and five slave women arrested at a candomblé, and merely instructed the subdelegado to let them off with a warning to stop "disturbing the peace." However, he would take a different line altogether with Gonçalo and Constança.

---

[75] Justice Minister Francisco de Paula de Negreiros Sayão Lobato to the president of the province of Bahia, Rio de Janeiro, April 10 and May 25, 1861, APEB, Ministério. Avisos do Ministério da Justiça, maço 900; José Pereira da Silva Moraes to the president of the province, May 6, 1861, APEB, Polícia. Correspondência, vol. 5747, fls. 14–15v; Antonio da Costa Pinto to the minister of justice, May 16, 1861, APEB, Presidência da Província. Correspondência, vol. 704, fl. 122. Moraes' behavior probably reflected a deep-rooted anti-African sentiment. Less than a month after Constança's deportation, he wrote that free Africans should all be deported at once, as recommended by the 1850 law that abolished the slave trade. José Pereira da Silva Moraes to the president of the province, July 17, 1861, APEB, Polícia. Correspondência, vol. 5747, fl. 119.

Figure 33. Vice President Manoel Messias de Leão (1799–1878), who deported Grato.

On June 26, 1861, Constança Nascimento was put aboard the *Novo Elizeo*, again a ship flying the Portuguese flag that was bound for West Africa. On that occasion, the police chief described her as follows: "Nagô, over 50 years old, average height and weight, black skin, with the marks of her homeland on her face, and on the left arm, perfect teeth, with considerably painted hair," meaning that it was streaked with gray.[76] The facial markings represented her original ethnic affiliation, and those on her arm probably designated her religious identity, for such scars were usually made during initiation rites. Eighty thousand reis were paid to transport the Nagô healer, the same amount paid for Gonçalo

[76] José Pereira da Silva Moraes to the warden of the Aljube prison, June 25, 1861, APEB, vol. 5745, fl. 117v.

Figure 34. President Antonio da Costa Pinto (1802–1880), who tried to prevent the deportation of Gonçalo Paraíso and Constança Pereira.

Paraíso's passage. Another Leão released this payment, the new president, Joaquim Antão Fernandes Leão. The money came from a secret Justice Ministry fund destined to combat the transatlantic slave trade – no less ironic than as being deported on a slave ship as Grato had been.[77]

Justifying Constança's expulsion to President Antônio da Costa Pinto, Chief José Pereira da Silva Moraes argued that it was necessary "more frequently to set an example, and deport similar witches and fortunetellers," underlining the targets of his wrath with his own hand.[78]

[77] José Pereira da Silva Moraes to the harbor master, June 25, 1861, APEB, *Polícia*, vol. 5742, fl. 321; Joaquim Antão F. Leão to the chief of police, March 19 and 21, 1862, APEB, *Polícia, correspondência recebida da presidência da província*, maço 6152.

[78] José Pereira da Silva Moraes to the president of the province, February 11, 1861, APEB, *Polícia. Correspondência*, vol. 5744, fls. 270v.

These words were written a year and a half before Domingos' imprisonment, and the chief of police who ordered his arrest, João Henriques,
in preparation for his new job, had certainly read this and other reports
from his predecessors regarding the deportation of alleged African sorcerers. That was how he got the idea of forcing Domingos Sodré to forswear Candomblé or leave the country. Did the priest faithfully comply
with the "obligation" imposed on him by the police chief to avoid being
deported? I would like to think he did not. There are signs in the pages
of O Alabama that he was active in the sphere of African beliefs at a
later date, as we have seen. Domingos may have become more discreet,
however, and stopped holding gatherings of African slaves and freedpersons at his home for divination sessions and other rituals, and may
even have avoided keeping a large amount of religious paraphernalia
there. But he could hardly resist the temptation to participate in and
contribute to African religious celebrations that took place around the
city, including his own neighborhood.

CANDOMBLÉ LIVES ON

While the campaign of repression continued, the drums of Candomblé
kept beating, and the temples kept recruiting more and more followers. Less than a month after Domingos' arrest, Maria Francisca da
Conceição, age twenty-six, a creole washerwoman; Luiza Marques de
Araújo, age twenty, a cabra seamstress, free and unmarried; and Anna
Maria de Jesus, age twenty-nine, a cabra seamstress, also free and unmarried, were arrested at a candomblé in the densely urban Santana parish.
None of them were African, none of them were tramps, and just one of
them was Brazilian black woman or crioula. Far and wide, Candomblé
was expanding beyond African borders. A few days later, Chief João
Henriques would send Subdelegado Pompílio de Castro to investigate a complaint that, in an alley near Domingos' house, there was a
place where "slaves and people of color gather and form Candomblé
and other immoralities."[79] In the same article published in 1869, which
complained about African tenements on Rua do Sodré and called them
quilombos, O Alabama stated that they "are constantly seething with
drums, dancing and shouting that go on all night." The newspaper

[79] Map of the House of Correction prison, August 17, 1862, APEB, Prisão.
Relação de presos, maço 6286. Chief Henriques to the subdelegado of São Pedro,
September 11, 1862, APEB, Polícia. Correspondência, vol. 5754, fls. 266v–267.

called attention to the "nauseating stench" of the animals sacrificed in those houses in honor of the divinities and ancestors. The reasons for those festivities varied: sometimes a funeral rite was being celebrated for a Candomblé priestess; sometimes the drumming sessions were held for a "major service"; or the drums were beaten "on the pretext, according to them [the Africans], of the Saint having gone to war, or because he had returned from war," probably a reference to the *Olorogun*, as warlords were called in Yorubaland, but in this case signifying a ritual that simulates a battle between devotees of Ṣàngọ́ and Obatalá, which sometimes marks the end of the ritual calendar after Lent. (Another explanation may be that a very real war was being fought in Paraguay, and hundreds of black soldiers were sent there from Bahia.) A few days later, *O Alabama* proclaimed: "These days the candomblés are at their height."[80] These bustling areas of the black city called quilombos on more than one occasion in *O Alabama* were also Candomblé temples – which corroborates the prevailing connotation at the time among officials and slaveholders that the African religion was an instrument of slave resistance.[81]

Opposition to slavery was on the prowl at other addresses in that neighborhood, on Rua do Sodré, in fact. Those African festivals were contemporary with literary soirees that Castro Alves started organizing at Sodré manor toward the end of that same year, 1869, after his return from São Paulo – the reader may remember that his family home had once housed Domingos' master's family.[82] The background music for the abolitionist poet's meetings was provided by African drums accused of beating for eight straight days. For some time, at least, the local residents, including the Alves family, seemed to tolerate those *batuques*

---

[80] *O Alabama*, May 6 and 13, 1869. The *Olorogun* ritual was suggested to me by Luis Nicolau Parés, personal communication, October 3, 2007. Regarding the black Bahian contribution to the Paraguay War, see Graden, *From Slavery to Freedom*, 56–61. Silva, *The Prince of the People* tells the story of some of those black Bahians. Many slaves actually *escaped* to the front lines to gain their freedom. See Hendrik Kraay, "'Ao abrigo da farda': o exército brasileiro e os escravos fugidos, 1800–1888," *Afro-Ásia*, no. 17 (1996): 29–56.

[81] In its August 24, 1869 issue, *O Alabama* also refers to a Candomblé terreiro as a quilombo. During the colonial period, the association between calundu and quilombo was made by the poet Gregório de Mattos and other colonials. See Roger Bastide, *As religiões africanas no Brasil* (São Paulo: Pioneira/Edusp, 1971), vol. I: 193; Souza, *O Diabo*, 266.

[82] Mattos, "A Bahia de Castro Alves," 283.

quite well, which would explain why they thrived to the point that they offended the ears and sensitivities of newspapermen.

But Candomblé was not just an instrument of slave, or more broadly speaking, African resistance. In his April circular letter to the subdelegados of Salvador Chief João Henriques wrote he was aware that "even people of a certain status go to gatherings" of Candomblé adepts.[83] As we have seen, some of Henriques' predecessors had also reached the same conclusion, and the press agreed wholeheartedly. Those "people of a certain status" not only tolerated the allegedly disorderly conduct of Candomblé devotees but were active participants in it. This was the case with Domingos Sodré's divination and healing business. In his report to the chief of police, subdelegado Pompílio Manoel de Castro focused his attack on the diviner's suspicious connections in the world of black slaves, but failed to mention that he also enjoyed good relations with the world of the free and whites. The *Diário da Bahia* took it upon itself to publish an accusation, complete with exclamation points, that the sessions at Domingos' home were not only frequented by African slaves but "it is said that tie-wearing and clean (!!) people attended them."[84] It goes without saying that the newspaper was referring to whites, defined in its prejudiced pages as the only people in the city of Bahia who were well-dressed and washed. I do not know if Domingos' lawyer, Mr. Albuquerque, was one of those people, but it was not uncommon for respectable whites to employ the services of African priests for numerous purposes, particularly spells related to classic human needs – health, love, money – as well as, in the second half of the nineteenth century, police investigations and party politics.

The presence and participation of whites in Candomblé, which was first described in the scholarly literature in the 1890s by Nina Rodrigues and in a fictional work by Xavier Marques, already had a long history in the province of Bahia.[85] *O Alabama* and other newspapers had already

---

[83] Circular letter from the chief of police to the subdelegados of Salvador, April 24, 1862, APEB, *Correspondência*, vol. 5754, fl. 111.

[84] *Diário da Bahia*, July 28, 1862. The symbols of power and prestige of the affluent people who frequented candomblés changed over time: in 1926, a high priest said to a newspaper that his temple received "people with cars." See Lühning, "'Acabe com este santo,'" 202.

[85] See Nina Rodrigues, *O animismo fetichista dos negros bahianos* (Rio de Janeiro: Civilização Brasileira, 1935 [orig. 1896]), 70–71, 91–97, 186–187, 194; Xavier Marques, *O feiticeiro* (São Paulo: GRD; Brasília: INL, 1975). This book

harped on that subject in the 1860s and 1870s. Even the militant Catholic press had noticed this phenomenon since the 1850s at the very least. That year, *O Noticiador Catholico* published an article by a certain Father Mariano that called for "forceful and uninterrupted police action" to uproot "witchcraft among us," and gave a detailed description of what it was all about:

> [R]ight here in the middle of our city, where nobody will say that enlightenment and knowledge have not spread, you see men running to the houses of sorcerers, so they can tell if the disease they are suffering is an <u>evil spell</u>, with which remedy they will be cured, if the child about to be born will be a boy or a girl, and other such foolishness, which is annoying even to enumerate: no wonder when, right here, you see women who go behind their husbands' backs to consult with sorcerers to ask them if their husbands have other loves, maintain other ties, often being involved in outrageous practices, and in all cases, opening their purses to such people.
>
> There are people who in fact do not belong to the lowest ranks of society who believe in such wretched things, and among the people, that is, the lower class of society, then who can unpersuade [*sic*] them of the power of a spell and a sorcerer.[86]

Having established the broad social base of belief in sorcery, Father Mariano goes on to describe the sorcerer as a caricature: "He is almost always some African who, being old and frail and good for nothing else, resorts to certain tricks and always makes them work to his advantage, exploiting the belief in magic spells that – why, no one knows – is widespread among the populace."[87]

---

was originally published in 1897 as *Boto & Cia*. A second, expanded edition appeared in 1922. I discuss the penetration of Candomblé in nineteenth-century Bahian society in "Sacerdotes, seguidores e clientes." The same phenomenon was found in Rio de Janeiro at the turn of the twentieth century as described by João do Rio, *As religiões do Rio*, esp. 34–41, where he writes the following about the city's residents: "Magic is our vice, our joy, degeneracy" (p. 35). For Rio, see also Sampaio, *Juca Rosa*.

[86] *O Noticiador Catholico*, II: 89 (1850): 365. The expression "evil spell" ("*coisa feita*") is underlined in the original.

[87] Ibid.

Even if they did not regularly profess the African religion or worship its divinities as they venerated Catholic saints, many whites,
including Catholic clerics, believed in the mystic power, the healing,
divinatory, and propitiating powers, of Candomblé specialists, who
were not always old black men. These whites – "why, no one knows,"
as Father Mariano lamented – simply believed in African witchcraft
and healing procedures. Poet Gregório de Mattos wrote about this in
the seventeenth century, and ever since that belief had grown among
the "well-dressed and washed," as the police chief who persecuted
Grato and the one who went after Domingos clearly understood.[88]
In 1854, in a house next door to the imposing Desterro Convent, of
the Poor Clares, a female African healer had a clientele made up of
large numbers of blacks from overseas as well as local whites. When
the subdelegado of Santana parish searched her house, "a white man
was found in [one] of the rooms, sick, and a Lady who said she was
his wife, and in the bedroom of that black woman (who was elderly),
a figure adorned with feathers, spattered with blood and surrounded
by some food." It must have been an African altar. The healer got off
with a warning from the official and the threat of imprisonment if
she continued conducting healing practices in her home.[89] In 1868,
O Alabama published a list of the typical attendees at a candomblé
house in Domingos' parish, including "married women, who go there
to find specific [ingredients] to ensure that their husbands do not overlook their conjugal duties; slaves who ask for ingredients to soften the
spirit of their masters; women seeking happiness and even merchants
wanting to ensure that their business goes well!"[90]
Candomblé was black territory, at the time still intensely African,
but a place where people from all classes and ethnic backgrounds
moved about and even mingled, from masters to slaves, particularly
in the numerous houses of diviners-and-healers who lived in the more
settled urban area of Salvador. Masters could even use Candomblé
in the domestic war against their slaves. I will repeat the newspaper
excerpt I have quoted before, about a woman who fell ill, and when

---

[88] On this subject in colonial Brazil, see Souza, O Diabo, 263–269, and passim;
and Sweet, Recreating África, passim; and by the same author, Domingos Álvares,
passim.

[89] José Eleutério Rocha to the chief of police, April 24, 1854, in Harding, Refuge in
Thunder, 194.

[90] O Alabama, September 2, 1868. See also Graden, From Slavery to Freedom, 116.

her husband consulted a diviner, he "cast his cowries and informed her that the lady was bewitched, and that [her] slave woman had cast the spell, and that it would be deadly if it were not circumvented without delay."[91] By doing so, the diviner got the slave woman into considerable trouble. A similar narrative surrounded the charge of witchcraft brought against Libânio José de Almeida as seen in Chapter 1, who was also said to have accused a slave woman of attacking her mistress with witchcraft.

In Bahia at that time, some whites even joined Candomblé temples as protectors, mediums, and leaders. Domingos Miguel, a Portuguese, was arrested a week after Grato's imprisonment, together with his common-law wife, a parda woman named Maria Umbelina, for holding gatherings "with dances and objects of witchcraft." He, too, was a foreigner, but because he was European, the chief of police did not even think of deporting him. There was also a white Brazilian high priestess, Maria do Couto, charged in 1873 of being the "owner or director" of a "large Candomblé" in Saboeiro, a good distance from the city center, unlike the Portuguese man's candomblé.[92]

Therefore it is not surprising that white people frequented Domingos Sodré's home. Although he provided most of his services to slaves who were at odds with their masters, he may have worked as a diviner and healer for whites as well. The well-dressed and washed folks who were said to consult him must have taken all sorts of problems to his divination table, possibly even seeking solutions for trouble with their slaves. Many times, as we have seen, slaveholders also needed help to "break" slaves whom not even the police could keep in line. The priest may even have understood problems of that nature, although he was an African and sympathized with his enslaved clients, most of whom were fellow Africans. However, his work may have followed the typical logic of a diviner and healer, handling clients on a case-by-case basis. After all, he was a slaveholder himself, as were some of his colleagues and friends. I will tell that part of his story later on. However, his involvement with the "well-dressed and washed" should be seen as no small achievement in a society that marginalized

---

[91] *O Alabama*, January 12, 1864.

[92] A. L. de Figueiredo Rocha to the vice president of the province, July 7, 1859, APEB, *Polícia. Correspondência, 1859*, fl. 258v (quotation); Reis, "Sacerdotes, seguidores e clientes," 68.

his beliefs as well as people of his background. By helping "civilized" people solve their problems, Domingos was, in a way, enslaving their minds to African values.

Nonetheless, it was not as a master or as a collaborator with slave-holders that Domingos Sodré was arrested in July 1862. His activities were seen as fostering slave resistance, which was harmful to the slave economy and seigniorial hegemony, and disturbing to the civilized order that the educated elite desired to cultivate on Bahian soil.

CHAPTER FIVE

WITCHCRAFT AND MANUMISSION

At the time of his arrest, Domingos Sodré was involved in a lawsuit against Elias Francisco de Seixas, an African freedman. Elias had been accused of murdering another African freedman and appropriating the money from a manumission society headed by Domingos. About seventy-four years old in 1862, Elias fathered four children born in Brazil, had a farm in the outskirts of Salvador, and owned several slaves. He lived in Mata Escura, within the boundaries of the second district of Santo Antônio parish, whose subdelegado was João de Azevedo Piapitinga, a name that is already familiar to us. Now we will get to know Elias better, as he was another significant figure in Domingos' life. Their dispute sheds light on several aspects of African life in Bahia, which included both solidarity and conflict within the group, the formation of clienteles around powerful characters, the use by Africans of the local justice system in conjunction with their own, and once again, it is another angle for observing the passage from slavery to freedom and Domingo's role in that process.

ELIAS FRANCISCO SEIXAS

Elias was the former slave of Maria Dorothea da Silveira Seixas. According to the terms of her will and testament, she had freed him upon her death on February 21, 1838, in Itapoã, a fishing village several miles north of Salvador, where she had taken refuge from a city besieged by the legal forces that crushed the Sabinada, a liberal revolt against the central government based in Rio de Janeiro, in a bloodbath.[1] That

---

[1] Souza, A *Sabinada*, 100–106.

lady had been widowed twice from her marriages to Captain Álvaro
Sanches de Brito and Comendador (an honorary imperial title) José
Venâncio de Seixas. Like Domingos, the freedman had been the slave
of powerful masters. Elias took his surname from his last mistress, sometimes adding his deceased master's middle name, Venâncio, as he did in
at least three notarized documents. Childless and with no direct heirs,
the widow Maria Dorothea had already freed several slave women and
dependents in her lifetime to reward their services, and their manumission was reiterated in her will. To those freedwomen and their children,
she bequeathed lifetime usufruct of a house, some money, jewels, and
even a slave. She also freed Elias before writing her will, on condition
that he paid her 40,000 reis, but the widow later changed her mind,
writing in a codicil: "The slave Elias, whom I had freed on condition of
paying 40,000 reis, is henceforth free, and that clause is null and void."[2]
He was the only male slave that Maria Dorothea manumitted unconditionally and without pay, which she must undoubtedly have done to
reward his loyalty and good service. The African freedman would have
been about fifty at the time.

Elias, who was a Nagô, prospered after receiving his manumission.
There are records since the early 1840s that he conducted various
transactions involving the purchase and sale of property. In 1842,
just four years after he gained his freedom, he purchased a woman
from the Tapa nation named Felicidade for 400,000 reis. She was a
laundress who did washing and ironing. The following year, he purchased a Nagô woman named Leopoldina for 200,000 reis.[3] By the
end of the decade, he possessed at least two more women, Benvinda,
a Nagô, and Delfina, whose African nation is unknown. A few years
later, he owned another slave named Ludovina, also a Nagô woman.
He also had dependents. Elias and his wife, Maria da Luz, freed one of
Delfina's children in October 1849. Aniceto, a creole, was four when
he received his freedom "due to the great love we have for him, having raised him as our own child." Elias and Maria da Luz, who were

---

[2]   APEB, *LRT*, vol. 25, fl. 164–170 (quotation on p. 168).
[3]   "Escritura de venda, paga, e quitação que faz Ignácio Manoel da Porciúncula a
      Elias de Seixas, de uma escrava de Nação Tapa por nome Felicidade, pela quan-
      tia de quatrocentos mil reis," APEB, *LNT*, vol. 277, fl. 151v–152; "Escritura de
      venda, paga, e quitação que faz Dona Joanna Maria de Jesus, ao Africano liberto
      Elias de Seixas, de uma escrava de nome Leopoldina, de Nação Nagou, pela
      quantia de Rs 200$000," APEB, *LNT*, vol. 278, fls. 86v–87.

childless, imposed the condition that the boy remain with them until they both died.[4]

Elias Seixas and Maria da Luz, an African freedwoman, were married in September 1840, two years after his manumission, in the parish church of Santana, where they probably lived by that time. Elias recruited prestigious witnesses for his marriage, members of his former mistress Maria Dorothea's family. They included Ignácio Carlos Freire de Carvalho, a lawyer and future judge who lived in São Pedro parish, and Second Lieutenant Domingos José Freire de Carvalho, the future commander general of the provincial police force, one of the officers responsible for the raid that led to Domingos Sodré's arrest in 1862. Ignácio was Maria Dorothea's nephew, godson, and heir. A long-term protector of Elias, in 1842 he signed the deed of purchase for Felicidade on the freedman's behalf. Second Lieutenant Freire de Carvalho was probably the son of another nephew and executor of Elias's former mistress's estate, Lieutenant-Colonel Manoel José Freire de Carvalho, a businessman and, mainly in the 1820s, a transatlantic slave trader. Like many freedpersons, Elias maintained ties of dependence with a powerful and influential seigniorial family. Its members not only engaged in prestigious professions, such as medicine, but held important public posts – including delegado, police chief, and assemblyman – as well as owning sugar plantations in the Recôncavo and trafficking slaves.[5]

In 1850, Elias freed a two-year-old creole named Christovão without charge. He was the son of his slave Benvinda, of the Nagô nation. Four years later he freed gratuitously another creole child, a three-month-old

4 "Liberdade do crioulinho Aniceto," APEB, LNT, vol. 293, fl. 56v. This is the first document I have found in which his name is given as Elias Francisco de Seixas Venâncio.

5 ACMS, Livro de registro de casamentos da freguesia de Santana, fl. 83; APEB, LRT, vol. 25, fls. 165 and 165v. Ignácio Freire de Carvalho held the post of judge in the First Civil Court according to documents attached to Marcolino Dias de Andrade's petition, dated March 31, 1874, APEB, Escravos (assuntos), maço 2886; and Silva, "Caminhos e descaminhos da abolição," 132 and 248, regarding another Freire de Carvalho, Manoel, being a prosecutor. Regarding Domingos Freire de Carvalho as commander general of the police force, see, for example, his signature in "Mappa dos prêsos durante o dia 21 de abril de 1860," APEB, Polícia. Presos, maço 6285. Regarding the Freire de Carvalho family's ownership of a sugar plantation, see Dorothea Seixas's will mentioned in note 2; and Manoel José Freire de Carvalho as a slave trader, see STVD, voyages # 204, 2919, 2948, 46833, and 46856.

baby named Thomazia, the daughter of the same slave. In Christovão's
case, he wrote that the manumission was granted "for the great love
I have, having raised him, and to ease my conscience, and for the good
services his mother has provided," although he also obliged the boy to
stay with him until his death. In Thomazia's case, he stated that she was
freed "to ease my conscience and for the good services her mother has
provided," but this time her manumission was unconditional.[6] One of
the reasons Elias gave for freeing these children – a heavy conscience –
led me to suspect they were his, with the slave Benvinda. And so they
were. Elias had another daughter, Francisca, with the same African
woman, and she was christened in Sé parish on Christmas Day 1859. In
her baptismal record, the mother's name is listed as Benvinda de Seixas.
Her master and the father of her children, Elias, had probably freed her
by that time, and in the process she had adopted his name. But they
were only officially married in March 1862, in the midst of his legal
battle with Domingos. Because he was a widower, they could not have a
church wedding. Instead, Canon Pedro Antonio de Campos, the vicar
of Santo Antônio parish, married them in the oratory of his home.[7]

Elias went from being these children's master to their father, and
from being the master of Benvinda, the mother of his children, to her
lawful husband. This set his relationships apart from conventional relations between white masters and their slaves. In the latter case, generally speaking, the transition was not as complete as it was in Elias's.
White slave owners often freed and sometimes even recognized the
children their slave women bore them, like Domingos' young master
did, but they only occasionally freed these women and rarely started
lawful families with them.

There is another observation to be made about Elias's family life. His
relationship with Benvinda began, and produced at least Christovão,

6 "Liberdade do crioulo de nome Christovão," APEB, *LNT*, vol. 295, fl. 127;
   "Liberdade da crioulinha de nome Thomazia," APEB, *LNT*, vol. 300, fl. 221.
   His name also appears in these two documents as Elias Francisco de Seixas
   Venâncio.
7 ACM, *Livro de registro de batismo. Freguesia da Sé, 1829–1861*, registro no. 330,
   December 25, 1859; ACMS, *Livro de registro de casamentos da freguesia de Santo
   Antonio Além do Carmo, 1840–1863*, fl. 179. This document shows another version of the African's name, here given as Elias Rodrigues Seixas, along with that
   of his wife, Benvinda Rodrigues. The vicar may have made a mistake by giving
   him his wife's surname as a freedwoman, possibly adopted from a master prior to
   her husband.

while he was still living with his first wife, Maria da Luz, who did not bear him any children. This conclusion comes from a simple calculation: in 1849, Maria da Luz and Elias Seixas jointly freed Aniceto, the child they raised, and the following year he alone freed his son Christovão, who was by then two years old. Aniceto may also have been Elias's son by another slave, Delfina. We do not know if Maria da Luz, his lawful wife – or should we now call her Elias' main or number one wife? – was aware of and in agreement with her husband's polygamy. In other words, Elias and Benvinda may have been more than just lovers. If this was the case, they would all have been involved in a reenactment of an African family traditions, or better yet, combining them with Brazilian norms, because Catholic marriages had also come into the conjugal – or cultural – mix. However, it would be good to question whether Africans were the only ones who entered into such marital arrangements, given the behavior of Domingos' masters, Colonel Francisco Maria Sodré and his son Jerônimo. As we have seen in Chapter 2, both were dedicated and public polygamists. However, there is no indication that the colonel lived with his wife and mistress under the same roof, as Elias, Maria da Luz, and Benvinda seem to have done.[8]

It seems that Elias had gradually eased himself out of his patron-client relationship with the Freire de Carvalho family, as they were not listed as witnesses for his second marriage. The individuals filling those roles were our old acquaintance Lieutenant Colonel João de Azevedo Piapitinga, the subdelegado of the second district of Santo Antônio parish, and Anna Ribeiro de Mello, a white widow. This shift may reveal an unusual dynamic of the paternalism that enmeshed freedpersons' lives: while some spent their entire lives in the orbit of former masters, others distanced themselves more and more from those webs of dependence as they became further removed from the experience of slavery. This social distancing was sometimes also geographic. Subdelegado Piapitinga was the highest police official in the district where Elias then lived and had the power to protect him when necessary. As we will soon

<hr>

[8] Mieko Nishida, *Slavery and Identity: Ethnicity, Gender, and Race in Salvador, Brazil, 1808–1888* (Bloomington and Indianapolis: Indiana University Press, 2003), 109, writes that "polygamous unions were exceptional" and only cites one case. Evidently, this sort of union was rarely documented. Isabel Cristina F. dos Reis, "A família negra no tempo da escravidão, 1850–1888," PhD dissertation, Unicamp, 2007, 116–117, mentions a Muslim who stated in his will that he was a polygamist with the blessing of Allah.

see, Piapitinga would testify in his favor against Domingos Sodré, who also had his defenders outside the orbit of his former masters.[9]

A small slave owner, Elias was not a kindly master. In 1855, his slave Ludovina, a Nagô woman, committed suicide by drowning herself in the water tank of a gunpowder factory in Mata Escura, where Elias lived in a place called Lagoa da Vovó (Granny's Lagoon), which still bears that charming name. Following procedure, the police examined Ludovina's body but did not find any signs of abuse from her master, which would have made her death a crime. However, after some investigation, the subdelegado discovered that "for stealing chickens, which she had taken from her master, his threat to punish her if she continued to do so [led] to her decision to run away from home and then to commit suicide."[10] This suggests that Elias did not feed his slave well, leading her to "steal" his chickens to eat, and punished his slave so harshly that she fled in despair and took her own life. The master's explanation to the subdelegado that he would only have punished her if she had done it again – or "if she continued" – does not seem to have been candid or at least Ludovina did not take it seriously, as she must have been thoroughly familiar with her master's methods of controlling his slaves. In short, she killed herself to put an end to the abuse. This says nothing about the dispute between Domingos and Elias, but it does shed light on Elias's possibly explosive temper.

Elias and the Death of João

Domingos Sodré had hired attorney Antonio José Pereira de Albuquerque, subdelegado of São Pedro parish, to represent him in his court case against Elias Seixas.[11] The case dragged on in the Bahian courts from October 1860 to November 1863, which puts the raid on the diviner's house and his arrest right in the middle of that legal battle. Domingos accused Elias of having dispatched another African named João to the afterlife. In the early morning of October 5, 1860, João was

[9] Piapitinga's African clientele is revealed in other weddings where he served as a witness, such as those of the freedpersons João Francisco da Costa and Juliana Josefa de Carvalho. ACMS, Livro de registro de casamentos. Santo Antonio, 1840–63, registered on May 26, 1860.

[10] José de Barros Reis to the chief of police, February 7, 1855, APEB, Subdelegados, maço 6234.

[11] This was not the first time Africans had hired Albuquerque as a lawyer. Three years earlier, he had defended three Africans who sued for their freedom from the Capuchin Piedade Convent. See APEB, Polícia, maço 3139-18.

said to have sought out Elias on his farm in the outskirts of Salvador, at Domingos' request, to reclaim the sum of a million reis that Domingos had entrusted to Elias. The accused never admitted any responsibility for João's death after the man's body was found floating in Dique do Tororó lagoon two days after their encounter. He also denied that he had received any amount of money from Domingos. The civil suit that Domingos had filed in the Third Municipal Court went on concurrently with the police inquiry conducted by the subdelegado of the first district of Santo Antônio parish. During the official inquiry, the subject of the stolen money came up in the background, whereas in the civil suit, it was the main focus of the case.[12]

Jugurta Caldas Pereira, of the Nagô nation, was baptized in February 1831, the year of the failed first attempt to abolish the transatlantic slave trade.[13] He had probably arrived in Bahia the year before, a time of intense slave importation. In 1862 – now a freedman of about forty years old who worked as a cobbler – he gave a detailed account of the events that led to João's disappearance, and his friends' and coworkers' reactions to these events. His words were repeated verbatim in all the inquiries against Elias, whom Jugurta had known for about eight years. The cobbler was Elias's main accuser in the criminal suit, while Domingos was the plaintiff in the civil suit. Some of the statements also claim that Jugurta – the Bahian slave with a Berber hero's name – was the dead man's nephew, although he does not say so himself.[14]

Jugurta belonged to Domingos' social circle and probably his ritual clientele as well. He had received his manumission recently; he was listed as a slave in January 1860, the year he christened Carlota, a creole girl, the natural daughter of Maria, an African woman, the slave of one Clara Efigenia. He may have gained his freedom with the help of a manumission society headed by Domingos as well as the latter's anti-seigniorial witchcraft.[15]

---

[12] The records of the two suits are in APEB, *Judiciária*, no. 26/921/16 and no. 28/978/10.

[13] ACS, *Livro de registro de Batismos. Freguesia da Sé, 1829–1861*, fl. 41.

[14] Jugurta was a risky name to give to a slave, being as it was the name of the Berber king of Numidia who defeated the Roman invaders in the second century B.C. What did his master have in mind when he baptized him with the non-Christian name of a noble North African warrior? Regarding the Berber hero, see Haouaria Kadra, *Jugurtha, un berbère contre Rome* (Paris: Arléa, 2005).

[15] ACMS, *Livro de registro de batismos. Freguesia de São Pedro, 1853–61*, fl. 328. In 1854 he had already baptized two children, also crioulos. ACMS, *Livro de registro de batismos. Freguesia da Sé, 1829–1861*, fls. 329v, 330.

Jugurta toiled as a street worker (or *ganhador*), and got together with other Africans in Mocambinho, a small square near Domingos' home. These groups of African workers were called *cantos*. This term means literally corners or, alternatively, songs, both of which may have been the origin of the term. The ganhadores gathered in specific parts of the urban geography – squares, alleys, docks, and especially street corners – that gave those groups their names; and the members of cantos usually performed their work while chanting African songs. Jugurta's group was called the Canto do Mocambinho. This place name, Mocambinho, means "small *mocambo*," this being an alternative expression to refer to *quilombo*, the usual term for maroon community. In this case, however, Mocambo became instead, and ironically, a reference to an African workplace, including slave labor. The idea of slave resistance, though, was probably not completely lost when Africans pronounced the word *Mocambinho*. Certainly these labor groups worked toward the enactment of African autonomy and ethnic identity, for they were usually organized on the basis of African ethnicity. Nagôs, Hausas, Jejes, Congos, Angolas, and so on ideally had their own cantos, many of them depending on the size of the African nation's population in Bahia.

Most of the workers organized around the cantos labored as porters, carrying all kinds of merchandise and people (in sedan chairs), but Africans with other occupations also joined these groups between jobs, including female street vendors, the ganhadeiras. Many actually doubled as porters and workers in other, more specialized trades such as bricklayers, tailors, smiths, and so on. Jugurta, for example, probably made and mended shoes while waiting for work as a porter. Domingos definitely did not engage in the portage trade – although one or another of his slaves might have – but he must have spent time in the Mocambinho and other cantos in his neighborhood. One of them, for example, gathered at the bottom of Ladeira de São Bento, just a few feet from his house. The cantos would have been a good place for the diviner to recruit clients and acolytes, meet up with friends and instruct his followers, chat, and catch up on the news – local, national, and African, veritable Atlantic conversations.[16]

The response of the African street workers to João's death clarifies several aspects of the micro-politics within the African community of

---

[16] Regarding cantos, see João José Reis, "A greve negra de 1857 na Bahia," *Revista USP*, no. 18 (1993): 6–29, and Reis, "De olho no canto: trabalho de rua na Bahia na véspera da Abolição," *Afro-Ásia*, no. 24 (2000): 199–242.

Figures 35, 36, and 37. African *ganhadores*, workers who gathered in *cantos* like the one on Mocambinho square.

Salvador, such as group solidarity, social hierarchy, political leadership, and family and friendship conventions. Hidden behind a web of events, there emerges a complex plot of murder, money, and witchcraft.

News of João's death and of his corpse being found in the Dique lagoon circulated in the African community, including the street work groups. We know from Jugurta's deposition that, when ganhadores at the Mocambinho canto heard about it, they immediately headed to João's house to confirm the news, and there they found Elias and the deceased man's common-law wife. Only then were they informed that the last person to have seen João was Elias, who they immediately

Figures 35, 36, and 37. (*continued*)

accused of having murdered João. The ganhadores forced Elias to march
with them, and after going from one authority after the other, the freedman was taken to the Aljube prison by two policemen, following the
orders of the commander of the police corps. The African ganhadores
then went to the chief of police to demand that a proper inquiry be
organized to investigate João's death, including a forensic examination
of his body before burial, which they managed to obtain. A detail: it
was Jugurta and his fellow workers, accompanied by a couple of police
inspectors, who rescued João's corpse from the Dique and took it to the
hospital to be examined. When asked why he thought Elias had killed

Figures 35, 36, and 37. (*continued*)

João, Jugurta answered that "it was because João's son had told him that his father had gone to Elias's farm and had not returned, and was later found dead in the Dique."[17]

The late João had probably belonged to the Mocambinho *canto*, which explains the unified response of its members to his death. If not, he had friends and coworkers who sympathized with him and joined in the effort to investigate his disappearance and death. Jugurta said he was his "kin," which means that they belonged to the same African nation, Nagôs, like Domingos, but also like Elias, the man accused of murder. Therefore, in ethnic terms, this was actually an internal affair. Jugurta was certainly speaking for the group when he said that "because [João] was his comrade, it was very hard that he should be buried without it being reported or legal measures being taken," giving us to understand that he was familiar with the law. His statement exposed the

---

[17] Domingos Sodré's civil suit against Elias Francisco de Seixas, APEB, *Judiciária*, no. 26/921/16, fl. 21v–22.

police authorities' lack of interest and the insistence of the Africans from the Mocambinho canto that the circumstances of João's death be investigated.

Jugurta explained that there was a small disturbance involving a group of fellow nationals and coworkers who believed Elias was the perpetrator. Elias was no stranger – he was part of Jugurta's circle (and Jugurta was "just as good a friend to him [João] as he was to the accused, Elias"), which also included Domingos. Elias may have been in the habit of stopping at the Mocambinho canto on his way from his farm to the city. But he did not consider himself on the same level as people who made their living in the streets because he was a successful, slave-owning farmer.[18]

The written correspondence from police officer Macário de Araújo Sacramento to his superior largely confirms Jugurta's statement. Sacramento wrote that Jugurta Caldas had arrived at the police station in Mouraria at 4 P.M. on October 7, 1860, with a group of Africans, bringing Elias with them, and everyone accused him of murdering João. Officer Sacramento's superior ordered him to take Elias to the Aljube prison (which he did) and then to go on to the Dique, from where he removed João's body with the help of another officer and some bystanders. The corpse was placed by the side of the road and examined. According to Sacramento, "I only found the marks of blows around the throat," which suggests that João had been beaten before he died. After that examination, Sacramento called in a constable from Santana parish to write a letter to the Misericórdia charity hospital requesting that the body be retrieved, which was the sort of charity that institution provided, among others. The hospital's director refused to accept the officer's request and demanded that the order come directly from the chief of police. With that order in hand, a stretcher was sent to carry João's body. Between the time the group led by Jugurta arrived and Sacramento returned to the police station at 11 P.M., seven hours had elapsed. The officer, who believed that Elias was guilty, also sent the police chief the accused man's umbrella,

---

[18] Civil suit brought by Domingos Sodré against Elias Francisco de Seixas, APEB, *Judiciária*, no. 26/921/16, fls. 19v-22. See also Pompílio Manoel de Castro to the chief of police, May 21, 1860, and João Pedro da Cunha, subdelegado of Santana Parish, to the chief of police, May 22, 1860, APEB, *Polícia. Subdelegados*, maço 6233.

because he had noticed that it was stained with "spots of the dead man's blood."[19]

Elias's situation worsened in the eyes of João's friends because of outbursts of arrogance on his part, mainly because he was much better off than most of the African freedpersons with whom he associated. Even before João's body was found, for example, Elias told Jugurta and other Africans that he would pay for the funeral himself, suggesting that he already knew about João's death. When he was taken to jail, Elias bragged to his associates that he had enough money to pay for his defense and, because of that, he would soon be cleared. Once under arrest, he was heard to say, "since you say it was me who killed him, I killed him, if you say so," words that seemed to confirm his guilt, but more probably, once again, evinced the dismissive arrogance of a man of means and good connections when confronting those underprivileged Africans.[20]

At first, Elias's accusers managed to convince the authorities of his guilt. In a letter from the police chief to the president of the province listing the arrests made on October 7, he included "the African Elias, a freedman, sixty years old, a farmer, indicted as the perpetrator of the murder of another freedman named João, whose body was dumped in the public Dike, from where it was removed for the coroner's inquest."[21]

Elias ended up in the Aljube jail, along with slaves who had escaped from and disobeyed their masters, or who had broken city ordinances, among other acts of resistance, as well as freed and free individuals arrested night and day for petty crimes. The same day Elias went to prison, he was joined by Isaltino de Santana, a mulatto cobbler, who was just 10 years old, jailed "for uttering obscene words"; Anselmo Machado, 29, a cabra seaman, "for drunkenness and insults"; João Antonio, 30, a white Portuguese, also a seaman, "on suspicion"; Epiphanio, 14, a creole slave who worked as a baker, for breaking a city ordinance; Balbina, 35, an African hire-out slave, at her master's request, for punishment; Felippe, 30, an African slave who worked as a

---

[19] Macário de Araújo Sacramento to the lieutenant colonel commander general of the police, October 8, 1860, APEB, *Mapas dos presos*, maço 6285. A copy of this document is also found in APEB, *Judiciária*, no. 28/978/10, fls. 4–4v.

[20] Witnesses in the case against Elias Seixas, October 20, 1860, APEB, *Judiciária*, no. 28/978/10, fl. 21v, 24v.

[21] Police Chief J. P. da Silva Moraes to the president of the province, October 8, 1860, APEB, *Correspondência do Chefe de Polícia*, vol. 5744, fls. 70–70v.

foreman, also at his master's request; Bernardo, 48, an African slave and seaman, for being found in the streets "after hours"; Damião Lopes, 19, a creole seaman, for being found in someone else's house under suspicious circumstances; and Isidoro Rocha, 18, a creole bricklayer, for the same reason. For nearly four months, the time it took to investigate the crime, these people would be typical cellmates for Elias, a rare African who had allegedly never seen the inside of a Bahian jail before, as he would claim during the inquest.[22]

João was only survived by two children and his common-law wife. As they had not been married in the Catholic Church, she is referred to as his *amásia*, or concubine, and sometimes his *camarada* in both suits – civil and criminal. Her name was Felicidade Francisca. She was an African freedwoman, more than sixty years of age, who made her living from trade. She and João had lived together in São Raimundo, in São Pedro Parish, which was less than ten minutes' walk from the Mocambinho *canto*. Felicidade was also a witness for the prosecution. She said that Elias had recently sought João out three times and, on Domingos Sodré's advice, he had gone to Elias's farm to "get something" – she did not know what – and had not been seen since. The African woman had even gone to Elias's house, which was three leagues away – a very long walk – to look for her man. Elias told her that João had left his home on the afternoon of the same day he arrived there and that he himself had accompanied the deceased "halfway" back.

Felicidade had reported João's disappearance to the police at Domingos' suggestion. When she returned home, she found Elias there, and "he asked her to give him the aforementioned João's coffer, asking if there was any money in it, and when she did not agree to it ... Elias had to leave because she did not want to give him ... hospitality."[23] Felicidade was implying that she already suspected that the accused had murdered her husband, and in any event, she had acted with the modesty of a married woman who could not receive a man in her home in her husband's absence. Jugurta had heard the same story, because he stated that Felicidade had not given "shelter" to Elias because it was

---

[22] "Mappa dos presos recolhidos à cadeia do Aljube durante o dia 7 de outubro de 1860," APEB, *Polícia. Presos*, maço 6285.

[23] Civil suit brought by Domingos Sodré against Elias Francisco de Seixas, APEB, *Judiciária*, no. 26/921/16, fls. 57–57v.

not proper for her to receive a man to sleep "in her home while João was missing."[24]

One of João's sons, by the name of Salustiano, helped remove his father's body from the lagoon. Salustiano had a half-brother by his mother named Felippe Neves, a twenty-five-year-old creole bricklayer who lived on Rua do Sodré, and was therefore one of Domingos' neighbors. Felippe would confirm all the charges against Elias, and even said that the farmer had repeatedly invited his stepfather to go and meet with him so he could give him the million reis owed to the manumission society, but that João had replied that "he would not go unless it was on the orders of the Plaintiff [Domingos], and that when he was told of that invitation, the Plaintiff had authorized João to go to the accused man's farm on Friday for the aforementioned purpose of fetching the money, and João had not returned that day or the next." This statement makes the chain of command clear: Domingos gave orders to João, as well as to his stepson, Felippe. The stepson also swore that he had often seen sums of money delivered to Elias. It is interesting that João had gone to Elias's farm on a Friday, the day of Candomblé meetings – or divinatory and healing consultations – at Pai Domingos' house.[25]

Elias Seixas gave a different version of João's visit to his farm. He said he had invited him to his home to discuss payment of a loan he had made to João, who had left his home in the evening of that fateful Friday. Before that, Elias said, he had invited João to stay at his house, as it was getting dark, but João refused, saying that he had not told his wife he would be spending the night away from home. Elias stated that he did not go all the way to town with João because he had business to take care of on his farm, but that he had accompanied him halfway. He claimed that it made no sense for him to kill João and carry his body a long distance from his home to deposit it in the Dique. In addition to Elias, one of his slaves had also seen João that evening. He confirmed his master's story. That slave was Aniceto, who was freed as a boy in 1849 on condition that he stay with Elias until his death. He was a freedman with a conditional manumission, but in his statement he said he was a field slave.

---

[24] Witnesses in the case against Elias Seixas, October 20, 1860, APEB, *Judiciária*, no. 28/978/10, fl. 26.
[25] APEB, *Judiciária*, no. 26/921/16, fls. 59v–60v.

The "doctors of medicine" examined the only physical evidence that Elias had murdered João, the red stain found on the farmer's umbrella, said to be the victim's blood, and came to a different conclusion: it was something else, but they did not determine the source of the stains. Furthermore, the results of the forensic examination attached to the records of the criminal investigation were inconclusive in other ways. João's body, found about three days after his death, was in an advanced state of decomposition, but the doctors were still able to find significant damage. They concluded that the cause of death was "asphyxiation by strangulation or drowning." In other words, he could either have been strangled and thrown in the Dique or have drowned there. When the police asked what sort of instrument was the cause of death, the answer was disappointingly vague: "A constricting instrument causing strangulation or water leading to drowning." Signs of a beating were also found, but the doctors did not bother to explain them.[26]

Like the doctors of that time, I do not know exactly what happened. Could João's death have been accidental, or even a suicide? The Dique do Tororó was one of the preferred places in the city of Bahia for Africans who chose to commit suicide, perhaps even for religious reasons. Since the early nineteenth century, there had been reports that there was a spring there called the Mother of Water (Mãe d'Água), the object of devotion and celebration. In the middle of that century, it is likely that the cult of Òşun – the Yoruba divinity of the eponymous river who became a divinity of fresh waters in Bahia – had already been established in the lagoon, and still exists to this day. During a visit to the Dique the year João was killed, Prince Maximilian of Habsburg came across what he believed to be elements of African spirituality:

In nearby fields, cultivated by the blacks, I saw, not without wonder, bull skulls stuck on long poles. They may have been scarecrows. I believe, however, that they are also traditions of the transatlantic fetish that persists, strangely, among the imported blacks, tacitly maintaining a sort of mysterious bond among them. In Africa, such bulls' heads are also seen. There, they are

[26] For the preceding two paragraphs, see Aniceto's statement, November 6, 1860, and interrogation of Elias, November 15, 1860, APEB, *Judiciária*, no. 28/978/10, fls. 35v–36, 41v–45, respectively; and "Auto de exame e corpo de delito," October 8, 1860, and the report on the examination of Elias's umbrella, December 14, 1860, idem, fls. 5–6, 51–52v, respectively.

considered a protection against the evil eye and against the influence of evil spirits.[27]

In 1902, a newspaper reported that, in the "vicinity of the Dique ... several Candomblé houses function day and night." In the 1930s, when American sociologist Donald Pierson did research in Bahia, the area was viewed as a "sacred lagoon" around or near which several Candomblé temples had been established, some in the previous century. One of them was the highly active Moinho, now known as Gantois.[28]

In Domingos' time, the Dique was a veritable sinkhole that swallowed up black people's lives. Over the course of one year, between 1849 and 1850, at least three Africans were found dead there, in addition to a free creole woman and an enslaved woman described as mulatto.[29] On May 21 and 22, 1860, two Africans were found dead in the lagoon, a man and a woman. She was removed one day and he the next. The African woman, whose body was in an advanced state of decomposition, was not described. The man was a man with a bushy beard and white hair, who appeared to be about fifty years old.[30]

Elias may have killed João (or, more likely, had someone else kill him) and dumped his body (or had it dumped) in the Dique, far from his home, to make his death look like a suicide or accidental drowning. The bruising around João's neck, identified by the police officer and confirmed during the inquest, suggests that he was beaten before he died. It may be that Elias had just wanted to intimidate him to make him pay his debt to the African farmer, but it may have gone too far, and the rest is history. This is just conjecture, a hypothesis. Historians often have to play the role of diviners. In any event, there was good reason to suspect Elias, although in both suits – the criminal and the civil – he accused Domingos Sodré of trying to frame him.

[27] Habsburgo, *Bahia 1860*, 212.

[28] Rodrigues, *Os africanos*, 243; Donald Pierson, *Brancos e pretos na Bahia* (São Paulo: Companhia Editora Nacional, 1971), 307. Regarding the Moinho candomblé, see Parés, *A formação do Candomblé*, 152.

[29] APEB, *Polícia. Correspondência*, vol. 5689, fls. 44, 47, 52–53, 62, 69, 81, 84. Brown, "'On the Vanguard of Civilization,'" 232, writes: "The police records are full of stories of slaves, many of them Africans, who killed themselves by jumping off rooftops, or drowning themselves in the ocean or the lagoon called Dique."

[30] Pompílio Manoel de Castro to the chief of police, May 21, 1860, and substitute subdelegado João Pedro da Cunha Vale to the chief of police, May 22, 1860, APEB, *Polícia*, maço 6233.

Figures 38 and 39. Dique do Tororó lagoon, ca. 1870.

THE MANUMISSION SOCIETY

Elias was never charged with João's murder, having been cleared on January 25, 1861. Domingos Sodré, however, continued to accuse him of the crime in the civil suit he brought against him to recover the million reis he claimed to have entrusted to Elias. The money was said to belong to a manumission society (or *junta de alforria*), a credit institution devoted to freeing enslaved Africans. Like the cantos, these societies were organized along ethnic lines, that is, African nations formed one or more manumission societies, again depending on the size of each group in the city. The Nagô societies, representing the largest African nation in Bahia in the mid-nineteenth century, were probably inspired by the *esusu*, a Yoruba credit institution that, according to late nineteenth-century Yoruba historian Rev. Samuel Johnson, was organized as follows: "A fixed sum agreed upon is given by each at a fixed time (usually every week) and place, under a president; the total amount is paid over to each member in rotation."[31] Thanks to Domingos' suit against Elias, we learn a lot more about how manumission societies functioned in Bahia, a subject on which there are very few records, although several authors commented on them at the turn of the past century.

According to Manoel Querino, each manumission society gathered "under the leadership of one of its members, the most respected and trusted."[32] That would have been Domingos in this case. In fact, during the investigation of João's death, African freedman Jorge Francisco Manoel de Castro, who made his living as a street worker, declared that the day João had disappeared, he was at a meeting with other society members, including Jugurta, at Domingos' home. The meeting was held to "distribute a certain amount" of money, a reference to the million reis Domingos had allegedly sent João to collect from Elias.[33]

The way the society was run sheds light on a different aspect of the diviner's leadership, which was probably associated with his religious activities. Lest we forget, the society met on a Friday, the same day that Candomblé meetings were held at his house, according to the police. Although we do not know the dynamics of power in that society, this is one indication that Domingos' leadership was somehow based on his

[31]   Johnson, *The History of the Yorubas*, 119; Reis, *Rebelião escrava no Brasil*, 365–367. See also a later, more detailed statement by William R. Bascom, "The Esusu: A Credit Institution of the Yoruba," *The Journal of the Royal Anthropological Institute of Great Britain and Ireland*, 82, no. 1 (1952): 63–69. There are also similarities between the *esusu* and the *ajo*, another kind of Yoruba credit institution. See Toyin Falola, "'My Friend the Shylock': Money-Lenders and Their Clients in South-Western Nigeria," *Journal of African History*, no. 34 (1993): 404.

[32]   Querino, *A raça Africana*, 146. This was a basic rule in Yorubaland, according to Bascom, "The Esusu", 68.

[33]   Witnesses against Elias Seixas, October 17, 1860, APEB, *Judiciária*, no. 28/978/10, fl. 11v.

ritual ascendancy over the other members. The credit institution does not seem to have held regular elections of its leaders. There are reports that Domingos had headed the organization since at least 1852, he may have founded it and being its chief since its creation. In precolonial Yorubaland eṣuṣu did not have permanent leaders; they were chosen on a rotating basis. And the figure of the *alajo*, who collected cash contributions and received a commission for his work, would only appear later on, in colonial Nigeria.[34]

The manumission society over which Domingos presided collected sums that were deposited on a weekly basis by enslaved and freed Africans who, at the end of a year, or, more precisely, fifty-two weeks, were distributed among its members "in proportion to each individual's contribution."[35] Here there appears to be another divergence from the Yoruba model, as it did not include deposits of fixed sums, as Johnson described the eṣuṣu, but in tune with Bascom's description. In Bahia, everyone contributed as much as they could and withdrew it proportionally. As for who could join these credit associations, at the time in question, it seems that they were not organized exclusively according to the ethnic background of their members, but also by parish. Therefore, according to Domingos' indictment, "the Africans residing in São Pedro Parish, like other parishes," had organized that manumission society.[36] Therefore, Domingos was apparently an important figure among Africans of various backgrounds in that densely populated parish, and not just among people of his own nation. Even so, at that point in the nineteenth century, nearly 80 percent of African slaves in Salvador were Nagôs, so most African organizations in the city would necessarily have had that predominant ethnic profile.[37] This is why the

---

[34] Regarding the African side, see Falola, "'My Friend the Shylock,'" 405. However, Bascom ("The Eṣuṣu"), doing research in the late 1930s in Yorubaland, observed that the founders of these societies would normally lead them for the duration of the group's life cycle.

[35] Civil suit brought by Domingos Sodré against Elias Francisco de Seixas, APEB, *Judiciária*, no. 26/921/16, fl. 5.

[36] Ibid., fl. 5.

[37] Reis, "A greve negra de 1857 na Bahia," 28. See also Maria Inês Côrtes de Oliveira, "Retrouver une identité: jeux sociaux des africains de Bahia (vers 1750 – vers 1890)," PhD dissertation, Université de Paris IV – Sorbonne, 1992, 107, where the author's data (which I have recalculated, taking into account specific ethnic terms) indicate that, between 1851 and 1890, 79 percent of African slaves in Salvador were Nagô.

creole Felippe Neves declared that the "savings fund" Domingos ran was ethnically restricted, once it had the "purpose of freeing his compatriots."[38] Because Domingos' compatriots were Nagôs, we can suppose that the territorial base of the parish largely, if not exclusively, overlapped the participants' ethnicity, which in this case I consider to be Nagô. However, even if he moved about in other circles that went beyond his ethnic borders, the priest was still a Nagô. As anthropologist Marshall Sahlins has aptly put it, the perimeters of identity serve as boundaries for "cultural communities" – like the African nations of Bahia – but not as "barriers to the flow of people, goods or ideas."[39]

Another aspect of this particular manumission society was that it was an all-male group. Felicidade, the merchant whose partner João was murdered, declared that she knew nothing about his dealings with Domingos and Elias "because it was men's business."[40] Like the labor cantos, manumission societies were predominantly, if not exclusively, male. According to studies of nineteenth-century Salvador, men – the majority in the enslaved population – had more difficulty obtaining manumission than women. This was because most domestics were female, which gave them an opportunity to form closer relationships with the master's family and put them in a better position to negotiate the terms of their manumission, even if they had to pay for it. But that was not all. Enslaved women generally had a lower market value than men, although many managed to engage in occupations, particularly as hire-out slaves, that made it easier to save up to buy their own freedom.[41] Therefore it is understandable that both for being the majority among slaves and for having a harder time obtaining their manumission, men were better represented than women in these credit societies.

For some, manumission societies were like savings banks from where each enslaved member withdrew a sum of money on a rotating basis, generally the exact amount he needed to buy his manumission. The withdrawer continued to contribute money to the fund to pay off the principal, plus interest, which could be as high as 20 percent, according

---

[38] Witnesses produced by the plaintiff, APEB, *Judiciária*, no. 26/921/16, fl. 59v.

[39] Marshall Sahlins, "Two or Three Things that I Know about Culture," *Journal of the Royal Anthropological Institute*, 5, no. 3 (1999): 415.

[40] Witnesses produced by the plaintiff, APEB, *Judiciária*, no. 26/921/16, fl. 57.

[41] Mattoso, "A propósito de cartas de alforria," 40–41; idem, *Da revolução dos alfaiates à riqueza dos baianos*, 193; Nishida, "Manumission and Ethnicity in Urban Slavery," 376.

to early twentieth-century chronicler Silva Campos. Here we find
another difference from the Yoruba eṣuṣu, which, according to Toyin
Falola, did not involve the collection of "any interest or the deduction
of fees."[42] In the case of Bahia, Silva Campos notes:

> In this city there were African banking companies that made
> loans for the purchase of manumission. After the amount had
> been settled and the loan obtained, once freed, the debtor
> started working on his own to pay off the debt. Amortization
> and interest rates were [calculated] weekly. That is, the debtor
> would make payments of 5$000 [five thousand reis] every
> Saturday, being 4$000 for amortization of capital and 1$000 in
> interest.[43]

Once his debt was paid, the freedman could stay on as a member of the
manumission society, this time as a creditor. Even a freedman who had
not been part of the society as a slave could theoretically join it. The
interest the debtors paid gave an excellent return on investment, and
at the same time, it encouraged the accumulation of capital available
for loans to enslaved members so they could buy their manumission.
This was an ingenious system for financing freedom, which was its main
purpose.

One of Domingos' witnesses, the mulatto tailor Dionizio Maximiano
de Albuquerque, age thirty-seven, emphatically described the manumission society as an "association of Africans for the purpose of freeing
their comrades."[44] In the charge brought against Elias, we see a confirmation that the society actually functioned as a mechanism for African
solidarity, but was also a business in which freedmen lent money to
slaves at interest:

> It will be proved that these weekly contributions were delivered
> to the Accused [Elias] as a trustee with the knowledge of the con-
> tributors, and from them the Plaintiff [Domingos] received the
> total result at the end of 52 weeks for distribution, being that this
> was done in assembly among everyone as all were Africans who do

---

[42] Falola, "'My Friend the Shylock,'" 404.

[43] João da Silva Campos, "Ligeiras notas sobre a vida íntima, costumes e religião dos
    africanos na Bahia," *Anais do Arquivo do Estado da Bahia*, no. 29 (1943): 297–298.
    See also Querino, *A raça africana*, 146–148.

[44] Witnesses produced by the plaintiff, APEB, *Judiciária*, no. 26/921/16, fl. 54.

not even know how to read, and because it was a *means for assisting the freedom of others through a profit*.[45]

"Through a profit ... " This was not a matter of pure philanthropy or group solidarity alone, as historian Maria Inês Oliveira has observed.[46] It was a credit system, in many ways similar to others, because the borrowers paid interest, and the lenders wanted to make a profit. The head of the group earned a bit more than the other members because he ran the system. Domingos was silent on this point, but it is confirmed by Manoel Querino and Braz do Amaral, who saw how those institutions operated first-hand in the late nineteenth century.[47] The freedman Jorge de Castro, age fifty, a ganhador and the only declared contributor to the manumission society to make a statement in the lawsuit, said that his "friend" Domingos was "the head of those Africans" and that he "makes a living from the society."[48] Therefore, we now know that, in 1862, Domingos' livelihood was based on running the society, divination and other ritual services, as well as the earnings of one or two slave women he owned.

One passage in this document gives a perfect demonstration of the different cultural territories in which our protagonist moved: the oral world of the manumission society, and the world of the written word, represented by notaries' offices and courts. There is some foundation to Elias's defense that "Africans do not entrust money without confirmation [a receipt], which they call 'paper,' which is public and common knowledge."[49] There were numerous property transactions registered by Africans in notaries' offices, and many of their dealings were not based on written documents but on trust, on their pledged word. For that reason they are harder to verify. This was the case with slaves who entrusted their savings to freedpersons, as well as the matter of manumission societies. Some masters may have been surprised, even appalled, that their slaves managed to amass savings to purchase manumission in a way that was outside their control.[50]

---

[45] Civil suit brought by Domingos Sodré against Elias Francisco de Seixas, APEB, *Judiciária*, no. 26/921/16, fl. 6v. My emphasis.

[46] Oliveira, "Retrouver une identité," 325.

[47] Querino, *A raça africana*, 147; Amaral, *Fatos da vida do Brasil*, 128.

[48] Witnesses produced by the plaintiff, APEB, *Judiciária*, no. 26/921/16, fls. 58, 59.

[49] Arguments of the defense, APEB, *Judiciária*, no. 26/921/16, fl. 85v.

[50] Silva, "Caminhos e descaminhos da abolição," 127.

Both Manoel Querino and his contemporary Braz do Amaral stressed that honest dealings generally characterized everyone involved in the verbal contracts of African savings and loan societies. Braz do Amaral expanded on the subject: "Imagine the amount of patience, energy, and hidden and honored effort that was necessary for this, as well as essential righteousness among all involved, lenders, trustees and debtors, to faithfully fulfill their contracts, made verbally, based on their word, without the slightest aid or protection of the law." And he concluded: "It should be noted that in some cases it was necessary to keep it a secret because of the opposition the masters raised to everything involved in freeing their slaves."[51] Historian Ubiratan Castro de Araújo has collected an oral tradition that gives an amusing portrayal of the struggle between master and slave about raising money for manumission. It is the story of an African slave who, while pretending to be a dullard, uses shrewd cunning to stop his master from getting his hands on his secret nest egg, making a fool of him and humiliating him to boot, pretending to reveal his savings' hiding place, which was instead a cesspit he had dug in his master's yard.[52] The protection of savings was not a concern to be overlooked, and explains Domingos' important role among the slaves, whether as a diviner-healer or leader of a manumission society.

According to Domingos Sodré, because they could not read and write, the members of the society gathered in an assembly to make decisions on a face-to-face basis. And here the verbal agreement jointly reached at the meeting implied a binding moral one with the same weight as a written and notarized contract. In another passage of the documents from the lawsuit, to justify the lack of a written document stating that Elias was holding money for the manumission society, Domingos claimed, through his legal representative, that "this money and that business belonged to and were dealt with among Africans who, for that reason, conducted such transactions in the best good faith."[53] However, there is another reason for this, aside from the Africans' lack of experience with Western writing: slaves could not legally sign contracts on their own behalf and would always have to be represented

---

[51] Amaral, *Fatos da vida do Brasil*, 128–129. Although Amaral attributes the initiative of starting manumission societies in Bahia exclusively to the Hausas, this was not the case.

[52] Ubiratan Castro de Araújo, *Sete histórias de negro* (Salvador: EDUFBa, 2006), 21–24.

[53] Domingos Sodré's rebuttal, APEB, *Judiciária*, no. 26/921/16, fls. 34v–35.

by trustees (usually their masters) in legal matters. This was the white man's law. According to the black man's law, the African's word was his bond, so they transacted the manumission society's business verbally. It was in the Africans' interest that these legal worlds be kept apart, because this prevented masters from sticking their vigilant noses into affairs related to their slaves' struggle for freedom, as Braz do Amaral observed. In fact, the same can be said of the system of justice and sanctions in the world of Candomblé, which was kept apart from the official legal system, despite the fact that, like the manumission societies, it sometimes came up in police inquiries and court sessions. Candomblé's rules regarding secret knowledge and rituals, mutual bond and solidarity, were often manifested in the manumission societies' dealings. Like the eşuşu in Africa, it is likely that "the members swore not to betray one another."[54] Candomblé and the manumission society had a lot in common and were not compartmentalized in Domingos' life.

Domingos' witnesses shed light on other aspects of the workings of a manumission society and its leadership, including the fact that some decisions required hiring people skilled in writing and accounting. This adds complexity to the cultural world of Africans in Bahia, which included dealing with and seeking the assistance of non-Africans as well. The bailiff for Sé parish and broker Manoel Francisco de Paula, age fifty-seven, an unmarried mulatto man, said he had witnessed the accounting of amounts received by Domingos on three occasions. But Domingos did not actually count and share out the money among the members of the society. Probably to ensure the transparency of the accounting process, he delegated that task to another bailiff, this time of São Pedro parish, Joaquim Francisco de Oliveira, age forty-six, another mulatto man whom Domingos also recruited as a witness in his suit against Elias. Joaquim Francisco declared that "everyone participated so that at the end of the year they could distribute and invest the total in freeing their comrades, a distribution that this witness carried out [and] for which he received payment."[55] Therefore, we can infer that the manumission society had hired a kind of accountant to assist it, someone whom the diviner trusted, who was also present as Domingos'

---

[54] Falola, "'My Friend the Shylock,'" 404.

[55] Domingos Sodré's rebuttal, APEB, *Judiciária*, no. 26/921/16, fl. 55. The information that Joaquim Francisco de Oliveira was a bailiff of the subdelegacia of São Pedro parish is in *Almanak. . . 1863*, 249.

witness in at least one other transaction that the freedman had registered in a notary's office seven years earlier.[56]

In both the criminal and civil cases brought against him, Elias Seixas
defended himself from the charge of murder by saying that Domingos
Sodré was trying to frame him, but that it had not worked because he,
Elias, was cleared during the police inquiry. His lawyers argued that
João's death had given Elias's accuser a chance to concoct a plot to
extort money from the accused, a prosperous farmer, family man, and
slave owner. In the police inquiry, Elias's lawyer called the subdelegado's attention to his client's exemplary behavior during the nearly forty
years he had lived in Bahia, "being an upright black man who lives
from his honest work to support his legitimate children and his wife
during his lifetime."[57] Elias' wife had been his slave and therefore had
helped – and certainly continued to help – support him. However, the
defense lawyer did not mention this because he needed to portray Elias
as a patriarch and provider to help bolster his image as a good, honest
man – everything in tune with mainstream Brazilian ways.

In both cases, Elias rejected the charge and claimed that he had
asked João to go to his home so he (Elias) could collect a debt of
120,000 reis, which he needed right away to help pay for two rural properties worth 300,000 reis (see box). The seller was Leonarda Thereza de
Jesus, an African freedwoman for whose child Elias had stood godfather
along with his wife, Maria da Luz, twenty years earlier.[58] To amass the
amount required, he said he had also requested a loan of 100,000 reis
from his friend Manoel Joaquim Ricardo, who confirmed that request,
but claimed that he had not made the loan because he did not have
enough money, which is hard to believe. The reader may have forgotten Manoel Joaquim. A wealthy African freedman, he was the master of the young creole whom the police found in Domingos Sodré's
house and was arrested along with the diviner, with whom Ricardo was
also friendly (see Chapter 6).[59] Notice the web being woven: Elias was

[56] See APEB, *Livro de notas do tabelião*, vol. 295, fls. 134–134v.
[57] Statement by Elias Seixas, November 15, 1860, APEB, *Judiciária*, no. 28/978/10,
fl. 42.
[58] ACMS, *Livro de registro de batismo. Freguesia da Santana*, illegible page, dated
March 15, 1843. This book is in very poor condition and was consulted on
microfilm no. 128–4581 of the Mormon Church's Family History Center, Igreja
de Jesus Cristo dos Últimos Dias, Salvador (FHC).
[59] Domingos Sodré's civil suit against Elias Francisco de Seixas and attachments,
APEB, *Judiciária*, no. 26/921/16, fls. 14–16v, 25v.

friends with Ricardo, who was friends with Domingos, who had once been friends with Elias. Elias must have been connected to the same religious circle in some way, even if he was just a devotee or client. Therefore, I suspect that Domingos was appealing to the white man's justice because the African kind – including divine justice – had failed him. I will return to this subject later.

Purchase of the Batefolha Farm by Christovão Seixas, Son of Elias, in 1864

Confirming the statements made by Elias Seixas two years prior, on May 10, 1864, the cabinetmaker Christovão Elias Seixas, the son of Domingos' rival, appeared as the purchaser, for 300,000 reis – paid on the occasion of the registration of the deed of sale to the African freedwoman Leonarda Thereza de Jesus – of "a piece of land beside São Gonçalo, second district of Santo Antônio Além do Carmo, called the Batefolha Farm, directly owned by Feliciana Pereira de Jesus." Said Feliciana had probably been Leonarda's mistress, but curiously enough, the São Gonçalo farm belonged to a married couple, Luiz José de Oliveira, a senator, and Maria José de Seixas, the daughter of Maria Dorothea Seixas, Elias's former mistress. The transaction between Christovão Seixas and Leonarda Thereza de Jesus was witnessed by subdelegado João de Azevedo Piapitinga, a familiar name. It should be noted that a "house of Candomblé" has existed on the Batefolha farm since 1838, as indicated by a map made by the legal forces combating the Sabinada rebels that year. Six years later, the police raided a house on that location, arrested its occupants, and confiscated religious objects. In that same neighborhood, in 1848, Elias Seixas had acquired from another African, Vicente Luciano, a mud house and several fields, including twenty-seven coconut trees, seven orange trees, two lime trees, and two mango trees. The land belonged to the São Gonçalo farm but was leased by Friar José de Santa Escolástica e Oliveira, who paid 6,000 reis per year. At the time, Elias already owned a farm in the same area, right next to the one being purchased. In other words, he was gradually adding adjacent properties to his dominions, purchased from other African freedpersons.

Source: APEB, *LNT*, vol. 285, fl. 173v, and vol. 375, fl. 79v. The candomblé in Batefolha is mentioned in Souza, A *Sabinada*, 101 and Abreu, *Capoeiras*, p. 84. See also Reis e Silva, *Negociação e conflito*, 61, for a report dating from 1832.

To give his client a better defense in the civil suit, Elias Seixas's lawyer described him as an "Apostolic Roman Catholic and god-fearing" man, and therefore incapable of denying his debts, much less committing murder. His lawyer in the police inquiry into João's death went even further by discrediting a witness for the prosecution from Domingos' circle, the freedman Jorge de Castro: "the witness is false and could not be otherwise because he has no Religion, as Africans do not, and therefore could not respect the sanctity of the oath," which was taken while placing their right hand on the Gospel, as all witnesses were required to do.[60] The religion Castro was referring to with a capital "R" was obviously the Catholic faith, as for him the African's Candomblé did not qualify as a religion. But the lawyer had gone overboard by casting a broad net that caught his own client because Elias was African as well, and as such was not supposed to be religious, only superstitious. His lawyer in the civil suit was more careful, merely underscoring his client's Catholic faith. Between the lines, he was implying that Elias was not a Candomblé adept, like Domingos and Castro. The lawyers most certainly knew about Pai Domingos' reprehensible ritual activities, no doubt from Elias himself.

It is too much of a coincidence that Domingos' arrest as a sorcerer occurred while the civil suit was under way. I suspect that Elias and his allies may have planned that episode, although there is no indication of this in the legal documents or the police correspondence regarding that case. The diviner's arrest, a scandal that made the pages of at least one newspaper in Salvador, was not mentioned in court. There were, however, subtle and indirect insinuations in Elias's defense lawyer's final arguments. After describing Domingos as a "sly and unscrupulous fellow," he accused the diviner of pocketing the manumission society's money because he had lived "for a long time from *alicantinas*," an untranslatable term that could mean either swindling or attempting to obstruct the course of justice. In an expression that was a little more directly related to the episode of his arrest, Elias' lawyer called Domingos a "big shot in this same Parish [of São Pedro Velho]."[61]

In fact, the police and even the press had spread the word that Domingos was the most important diviner and sorcerer in the city. He was even more of a big shot because one of his witnesses in his

[60] Rebuttal to Jorge de Castro's testimony, APEB, *Judiciária*, no. 28/978/10, fl. 13v.
[61] Final arguments of the defense, APEB, *Judiciária*, no. 26/921/16, fls. 92v–93.

civil suit against Elias was the bailiff of the substitute subdelegado who arrested him, as well as having the subdelegado of São Pedro himself as his lawyer in a civil suit against yet another African freedman. The defense could not risk attacking the subdelegado, a respectable man with a law degree. However, the bailiff, a mulatto man, was accused of spending "night and day soaked in liquor and almost always at the table" of the freedman Domingos.[62] For anyone who had been keeping track of recent police activities in that parish, it was understood that the bailiff, who lived nearby, was one of Pai Domingos' best clients, and as a result his faithful witness. In fact, in the criminal suit in which Elias was charged with murder, Joaquim Francisco Oliveira, the mulatto São Pedro parish bailiff, swore "on his conscience that he believed the accused is innocent," but in the civil suit, he accused him of stealing money from the manumission society. Domingos was always surrounded by allies who helped him with the police bureaucracy. The mulatto bailiff from the Curato da Sé and accountant of the manumission group, Manoel Francisco de Paula, declared that, as he "habitually frequented Domingos Sodré's home," he had heard about João's death through the diviner.[63] He probably had other reasons for visiting Domingos besides counting the manumission society's money, which he also did. Of course, both public officials were well aware of Domingos' skills as a diviner-healer, and probably made use of them.

Elias Seixas chose better witnesses to defend him from the charge of appropriating the manumission society's money. Domingos' witnesses included two African-born individuals, one being João's widow, as well as two creoles, including João's stepson; and three mulattos, two being the bailiffs. None of them was white. Elias had three whites, a mulatto, a creole, and two African freedmen on his side. The most eminent white man among them was the subdelegado of Santo Antônio parish, the district where the African lived, Lieutenant Colonel João de Azevedo Piapitinga, whom we have come across several times in this book – even as a witness to Elias's wedding. As I have said, Elias was part of the subdelegado's African clientele, as Piapitinga stated that "he was most certain that the Accused was not a member of any sort of manumission society, and never held any sort of meetings at his home. On the contrary, he only associated with his own family," which was

---

[62] Ibid., fl. 89v.
[63] Witnesses at Elias's arraignment, APEB, *Judiciária*, no. 28/978/10, fls. 14v, 22.

absolutely false. As for holding money, he said that the African "had never communicated" such a thing to him, and boasted that he would have known, "because all Africans sought him as a witness in their business dealings." He saw himself as the great patron of freedpersons in Santo Antônio parish. Finally, he guaranteed – in both suits – that he had witnessed Elias's purchase of Leonarda's properties and could vouch for the African's honesty and probity, because he exercised "constant inspections and vigilance of all residents in his District, particularly the Africans."[64] As we have seen, a few months earlier, Piapitinga had assured the chief of police that he had done away with the Candomblé houses in his parish – a feat his superior questioned.[65]

Elias entrusted his business to other people who were higher up on the social ladder, all of whom resided in Sé parish in the center of the city, where he had lived as a slave of the Seixas family. Ricardo de Abreu Fialho Jr., a twenty-five-year-old white man who worked as a clerk in a notary's office and had stood godfather to Elias's daughter Francisca, stated that the African always consulted him about business matters, but had never said anything about the manumission society's money. If he was holding other people's money, he concluded, "being as scrupulous as he [Elias] is, he would have told him [the notary clerk]." Bernardino Andrade e Almeida, a mulatto cobbler, declared that Elias never did anything without consulting both an unnamed tradesman at his shoemaker's shop and Francisco Ribeiro de Mello Nabuco, a twenty-five-year-old white musician, who also testified on Elias's behalf. His testimony was even more damaging to Domingos' case. The musician declared that he had been the intermediary for a proposal made by Domingos to drop his suit against Elias. The diviner had initially demanded 500,000 reis, half of what he accused Elias of stealing, but was later content with just 250,000 reis. This incident convinced Nabuco that Elias did not owe the manumission society any money because, if Domingos' charge had been true, he "would not have given up three-quarters of the amount owed."[66]

Elias was eventually acquitted on November 30, 1863, more than three years after the civil suit in which he was accused of taking the

[64] Ibid., fl. 89v; "Witnesses for the defense," APEB, *Judiciária*, no. 26/921/16, fl. 71.
[65] João de Azevedo Piapitinga to the chief of police, May 26 and May 16, 1862, APEB, *Polícia*, maço 6195.
[66] Witnesses for the defense, APEB, *Judiciária*, no. 26/921/16, fls. 63 (quoting Nabuco), 65v–66 (quoting Fialho), and 69v.

manumission society's money began. Domingos had to pay the court costs – 37$800 reis (37,800 reis) – as well as his lawyer's fee, which I have been unable to ascertain.

DOMINGOS, THE AVENGER

Obviously, it is not for us to retry this case, but it is strange that ten years earlier, in 1852, Domingos told a similar story about a loan allegedly made to Cipriano José Pinto, a freed Hausa merchant, and Candomblé leader whom we met briefly in the last chapter and will get to know better in the next. In that suit, Domingos claimed the following about the alleged loan: "and knowing that the same [Domingos] held money for other African freedmen, he [Cipriano] had borrowed the amount of two million five hundred thousand Réis to purchase goods for sale." Here too we find that the money involved belonged to the manumission society. Domingos was said to have received as a guarantee a locked chest containing a mysterious "object of great value," but when the debt was not honored and the chest opened, all he found was "some pine boards."[67] This is certainly a preposterous story, which Cipriano vehemently denied.

Before I compared these two stories, I had gone so far as to imagine that Domingos believed he had seen in his divination game that Elias killed João because the dead man owed him money. He may have in any case interpreted João's death in terms of witchcraft, according to which logic an untimely death is not a part of the natural workings of life, and believed that Elias was somehow behind this plot no matter what caused João's tragic end: murder, an accident, or even suicide could all be explained as a result of witchcraft. I still ponder that, through divination or other means, Domingos was convinced that Elias Seixas had somehow, through whichever method, murdered his friend, fellow manumission society member, ethnic kinsman, and possibly a participant in the diviner's Candomblé circle.

The depositions in the lawsuit – that of Felippe Neves, for example – make plain that João was part of Domingos' social circle, as were his widow, the freedman Jugurta, and other workers at the Mocambinho canto, who had seized Elias that day in October 1860. Domingos held sway over them all. It was up to him to avenge the death of his friend,

---

[67] APEB, *Tribunal da Relação. Execução cível*, no. 22/0768/14, fl. 38.

ally, or dependent – whichever he was – and thereby validate his leadership of the group. The relationship between Domingos and Elias would have been between peers, and they were on good terms before João's death. A witness for the defense in the civil suit, when asked by Domingo's attorney why the diviner "imputed João's death to Elias," answered, "perhaps because of a falling out, because before João's death they got along well."[68] The falling out was probably due to the fact that Elias was held responsible for the death of one of Pai Domingos' people.

Domingos took on the role of avenger. Because of the bruises and wounds found on João's body, the cause of his death did not seem to have been witchcraft commissioned or prepared by Elias, and therefore the method of the latter's punishment should be secular, or both ritual and secular. If there was any, the documents do not reveal anything about ritual revenge – through witchcraft, for instance. About worldly revenge there is plenty. Domingos decided to sue Elias for stealing money from the manumission society, paying him back in the same coin. This is because he believed that financial motives had led Elias to murder João, who was killed, perhaps accidentally, on account of a debt. Therefore, Elias should pay for the crime in kind. This was the only plan left because the criminal investigation had come to nothing. Domingos guided his lawyer in the construction of a narrative of larceny that ran parallel to and overlapped with the one of murder. However, this plot became a collective effort because the diviner had enlisted witnesses who all got their stories straight in their sworn testimony against Elias. The main flaw was its similarity to the charge of larceny brought against Cipriano ten years earlier, of which Elias's defenders were apparently unaware.

Could Domingos have been inspired by a real story – Cipriano's – to attack Elias, or did he fabricate both charges? It is unlikely that, as clever as he was, Domingos could have been that easily swindled out of the manumission society's money on two occasions. What sort of theories would a good detective produce to solve this case? Was the diviner hopelessly naive or a complete scoundrel? There is a third possibility – that nothing was stolen because the manumission society did not have any money to distribute at that particular time. Domingos would have been acting according to a cultural code in which the methods of confrontation he chose may have been part of the game of life. In other

---

[68] "Witnesses for the defense," APEB, *Judiciária*, no. 26/921/16, fl. 66v.

words, Domingos the avenger was convinced – and had convinced his allies and dependents – that the accusation of stealing money from the society was a punishment, not the most fitting, but the only one possible, for the murder of João. The diviner may have sensed that his strategy would work. I do not even want to speculate what Domingos would have done with a million reis if he had won his suit against Elias.

As an African priest, Domingos had been trained to meet the demands of complex negotiations in the sacred sphere, which must have influenced, or at least inspired, him to reproduce them in the secular world. The practice of divination consists of a vast range of possibilities, from total success to absolute failure, depending on the diviner's performance in interpreting the symbols, consequent identification of the exemplary tales that they represent, and the corresponding sacrifices. Through offerings, prayers, and incantations, the diviner appeals to the gods and goddesses to identify the cause of a misfortune and advocate a solution. In a lawsuit, an exemplary narrative is also build up to convince the judge and jury that the cause is just, as Natalie Davis has observed in requests for pardons by people convicted of capital crimes in sixteenth-century France.[69] Domingos would have been in his element when he filed his papers – I almost wrote, his fiction – in court. Divination and so-called witchcraft had something in common with court proceedings, including a morality – or an apparent lack of it – that the non-initiated may find outlandish. Of course, here again the deeper cultural meanings of the lawsuit Domingos and his associates brought against Elias regarding the manumission society's money will never be completely clear to us.

We know, however, that these societies' business dealings were not always aboveboard, which may be why Domingos failed to convince some people with his story. Shady deals, swindles, and even witchcraft involving manumission societies may have been facilitated by scanty record keeping, which was not always based simply on its members' memories. There were codes that, even if they were not secret, could not be easily deciphered. Silva Campos has mentioned that accounts of deposits and withdrawals from the societies were done with strokes of a pencil or a piece of charcoal on a wall, while Querino and Amaral describe a more reasonable method, according to which the

[69] Natalie Zemon Davis, *Fiction in the Archives: Pardon Tales and Their Tellers in Sixteenth-Century France* (Stanford, CA: Stanford University Press, 1987).

contributions were marked with incisions on a wooden rod that each member kept in his possession. Amaral gave a more detailed description of this accounting method:

> Because they were not familiar with the numbers and lacked books and paper, they made incisions in a piece of wood or a stick, usually a piece of bamboo, corresponding to the members' entries, and the banker had a stick for each of his clients. It is a wonder that they did not get them mixed up and that they were able to do the calculations and adjust them with rudimentary accounting processes.[70]

I am not convinced that the Africans used this code to manage their finances instead of writing them down merely because they were unfamiliar with "the numbers" and "lacked books and paper." Nor was this a matter of "rudimentary accounting." Many members of the society were street workers and merchants who were perfectly capable of doing the math, and could buy books and paper, which were easily affordable for black ganhadores. If someone like Domingos Sodré could file lawsuits and pay lawyers' fees, why couldn't he buy paper? Doing the accounts by marking bamboo or another type of wood as well as marking contributions on walls were both Yoruba methods of accounting, and the Nagôs may have reproduced both in Bahia.[71] At the same time, these accounting methods would be another way for Africans to keep their business confidential. It is also possible that different groups used different means of keeping track of the society's members' deposits. But when these accounts were done, by whichever method, they had to be witnessed by a general assembly of the society.

Querino's and Silva Campos's informants at the turn of the twentieth century told them about disputes involving the funds of manumission societies. Silva Campos recounts the case of a water carrier, a freedwoman who was swindled by the organizers of one such association. Suspecting she had been cheated, she asked university students for whose collective residence she supplied water to help her calculate her contributions, and they concluded that she had already paid much more than she owed, so she took the society to court. Querino's comments on the subject are vaguer. He merely admits that there were many disputes

---

[70]   Amaral, *Fatos da vida do Brasil*, 128.
[71]   For markings on wood, personal communication from Toyin Falola, January 31, 2008; for markings on walls, see Bascom, "The Eṣuṣu," 66.

when the capital and dividends were distributed but, in the end, the complaisant author guarantees that everything was resolved without any need for "police intervention."[72] As we have seen, this was not always true.

The African manumission societies were a collective effort of solidarity for many, a business opportunity for some, and a chance for embezzlement for others. Domingos may have engaged in a bit of each, as his confrontations with Elias and Cipriano suggest. The course of his life, like those of many Africans who came to Brazil as slaves, was probably not free of moral turpitude. To achieve individual uplift, leaving behind the condition of slavery, and once freed, establishing themselves in the world of the free and surviving and thriving there, many Africans had somehow to trample some of their own people while extending a hand to others.

However, unlike most Africans, Domingos' position as a religious leader must have made his life easier, because he could make himself more respected, feared, obeyed, and served. Even so, it would not have got him very far if he had systematically let down his partners, associates, fellow Candomblé devotees, and clients, including the slaves who sought him out as one of their strategies for attaining freedom and resisting their masters. He had been accused of seeing slaves who asked him for his aid in gaining their manumission through his knowledge of herbs and his power to communicate with the gods. Freedom and witchcraft seemed to be closely linked in these transactions.

Whether as a diviner-healer or a manumission society leader, Domingos' activities interfered with a domain in which the slave owners did not admit any competition. Manumission was a key expedient in their policy of paternalistic control, and Brazil was the leading slaveocracy in the Americas in this regard, having formed a very large population of freed and free blacks, which at the time of Domingos was much larger than the slave population, and included many thousands Africans countrywide.[73] Many slaves believed that good service and loyalty would win them their freedom, particularly when their masters, when preparing for a good death, wrote their wills and sought to pay for their sins with this type of charity. Nevertheless, most letters of

---

[72] Campos, "Ligeiras notas," 298; Querino, A raça africana, 146–147.

[73] Klein and Luna, Slavery in Brazil, esp. chap. 9. See also Rafael Bivar Marquese, "A dinâmica da escravidão no Brasil: resistência, tráfico negreiro e alforrias," Novos Estudos, no. 74 (2006): 107–123.

manumission were sold, and that is why slaves knew it was essential to
save money before they could nurture hopes of freedom. And how big
did their savings have to be to purchase manumission? In this respect,
historian Kátia Mattoso aptly observes that the price of manumission
varied according to the relationship each slave established with his or
her master. She writes:

> It depends on the degree of intimacy that the slave enjoys with his
> master, feelings that are impossible to evaluate monetarily, which
> form a continuum between nuances of friendship and indiffer-
> ence. We can say there is a parallel market where the value of the
> slave is reduced if the master is determined to encourage manu-
> mission, [and] increased if he is against it. The letters of manu-
> mission granted at a price based on what was estimated between
> owner and slave undervalue the slave, while the price in other
> cases is close to the market price for slave labor.[74]

In other words, even paid manumission passed through the sieve of
paternalism. This is why, even with cash in one hand, the master generally wrote with the other that the slave's manumission was being
granted because of good service, loyalty, obedience, and so forth. Slaves
could not even buy their freedom without their master's consent, and
it was the slave owner who set the price of their manumission, at least
until the law of September 28, 1871 guaranteed the slaves' right to their
savings and ordered that it was up to a judge to set the "fair" price of
manumission whenever there was a dispute between the two parties.
Before that law, slaves were at the mercy of their masters as to their
right to their own savings, the price of their manumission, and even the
concession of freedom itself. This is where Domingos Sodré came in.

I suppose that Domingos' divination sessions counseled slaves to
seek freedom through the manumission society that he led, and as we
have seen, the healer's potions helped put the master in the right frame
of mind when negotiating terms – not only granting manumission but
doing so under favorable conditions, for a good price, if not for free.
Domingos' religious activity – or, if you like, his ability to manipulate
the spiritual order – attracted slaves to the manumission society he led,
and they filled its coffers, at least in part, with objects and money stolen from their masters. The police did not perceive this connection,

---

[74] Mattoso, *Être esclave au Brésil*, 210.

although interim subdelegado Pompílio Manuel de Castro wrote that slaves gave Domingos stolen items "as offerings to achieve their freedom." These "offerings" may have been votive, the diviner's payment, or deposits in the manumission society's account. In the statement of obligation he signed, Domingos promised to stop "enticing slaves and as a diviner making them grand promises of freedom."[75] I am convinced that these promises of freedom involved the manumission society, but the police were focused on witchcraft, or better yet, fraud disguised as witchcraft. They failed to make the right association between witchcraft and manumission. The suit against Elias – about which Subdelegado Pompílio must have known – and Domingos' arrest were therefore not interpreted as part of the same African method for negotiating freedom. But they were.

[75] Letter from Pompílio Manuel de Castro to the chief of police of the province of Bahia, July 27, 1862.

CHAPTER SIX

Meet Some Friends of
Domingos Sodré

The police accused two people of consorting with Domingos Sodré in relation to Candomblé in 1862. They were Manoel Joaquim Ricardo and Antão Pereira Teixeira, also African freedmen. In searching the archives, I have found another freedman who enjoyed Domingos' friendship and had been arrested about ten years earlier for running a small Candomblé terreiro in the sugar plantation Recôncavo. His name was Cipriano José Pinto. A summary of the biographies of these three supporting characters, their strategies for survival and success in Bahian society, their victories and defeats, sheds further light on the complex experience of a segment of the African community, the freedpersons or *libertos*, to which Domingos belonged and in which he circulated. Slave/master relations, family, work, property – including property in slaves – business acumen, intra-African solidarity, competition, and conflict, relations with state authorities, especially the police, spiritual afflictions, and religious affiliations are some of the themes explored in the lives of the three individuals portrayed here. Through them we will further explore the complexities of both slavery and freedom in nineteenth-century Bahia.

Manoel Joaquim Ricardo

João, the young slave arrested in Domingos' home in 1862, belonged to a successful transatlantic merchant, businessman, and slaveholder, Manoel Joaquim Ricardo[1], a Hausa freedman who then lived in Cruz

---

[1] A longer essay on this man is João José Reis, "From Slave to Wealthy Freedman: The Story of Manoel Joaquim Ricardo," in *Biography and the Black Atlantic*, ed. Lisa Lindsay and John Sweet (Philadelphia: University of Pennsylvania Press, 2014), 131–145.

do Cosme, the rural district ruled by subdelegado João de Azevedo Piapitinga, which was also home to Libânio José de Almeida and others charged with practicing witchcraft and Candomblé in Chapter 1 of this book. Manoel Joaquim, for instance, met Libânio in church, having at least once, in 1862, performed a baptism together in which the latter stood godfather and the former "touched Our Lady's crown" – meaning that the Mother of God was the godmother – on behalf of a creole child. Ricardo, it should be recalled, was a friend and neighbor, but also a compadre of Elias Seixas, who chose him and his wife as the godparents for his baby daughter.[2] At the time of Domingo's arrest in 1862, Subdelegado Pompílio Manoel de Castro charged Manoel Joaquim Ricardo with having a "house for these meetings" of Candomblé in Cruz do Cosme, adding that Domingos maintained "close relations" with him.[3] In short, the two were believed to be both good friends and coreligionists. The subdelegado must have known Manoel Joaquim; the freedman's deceased master was the common-law husband of Pompílio's sister-in-law, Umbelina Julia de Carvalho. Although in 1873, when she died, she was living in the outskirts of Salvador, Umbelina owned a house on Rua do Sodré, in Domingos' neighborhood. I suspect that this house had once belonged to Manoel Joaquim Ricardo's former master, who purchased a piece of land on that same street in 1836.[4] Domingos Sodré and Manoel Joaquim Ricardo may have met for the first time in that neighborhood.

In 1845, when he still lived in the port parish of Conceição da Praia, Ricardo purchased for 195,000 mil reis (the approximate price of a slave) two small adjacent plots of land in Cruz do Cosme, each from an African-born freedwoman, another example of an intra-African property deal. All told, the plots covered a 314-m^2 area, forming a small farm or roça, but Ricardo would add more land when he moved from the city to Cruz do Cosme. In September 1862, at a time when land prices had

---

[2] ACMS, *Livro de batismos da freguesia de Santo Antônio, 1852–1869*, fls. 167 and 178v.

[3] Pompílio Manuel de Castro to the chief of police of the province of Bahia, July 26, 1862.

[4] Probate records of Umbelina Julia de Carvalho, APEB, *Judiciária*, 07/3069/04. Pompílio appears as Umbelina's chief executor. She was not legally married to Manoel Joaquim's master, but inherited assets from him under usufruct. The purchase of the land in 1836 is registered in a "deed of purchase" for 60,000 in March 1, 1836. APEB, *LNT*, vol. 251, fl. 132v.

soared, he purchased a 154-m² plot for 1,200,000. It, too, was adjacent to the previously acquired properties.[5]

I have become better acquainted with Manoel Joaquim Ricardo through the extensive documents linked to a lawsuit begun in 1847, when he and another African freedman, Joaquim Antonio da Silva, both claimed ownership of two slave women, Constança and Francisca.[6] According to the court records and a few other sources, Manoel Joaquim's ex-master, Manoel José Ricardo, was a transatlantic trader whose ships crossed the ocean bound to both Lisbon and the Slave Coast in the Bight of Benin region. His slave Manoel Joaquim was brought to Brazil in the hold of one of those ships, the *Ceres*, in the early nineteenth century.[7] On his death in Bahia in 1841, Manoel José had freed fifteen slaves free of charge "in exchange for good service," one of them being Domingos' friend. While still enslaved, Manoel Joaquim Ricardo's owner allowed him to live like a freedman, running a rented shop since at least 1830, where he sold beans, rice, corn, and manioc flour in the Santa Bárbara Market, a major commercial hub in the port district where he also resided. According to receipts for the purchase of goods and payment of rent for the store and the house where he lived away from his master – documents that were included in the lawsuit – he, a slave, was treated by his creditors and landlords as "*Senhor* Manoel Joaquim." *Senhor* was a respectful treatment, roughly meaning Mr.; it also meant master or, according to a late eighteenth-century dictionary, "someone who has dominion over any slave or thing."[8] According to Manoel

5 "Deed of sale, with payment in full, made by Florência Maria de Jesus to Manoel Joaquim Ricardo for six *braças* of land for the amount of 90$000, as stated below"; "Deed of sale, with payment in full, made by Simianna de Souza, to Manoel Joaquim Ricardo, for six *braças* of land for the amount of Rs$105$500, as stated below," October 13, 1845, APEB, *LNT*, vol. 279, fls. 118v–119v; and "Deed of sale, with payment in full, made by Petronilio Ferreira da Conceição, to the minors Damazio, and Olavo, represented by their Father and guardian Manoel Joaquim Ricardo ... for a small farm, seventy *braças* wide, located in Cruz do Cosme, for the amount of Rs1: 200$000," APEB, *LNT*, vol. 361, fls. 93v–95.

6 APEB, *Judiciária*, no. 51/1821/04.

7 Manoel José Ricardo appears as a ship owner in the Bahia-Lisbon trade in Eduardo Frutuoso, Paulo Guinote, and António Lopes, *O movimento do porto de Lisboa e o comércio luso-brasileiro (1769–1836)* (Lisbon: Comissão Nacional para as Comemorações dos Descobrimentos Portugueses, 2001), 505–575, and as the owner of the *Ceres* in The Slave Trade Database (TSTD), voyages # 51234 (1795), # 51282 (1797), # 51434 (1806), and # 51476 (1807).

8 Antonio de Moraes Silva, *Diccionario da língua Portugueza* (Lisbon: Officina de Simão Tadeu Ferreira, 1789).

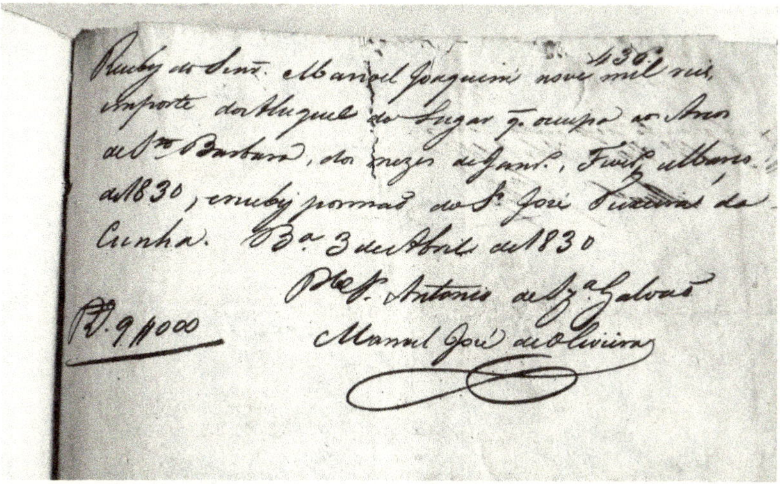

Figures 40, 41, 42. Receipts given to Manoel Joaquim Ricardo referring to him, a slave, as "Senhor," 1830, 1837 and 1838.

Joaquim, in addition to having "ample license" to do business and reside outside his master's house, he was authorized to be a slaveholder himself, because the slave owned an African girl named Thomazia, purchased in 1833 for 150,000 reis when she was twelve years old. Two years later, he had had her christened in Sé parish, where she was registered as belonging to the Tapa nation. Manoel Joaquim also said he actually owned several slave women before he obtained his freedom in 1841. He was attempting to contradict the opposing counsel's argument and convince the judge that the slave women at the center of the dispute could have been purchased before his manumission, in view of his very special relationship with his own master.[9]

---

[9] APEB, *Judiciária*, 51/1821/04, fls. 430v–436 (the quotations are on fls. 418 and 431). Thomazia was baptized on November 7, 1835, according to ACMS, *Livro de registros de batismo da freguesia da Sé, 1829–1861*, fl. 36v. Feliciana's sale is registered in AMS, *Escrituras. Conceição da Praia*, vol. 66.1, fls. 140v–141v. There is increasing evidence that slaves owned slaves in Brazil. See, for example, Reis, "From Slave to Wealthy Freedman" and "Social Mobility among Slaves in Brazil," paper presented at the *Heterodoxies* seminar, Vanderbilt University, 2013; Robson Pedrosa Costa, "A Ordem de São Bento e os escravos do Santo, Pernambuco, séculos XVIII e XIX," PhD, Universidade Federal de Pernambuco, 2013), chap. 3; Juliana B. Farias, Carlos Eugênio L. Soares, and Flávio Gomes, *No labirinto das nações: africanos e identidades no Rio de Janeiro, século XIX* (Rio de

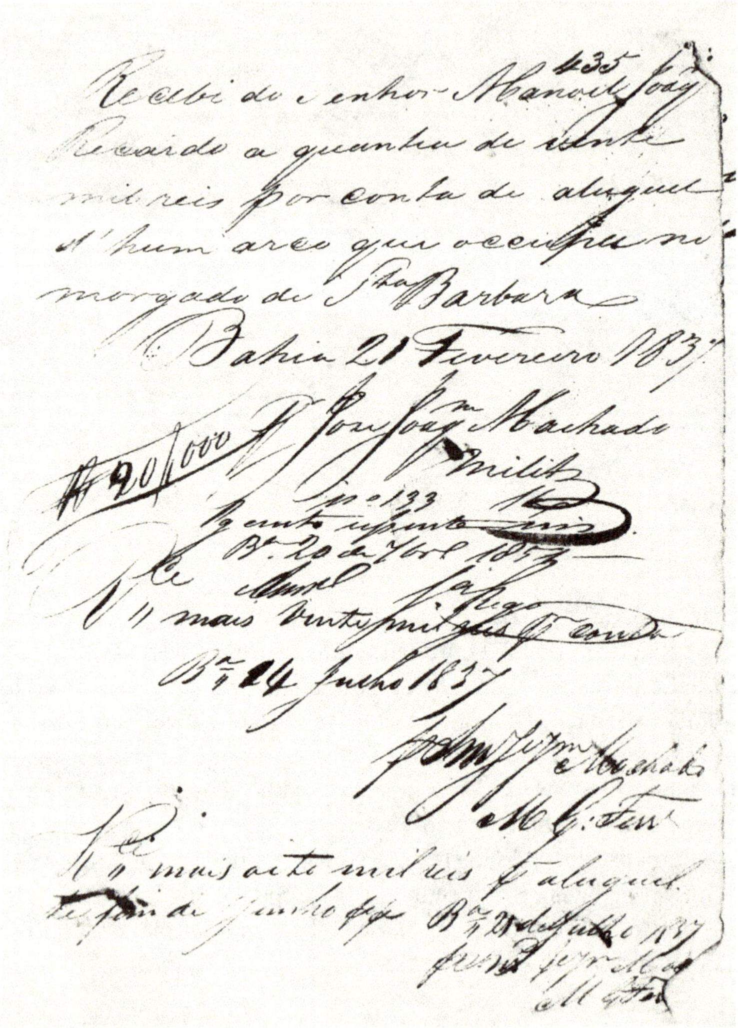

Figures 40, 41, 42. (*continued*)

While still a slave, Manoel Joaquim Ricardo had followed in his master's footsteps and become a transatlantic trader. Since at least 1839, he

Janeiro: Arquivo Nacional, 2005), 48. The custom of a slave offering one of their slaves in exchange for manumission is well documented. For nineteenth-century Salvador, see Oliveira, "Viver e morrer no meio dos seus," 187–188; Nishida, *Slavery and Identity,* 79–84; idem, "Manumission and Ethnicity," 387–390.

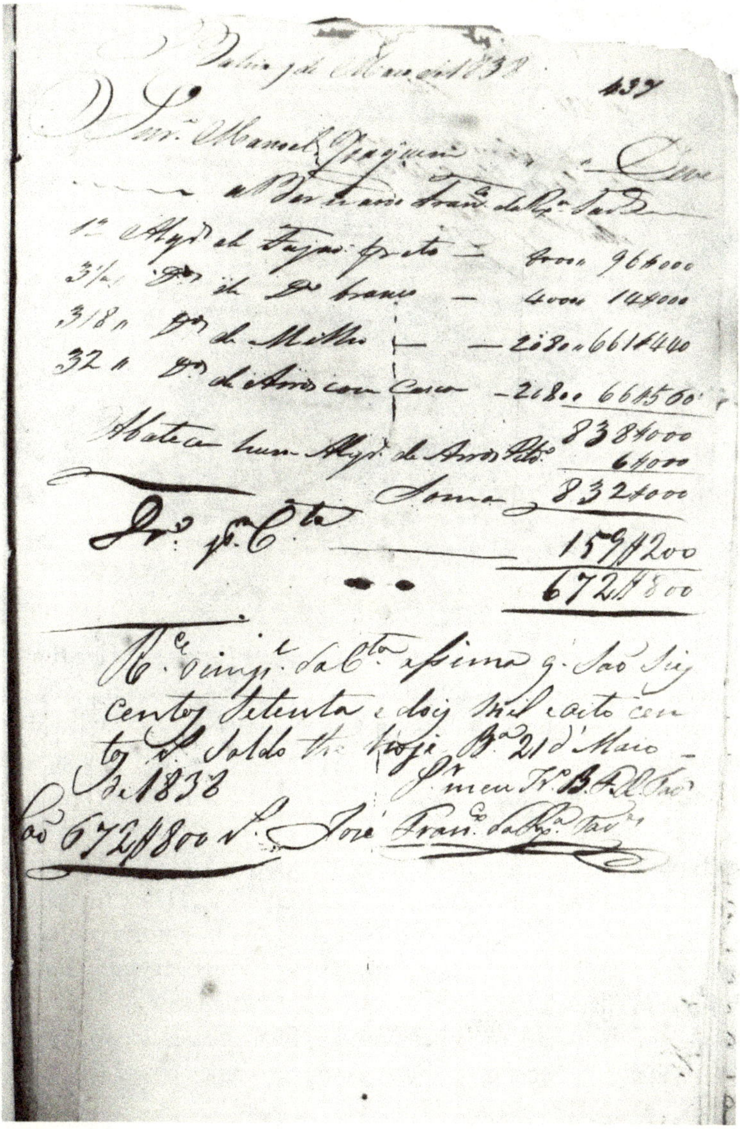
Bahia 9 de Maio 1838 437
Sr. Manoel Joaquim Deve
a Bernardino Franco da Rocha Pardo
Abateu hum Alqr. de Arroz 838$000
6$000
Soma 832$000
1598$200
672$800
Ba. 21 d'Maio de 1838

Figures 40, 41, 42. (*continued*)

had extended his business dealings to West Africa in partnership with Joaquim Antonio da Silva, the opposing party in the lawsuit, and Pedro Autran, a Nagô freedman both based in Ouidah (Autran stayed there permanently). Perhaps because he was already a freedman, it was Joaquim Antonio da Silva, not Manoel the slave, who crossed the ocean from time

Figure 43. Santa Bárbara Market in the Lower City, where Manoel Joaquim Ricardo ran a business.

to time, apparently to smuggle human cargo under the cloak of legitimate commerce. This is not to say that the only possible business with Africa at that time involved human trafficking. Other commodities included grass mats, baskets, gourd bowls, black soap, palm oil, kola nuts, starch, and other items consumed in Bahia, mainly by the Africans themselves, and sometimes for ritual purposes. If Manoel Ricardo and his associates dealt in such products, there are indications that they also slaves. According to British officials in Sierra Leone, Manoel Joaquim and his partners used the phrase "kola nuts" as code for "slaves" in their correspondence to mislead the anti-slave-trade authorities.[10] They also had business dealings with Joaquim Alves da Cruz Rios, who, along with his father, José, is on the list of major Bahian slave traders compiled by Pierre Verger, and was named as the leading slave trader in an investigation the French consul conducted in Bahia in 1846. He was also an important planter.[11]

[10] Walter W. Lewis and M. L. Melville, "Report of the case of the Brazilian brigantine 'Nova Fortuna,' Francisco José da Mota, Master," Sierra Leone, June 22, 1841, House of Commons Parliamentary Papers, Class A, *Correspondence with the British Commissioners Relating to the Slave Trade* (London: William Clowes and Sons, 1842), 152.

[11] APEB, *Judiciária*, no. 51/1821/04, fl. 97. Verger, *Flux et reflux*, 456–457 and passim; and Araújo, "1846: um ano na rota Bahia-Lagos," 91. Cruz Rios did business

So here we come across another peculiar situation: the slave Manoel Joaquim Ricardo was not only a slave owner but a slave trader. Several studies have found that African freedpersons were minor players in the transatlantic traffic in human beings.[12] But it was unusual, although not unknown, for slaves to get involved in this business. In Ricardo's case, the evidence is clear. There are records of goods he shipped to Africa from Bahia in 1839 and 1840, including crockery, coral beads (beads again), textiles, tobacco, and sugarcane brandy (*aguardente*), all – except the crockery – typical products used in the slave trade with the Bight of Benin, particularly tobacco. All that was lacking were rifles and gunpowder, but those were for major players. While he kept records of the goods he exported to Africa, Manoel Ricardo was suspiciously silent about his imports, except in private letters to his business partners, where he mentioned dealing with "kola nuts." Again, the slave trade was illegal, so the dispute between the partners over the two slaves could not have been conducted entirely and openly about that subject in a court of law.[13]

---

with other small African slave traders who owned slaves in Bahia, according to Verger, *Os libertos*, 117–118. Also regarding connections between Joaquim da Cruz Rios and the slave trade, see Pierre Verger, "Influence du Brésil au Golfe du Benin," in *Les Afro-Américains* (Dacar: IFAN, 1952), 59 et seq.; and regarding Cruz Rios as a plantation owner, see Barickman, *A Bahian Counterpoint*, 136.

[12] Regarding the involvement of African freedpersons in the transatlantic slave trade, see Verger, *Os libertos*, 9–13, 46–47, 55–65, etc.; Oliveira, "Viver e morrer no meio dos seus," 188–189; Reis, *Rebelião escrava*, 485–491; Nishida, *Slavery and Identity*, 86–87; Reis, "Social Mobility"; Luís Nicolau Parés, "Milicianos, barbeiros e traficantes numa irmandade católica de africanos minas e jejes (Bahia, 1770–1830)," *Tempo*, no. 20 (2014): 1–32 <http://www.historia.uff.br/tempo/site/>. Regarding relations between a major slave trader, Francisco Félix de Souza, or Chachá, with small traders, see Silva, *Francisco Félix de Souza, mercador de escravos*, 122. The story of an African freedman with some experience in that business is recounted in João Reis, Flávio Gomes, and Marcus Carvalho, *O alufá Rufino: tráfico, escravidão e liberdade no Atlântico negro (c. 1822 – c. 1853)* (São Paulo: Companhia das Letras, 2010).

[13] The goods Ricardo listed were precisely those most commonly imported by a famous slave trader from Ibadan. See Bolanle Awe, "Iyalode Efusetan Aniwura (Owner of Gold)," in *Nigerian Women in a Historical Perspective*, ed. Bolanle Awe (Ibadan: Bookcraft, 1992), 62. Regarding the role of tobacco in the slave trade in the Bight of Benin, see Verger, *Flux et reflux*, as well as idem, *O fumo da Bahia e o tráfico de escravos do golfo de Benin* (Salvador: Universidade Federal da Bahia, 1966). Regarding rifles and gunpowder, see Araújo, "1846: um ano na rota Bahia Lagos," 86.

Here are the arguments on both sides: Joaquim Antonio da Silva claimed that he had left two hire-out slaves, Francisca and Constança, both Jejes, under the "administration" of a third character in this story, Manoel José d'Etra. The latter was a forty-four-year-old creole, the son of an enslaved African woman, and the ward of (or born in the house of) José Antonio d'Etra, who was also African and died childless in 1829, leaving three slaves and some other less valuable property to Etra.[14] Since then, Manoel d'Etra had prospered: he was a barber-surgeon, the owner of a competent band of slave barber-musicians, and lent money to slaves at interest so they could buy their manumission. He was a trusted friend of Manoel Ricardo, four times his *compadre* – having stood godfather to four of Ricardo's children – and a constant presence in his business transactions. He wrote business letters and witnessed deeds of sale and manumission documents for Ricardo. (Manoel d'Etra, incidentally, must have known Domingos Sodré, for he lived just down the street from the diviner's residence on Rua do Sodré).[15]

According to Joaquim Antonio da Silva, the alleged owner of the slaves in question, during his absence in Africa the women were supposed to work for their own living and only turn to his business partner Manoel Ricardo in case of need. However, having heard that Joaquim Antônio was seriously ill in Ouidah, and believing he would die there, Manoel Ricardo, with the help of his good friend Manoel José d'Etra, allegedly plotted to take illegal possession of his human chattel by having the former register and baptize the African women as his own slaves. This transpired between 1845 and 1846. The baptismal records for Constança and Francisca in Conceição da Praia Church show the names of four other slaves that Ricardo owned.[16]

---

[14] "Registro de testamento com que faleceu José Antonio de Etra em sete de Maio de mil oitocentos e vinte oito...," APEB, *LRT*, vol. 16, fls. 100–102.

[15] In August 1843, Manoel d'Etra loaned 400,000 reis to Alexandre José da Fonseca Lessa so he could purchase his manumission from João Antonio da Fonseca Lessa. The debt was to be repaid in six years at monthly interest of 1.5 percent. See Arquivo Municipal de Salvador, *Livro de escritura de escravos*, no. 80.2, fl. 1. The *Almanach para o anno de 1845* (Bahia: Typ. de M. A. da S. Serva, 1844), 247, lists "Manoel José de Etra, owner of a band [of barbers], on Rua das Grades de Ferro: the best." This address is where Manoel Joaquim Ricardo also lived at the time.

[16] APEB, *Judiciária*, no. 51/1821/04, fls. 12v, 72v.

This baptism, carried out fourteen years after the slave trade was banned in 1831, adds to the suspicion that Constança and Francisca were imported illegally. That would explain why neither of the parties in the lawsuit could produce deeds of purchase or sale for these women. The 1846 tax registration of his slaves also suggests Manoel Ricardo's participation in the illegal trade. In addition to the two slaves in question, only five years after his manumission, the alleged Candomblé priest who was Domingos' friend had also registered ownership of another fifteen captives, all Africans like him – four men and eleven women, including Thomazia, his first slave, who was now twenty-four years old. Most were between eighteen and twenty-five years old, the typical age group of recently imported Africans.[17] Except for two men – a sailor and a domestic – all were vaguely described as working "for hire." If at this point, the mid-1840s, Manoel Ricardo was no longer engaged in the transatlantic slave trade, he was active in the internal trade, which was still legal: three of his slave women were sold to Rio de Janeiro that same year, 1846.[18]

Manoel Ricardo's version in the lawsuit was different. He confirmed that he had been Joaquim Antonio da Silva's friend and business partner, so much so that, after Silva returned from Africa, he had put him up for some time as "his protégé" in his house on Rua das Grades de Ferro. Later on, Silva had gone to live in his own place, but because he was still sick, Manuel Ricardo, "in consequence of the great friendship they had then," allegedly loaned out Felicidade and Constança to take care of him.[19] After that they purportedly agreed that Joaquim Antônio would buy the two women for one million reis, a sum that was never paid.

Manoel Ricardo also maintained that, when he left Bahia for Africa, his former partner owned just two slaves, Maria Roza and Jacinto Antonio da Silva, a mother and her son whom he left in Ricardo's care.[20]

---

[17] Out of a group of 234 slaves seized as contraband in 1836, the ages of 72.6 percent were estimated to be between eighteen and twenty-two. See APEB, *Polícia*, maço 2885. In Rio de Janeiro, 36 percent of a sample of 654 slaves that were embarked in 1852 were between twenty and twenty-nine years old. See also Herbert Klein, *The Middle Passage: Comparative Studies in the Atlantic Slave Trade* (Princeton, NJ: Princeton University Press, 1978), 102.

[18] APEB, *Judiciária*, no. 51/1821/04, fl. 13.

[19] Idem, fl. 10.

[20] This information is contradicted by a witness who states that Joaquim Antonio da Silva had two more slaves, Antonio and José. However, the documents for the lawsuit contain the registration of these slaves on August 20, 1847, a later date. See APEB, *Judiciária*, no. 51/1821/04, fls. 156 and 230.

Joaquim Antonio had a special relationship with Jacinto, to whom he had already given his surname, although he was not his son. The slave owner had taken the precaution of writing a conditional letter of manumission for mother and son that would have gone into effect if he had died on the other side of the Atlantic. Manoel Ricardo included this letter among the legal documents for the suit in an attempt to prove his honesty because he had never denied that his opponent owned the slaves mentioned therein. By the way, at the time, 1838, Ricardo was himself a slave.[21] Joaquim Antônio died in 1849 while the legal dispute with his former business associate Manoel Ricardo was still under way. The squabble would continue through his grandson (his daughter's child) and heir, Manoel Antônio da Silva. As the heir was still a minor, his legal representative in the case was his father, Manoel Francisco Duarte (there are several Manoels in this story), a typical character in the Atlantic world. Recently returned to Brazil from a stay on Príncipe Island, on the African coast, Duarte had also lived in Recife, where his son – now the plaintiff – was born. In an added twist to this complicated plot, two years later, the deceased's daughter, Ângela Custodia do Reino, would also step in to claim a share of her father's estate. She lived in Recife and made a point of being named as co-heir and a party in the lawsuit regarding ownership of Constança and Felicidade.[22]

The slaves being disputed never deposed, although they were in the best position to shed light on the case. We know that in 1846, Constança was thirty-five and Francisca forty. Both were Jejes and worked as hire-out slaves. Francisca sold African gourd bowls "a long time after the Sabino War," according to the African freedwoman Henriqueta da Silva Pimentel in her statement, which marked the passage of time in the African way with an important milestone event, in this case the liberal Sabinada Revolt (1837–1838). But the records show that both slave women also sold "foodstuffs."[23] While the court battle between the two African freedmen was under way, the disputed slaves went on with life as usual, including their personal lives. Constança gave birth to a child, and Francisca had two daughters. As a result, the victor's spoils were growing.[24]

[21] APEB, *Judiciária*, no. 51/1821/04, fls. 43–45v.
[22] APEB, *Judiciária*, no. 51/1821/04, fls. 450–460.
[23] APEB, *Judiciária*, no. 51/1821/04, fls. 13 and 153.
[24] APEB, *Judiciária*, no. 51/1821/04, fl. 195.

In short, a reading of the court documents provides plenty of evidence for both sides, and the only certainty is that, once they had dissolved their partnership because of a disagreement over the accounts – and there are several documents about this in the records of the lawsuit – one piece of unfinished business between the two merchants involved ownership of the two women. In April 1852, five years after it began, the suit went to the Court of Appeals, and after that, it vanished from the records. However, we know that Ricardo came out at least a partial winner. Francisca may have gone to his partner's heirs, but baptismal books show five of Constança's children registered as Ricardo's creole slaves. His 1865 probate records also included Constança, described as "*velha,*" an elderly woman (she would have been about sixty-five by then) who worked for hire and was valued at 400,000 reis. They also listed two of her children – the other having either died or been sold – including a fourteen-year-old creole boy named João, the same João who was arrested in Domingos' home in 1862.[25]

Like other masters, Manoel Joaquim Ricardo had trouble keeping his slaves in line. In the same month and year in which his suit against his former business partner went to the Court of Appeals, Ricardo's slave Geraldo disappeared. According to his owner, Geraldo was a "twenty-something-year old" creole. Ricardo made the complaint in July 1852, at least three months after his slave had vanished, as the freedman had learned that Geraldo was being harbored on a farm in Cotegipe parish in the completely rural outskirts of Salvador. Ricardo explained to the chief of police that the people sheltering his slave were a creole woman and one of her children, both of whom he promised to sue because "from this city they took the said slave enticed from a farm the Plaintiff owns in Cruz do Cosme." He asked the police chief to order the local subdelegado to capture Geraldo in name of the "guarantee of property rights,"[26] but that authority suggested that Manoel Joaquim put his request directly to the subdelegado. That same day, the freedman returned to the charge and argued that it would be more efficient if the police chief himself issued an order of capture to the subdelegado, who could easily implement them because

[25] Baptismal records of Constanças' children: ACMS, *Livro de batismos da Conceição da Praia, 1844–1889.* fls. 139v, 170v–171; and Ricardo's probate records, APEB, Inventário no. 04/1457/1926/18, fls. 13v, 14.
[26] Petition from Manoel Joaquim Ricardo to the chief of police, n.d., expedited on July 9, 1852, APEB, *Polícia,* maço 6317.

he owned a plantation facing the farm where Geraldo was hiding. Ricardo offered to take the order to that local authority as quickly as possible so the fugitive would not have time to flee again. The chief agreed, but by that time Geraldo had moved on, so he was not caught. At least, not yet.

It was only in mid-September, after nearly six months on the run, that Geraldo was finally arrested in Matoim parish, also on the outskirts of Salvador. On that occasion, Ricardo asked the police chief to hold his slave in the House of Corrections "until his fate was decided."[27] If the master wanted to use his slave's services again, he would have asked that the slave be returned immediately, after, perhaps, being punished with whipping or a beating with a ferrule by the police, as was the custom. But the punishment would be even more severe. By asking for him to be kept in jail, Ricardo signaled his intention to sell the slave. This was the usual expedient for punishing slaves who were disobedient, loafers, or prone to flee – in short, rebellious. It is also possible that Geraldo had fled to avoid being sold outside the province in the first place. After all his master was not only a farmer and merchant but a long-time slave trader. Geraldo's name does not appear in Ricardo's probate records in the mid-1860s, which confirms that he was sold prior to that period.

Another slave of Manoel Joaquim Ricardo gave him considerable trouble in early 1858. In a letter to the police chief, the freedman requested the release of an African named José whom he, his master, had ordered imprisoned two days earlier in the Aljube jail. Ricardo had sent his slave to jail "for disobedience, in order to dispose of him, because he does not want to behave and continue serving me." Like Geraldo six years earlier, José would now be sold, and Ricardo had hired a broker to "dispose of him." At Ricardo's request, that agent had gone to jail to fetch the clothes the slave had left there, only to find him behind bars once again. Ricardo then asked for his release because there was "no reason at all" for him to be jailed, as he supposed in his petition to the chief of police. But there was a reason. When consulted, the jailer informed his superior that José had been imprisoned again because he had tried to introduce a bottle of sugarcane brandy into the slaves' prison. The police chief ordered the jailer to send him to the

---

[27] Petition from Manoel Joaquim Ricardo to the chief of police, n.d., expedited on September 11, 1852.

Barbalho prison, where he would be given two dozen strikes of the ferrule for the offense and be immediately returned to his owner.[28]

Possibly because he had a reputation for insubordination, José was
not purchased, at least he had not been sold by June 25 of that same
year, 1858, six months after trying to slip brandy into the prison. On
that date he was arrested once again, this time for theft, by the subdelegado of Pilar, a parish next to Conceição da Praia. When he was
booked in prison, José was listed as a Nagô hire-out slave, twenty-eight
years old, almost certainly imported after the 1831 prohibition of the
transatlantic slave trade, but registered as legally "belonging to Manoel
Joaquim Ricardo."[29] José seemed to be one of those incorrigible slaves
whose masters, whether African or Brazilian, eventually gave up trying
to "tame." It is likely that José spent many years in thrall to the African
freedman because in 1846, when the tax registry of Ricardo's slaves was
made, an African named José appeared on the list. Like Geraldo, José is
not mentioned in the list of Ricardo's slaves inventoried seven years later.
He must have been sold as well.

The stories of Geraldo and José are similar to those of many other slaves
whose masters regularly sent them to jail for punishment. When they were
considered incorrigible, many were immediately sold, often outside the
province. This was a harsh punishment indeed, because it placed them far
away from their social networks and often their kinfolk in Bahia. Slave sale
advertisements from time to time required as a condition for the deal that
the purchaser send the acquired slave outside the province. Punitive sales
were a time-honored method of seigniorial control. Slaves who did not
toe the line knew they could be exported far away from their friends and
relatives, transferred from an environment they had learned to manage to
an unknown destination, an unpredictable and possibly even harsher form
of slavery. Historian Sidney Chalhoub observes that this form of punishment must have been worse than the whip, which opened wounds that
healed in time, while being sold did not. I agree. Geraldo the Crioulo may
have had a mother and siblings in Salvador, if not among Ricardo's other
slaves. Both Geraldo and José were removed from a slave community that,
although not as large as some, consisted of nearly thirty people, as we will

[28] Petition from Manoel Joaquim Ricardo to the chief of police, January 29, 1858,
APEB, *Polícia*, maço 6322; Maximo Joaquim da Silva Pereira, jailer at Aljube, to
the chief of police, January 28 and 29, 1858, APEB, *Polícia*, maço 6271.
[29] "Mapa de presos recolhidos na Cadeia do Aljube durante o dia 25 de junho de
1858," APEB, *Polícia*, maço 6271.

see shortly. For that reason, by the way, Manoel Ricardo felt he had to give
his slaves exemplary punishments to prevent insubordination from spreading to other members of the slave quarters. The African freedman seems
to have been a model slave owner. There is even more evidence of that.[30]

In December 1861, Manoel Joaquim Ricardo freed a Nagô woman by
the name of Esperança, who had paid him 2 million reis for her manumission.[31] This slave was probably the same Esperança whom he had
baptized and registered along with Constança, Francisca, and José in
1845. At the time she was about thirty-five and worked for hire in an
activity in which she seems to have prospered enough to pay twice the
amount of the average price of a slave in around 1860 – in fact, a time
when the price of manumissions reached its highest peak in the nineteenth century.[32] And when Esperança became a freedperson she was
no longer a young woman at the height of her productive strength, but,
for those times, an old lady of about fifty. Joaquim Ricardo had allowed
her to make and save money while she was enslaved, but he set a high
price for her freedom, on top of more than fifteen years of service. It
was a mean-spirited move. He did not even take into account that she
was the mother of at least three of his creole slaves, having thus further
contributed to Ricardo's prosperity.

[30] Regarding the internal slave trade, see, among others, Richard Graham, "Nos
    tumbeiros mais uma vez? O comércio interprovincial de escravos no Brasil, *Afro-
    Ásia*, no. 27 (2002): 121–160; Robert Slenes, "The Brazilian Internal Slave
    Trade, 1850–1888: Regional Economies, Slave Experience and the Politics of a
    Peculiar Market", in *The Chattel Principle: Internal Slave Trades in the Americas*,
    ed. Walter Johnson (New Haven, CT: Yale University Press, 2005), 325–370;
    Silva, "Caminhos e descaminhos da abolição," chap. 3. The interesting case of
    a slave who in 1875 attempted to kill her mistress for wanting to sell her out-
    side the province is reported in Reis, "A família negra no tempo da escravidão,"
    40–61. Also regarding sales, the tensions this generated, the rebelliousness
    of slaves imported from the north, and other related subjects, see Chalhoub,
    Visões da liberdade, especially chap. 1. Not all authors agree that slaves imported
    from the north would typically be rebels in the south. See Maria Helena P. T.
    Machado, *Crime e escravidão: trabalho, luta, resistência nas lavouras paulistas,
    1830–1888* (São Paulo: Brasiliense, 1987), esp. 48–49, n. 17.
[31] Letter of manumission for Esperança, December 17, 1861, APEB, *Livro de notas
    do tabelião*, no. 360, fl. 140v.
[32] See Kátia Mattoso, Herbert Klein, and Stanley L. Engerman, "Notas sobre as
    tendências e padrões de preços de alforrias na Bahia, 1819–1888," in *Escravidão
    e invenção da liberdade: estudos sobre o negro no Brasil*, ed. João José Reis (São
    Paulo: Brasiliense, 1988), 66.

The year of Domingos' arrest, Manoel Joaquim Ricardo's name appeared, a few months earlier, in a correspondence from Subdelegado João de Azevedo Piapitinga to the chief of police. Lest we forget, Chief João Henriques had accused this subdelegado of tolerating candomblés in the district under his charge, which included the rural neighborhood of Cruz do Cosme, Ricardo's address. Piapitinga's letter does not refer to Manoel Joaquim Ricardo as a Candomblé practitioner, but the freed-man does appear as a major reveler. He had asked and received "permis-sion to dance" from a prior police chief – at Subdelegado Piapitinga's recommendation – who authorized him to hold a three-day party to celebrate his marriage to Rosa Maria da Conceição, in 1860.[33] I have no doubt that it was the real reason for those festivities. Piapitinga himself mentioned the episode as an example of the kind of African pastimes he did in fact tolerate because no harm to public morals and order would result from it, while stating that he had put an end to the Candomblé celebrations in his district. Now, he maintained, thanks to his good counsel, Africans had found a new way of life: farming. Ricardo was himself a farmer, as well as a merchant, landlord, and a slaveholder, so he was more than entitled to receive a party permit.[34]

As another example of the type of African festivities he tolerated, Piapitinga mentioned the Cruz do Cosme farmers' harvest festival, suppos-edly without suspecting that the dances held during the event might have formed part of African agricultural fertility rites, which were, of course, pagan religious expressions. This was the case with the feast of the New Yam, which paid tribute to Obatalá and marked the beginning of the sea-son of public ceremonies at some Bahian candomblés. A careful observer of the African religion in Bahia, O Alabama reported in 1870 that this festival "consisted of the consecration of the first fruits of each year's har-vest to the African divinities. Before this ceremony is held, the proselytes of the African sects are prohibited from eating them."[35] As I mentioned in

---

[33] I have not been able to find the parish record of this marriage.
[34] João de Azevedo Piapitinga to the chief of police, April 26 and May 16, 1862, APEB, Polícia, maço 6195.
[35] O Alabama, November 24, 1870, 4. Graden, From Slavery to Freedom, 121–122, comments on the festivities, based on a report published in 1867, again in O Alabama. Regarding the New Yam festival, see also a brief description by Querino, A raça africana, 52–53. A similar ceremony was held in Sergipe in the late nineteenth century, as documented by Sharyse Piroupo do Amaral, "Um pé calçado, outro no chão": liberdade e escravidão em Sergipe (Cotinguiba, 1860–1900) Salvador: EDUFBA; Aracaju: Editora Diário Oficial, 2012), 318–319.

the first chapter, yam farming was one of the main economic activities of Africans living on the outskirts of Salvador, particularly in Cruz
do Cosme, and their religion permeated farming activities and eating
habits. On the occasion of the harvest festival – and other occasions –
as Subdelegado Piapitinga wrote to his chief, "families and young men
of different classes" came from town to "frolic" with the Africans. If
we associate this information with Manoel Ricardo's reputation as a
Candomblé practitioner linked to Domingos, it is easy to imagine that
the subdelegado was pulling the wool over the police chief's eyes and
did in fact tolerate candomblés in his district, depending on who was
in charge. Either that or the Africans – perhaps Ricardo himself – were
duping him by celebrating religious rituals like the New Yam festival
under the pretext of holding dances that were "no threat to morals," in
that police authority's jargon.[36]

The marriage feast that took place around 1860 celebrated Ricardo's
long-term conjugal relationship with Rosa Maria da Conceição. At that
point, he was about seventy years old. In a statement given in 1850,
related to the lawsuit against Antonio Joaquim da Silva's heirs, he
declared that he was single. A witness in the same lawsuit stated that, in
about 1847, he was living in the house on Rua das Grades de Ferro, and
living well and comfortably, with a woman who helped him manage
his hire-out slaves. She was Rosa Maria da Conceição.[37] Ricardo and
Rosa's surviving children included three sons and one daughter. The
eldest was their daughter, Benta, born in 1834, followed by Martinho
in 1840. The others, Damazio and Olavo, were born in 1843 and 1845,
respectively.[38]

Two of Manoel Ricardo and Rosa Maria da Conceição's children frequently appear in the records – Damazio and Olavo Joaquim
Ricardo. Esperança's letter of manumission, issued in 1861, was signed
by Damazio. Now a grown-up and literate, he had replaced Manoel
d'Etra as his father's scribe. In late August of that year, Manoel Joaquim
Ricardo purchased land in both their sons' names, "a small farm ... with

[36] Subdelegado João de Azevedo Piapitinga to Chief of Police Henriques, April 26
      and May 16, 1862, APEB, *Polícia*, maço 6195.
[37] APEB, *Judiciária*, no. 51/1821/04, fls. 150, 156v, 157.
[38] Baptismal records for Ricardo's children in ACMS, *Livro de registro de batismos.
      Freguesia da Conceição da Praia, 1834–1844*, fls. 160, 275; ACMS, *Livro de reg-
      istro de batismos. Freguesia da Conceição da Praia, 1844–1889*, fls. 1v, 29v; ACS,
      Livro de registro de óbitos da C. da Praia, 1847–1895*, fl. 7v.

a mud hut and a tiled roof located in Cruz do Cosme." But in the notarized deed, the father stated that his sons could not

> dispose of the property, nor anything related to it ... or mortgage
> it to anyone while their father Manoel Joaquim Ricardo, and his
> wife Rosa Maria da Conceição, are still living, who because of the
> amount lent [to their children] are in possession and enjoyment of
> the property acquired, and the children have no right to the prop-
> erty while their said Parents are living, just as they [the Parents]
> have no right to demand the amount of the loan from their chil-
> dren, unless at any time their children plan to take possession of said
> property, and the transfer will not be effected unless they immedi-
> ately pay not only the price but all expenses and improvements
> which their Parents have carried out to add value to the property.[39]

That way, the couple was forestalling a future filial mutiny. But why didn't
Manoel Ricardo and his wife simply buy the land in their own names?
Although they already owned land, such as the farms acquired in 1845,
they did so illegally because according to chapter 2 of Provincial Law
no. 9, passed after the African uprising in 1835, Africans were prohibited
from purchasing real estate property. That law does not seem to have
been strictly enforced, enabling Ricardo to buy those farms and other
properties with impunity. However, in 1847, the Provincial Assembly of
Bahia reaffirmed the law "after a heated debate," according to a news
report in Correio Mercantil.[40] When he registered his not-so "small farm"
in 1861 in his sons' names, and included suspensive clauses in the deed,
Ricardo was trying to find a way around the law while ensuring that he
and his wife could use the property without fear of seeing it confiscated
by the government. In fact, Ricardo himself confessed as much in his last
will and testament, written that same year, 1861: "I hereby declare that
before I was married, and even afterwards, I purchased some properties
and other real estate in my children's name because I was prohibited from
purchasing it in my name by Provincial Law no. 9 of May 13, 1835."[41]

One important aspect of Manoel Ricardo's life is his ethnic affiliation in Bahia. In the clause of his will that freed Ricardo, his master merely mentioned that he was "African," and from then on this
was how the freedman described himself and how he was referred to in

[39] APEB, LNT, no. 361, fl. 94.
[40] Correio Mercantil, March 11, 1847.
[41] APEB, Judiciária. Testamento, no. 04/1457/1926/18.

numerous documents. But Manoel Ricardo is listed as Hausa in several baptismal records in which he stood godfather to adult African slaves between 1826 and 1830 in Conceição da Praia parish.[42] Later on, in an 1850 petition to the municipal judge during that lengthy lawsuit, his opponent stated that Ricardo belonged to the "Hausa Nation."[43] This is the only ethnic reference attributed to Manoel Ricardo in a case that produced nearly 500 pages of documents, and while it confirms the baptismal records it also points to a vanishing public identity. The fact that Manoel Ricardo stopped describing himself as a Hausa may have been a precaution to avoid being identified as a *mussulmi* (Hausa Muslim) after the 1835 rebellion, when some members of his ethnic group, most of them freedmen, were arrested and tried, although only a couple were found guilty. The fact is that his African origins ended up fading into the background, at least to those unfamiliar with the African community to which he belonged. Nearly three decades later, for example, merchant Antonio dos Santos Coimbra, age fifty-three, a witness in a police inquiry, referred to Olavo Ricardo as the "son of Manoel Joaquim, a black Jeje man, deceased."[44]

Manoel Joaquim Ricardo died "of an internal ailment" on June 20, 1865, at "the presumed age of ninety," according to the vicar of Santo Antônio Além do Carmo parish. His body was dressed in a black Franciscan habit, a very popular shroud among freedpersons, and the following day he was buried in the Quinta dos Lázaros cemetery, in a funeral accompanied by an orchestra and lit by numerous torches. There, after being commended by a Catholic priest in a lavishly decorated funeral chapel, he was laid to rest in one of the niches of the Franciscan Order. This African had died in style.[45]

Manoel Joaquim Ricardo was a wealthy man: he owned twenty-seven slaves worth 19,100,000 reis, representing half of his estate when he died, the other half being two plots of land and four houses, including the three-story townhouse on Rua das Grades de Ferro, where he spent

---

[42] ACMS, *Livro de registro de batismos. Freguesia da Conceição da Praia, 1826–1844,* fls. 39, 39v, 44, 215, and 234v.

[43] APEB, *Judiciária. Processo-crime,* no. 51/1821/04, fl. 213.

[44] APEB, *Judiciária. Processo-crime,* no. 22/949/16 (1873), fl. 14.

[45] ACMS, *Registro de óbitos. Santo Antônio Além do Carmo, 1851–1866,* fl. 315. Several studies confirm the popularity of the Franciscan shroud among freedpersons in Bahia: Mattoso, *Da revolução dos alfaiates à riqueza dos baianos,* 244; Oliveira, *O liberto,* 96; and Reis, *A morte é uma festa,* esp. 125–126.

most of his life as a freedman, and a three-bedroom terraced house to which he moved in Cruz do Cosme, built next to a "large slave quarters with a tile roof divided into rooms for slaves." His inventoried estate reached an exact total worth of 42: 302$740 (42,302,740 reis). He belonged to the wealthiest 10 percent of Salvador (including white proprietors) even after paying his debts, such as bank loans, taxes, and funeral and probate expenses.[46] He left assets with a net value of 36 million reis, half of which went to his four children and half to his widow, as established by law. In addition to their inheritance, three of his children plied a trade: Damázio was a merchant and Olavo and Martinho were carpenters. They were all literate, including Benta, who had by then married a creole teacher born in Bahia.

Manoel Ricardo's contingent of slaves consisted of fifteen Africans and twelve creoles. The Africans included five men and ten women. All of the women were listed as working in the streets as earners, even the two described as "elderly." Four of the men were listed as farm laborers – one also worked as a litter bearer – and one was a barber. Most of the creole slaves were the children of his African slave women. Just three are listed without an occupation and described as having a "chest" ailment, including João, who was arrested in Domingos Sodré's home in 1862. The work of his slaves was without a doubt the most important source of income for Manoel Ricardo, and his main means of capital accumulation. Unlike his master, Manoel Ricardo did not free any of his slaves in his will. His houses and land, marriage, and legitimate children, as well as numerous slaves, made him one of the most successful African freedpersons in Bahia during his time. Other friends of Domingos did not attain the level of prosperity Ricardo achieved.

If he was an important figure in the Candomblé of Bahia, Manoel Joaquim Ricardo may not have been persecuted because he had enough money to buy the silence of the police, including that of Subdelegado Piapitinga. This possibility should not be discarded. However, apart from Subdelegado Pompílio de Castro's accusation in 1862 that Ricardo was the leader of a Candomblé terreiro, the evidence is scarce and limited to people in his circle of friends and business partners. There was his partnership with Pedro Autran, the husband of a famous Nagô priestess, and himself a priest of S̩àngó̩ exiled to Ouidah after the Malê Revolt. There was Marcelina da Silva, better known as Obatossi, who succeeded

---

[46] For wealth distribution in Salvador, see Mattoso, *Bahia*, 607.

Autran's wife as high priestess of Ilê Axé Iyá Nassô Oká, better known as Casa Branca (White House), whose slave Delfina had declared to the police she was Ricardo's slave but was indeed Marcelina's, indicating a close relationship between the two.[47] In terms of religion, so far I have found nothing linking Ricardo with Islam, the religion usually associated with the Hausas, but he could have been knowledgeable about *Bori*, a Hausa possession cult highly syncretized with Islam that would have facilitated his conversation with practitioners of other traditions of spirit possession religions, people like Domingos Sodré or Cipriano José Pinto.[48]

Cipriano José Pinto

Domingos Sodré had another Hausa friend, the freedman Cipriano José Pinto, who was a confessed Candomblé practitioner. As we have seen in the previous chapter, Domingos had accused Cipriano of failing to repay a large business loan. Let us dig deeper into this story.

A small merchant with a shop on Carmo hill, only a couple of steps from an imposing Carmelite convent, Cipriano sold African shawls, clothing, shoes, raffia baskets, berimbaus (the musical bows associated with capoeira), rosaries, skullcaps, mousetraps, funeral wreaths, pens, inkwells, fish hooks, toothbrushes, and sundry items like buttons, thread, and pins, among other goods from an extremely varied inventory, including cultural variety. Some items could have been used in African rituals, such as the shawls and baskets, berimbaus, and skullcaps, the latter being very popular among Malês and well-to-do Africans. In the hands of a Malê, a pen and ink could become a religious instrument used to copy verses from the Qur'an and make written amulets.

---

[47] José Pereira da Silva Moraes to the jailer at Aljube, June 26, 1861, APEB, *Correspondência*, vol. 5745, fl. 119. Regarding the Casa Branca terreiro, see Silveira, *O candomblé da Barroquinha*, esp. chaps. 8 et seq., in which he systematically studies that temple's rich oral tradition; and Castillo and Parés, "Marcelina da Silva e seu mundo," which contains an abundance of fresh empirical data on this subject. That Autran was a priest of Ṣàngọ́ is information I obtained from Lisa Castillo, who has interviewed his descendants at Ouidah. Personal correspondence, September 28, 2013.

[48] Regarding *bori*, see Freemont E. Besmer, *Horses, Musicians, and Gods: The Hausa Cult of Possession Trance* (South Hadley, MA: Bergin & Garvey, 1983); and Jacqueline Monfopuga-Nicolas, *Ambivalence et culte de possession: contribution à l'étude du Bori Haoussa* (Paris: Anthropos, 1972).

Cipriano himself, who was a Hausa – a predominantly Islamic and rel-atively literate (in Arabic) group – may have produced amulets for sale in his shop. And he also sold rosaries and funeral wreaths for the con-sumption of Africans, Brazilians, Portuguese, and other Europeans who in different ways followed or used customs of the Catholic faith.

In October 1852, Cipriano was sent to the Aljube prison because, as of late July, he owed 25,000 reis for eight months' unpaid rent on his store. His merchandise, valued at a little more than 500,000 reis, was confiscated to pay that debt and other, much larger ones that arose dur-ing the course of the lawsuit. A year earlier, he had borrowed 600,000 reis from a neighbor. In the document recording that transaction, Cipriano stated that the money, which was to be paid in six months (a deadline that had already expired), would be used "to sell bric-a-brac on Carmo Hill." But Cipriano's biggest creditor was apparently none other than our own Domingos Sodré, who claimed to have lent the Hausa merchant the small fortune of 2,500,000 reis, roughly five times the value of the merchandise confiscated from Cipriano's shop. According to Domingos, the creditor and debtor maintained "relations of friend-ship," which had facilitated the transaction intended as an investment in Cipriano's store. Cipriano contested that debt, and said that it was "an invention" on Domingos' part. However, Domingos won this law-suit, although he only received 128,000 reis of the 2.5 million he had demanded, because all the debtor's worldly goods – the inventory of his store – were simply not enough to cover that massive, perhaps implau-sible debt.[49]

The two African freedmen's friendship probably had something to do with religion. Cipriano was not just a merchant; the following year we will again find him involved with the police, this time charged with running a candomblé. While his creditors were haggling over the spoils from his store, the freedman sneaked out of Salvador and started a new life in the Recôncavo, probably with some of the money he had hid-den from the courts when declaring his assets. There, he established a Candomblé house on land belonging to a sugar plantation and opened a small business in the village of Paramirim, within the limits of the important sugar-producing town of São Francisco do Conde.[50]

[49] APEB, *Judiciária. Tribunal da Relação. Execução cível*, 22/0768/14 and 12/411/14. The quotations are from fls. 41v, 37, 38.
[50] See inquiry in APEB, *Polícia*, maço 6185. Although there are problems with the transcription, the main documents related to this candomblé have been published and analyzed by Soares in "Resistência negra e religião," 133–142.

The experiment was short lived. In mid-1853, the police raided Pai Cipriano's candomblé, where, according to the local delegado's report, they found "a room richly decorated with fabric on the walls, trimmed with cowries, beads, coral and further adornments and other ingredients from the Mina Coast, a throne, benches and additional articles whose names we do not know." They found offerings of palm oil, wine, brandy, and chicken feet and blood, among others. There were also stones, bones, and "a bag full of bits of paper with Malê writing on them," in other words, amulets written in Arabic that reflect the Hausa priest's mussulmi influence. These pieces of paper could have been the work of the African himself. However, he did not profess the religion of Mohammed, at least, not exclusively. Cipriano may have been a Hausa Bori priest. When questioned, he declared that he had set up a house "for his saint from his land," which was certainly not Allah. His presumed Bori had adopted other ingredients in Bahia that were unknown in his homeland, such as offerings of palm oil and brandy. This was yet another case of cultural mixing.[51]

In addition to worshipping the divinity he had brought with him from Africa, Cipriano used the terreiro, in his words, "as his pastime and to sell [goods] to other blacks and thus do business," meaning that, through religious rituals – "his pastime" – he attracted clients to his, say, legitimate business. If this was true, his stock of merchandise, compared with what he had had in Salvador, was still modest, because it only included a few African shawls found in the Candomblé temple, crockery, and manioc flour arranged on shelves in his house in the village. Without being asked, he declared that the rent on that house had been paid in advance, which was his way of saying that he no longer cheated his landlords.

The police confiscated ritual objects and arrested Cipriano, his partner, Sofia da Matta – from the Efon nation, a Yoruba-speaking subgroup (more mixing) – and an elderly black man, Venceslao Marinho, whose ethnic affiliation is not specified in the documents. A report from the chief of police dated April 30, written in the margins of the letter from the São Francisco do Conde delegado who had sent the African prisoner to Salvador, refers to the charge Domingos and other creditors had brought against him: "Cipriano had already been investigated for larceny." It was a statement that almost condemned him outright, but even worse suspicions were soon to come.

Together with Venceslao and Sofia, Cipriano was jailed in Aljube on March 30, 1853. The old man would be freed a few days later, on April 6.[52] I do not know when Sofia was released, but Cipriano remained behind bars. He had had the very bad luck of being arrested shortly before rumors that Africans were planning a revolt began to stir in Salvador. The alarm was sounded in early April, when a subdelegado from Salvador confiscated Malê writings from an African, and the authorities became increasingly apprehensive in the weeks that followed.[53] In mid-May, the police began arresting suspects and sending them to Aljube. On May 21, twenty-two Africans, with Cipriano at the head of the list, were transferred in Navy longboats to a fortress in the port of Salvador considered a high-security prison because surrounded by water. In 1835 the Sea Fortress – known today as Fort São Marcelo – had been used to hold Africans arrested during the Malê rebellion.[54]

We have a report describing fears of African revolt that year, penned by the British consul John Morgan Jr., situating the height of the rumors at the beginning of the second week in May. Residents of Salvador were alarmed by the mobilization of armed troops. The press that sided with the government kept quiet to avoid alarming the public even more, but it was impossible to hide the large contingent of cavalry that occupied the streets at night, while the infantry maintained a state of high alert in the barracks. Word was going around that weapons had been confiscated in the homes of Nagô freedmen – Domingos' people. Banners and clothing similar to those worn by the Muslim rebels in 1835 had allegedly been seized. The police ransacked houses in a "deplorable" fashion, according to the consul, and filled the jails with African suspects. Morgan believed that the evidence gathered did not justify the authorities' arbitrary behavior, and that the rumors were being used as an excuse to deport African freedmen who fell under suspicion, just as the government had done in 1835.[55]

---

[52] André Chichorro da Gama to the president of the province, March 31, 1853, APEB, Polícia. Correspondência, 1852–53, vol. 5712, fl. 140.

[53] Manoel Francisco Borges Leitão to the chief of police, April 4, 1853, APEB, Polícia, maço 6230. See also Graden, From Slavery to Freedom, 105.

[54] André Chichorro da Gama to the president of the province, May 21, 1853, APEB, Polícia, maço 3133.

[55] John Morgan Jr. to Clarendon, May 13, 1853, British National Archives, Foreign Office 84: 912. Also transcribed by Verger, Flux et reflux, 537–538.

Figures 44 and 45. The Sea Fortress, where Cipriano was imprisoned.

Domingos Sodré himself would be briefly arrested in late May, but he was not interned in the Sea Fortress, where he might have been reunited, and probably quarreled extensively, with his former friend and debtor Cipriano. As I have indicated, Domingos managed to convince the authorities that he was a well-behaved, pro-white African, and even proved himself a veteran of the war of independence in Bahia – and was allowed to go free. Other Africans were not so lucky. In June, Roberto Argolo, a Nagô freedman, begged in vain to be released from Aljube because "no object that could be used in an insurrection or even an indication of that" was found in his house, which was confirmed by the constable responsible for conducting the search.[56] As for Cipriano, he was a perfect suspect because he had been arrested in São Francisco do Conde with Arabic writings in his possession that, apparently, he used either in his Candomblé rituals or as amulets. However, remembering the 1835 Malê Revolt, the police saw them as a sign of a high African conspiracy. Profiled as a dangerous fellow, Cipriano was transferred from Aljube to the Sea Fortress.

In addition to Muslim writings, Bahian authorities were concerned with another form of the written word in those days, despite the fact that it contained a considerable dose of Christian sentimentality. In July, booksellers J. Baptistas Martin and Carlos Pogetti were ordered to surrender copies – eighty-two from Martin's shop and thirty-six from Pogetti's – of a particular book to police headquarters. It was Harriet Beecher Stowe's abolitionist novel *Uncle Tom's Cabin*, which had been translated into Portuguese, published in Paris and available in Brazil with enormous speed, sometime during the first semester of 1853. The book had come out in the United States the previous year and became a best-seller, only outsold by the Bible, which was certainly its devout author's favorite book. Despite the passivity of the slaves it portrayed, the novel openly denounced the suffering inflicted on them by their masters, and therefore condemned the institution of slavery. This seemed sufficiently dangerous in the eyes of Bahia's apprehensive authorities, at least during those tense times when public order seemed to be under threat. What if the book fell into the hands of a literate slave or was read aloud by a sympathetic free person to a slave audience? Better not to risk it.[57]

[56] Petition from Roberto Argolo to the chief of police, n.d., expedited on June 7, 1853, APEB.

[57] For police confiscation of copies of the book, see APEB, *Polícia*, vol. 5645–1, fls. 34v–35. The Portuguese edition is Harriet Beecher Stowe, *A cabana do Pai*

In a report to the president of the province about fears of rebellion, Police Chief João Mauricio Wanderley justified the measures he had taken: "Your Excellency is aware that in May of this year, there were serious fears that African freedmen and slaves would attempt a rebellion: precautionary measures were taken, the main one being the arrest of the most suspicious African freedmen for deportation; and the fact is that not a few were captured and imprisoned in the Sea Fortress, where they are still being held for that purpose."[58] The tension went on until mid-September, when the chief of police once again wrote to the president to give an explanation about a freedman whose arrest the Uruguayan consul had denounced as arbitrary: "since the fears have dissipated of an insurrection that led to the arrest of said African and others, who are now in the Sea Fortress, I think they should all be removed to the Aljube prison in order to be examined and so that those who are not suspects can be released, and the others deported as soon as possible."[59]

These words were written on September 12, 1853. Four days later, Cipriano José Pinto would be taken back to Aljube after spending 128 days in the Sea Fortress. The Hausa freedman then occupied cell number 4 of that jail. Ten years earlier, Dr. João José Barbosa described that particular cell as "the worst" in Aljube in his medical school graduation thesis: "made of bricks, very poorly cleaned, dark; humidity; some heat; just 2 windows."[60] At the time, between twenty and twenty-five people were imprisoned there. When Cipriano was in jail, there were fewer in that cell, ranging from thirteen in February to seven in June 1854. In February, the cell housed an African slave, eight freedmen, including one who claimed to be free but whom the police suspected of being a runaway slave, and four creoles – two slaves, a freedman, and one who also claimed to be a free man. The number of prisoners in the entire jail averaged ninety at the time. The inmates were mainly black and mulatto, but some were white, which was against the jail's regulations, as it was in theory reserved exclusively for slaves.

Thomaz ou a vida dos pretos na America, translated by Francisco Ladislau Alvares d'Andrada (Paris: Ray & Belhatte, 1853).
[58] Chichorro da Gama to the president of the province, August 23, 1853, APEB, *Polícia*, vol. 5645–1, fl. 278.
[59] Chichorro da Gama to the president of the province, September 12, 1853, idem, fls. 298–298v.
[60] João José Barbosa de Oliveira, *As prisões do paiz, o systema penitencial ou hygiene penal*. (Bahia: Typ. De L. A. Portella e Companhia, 1843), 23.

The prisoners were being held for all kinds of offenses. Some were awaiting arraignment for serious crimes, including murder. Most were jailed for disorderly conduct, breaking the city regulations, fighting, gambling, and running away from their masters. Manoel Damião de Jesus, a free cabra, was arrested for walking the streets with a snake around his neck, followed by a crowd of children who made a ruckus, disturbing the peace. The *Jornal da Bahia* thought that he was using this ruse to take "money from ignorant Africans." Many slaves were detained in Aljube for a few days or even hours to receive corporal punishment, generally at the request of their masters. Day after day, Cipriano, who may have received that sort of punishment himself in the past, would awake to the screams of pain of the slaves imprisoned for whippings and blows of the ferrule, which, according to the regulations, were administered between 5 and 7 A.M. At night, there was another kind of suffering in store for many African inmates: after the curfew bell rang, they were supposed to kneel and recite "prayers of Christian doctrine" before going to bed.[61]

Aljube would be Cipriano's last residence in Brazil. A decree from the chief of police ordering his deportation to West Africa was published on January 11, 1854. But he would not be embarking right away, possibly because he had to wait for a place on a ship that could transport him, and the line of deportees was apparently long. On September 19 of the previous year, for example, Miguel Viana, a freedman arrested during the conspiracy scare of 1853, and transferred in the same group as Cipriano to the Sea Fortress, was released from Aljube on condition that he leave for West Africa within six months. He was given that time to "put his affairs in order [before] his voyage." The police justified his expulsion "because he had become a suspect."[62] Their suspicions must

---

[61] Regarding Cipriano's time in Aljube, see several reports from his jailer, Antonio Peixoto de Miranda Neves, to Chief of Police. For example, "Relação de prezos existentes na cadeia do Aljube em 31 de 10ᵇʳᵒ de 1853"; "Relação de prezos existentes nesta cadeia do Aljube athé 28 de Fevereiro de 1854"; "Relação de prezos existentes nesta cadeia do Aljube athé 30 de Junho de 1854"; and a letter dated March 13, 1854, APEB, *Polícia. Cadeias, 1850–54*, maço 6270. The same packet and dozens of others record the whippings and beatings of slaves imprisoned in Aljube. The prison's regulations, dated 1842, can be consulted in APEB, *Polícia*, maço 6242. The quotation from *Jornal da Bahia* is from Verger, *Flux et reflux*, 535.

[62] "Termo de obrigação," September 19, 1853, APEB, *Polícia*, vol. 5645-1, fl. 97.

not have been too serious, as he was freed on his own recognizance for six months before setting sail. In early February 1854, a more important suspect in that supposed conspiracy left Aljube to be extradited. Thomé Dourado, a freedman who had also been imprisoned in the Sea Fortress along with Cipriano, was taken directly from Aljube to a Portuguese patache, the *Cezar*, bound for Africa.[63] Miguel Viana, Thomé Dourado, and Cipriano himself would be deported on suspicion of conspiracy, like the others punished according to Law no. 9 of 1835, which dated from the time of the Revolt of the Malês.

While he was awaiting his own deportation, Cipriano would only leave Aljube once, in mid-February 1854, when he and two other occupants of Cell 4 and five other cells were taken to the Barbalho prison, where they were put to work doing maintenance and cleaning. Nine days later, they were back in Aljube. Finally, on August 8, Cipriano was transferred to the brig *Dois Irmãos*, which took him back to Africa. The police did not give him any time at all to get his affairs in order in Bahia before embarking.[64]

In a letter to London in which he protested that the government of Bahia wanted to force the captain of a Dutch ship to convey a suspect African freedman, the British consul was even more emphatic in his criticism of the persecution of Africans in 1853: "He [the Bahian chief of police] was ready to make foreign flags bound for West Africa the instruments of such an injustice, which is transporting a class of people whose freedom constitutes the greatest of all crimes, freedom that had been purchased after years of hardship and savings." And he concluded: "These Africans are now being torn from their wives and children with the same barbarism with which the infamous robbers of men had previously torn them from their native land."[65] The consul clearly had his own agenda as the representative of a nation that was now involved in an international abolitionist campaign, but for all that his words were nonetheless apt, given the situation that African freedpersons endured in those circumstances.

---

[63] Francisco Bento de Paula Bahia to the chief of police, February 3, 1854, APEB, *Polícia. Cadeias, 1850–54*, maço 6270.

[64] Antonio Peixoto de Miranda Neves to the chief of police, February 17 and August 7, 1854, APEB, *Polícia. Cadeias, 1850–54*, maço 6270.

[65] Consul Morgan Jr. in Verger, *Flux et reflux*, 538.

Antão Pereira Teixeira

Subdelegado Pompílio Manoel de Castro wrote the following about Domingos Sodré at the time of his arrest: "I have been informed that this African has long made a living by this means [Candomblé] and in association with an African by the name of Antão, also a freedman, who, to my knowledge, lives in this Parish, but I have not been able to learn more about him, and during this investigation I am better situated to get to the bottom of it." At the time, Antão Pereira Teixeira lived on Ladeira de Santa Tereza, the small street where Domingos also lived, but apparently Pompílio did not fulfill his promise to go after him.[66]

Antão was a relatively successful freedman, although nowhere near as well-to-do as Manoel Ricardo or even Cipriano José in his heyday as a shopkeeper. There is no record of his owning slaves, but he had the wherewithal to do so. He found another way of profiting from slavery that he may have used more than once. In 1856, he loaned 815,000 reis to Sebastião, a Jeje slave, so he could purchase his manumission in exchange for services and at the heavy, if official, interest rate of 2 percent per month. This was apparently a very good deal for Antão: in a little over four years of interest alone he would have recovered the amount of the loan, and Sebastião would still owe the principal. However, Sebastião did not honor his side of the bargain, registered in a notarized contract of "debt, obligation and subjugation." He may have come to the conclusion that the deal was only good for Antão and, in mid-1857, the debtor tried to leave town, but before he could flee his creditor had him arrested and jailed in Aljube as if he were a fugitive slave. In an official request to the chief of police from the justice of the peace of São Pedro parish, we read that Sebastião was to be sent from Aljube to the police chief "to deal with the lawsuit due to the obligation he had undertaken to hire out his services ... in consequence of which the slave had been freed, and had absented himself without repaying the loan." So far, Antão had managed to keep Sebastião in line with the help of the white man's law and police.[67]

---

[66] Pompílio Manuel de Castro to the chief of police, July 26, 1862. Antão said he lived with his wife in Santa Tereza in a petition to the police chief dated December 4, 1857, APEB, *Polícia*, maço 6480.

[67] See petições from Antão Pereira Teixeira to the chief of police, August 1 and 5, 1857, and "Precatório passado a Requerimento de Antão Pereira Teixeira etc.," July 31, 1857, APEB, *Escravos*, maço 6231.

Three years later, we find Antão writing to the chief of police once more, again asking him to thwart the Jeje freedman's fresh escape plan. Antão claimed that Sebastião, "if he has provided services on some occasions ... he has often and repeatedly sought ways to flee this city, as he did in 1857." And he reported: "Now, the Appellant has received word that said Sebastião is about to set forth by tomorrow for someplace in Rio Grande do Sul, either as a passenger or as a registered seaman aboard a ship."[68] Along with Rio de Janeiro, that province in the extreme south of Brazil was the destination of many Africans who lived in Bahia, including both those transported there by the domestic slave trade and freedpersons who decided to try their luck in other parts of the country. Rio Grande do Sul and Rio de Janeiro both housed sizeable communities of blacks from the Mina group, an ethnic catch-all term used in those provinces that included Nagôs, Jejes, Hausas, and other groups imported from the Bight of Benin in West Africa, and who took on more specific ethnonyms in Bahia, usually their first home in Brazil.[69] Sebastião must have been well aware of that, and perhaps even knew people who would help him when he reached his destination, which was as far as possible from his creditor.

Antão asked the police to take steps to stop Sebastião from setting sail, claiming that he could not "suffer a loss when he did a favor so the abovementioned could get his freedom, nor allow him to triumph when scoffing the laws that govern us." The chief of police once again complied with Antão's request and advised the port authority to prevent the

---

[68] Petition from Antão Teixeira to the chief of police, with annotations from the latter dated June 17 and 20, 1860, APEB, *Polícia*, maço 6324.

[69] Regarding Africans of the Mina nation in Rio Grande do Sul, see Paulo Roberto Staudt Moreira, *Faces da liberdade, máscaras do cativeiro: experiências de liberdade e escravidão percebidas através das cartas de alforria – Porto Alegre (1858–1888)* (Porto Alegre: EDIPUCRS, 1996); and idem, *Os cativos e os homens de bem: experiências negras no espaço urbano* (Porto Alegre: EST Edições, 2003); regarding Rio de Janeiro, see, among others, Farias, Soares, and Gomes, *No labirinto das nações*, esp. chaps. 3, 5, and 6; Mariza de Carvalho Soares (ed.), *Rotas atlânticas da diáspora africana: da Baía do Benim ao Rio de Janeiro* (Rio de Janeiro: EDUFF, 2007); João José Reis and Beatriz Mamigonian, "Nagô and Mina; The Yoruba Diaspora in Brazil" and Mariza de Carvalho Soares, "From Gbe to Yoruba: Ethnic Change in the Mina Nation in Rio de Janeiro," in *The Yoruba Diaspora in the Atlantic World*, eds. Toyin Falola and Matt Childs (Bloomington and Indianapolis: Indiana University Press, 2004), 77–110 and 231–247, respectively.

escaping freedman from embarking. I do not know if Sebastião managed to escape his contractual obligation this time around.[70]

Do not think that Antão and Sebastião were the only ones to sign a contract involving freedom and indenture. Arcangela, age sixty, an African woman of the Tapa nation, was valued at 50,000 reis in the mid-1850s upon the death of her mistress, Leonor Argolo Peró, whose son and heir refused to accept a penny less than the already rather low price – low because of her advanced age. Therefore, Arcangela, who worked as a slave on the Pitanga plantation, borrowed the amount required for her manumission from Ezequiel, a freedman from the same Tapa ethnic group who lived in Salvador. In return, she worked for him for three years, at the end of which she protested that she considered her debt paid. However, Ezequiel disagreed and refused to return her manumission papers, which he held onto as a guarantee that the freedwoman would keep to her side of the contract. And he went even further. Throwing ethnic solidarity to the winds, he sold his fellow Tapa "in bad faith" – as she described his misdeed – to the town of Caravelas in the south of the province of Bahia. The African woman's complaint landed on the police chief's desk in December 1857, but I do not know how it turned out.[71]

I have also found another episode involving an African who purchased his freedom this way – Gervásio, ethnic group unknown. He borrowed 400,000 reis again from a freedman, Antonio Gomes, and used part of that sum to obtain his manumission. The loan contract was notarized on May 29, 1877.[72] In this agreement, Gervásio, the debtor, had taken out the loan not only to buy his freedom but also to pay other undisclosed expenses, possibly money he needed to help him begin his new life as a freedman. The contract specified that the daily payment his creditor expected to receive was very low, only 500 reis per day – the normal daily rate ranged from 3,000 to 4,000 reis[73] – because the debtor

[70] Antão Teixeira's petition to the chief of police, with the latter's reports dated June 17 and 20, 1860.

[71] J. B. Madureira to the subdelegado of Rua do Paço parish, December 24, 1857, APEB, Polícia. Correspondência expedida, vol. 5729, fl. 26.

[72] "Escriptura de locação de serviço que fazem entre si, como locador o Africano liberto de nome Gervazio, presentemente em casa de Leocádio Duarte da Silva ... e como locatário o Africano liberto de nome Antonio Gomes etc," AMS, Escrituras. Freguesia de Santana, 1877, vol. 28, fls. 10v–11v.

[73] "Conta dos rendimentos dos prédios e escravos do casal do finado Antonio Xavier de Jesus [April 24, 1873]," APEB, Inventários, no. 07/3023/01, fl. 77v.

was an old man. The creditor undertook to take care of the debtor's health, food, and housing if he should decide to keep him in his company, but could rent him out to another household or allow him to live and work on his own. Finally, according to the contract, "if the lessor [Gervásio] does not comply with this Agreement, he will be subject to the penalties of law in such cases, and the lessee [Antonio Gomes] can concede the lessor's services to any other person." I do not know if Gervásio and Antônio Gomes kept to the agreement or a conflict eventually arose, as it did between Arcangela and Ezequiel, as well as Antão and Sebastião.[74]

Although these agreements should not be directly attributed to customs brought over from West Africa, in many ways they are similar to human pawnship, which was a widespread practice there. To describe the system of pawnship, the Yorubas used the term *iwofa*, the Ewe, *awubame*, the Fon, *gbanu*, the Ga, *awoba*, the Edo or Benin, *iyoha*, and the Akan *awowa*. Although some much more than others, all these peoples were represented among the enslaved Africans in Bahia. Pawnship involved an obligation to provide services to the creditor, whether by the debtors themselves or a dependent, usually their children, other relatives, or slaves. Political leaders also pawned their subjects. Studying the Yoruba, historian E. Adeniyi Oroge associates this custom with the development of a monetary economy, linked to the introduction of the cowry as a form of currency, at least since the sixteenth century. This, in turn, was linked to the development

---

[74] Contracts and agreements of this nature did not just involve African freedpersons. There are several others in which the loan intended for purchasing manumission was made to a slave by a free person. One brief report on this documentation can be found in José Fábio Barreto P. Cardoso, "Modalidades de mão-de-obra escrava na cidade do Salvador (1847–1887)," *Revista de Cultura Vozes*, 73, no. 3 (1979): 13–17. For a discussion of the laws governing "service labor" in nineteenth-century Brazil, but focused on immigrant labor, see Maria Lúcia Lamounier, *Da escravidão ao trabalho livre: a lei de locação de serviços de 1879* (Campinas: Papirus, 1988). Similar contracts to those found in Bahia were established elsewhere. See Regina Célia Lima Xavier, *A conquista da liberdade: libertos em Campinas na segunda metade do século XIX* (Campinas: Centro de Memória da Unicamp, 1996), 97; and more extensively (dealing with contracts similar to the ones I found for Bahia), see on Santa Catarina province Henrique Espada Lima, "Sob o domínio da precariedade: escravidão e os significados da liberdade de trabalho no século XIX", *Topoi*, 6, no. 11 (2005): 289–326.

of the transatlantic slave trade and the concomitant growth of slavery in that region. In nineteenth-century Yorubaland, which was scourged by wars that produced thousands of slaves, families went into debt to rescue their members from slavery and pawned off other members to their creditors to pay their debts. This became yet another system for recruiting forced labor, because pawnship was in any way a form of temporary slavery. Another form of pawnship directly related to the slave trade was the requirement by European merchants of using African individuals as a guarantee against advance payment for merchandise. West African traders used those goods to purchase slaves in the interior. However, the creditors frequently ignored the terms of the contract and sold individuals held in "guarantee" to the slave trade, including members of the mercantile and political elites.[75]

It could be suggested that the principle of human pawnship existed in strict connection with and constituted an aspect of the business culture of the slave trade on both sides of the Atlantic. Antão the freedman and Sebastião the slave, who entered into a contract in which Sebastião would work off his debt, may have recognized in Bahia a system with which they had been familiar in Africa. However, one difference stands out between the African and Bahian systems: in Africa, pawnship could lead to slavery, but payment of the debt restored the individual's freedom; in Bahia, the work agreement intended a transition to free labor, although it actually meant that the freedperson was delaying the full exercise of their freedom, like a conditional

[75] On this subject, see E. Adeniyi Oroge, "Iwofa: An Historical Survey of the Yoruba Institution of Indenture," *African Economic History*, no. 14 (1985): 75–106; Toyin Falola, "Slavery and Pawnship in the Yoruba Economy of the Nineteenth Century," *Slavery & Abolition*, 15, no. 2 (1994): 221–245, which is a critique of Oroge's work. Both authors write about Yorubaland. Three works closely associate pawnship with the slave trade: Ojo, "The Organization of the Atlantic Slave Trade," esp. 95–97; Paul E. Lovejoy and David Richardson, "The Business of Slaving: Pawnship in Western Africa, c. 1600–1800," *Journal of African History*, 42, no. 1 (2001): 67–89; and Paul E. Lovejoy and David Richardson, "Trust, Pawnship, and Atlantic History: The Institutional Foundation of the Old Calabar Slave Trade," *The American Historical Review*, 104, no. 2 (1999): 333–355, where the authors argue that human pawnship was a common commercial mechanism in Calabar. Incidents in this region where Africans pawned by the Calabar elite were kidnapped and transported across the Atlantic are recounted by Sparks, *The Two Princes of Calabar*, esp. 25, 47–49, 73.

manumission, where repayment of a debt was involved. In the city of
Desterro, Santa Catarina province, contracts with the expression "to
serve as if a slave" were common.[76] At the same time, purchasing freedom with loans was a risky business. We have seen that Ezequiel was
able to sell Arcangela – illegally, it is true – and Antão had Sebastião
arrested – legally this time – as if he were just another runaway slave.

It may be that Sebastião was not just trying to escape a debt but
fleeing from a temperamental creditor. In December 1857, six months
after sending Sebastião to jail, Antão himself would end up behind bars
for breaking into the home of a city policeman, his neighbor. Antão
was looking for his woman, who had sought refuge from the African's
drunken rage. He wanted to force her to return home and used violence to get his way. In yet another petition to the police chief, Antão
claimed that he had been under the influence of alcohol, said he was
sorry, and asked to be released. The police chief granted his request;
after all, the freedman had only beaten an African woman.[77]

The partner Antão was harassing may have been Rita Mamede or
Gertrudes da Silva Friandes, both of whom were African freedwomen
with whom he had intimate relations. In August 1856, a creole baby
named Manoel, Antão and Rita's natural child, was baptized in São
Pedro parish at the age of seven months: we are already acquainted
with the baby's godfather, Manoel José d'Etra, who was also a compadre of Manoel Joaquim Ricardo – yet another link in the social network our characters formed. A few months later, in early 1857, Antão
and Gertrudes appeared in Sé parish as the godparents of Cirillo, a
six-month-old creole, the child of an African slave woman.[78] We cannot be sure if they were already in a relationship at the time, but Antão
and Gertrudes eventually got married.

In 1869, by which time he was living in Cruz do Cosme – and was
therefore one of Manoel Joaquim Ricardo's neighbors – we find Antão
involved in a lawsuit regarding his late wife's last will and testament.
Gertrudes Friandes had left a four-windowed house with a tile roof and
two thatched huts to Antão, who was her lawful husband. According

[76] Lima, "Sob o domínio da precariedade," 303, 304, 305 for example.
[77] Petition from Antão Teixeira to the chief of police, December 4, 1857, *Polícia*,
maço 6480.
[78] Registry of Cirillo on February 6, 1857, ACMS, *Livro de Registro de Batismo.
Freguesia da Sé, 1829–1861*, caixa 25, fl. 369; ACMS, *Livro de registro de batismos.
Freguesia de São Pedro, 1853–1851*, fl. 146v.

to the terms of her will, the freedman, who was also her executor, was supposed to deduct a sum to pay a 400,000-reis inheritance to Josefa Carolina Xavier de Jesus, then aged five. She was Gertrudes' goddaughter, the child of one of her former slaves, possibly Maria, whom she had freed sometime between 1863 and 1865. However, Antão questioned the validity of the will, claiming that nobody had signed it on the testatrix's behalf, as she could not read or write. Furthermore, he contested the legitimacy of the girl's (court-appointed) guardian and godfather, Antonio Xavier de Jesus – who had given the girl his surname – the person responsible for managing that bequest. Antão claimed that because the child's mother was still living, she did not need a guardian.

Josefa Carolina's guardian certainly did not need her bequested money. Antonio Xavier was one of the most prosperous freedpersons in Salvador's African community at the time. He had been a transatlantic slave trader, owned a wide range of shops and taverns and eight slaves, and was the proprietor and landlord of several buildings, most of which he had inherited from a former master, who was also African, a slave trader, and had been expelled from Brazil in the wake of the 1835 Malê Revolt. On his death in 1872, Antonio Xavier's fortune was valued at more than 66 million reis – almost twice the net estate left by Manoel Ricardo – which went to his seven children. His wife and their mother was an African freedwoman, Felicidade Francisca Friandes, who had died before her husband. By her surname we can guess that she had been the slave of the same master as Antão's wife, Gertrudes Friandes. The two women were friends. In 1838, Felicidade named a daughter after Gertrudes.[79] Most certainly referring to her, Gertrudes Friandes kindly left an African shawl in her will to "my friend Felicidade, of the Jeje nation."[80]

After losing a three-year legal battle in municipal court, Antão turned to the Supreme Court of Appeals. I have not been able to find any records

[79] ACMS, *Livro de registro de batismos da Conceição da Praia, 1834–1844*, fl. 76v.
[80] The records of Antão Teixeira's lawsuit against Antonio Xavier, including a copy of Gertrudes's will, can be found in APEB, *Judiciária*, no. 25/0876/05 (1869), fl. 12 (citação). See Antonio Xavier's probate records and APEB, *Judiciária*, no. 07/3023/01. Regarding Antonio Xavier de Jesus, see also Verger, *Os libertos*, 55–65, 125–37; regarding his master, see Reis, *Rebelião escrava*, 485–90; regarding both, the most complete study is Elaine Santos Falheiros, "Luis e Antonio Xavier de Jesus: mobilidade social de africanos na Bahia oitocentista," MA thesis, Universidade Federal da Bahia, 2014. Regarding Maria, the slave freed by Gertrudes, see APEB, *Índice de alforrias, 1863–65*, maço 2882, fl. 22.

of this final stage of the lawsuit, begun in October 1871. A year later, the girl's guardian, Antonio Xavier, passed away. His probate records do not mention the lawsuit with Antão or even his godchild and ward, who was at the center of the dispute. Could Antão have had something to do with Antonio Xavier's death? Have we come across a war involving poisoning by witchcraft? There are signs that, like Manoel Joaquim Ricardo, Antonio Xavier was linked to the Candomblé high priestess Marcelina da Silva, or Obatossi, whose daughter Maria Magdalena had stood godmother to the wealthy freedman's daughter Maria Vitória in 1865.[81] I do not believe that Xavier would have involved himself in a conflict with Antão without seeking protection from powerful members of the African religious community, like Magdalena and particularly her mother, Marcelina, because Antão was known to be a dangerous practitioner of witchcraft, poisoning included.

Antão may not have been able to see the lawsuit through. He was arrested in late 1872, charged with giving a young woman a beverage "claimed to be a refreshment" that left her unconscious, and violently deflowering her. The accuser was Maria Isabel da Conceição, a poor mulatto woman who was more than twenty-four years of age. Here is the victim's statement in her complaint to the police chief:

> As the plaintiff, who is a person of good character, lives in the company of her married cousin, who is well known in this city, Manoel Zacarias de Santa Isabel, on November 14 of last year she went to spend the day on a small property there [in Cruz do Cosme] that her same cousin owns, and while on an outing having gone to the farm of said Antão, with whom they were acquainted, spent some time there. This barbarian took advantage of a time when he was alone with the plaintiff, offered her as refreshment a concoction that made the plaintiff lose consciousness before it had barely touched her mouth. Then, removing her to a room in which he locked himself, he violated her there, producing on her the offenses which the attached forensic examination reports.[82]

We have already seen that Antão could be violent with women, as he was arrested for trying to beat his wife. Now, the forensic examination

---

[81] Lisa Earl Castillo, personal communication, March 9, 2007.
[82] Petition from Maria Isabel da Conceição to the chief of police (day illegible) March 1873, Arquivo Nacional, Gabinete do Ministro da justiça, Rel 28-seção dos ministérios, IJ1–428, folhas avulsas, 1870–1880.

confirmed the mulatto woman's accusations. She was subjected to more male manipulation of her body by the doctors. Two of them examined Maria Isabel in her home in the city center and "noted in various parts of the vagina signs of contusions, and the patient complained of intense pain in her thighs, revived by the movement and introduction of the speculum, from which they gather that the above-mentioned injuries were the result of violence from blunt force trauma or a disproportionally sized organ."[83] However, they concluded that she had not been deflowered as a result of the rape; in other words, according to them, she had not been a virgin before Antão's attack.

In the same complaint, Maria Isabel regretted that she did not have the financial means to sue the African freedman, and her case was hampered by the lack of witnesses. She also mentioned similar crimes Antão had committed that had been reported, but he was still free and unpunished. He must have had protectors. The victim (or the person who wrote the complaint on her behalf) stated that society could not remain "exposed to the brutal and cunning lechery of this perverse man whose profession is to cast spells and curses that are harmful to the health and damage the reason of the fools who have the misfortune of trusting him." And she concluded that Antão should be punished with extradition to West Africa, "as a public safety measure."[84]

The chief of police immediately sent Maria Isabel's complaint to his superior, the president of the province, accompanied by a letter in which he stated that he knew of Antão's reputation, and there were "constant ... complaints against said African." He was allegedly known as "an agent of a candomblé in Quinta das Beatas, where he says he has a farm, and from which he makes a living almost exclusively from filching money and jewels from the unwary through artifice and witchcraft, even from ladies," certainly meaning white women. What we have here is a man known for activities very like those that landed Domingos in jail, aside from the serious charge of rape, of course. However, the chief of police added a discordant note to Maria Isabel's story. She said she had gone to the African's farm for no particular purpose, "on an outing," but the authority wrote that although she was a "decent young woman," she had gone there for a divination session. In other words,

---

[83] Idem: Forensic report dated November 17, 1872, attached to the aforementioned inquest.

[84] Idem: Petition from Maria Isabel da Conceição to the chief of police (day illegible), March 1873.

the young woman knew of Antão's occupation and had sought him out for his ritual services. But the chief of police was not interested in that detail – or in presenting Antão's version of events – and recommended to the president that the freedman be deported.[85] The president of the province agreed with that measure and sent on the request to the minister of justice, attaching copies of the forensic report and Maria Isabel's complaint, as well as a copy of the letter he had received from the chief of police.[86]

In the long report he issued on this case, the minister of justice agreed with the Bahian authorities but lamented that there were no means of prosecuting Antão in Brazil, to punish "the criminal in the presence of his victims, and chief among those – the society which he mocks with impunity." This was an old complaint – that those Africans did not leave any evidence of their alleged crimes – as it was an old argument that Candomblé was a den of iniquity and sexual abuse. The minister also took the opportunity to compare Antão with a well-known Candomblé priest from Rio de Janeiro, Juca Rosa, whom the authorities in that city had prosecuted for larceny in 1870:

> The African in question proceeds in Bahia just as the black Crioulo fraud and libertine known as "Juca Rosa" did here in the capital. He must therefore be prosecuted and punished for crimes against morality and chasten other "fortunetellers" that must exist in that province as unfortunately is the case in the Imperial Capital, but without such audacity and impudence.[87]

He therefore concluded that the freedman should be deported – or "shipped" as the president of Bahia expressed in the language of slave traders – to Africa, "whose hinterlands he should never have left." Of course, the African had never asked to be removed from his hinterlands and shipped to Brazil in the first place.

These documents confirm what we have already seen in Chapter 4: the war against Africans accused of witchcraft in imperial

---

[85] Idem: Aurélio Ferreira Espinheira to the president of the province, March 14, 1873.

[86] Idem: João José Almeida to the minister of justice, April 3, 1873.

[87] Reply from the minister of justice to the letter from the president of the province of Bahia, April 15, 1873. However, the reply is not signed by the then-minister, Manuel Antonio Duarte de Azevedo, but by A. de S. Barros, followed by the observation "Viewed" by A. Fleury dated April 18, 1873.

Brazil could reach the ministerial level, so government ministers were reflecting on a truly national phenomenon. Their thoughts and comparisons show that Bahia was seen as the land par excellence of audacious sorcerers. And competent ones, to boot. Juca Rosa himself had traveled north to that province at least once, presumably in search of esoteric knowledge (from Domingos? Antão?), as well as going on a pilgrimage to the Church of Senhor do Bonfim, one of his Catholic devotions. Shortly after returning to Rio, Juca Rosa, the Brazilian-born son of an African mother, would be charged with sexual scandals involving black, mulatto, and white women, ranging from prostitutes to elegant ladies, all part of his following. Because he got involved with the mistress of a powerful man in Rio, he had ended up in hot water. Because he was a Brazilian, he could not be deported or incriminated for witchcraft or quackery, crimes that were not technically illegal, so he was charged with and convicted of larceny.[88]

According to a report in the Catholic newspaper *Chronica Religiosa*, published in 1875, Antão Teixeira was only deported that year. Folklorist Silva Campos, who provided this information, referred to him as "one of the most famous sorcerers in the city," and said that he knew through a contemporary of the African that he had made a big mistake to merit deportation: "he dared to cast a spell on a certain big shot."[89] According to this account, it seems that the police and legal authorities had worked on the basis of belief in witchcraft, retaliating against an attack on a powerful Brazilian by an African priest whose ritual powers were not that strong after all.[90] But now we know that Antão's deportation had nothing to do with a state that feared witchcraft as a belief, although it was still considered a threat against good customs, public order, and civilization. It is always possible that the African had cast a spell on an influential person, one eventually involved in the decision to deport him, but we must also consider that the oral tradition that reached the folklorist may have been an attempt to rehabilitate the

---

[88] Regarding Juca Rosa, see Sampaio, *Juca Rosa*, and, idem, "Tenebrosos mistérios: Juca Rosa e as relações entre crença e cura no Rio de Janeiro imperial," in *Artes e ofícios de curar no Brasil*, ed. Sidney Chalhoub et al. (Campinas: Editora Unicamp, 2003), 387–426.

[89] Campos, "Ligeiras notas," 304.

[90] Regarding the state as an involuntary legitimizer of the belief in witchcraft at the turn of the twentieth century, see Yvonne Maggie, *Medo do feitiço: relações entre magia e poder no Brasil* (Rio de Janeiro: Arquivo Nacional, 1992).

African priest by replacing the villain who raped a woman of the people with a folk hero who had fought a member of the elite. This more edifying story could be a sort of counter-narrative in defense of the values of a persecuted religion whose priests were probably good, decent people, for the most part.

Silva Campos also erred on the date of Antão's deportation from Bahia. He was expelled from the country one month after the minister of justice had taken his decision. In preparation for his trip, on May 16, 1873, Antão obtained permission from the chief of police to leave the jail to put his affairs in order, which may have included his lawsuit regarding his late wife's young heiress. Escorted by the Urban Guard, he left at 10 A.M. and returned at noon, according to the jailer's careful report. Five days later he was on board the Brazilian schooner *Tejo*, bound for West Africa. On the occasion, the ship's captain acknowledged that he had received the African aboard, and described him as follows: "60 years of age, fat, tall, color a bit pale [cor um pouco fula], thick beard, long face, black eyes, good teeth, and marks from his nation on the face." The *Tejo* deposited Antão in Lagos on July 8, but "proceeded to Porto Novo as he could not be received in this settlement," according to the local English customs clerk, who did not state why Antão was not allowed to stay in Lagos, Domingos' homeland.[91]

Domingos Sodré's relations with Manoel Joaquim Ricardo, Cipriano José Pinto, Antão Teixeira, Mãe Mariquinhas – mentioned in Chapter 3 – and others accused of witchcraft suggest that he played an active role in an African social and religious network. It is interesting that it was not an exclusively ethnic network, even though ethnic ties were an important part of the city's cultural makeup, as it gravitated around its African "nations." Although all the fellow Candomblé practitioners I have been able to identify among Domingos' friends and acquaintances were African, not all of them were members of the Nagô nation, the most numerous African ethnic group in Bahia at the time. Domingos the Nagô had dealings with the Hausas Manoel Ricardo and Cipriano José, and with the Jeje Mãe Mariquinhas – and, as we have seen, the first two also moved in various ethnic circles.[92]

[91] João José da Rocha, Carcereiro da Casa de Correção, May 16, 1873, APEB, *Mapa de presos, 1872–1874*, maço 6276. The documents related to Antão's trip are in APEB, *Policia do Porto*, maço 6428.

[92] I do not know to which nation Antão belonged. The Jeje origins of Mãe Mariquinhas are suggested by Parés, A formação do candomblé, 175–176.

By not closing himself off behind the borders of his own African nation, Domingos may have been following a habit acquired in his homeland, because the port kingdom of Lagos was highly cosmopolitan, a melting pot of natives and strangers attracted by bustling commerce that was closely linked with the transatlantic slave trade. This cosmopolitanism was comparable to Salvador's, which was also due to the slave trade, and had an equally religious dimension. Although without the typical pomp of the other Yoruba kingdoms, Lagos was home to many devotions of Orişa worship and the cults of other West African divinities, much like Bahia. If there was any competition for ritual space or possibly mutual hostility, religious leaders were not segregated, as Domingos' experience suggests. The free movement of priests and priestesses, diviners and healers in the world of Candomblé, both of their and other nations, and their involvement in different rituals were part of the religious life of nineteenth-century Bahia. These men and women probably both held and exchanged ritual experiences and knowledge, some of which complemented and enriched the experiences of others. From the ethnic standpoint, relations between Jejes and Nagôs are the best known, according to Nina Rodrigues's first-hand account, dating from the turn of the twentieth century.[93]

In the world of nineteenth-century Bahian Candomblé, the freedpersons called the shots. The backgrounds of Domingos' friends, as well as his own, confirm this. Freedpersons had the resources and social mobility required to organize and benefit from the ritual experience with greater autonomy, despite heavy pressure from the government and society. Nevertheless, they did not represent a uniform group in the social and economic hierarchy. Very few achieved the success of Manoel Joaquim Ricardo, for example. Cipriano José Pinto was just a small merchant who prospered enough to take out large loans.

---

[93] See, for example, Rodrigues, Os africanos, 230–231, where he coins the expression "Jeje-Nagô mythology" to refer to what he considered the most "elevated" part of the Afro-Bahian religious complex. The Jeje-Nagô relationship is discussed (in fact, consigned in the very title of his book) by Lima, A família-de-santo. See also Yeda Pessoa de Castro, "África descoberta: uma história recontada," Revista de Antropologia, no. 23 (1980): 135–140; Harding, A Refuge in Thunder, 44–52; and, particularly, the well-documented study by Parés, A formação do candomblé, esp. 142–162. A more subtle and therefore as yet little-studied syncretism arose among the various Nagô-Yoruba subnations and the Tapa-Nupe. See in this regard Silveira, O candomblé da Barroquinha, 491–496.

However, he failed to honor them, and landed in jail. Antão Teixeira suffered the same fate for another reason, a sex crime. Although he had managed to accumulate more material wealth, he was also jailed. Both Cipriano and Antão ended up being banished back to Africa as a result of a series of events that were not lacking in African religious practices. It is symptomatic that Manoel Joaquim Ricardo, the wealthy owner of many slaves and extensive real estate, was the only member of the group who did not experience an unpleasant encounter with the police – as far as we know – despite their suspicions that he, too, was involved in Candomblé.

CHAPTER SEVEN

Domingos Sodré, *Ladino* Man

of Means

Ladino: in the days of slavery in Brazil, the term identified Africans who were familiar with and could decode or adopt the local customs, including the language. Like many ladino African slaves and freedpeople, Domingos Sodré did not profess just one religious belief. He was both a Candomblé priest and a Catholic devotee. Like whites and other ladinos and Crioulos, he had learned to manipulate the means to get ahead in business and move forward in society. This is not to say that these values were absent in the Africa he had left behind, but once in Bahia, Domingos would begin to control new ways of manipulating, innovating, and transcending his circumstances. Let us start with religion.

Saint and Orișa

When he dictated his second will and testament in 1882, Domingos stated at the outset that he was a "true Christian," with an emphasis that was far from the norm in such documents by the late nineteenth century. And he recalled being baptized in the catholically named plantation of Trindade (Trinity), which his former master owned in Santo Amaro da Purificação. He also remembered his marriage in 1871, before the Catholic shrine in his house, celebrated by an important member of the clergy, thereby legitimizing his long-term "illicit union" with his partner, Maria Delfina da Conceição, according to Canon Raymundo José de Mattos, the vicar of São Pedro parish, synodal examiner and professor of religious history at the Archiepiscopal Seminary in the Convent of Santa Tereza, a few yards from Domingos' home.[1]

[1] ACMS, *Livro de registro de casamentos. Freguesia de São Pedro, 1844–1910*, fl. 128v;

This was Domingos' second marriage. His first wife had been
Maria das Mercês Rodrigues de Souza, with whom he also lived in a
common-law union before they were married by the Catholic Church
on June 9, 1850. She was seriously ill at the time and died about a
month later. When she was buried in the Church of the Rosário dos
Pretos Confraternity in São Pedro parish, the funeral rites were accompanied by confraternity members in full regalia, a sacristan, and two
priests. She also dictated her will, which I have unfortunately not been
able to find, appointing her husband as its executor.[2] She had been a
prosperous enough freedperson to become a slave owner during her
lifetime. In 1840, she purchased a Nagô woman named Francisca for
460,000 reis. When Maria das Mercês died ten years later, she owned at
least one other slave, Ana, whom Domingos freed in 1853 for 300,000
reis, an amount that was probably set in his late wife's will.[3]

Besides marrying twice according to Catholic rites, Domingos Sodré
often appeared in church for numerous baptisms, as shown in the following box. The first records of the freedman standing godfather date
from 1845, the year after he officially obtained his manumission, and
go on until 1878, when he was about eighty years old. These baptisms,
fourteen all told – and there may be others whose records are yet to be
found – were mostly for adult African slaves and enslaved children born
in Brazil, principally to African mothers.

One question that is usually raised when it comes to slave baptisms
is who chooses the godparents. To start with, I suspect that Domingos,
like other African freedpersons, was often chosen as godfather at ran-
dom by masters of slaves to be baptized. On three occasions, for example, he stood godfather to the slaves of different masters on the same day
in 1845, 1847, and 1854. It is possible that while he was in church for
one baptism, he was also roped in by a master looking for a godfather for
his slave. For example, when Domingos went to the Conceição da Praia
parish church on August 15, 1847, to stand godfather to Paulina, having previously agreed to it with her master, mother, or possibly father
(who was usually out of the picture if not officially married) – or perhaps with just one of them – he may have been invited to be Sabino's

Almanak ... de 1873, 63. It would add a lot to our discussion if the Catholic
   cleric knew about Domingos' arrest as a Candomblé practitioner a decade earlier.
[2] ACMS, *Livro de registro de casamentos. Freguesia de São Pedro, 1844–1910*, fl. 37;
   and ACMS, *Livro de registro de óbitos. Freguesia de São Pedro, 1848–1850*, fl. 67v.
[3] APEB, *LNT*, no 308, fl. 71; AMS, *Escrituras. S. Pedro*, vol. 1, fls. 132–133.

godfather by her mother, father, or, more likely, his master. While his role in the baptism of Paulina would have reflected social and possibly emotional ties already formed by the individuals involved, standing godfather in Sabino's would have been a mere formality. There were also collective baptisms of adult slaves recently arrived from Africa, which were typically just formalities as far as the choice of godparents was concerned: slaves needed to be baptized, according to civil and canonical laws – but also to formalize property rights with another document besides (or in the absence of) a bill of sale – and any godparent would do, sometimes one person serving as godfather to three, five, seven adult Africans. Domingos, however, to my knowledge, did not stand godfather in such capacity.

Domingos Sodré's Godchildren, 1845–1878

1. Cosma, four months, Crioula, daughter of Maria, African, slaves of Domingos de Oliveira Pinto, married, white. Conceição da Praia Parish, November 16, 1845.
2. Damiana, twin sister of Cosma.
3. Domingos, two months, Crioulo, son of Maria, Crioula, slaves of Manoel Vargas, white, married. Conceição da Praia Parish, November 16, 1845.
4. Ventura, ten months, son of Lucia da Silva, godmother Francisca Maria da Pureza, African freedwoman. Sé Parish, May 16, 1846.
5. Paulina, Crioula, two months, daughter of Maria, African, slaves of Domingos de Oliveira Pinto, white, married. Conceição da Praia Parish, August 15, 1847.
6. Sabino, Crioulo, one month, son of Maria, Crioula, slaves of João José da Rocha. Conceição da Praia Parish, August 15, 1847.
7. Maria, adult, African, slave of Benedicto José de Araújo Sé Parish, March 12, 1848.
8. João, two years, Crioulo, free, son of Gertrudes, African freedwoman, godmother Joana Maria da Cruz. Conceição da Praia Parish, September 1, 1848.
9. Rachel, adult, African, slave of Dr. Thomaz de Aquino Gaspar, white, married, godmother the Virgin Mary. São Pedro Parish, June 13, 1854.
10. Henriqueta, adult, African, slave of Hermenegildo José do Valle, godmother Rosa, African slave, probably of the same master. São Pedro Parish, June 13, 1854.

11. Christovão, older than thirty, African, slave of Agostinho Moreira de Souza. Sé Parish, July 21, 1857.
12. Filomena, Crioula, daughter of Febrônia, African freed-woman, godmother Esperança, African freedwoman. Sé Parish, December 9, 1860.
13. Fausto, three years, *cabra*, legitimate son of José Martins Rosendo dos Santos Moreira and Silvéria Maria da Rocha, second godfather Miguel Domingos José Martins. São Pedro Parish, September 23, 1866.
14. Amélia Maria, four months, *parda*, daughter of Adrelina Maria da Conceição, unmarried, godmother Maria Delfina da Conceição. São Pedro Parish, August 15, 1878.

Sources: ACMS, *Livros de registro de batismos. Freguesia da Conceição da Praia, 1844–1889,* fl. 11v (Cosma and Damiana), fl. 12 (Domingos), fl. 37 (Paulina and Sabino), fl. 53 (João); *Freguesia da Sé, 1829–1861,* fl. 201v (Ventura), fl. 249 (Maria), fl. 392v (Christovão), fl. 461 (Filomena); *Freguesia de São Pedro, 1853–1851,* fl. 44 (Rachel and Henriqueta); *Freguesia de São Pedro, 1865–1872,* fl. 21v (Fausto); *Freguesia de São Pedro, 1872–1881,* fl. 139v (Amélia Maria).

The merely formal christenings in which Domingos may have participated would have involved his four African godchildren baptized in 1848, 1854, and 1857, who may have arrived after the first ban on the slave trade in 1831. Whether slaves arrived before or after that year, masters often did not have them christened right after they arrived in Brazil. In fact, there are numerous cases in the parish records of African and creole slaves, but also freed and free people, including whites, who were baptized many years after they were imported to or born in Brazil. All this is to say that Africans who had lived in Bahia for some time – in this case Maria, Rachel, Henriqueta, and Christovão – may have known Domingos before they got together at the baptismal font, and therefore may have chosen him as their godfather. In this case, baptism would have functioned as a mechanism for the reaffirmation, if not creation, of African solidarity. This network of solidarity would also have included the parents, particularly the African mothers of the creole godchildren. And women who stood alongside Domingos as godmothers should also be included in this network, through which they also became a part of his African circle, if they were not already, including his Candomblé circle.[4]

Whether he was an accidental godfather or not, Domingos would, in principle, have undertaken the same commitments to protect and support all of his godchildren. In the case of his nine enslaved godchildren (five creoles and four Africans), for example, he would be responsible for helping them obtain their manumission. This was a golden rule at the time, a moral undertaking, as well as an expression of Christian charity that dated back to colonial times. This is why masters did not stand godfather to their own slaves – and when they did, they generally planned to free them. There was a contradiction between playing the roles of master and godfather of a slave at the same time, as Gudeman and Schwartz suggest.[5] Of course, it would have been impossible for Domingos to purchase the manumission of so many enslaved godchildren, but he may have helped them obtain their freedom in other ways. After all, he was an expert in that field.

Unfortunately, I have not been able to determine the social status held by masters of the slaves for whom Domingos stood godfather to determine whether he was building vertical or horizontal alliances. It is likely that some were African freedpersons like himself. Three of those masters, however, are positively identified in the baptismal records as white. Domingos de Oliveira Pinto was Portuguese, a businessman with a dry goods shop on Rua das Grades de Ferro – therefore a neighbor of Domingos' friend Manoel Joaquim Ricardo, the freedman introduced in the previous chapter. He owned three slave women and five slave children when he died in 1849. Of these, Domingos Sodré stood godfather for the twin sisters Cosma and Damiana, in 1845, and Paulina, in 1847, daughters of Maria, of the Nagô nation like her compadre. The mother probably had or developed a solid

---

[4] For an author who emphasized baptism as a means of forging African solidarity, see Moacir Rodrigo de Castro Maia, "O apadrinhamento de africanos em Minas colonial: o (re)encontro na América (Mariana, 1715–1750)," *Afro-Ásia*, no. 36 (2007): 39–80.

[5] See Stephen Gudeman and Stuart Schwartz, "Purgando o pecado original: compadrio e batismo de escravos na Bahia no século XVIII," in *Escravidão e invenção da liberdade: estudos sobre o negro no Brasil*, ed. João José Reis (São Paulo: Brasiliense, 1988), 33–59; and Stuart Schwartz, *Slaves, Peasants, and Rebels: Reconsidering Brazilian Slavery* (Urbana and Chicago: Illinois University Press, 1992), chap. 5.

relationship with Domingos, having given him three of her children to baptize. Another white man whose slave became Domingos' godchild was Dr. Thomaz de Aquino Gaspar, a physician and builder who lived in Domingos' neighborhood. Gaspar was married, owned at least six slave women and three of their children, and was connected through ties of godparentage to two powerful political figures of the Empire of Brazil, Manoel Pinto de Souza Dantas and the Baron of Cotegipe. On June 13, 1854, in São Pedro parish, Domingos stood godfather to Rachel, one of Gaspar's adult African slave women. The same day and in the same parish, Domingos stood godfather to Henriqueta, also an adult African slave, whose master was Hermenegildo José do Valle, about whom I have not found any further information. The godmother, alongside Domingos, was Rosa, an African slave, probably of the same master.[6]

Two godchildren stand out among the creoles and Africans, mostly enslaved, whom Domingos helped baptize. Fausto and Amélia Maria were free, lighter-skinned children – the first was a *cabra*, a dark-skinned mulatto, and the other was registered as *parda*, or light-brown mulatto. Furthermore, Fausto was born in wedlock. When he became their godfather, Domingos climbed up a few rungs on the social ladder of the *compadrio* system – a black African standing godfather to mixed-race Bahians. It may be that Fausto's parents and Amélia Maria's mother invited him to be their children's godfather in recognition of some sort of service he had provided to them or their children, such as curing a disease with African medicine or some other ritual procedure. It should be noted that Fausto's christening in September 1866 took place just four years after Domingos' scandalous arrest for practicing Candomblé, a fact that must have been well known to the godchild's parents, as they all lived in the same parish, São Pedro, where the African freedman

---

[6] ACMS, *Livros de registro de batismos. Freguesia da Conceição da Praia*, 1844–1889, fl. 11v (Cosma and Damiana), fl. 37 (Paulina); Domingos de Oliveira Pinto's probate records, APEB, *Judiciária. Inventários*, no. 07/2833/05; ACMS, *Livro de registro de batismos. Freguesia de São Pedro*, 1853–1851, fl. 44 (Rachel and Henriqueta). This book records other slaves and dependents of Aquino Gaspar between 1854 and 1857. See also ACMS, *Livro de registro de batismos Freguesia de São Pedro*, 1861–1865, fl. 117v. For Gaspar as physician and builder, see *Almanak administrativo, commercial e industrial da Província da Bahia para o anno de 1873*, compiled by Albino Rodrigues Pimenta (Bahia: Typographia de Oliveira Mendes & C., 1872), Part iv, 5, 13, and 18.

and his wife resided. However, this did not prevent them from choosing Domingos to be Fausto's godfather.

Amélia Maria's mother included Delfina in the godparentage arrangement. This was the only time when Domingos and his wife, now married, appeared side by side before the priest in a baptismal font, and it is likely that Delfina was the main link to the baby's mother. Her name, Adrelina Maria da Conceição, suggests a special relationship that could have involved some type of devotional partnership between her and Maria Delfina da Conceição.

Christenings produced symbolic kin. In exchange for his protection, his godchildren and their parents could become Domingos Sodré's dependents and future supporters. If it was an act of solidarity, it also meant a hierarchical commitment that both reflected and reaffirmed the diviner's prestige inside and outside the African community.[7] But through rituals of godparentage, the freedman not only expanded his social alliances with mothers, fathers, and masters of his godchildren but also somehow extended his commitment to the hegemonic religion. I suppose that, at the same time, the godparentage ties that Domingos formed could also have been derived to some extent, or in some cases, from his position as a diviner and healer – that is to say, his skills in the field of ritual knowledge could have been somehow responsible for his involvement in the fundamental Catholic initiation rite of baptism. Similarly, standing godfather in church could represent a means of recruiting future clients and Candomblé followers – including his own godchildren and their parents.

Nothing I have said in the previous paragraph can be confirmed through documents that demonstrate the real importance of godparentage in Domingos' life. I have not yet found any evidence that the freedman shared the lives of his godchildren and their parents, or even their masters. Building bonds of solidarity, expanding social networks, forming a clientele – all this remain within the realm of possibility in a society in which godparenthood is known to have served for all these things and more, including the promotion of Catholicism.

[7]   During the mining boom era in Minas Gerais, its governor, Count Assumar, strongly recommended that masters avoid choosing other slaves and freedpersons as their slaves' godparents, arguing that the latter's ascendancy over the former could present a danger to the colonial and slave-owning order. See Maia, "O apadrinhamento de africanos," 46–49, 54–55.

In addition to two marriages and several baptisms, other factors point to Domingos being a full member of Catholic society. In his 1882 will, the African freedman declared that he was a member of the Our Lady of the Rosary brotherhood of his parish, to which both his wives also belonged. The confraternity was founded in 1689 in the parish church of São Pedro and later moved to its own church, probably built in the mid-eighteenth century on land leased from the Benedictine monastery, which stood imposingly on the edge of that parish, very close to where Domingos lived. Our Lady of the Rosary had been the most popular Catholic devotion among black people in Brazil since colonial times. In Salvador, there were several confraternities dedicated to that saint, and the one in São Pedro parish counted among the most important for African freedpersons in particular. In the late eighteenth century, it was run by blacks from the Benguela and Jeje nations, but Africans from other nations and creoles must have joined its leadership over the course of time.[8]

By the late nineteenth century, the old ethnic barriers had certainly given way, and a Nagô like Domingos could probably have become part of the leadership in that institution, but it seems that he was just an ordinary member. At that time, the confraternity, whose altar bore a splendid statue of São Domingos (St. Dominic), may not have been the wealthiest, but it had enough property – including a small house close to the freedman's on Rua do Sodré – for its directors to be frequently accused of embezzlement.[9] But the confraternity had overcome these crises and continued to play its traditional role of burying its members,

[8] Luiz Monteiro da Costa, "A devoção de N. S. do Rosário na Cidade do Salvador," *Revista do Instituto Genealógico da Bahia*, 11, no. 11 (1959): 159–160; Reis, *A morte é uma festa*, 56; Oliveira, *O liberto*, 86–87. Regarding black Catholic devotions in Bahia during slavery, see Tânia Maria de Jesus Pinto, "Os negros cristãos católicos e o culto aos santos na Bahia colonial," MA thesis, UFBA, 2000. Specifically regarding the devotion to the Virgin of the Rosary (Rosário), see Lucilene Reginaldo, *Os Rosários dos angolas: irmandades de africanos e crioulos na Bahia setecentista* (São Paulo: Alameda, 2011); and Sara Oliveira Faria, "Irmãos de cor, de caridade e de crença: a Irmandade do Rosário do Pelourinho na Bahia do século XIX," MA thesis, UFBA, 1997.

[9] See documents related to the Rosário do João Pereira Confraternity in APEB, no. 21/741/01 to 48, and *Tombo dos bens das ordens terceiras, confrarias e irmandades da cidade do Salvador instituído em 1853*. Publicações do APEB, vol. VI (Salvador: Imprensa Oficial, 1948), 84–85 (house on Rua do Sodré), 181–184 (inventory of statues, furnishings, etc.).

Figure 46. On the far right, the grilled entrance to the Church of the Confraternity of Rosário dos Pretos of Rua de João Pereira, in the late nineteenth century.

and Domingos knew that. In his last will and testament, he asked to be "carried and buried" by Rosário members, like his first wife had been – evidence of his attachment to the Baroque style of death he had learned in Catholic Bahia. And he expressed this pious wish at a time when nearly 100 percent of African freedmen no longer belonged to religious confraternities.[10]

Twenty years earlier, when the police raided Domingos' home, they had found a gold rosary, framed pictures of Catholic saints on the walls, and a well-tended shrine. The pictures in their frames – thirty all told, one of which was gilded – and the wooden shrine with its clothed statues of saints were still there in 1887 when his estate was inventoried. At the time of his arrest in 1862, Subdelegado Pompílio Manoel de Castro reported that pictures of "our saints" hung on the walls in Domingo's living room, arrogantly suggesting that the saints belonged exclusively to Brazilians, but at that point they also populated the imaginary of those Africans who, like Domingos, had been "Brazilianized" and

[10] Oliveira, *O liberto*, 84, establishes that 96.1 percent of freedmen and 84.2 percent of freedwomen did not state in their wills that they participated in Catholic confraternities between 1850 and 1888.

had chosen to try a double religious immersion because their original faith did not demand exclusive adherence to one faith. However, his Catholic faith, populated as it was with these celestial mediators, was typical of a sort of folk Catholicism that gravitated around a "religious economy of give-and-take" between devotee and devotion, humans and saints, according to Laura de Melo e Souza. In short, it was a form of Catholicism that strongly resembled the economy of sacrifice in Candomblé: the Orişa (or the Vodun of the Jejes and the Nkisi of the Angolas) is empowered with offerings from the devotee, who in turn is empowered by the Orişa.[11]

While Catholic saints occupied Domingos and Delfina's living room, African divinities occupied the backrooms. In Subdelegado Pompílio's complete wording: "we found in the living room ... several pictures of our saints, and even a shrine, but in the bedrooms he had the mixtures [ritual ingredients, leaves etc.], clothes and emblems of his superstitious trade."[12] In other words, Domingo's devotional world was spatially and apparently ritually divided. There are some who claim – and the police insinuated – that the religious symbols displayed in the living room were just a front, a devotion for whites to see and approve, while he hid his true faith, Candomblé, in the backrooms. The fact that one was on display and the other was concealed had an obvious strategic reason, but it does not mean that Domingos was just pretending to be Catholic. He was baptized, stood godfather, belonged to a Catholic brotherhood, married, and died in the Church. He lived as a Catholic, although not exclusively. The fact that he kept his saints and orişas separate indicates that instead of being a syncretist Domingos held both religions as complementary. Although I do not agree with Nina Rodrigues when he wrote in the late 1800s that "the fetishist beliefs and practices" of the Africans "did not change at all" when they came into contact with Catholicism, I agree with this early student of Candomblé that, in their conception, Orişa and saints were "perfectly distinct." Africans did not "convert" to Catholicism in the manner that Rodrigues and others after him conceived conversion. Instead, Africans incorporated both religious systems into their complex spiritual experience, which

---

[11] Souza, *O Diabo e a Terra de Santa Cruz*, 115.

[12] This quotation is from the already much-cited letter from Pompílio Manoel de Castro to the chief of police, July 27, 1862.

included and even promoted the accumulation of esoteric knowledge and ritual power derived from a variety of sources. As a result, being a Candomblé follower did not mean a rejection of Catholicism – it meant rejecting the conventional model of Catholicism that Nina Rodrigues had in mind.[13]

The Burden of Independence and Networks of Dependency

In addition to the religious aspect, other signs of Domingos' adherence to the local society and culture abound in the documents related to him, along with evidence of his indisputable connection to the life and values of the African community in Bahia. Let's start with a detail: those flower vases observed by the police in the windows of his house signified that he was Brazilianized, because the decorative use of flowers was not part of Yoruba culture or any other in West Africa.[14] More than just a detail, when he was arrested in his home in 1862, Domingos was wearing his uniform from the war for independence – he had probably put it on while the police searched his house – and still wore it when he walked through the busy center of the Upper City to the House of Correction jail with a police escort. This gesture, somewhat altered and romanticized by oral tradition, reached the ears of Manoel Querino, black abolitionist, geometric drawing teacher at the local Lyceum (primarily a vocational education school for low-income youth), and scholar of African history and culture in Bahia: "It is said that the African Domingos so-and-so, who lived on Ladeira de Santa Teresa, used to hold Candomblé functions there, and on one of those occasions, his house was surrounded by the police. Because he displayed his rank as a militia lieutenant, he had to be held in the free room in

---

[13] Rodrigues, *O animismo fetichista*, 168–169. Regarding the reshaping of African sacred space in Bahia, see Silveira, *O candomblé da Barroquinha*, 272–273. Harding, *A Refuge in Thunder*, 50–51, also comments on the spatial division between Catholic and African religions in Domingos' house and seems to agree with Nina Rodrigues' interpretation. Regarding the parallels between Africans' Christian and pagan beliefs, see Mattoso, *Être esclave au Brésil*, 166. For a critique of the tendency to judge Africans' Catholicism through the prism of "official" Catholic faith, see Anderson José M. de Oliveira, *Devoção negra: santos e catequese no Brasil colonial* (Rio de Janeiro: Quartet/FAPERJ, 2008), esp. 25–38.

[14] As Silva recalls in *Francisco Félix de Souza*, 9–10.

Aljube."[15] Domingos did not wear a lieutenant's badge but the uniform of a veteran of Bahia's War for Independence, a conflict in which he had fought and in which he was wounded, as I mentioned some chapters earlier. And the African freedman was not sent to the privileged "free room" in the Aljube prison either. In fact, Aljube, a jail I have mentioned several times in this book, had been shut down the year prior to Domingos' arrest because it stood "in the center of the city, in a narrow street, going against all standards of hygiene and public morals."[16] It had been replaced in its function by the House of Correction where Domingos was imprisoned that day.

The value of Querino's report does not lie in the accuracy of the facts, but in that it attests to the enduring memory in Bahia of a striking aspect of Domingos' arrest. In other words, it was the diviner's defiant stance in wearing that green uniform – in contrast with the blue-and-white uniforms of the officers who arrested him – which garnered him lasting symbolic dividends and perhaps immediate political support because he did not stay in jail for long.[17]

Subdelegado Pompílio Manoel de Castro described the uniform incident as "cunning" on Domingos' part, by wearing it to embarrass a police authority who dared to arrest a former soldier, a hero who had fought for the country against the hated colonial army. In his report, the subdelegado stated: "Also, I am told that this African Domingos was freed by the late [Colonel] Sudré in 1836, however he had the cunning to cover himself with the uniform of an Independence veteran and habitually wear it, as he did when he was sent to the House of Correction, when at the time of our Independence he was a slave and

[15] Querino, A raça africana, 42. Querino originally published information on this subject in 1916. The "free room" in Aljube was where "only people who were not presumed guilty of a crime" were held, according to Oliveira, As prisões do paiz, 20. On Manuel Querino's life and ideas, see Maria das Graças de Andrade Leal, Manuel Querino entre letras e lutas: Bahia, 1851–1923 (São Paulo: Annablume, 2009); and Sabrina Gledhill, "Travessias racialistas no Atlântico Negro: reflexões sobre Booker T. Washington e Manuel R. Querino," PhD dissertation, Universidade Federal da Bahia, 2014.

[16] Relatório apresentado ao excelentíssimo Senhor Conselheiro Joaquim Antão Fernandes Leão, Presidente da Província da Bahia, pelo 4o Vice-Presidente excelentíssimo Senhor Doutor José Augusto Chaves no acto em que passa-lhe a administração da Província da Bahia (Bahia: Typographia Antonio Olavo da França Guerra, 1862), 6–7.

[17] Description of the Urban Police uniform in the "Regulamento" of May 18, 1857, Art. 14, APEB, Polícia, maço 2946.

remained so on the Plantation of the same late Sudré much later [after the war]."[18] I have to agree with the subdelegado that the African freedman was clever. According to Pompílio de Castro, Domingos could not have been a veteran of the War for Independence because he was still a slave during the campaigns of 1822–1823, and only obtained his manumission years later, in 1836 (or in 1844 as we have seen in Chapter 2). However, the police authority was either uninformed or malicious, for many slaves had passed themselves off as freedmen and some fought the Portuguese while still enslaved – with or without their masters' permission – and many were granted manumission by the imperial government or their masters manumitted them under pressure from the same government. In regard to these men, the commander in chief of the anti-Portuguese forces, José Joaquim de Lima e Silva, wrote in a letter to one of the official founding fathers of Brazil, José Bonifácio de Andrada e Silva: "I have always observed proof of valor and intrepid courage in them, and a decided enthusiasm for the cause of the Independence of Brazil." Then, he asked that the recently founded Empire of Brazil pay for the manumission of those brave soldiers, and many of them received it.[19] However, this was certainly not the case with Domingos, who remained a slave after independence, about which Subdelegado Pompílio was correct.

Domingos' behavior reflected sagacity and sensitivity to Bahia's patriotic culture. Every year, thousands of Bahians – the British consul calculated about 50,000 at the time – took part in the Second of July parade in celebration of a war that had become a veritable founding myth for their local identity.[20] On that civic date in 1862, which marked forty years since Brazil's declaration of independence, shortly after Domingos' arrest, the Independence Veterans' Society was created, and the clever

---

[18] Pompílio Manoel de Castro to the chief of police, July 27, 1862.

[19] José Joaquim de Lima e Silva to Minister José Bonifácio de Andrada e Silva, July 16, 1823, BNRJ, Seção de Manuscritos, II-31, 35, 4. See also Hendrik Kraay, "'Em outra coisa não falavam os pardos, cabras, e crioulos': o 'recrutamento' de escravos na guerra da independência na Bahia," *Revista Brasileira de História*, 22, no. 43 (2002): 109–128. Regarding the episode where Domingos was sent to jail in uniform, see p. 118.

[20] The numbers the British consul provides are in a letter from John Morgan Jr. to the Foreign Office, March 16, 1858, BNA, FO, 13, 365, fl. 53v. Regarding the celebrations of Bahia's independence at the time, see Hendrik Kraay, "Entre o Brasil e a Bahia: as comemorações do Dois de Julho em Salvador no século XIX," *Afro-Ásia*, no. 23 (2000): 49–88.

freedman must have been paying attention to this novelty, and perhaps had been accepted as a member of that society.[21] Trained to
decode and manipulate African symbols, he applied his knowledge to
the symbolic universe of Bahia. Wearing that uniform also signified,
as Rachel Harding suggests, that the freedman wanted "to remind the
arresting officers, society at large, and himself that he claimed (and
indeed was owed) a stake in the emerging independent nation."[22] In
this sense, we have a priest of the Nagô nation who struggled to legit-
imize himself as a member of the Brazilian nation, in which he was
marginalized as a noncitizen. Among other mishaps, it meant that he
could be deported from the country at any time for a single misstep.
As I have said, his arrest was part of a kind of war, and Domingos had
gone into battle wearing the uniform of Bahia's independence, and
may at the same time have invoked the Nagô warrior gods, the owners of the swords confiscated in his home on Ladeira de Santa Tereza
by the police.

Going beyond flowers and uniforms, there are other signs that
Domingos sought and gained some ground in Brazil's mainstream society. His home was frequented by well-dressed, "tie-wearing" people,
representatives of his extra-African social networks. But they were not
just there for divination and healing rituals, to learn about their present ailments and ways to improve their future, or to cure them and
their loved ones from sickness, bad luck, or witchcraft. His marriage
to Delfina, celebrated before a Catholic shrine in his home, was witnessed by Antonio Clemente de Moura Florence and Miguel Gehagen
Champloni. At the time of Domingos' arrest, Florence was a small merchant listed in the *Almanak* of 1859–1860 as the owner of a stall that
sold "sundry items" in Coberto Grande, a market in the Lower City.
I know more about Miguel Champloni. He was married and the son
of a man of the same name who had committed suicide in 1838, and
whose business dealings included the slave trade after it became illegal. Born in Bahia, Domingos' best man had lived with his family in
Porto Alegre, where he had served in the National Guard, and from
where he returned in the early 1850s.[23] The year of Domingos' arrest,
Champloni Junior was a constable in Barris, a neighborhood in São

---

[21] For the founding of the Veterans' Society, see *Almanak . . . 1863*, 295.
[22] Harding, *A Refuge in Thunder*, 95.
[23] Silva, "Caminhos e descaminhos da abolição," 2007.

Pedro parish, where he lived with his mother in a comfortable two-story house with six windows facing the street, "surrounded by walls and with an iron gate on pilasters." Champloni had also worked as a clerk in São Pedro parish from 1872 to 1891, at least, probably recommended by Antônio José Pereira de Albuquerque, the subdelegado of São Pedro and Domingos' lawyer in his case against Elias Seixas. The network is expanding.[24]

Champloni takes us into another part of Domingos' web of extra-African associations. After her husband's death, Champloni's mother married Francisco José Pereira de Albuquerque, the brother of subdelegado Antonio José Pereira de Albuquerque, a bachelor who had stood godfather to two of his nephews. We are getting close to a group of people from the same family who were associated with our African freedman in several ways. I have already said in a previous chapter that I suspect that Subdelegado Antonio José had intervened on Domingos' behalf to get him out of jail and prevent his deportation. Now we find the subdelegado's clerk, who was also his brother's stepson and the half-brother of his nephews and godchildren, as a witness to Domingos and Delfina's wedding. It is not that complicated.[25]

Although they did not belong to the crème de la crème, the witnesses at Domingos and Delfina's wedding, particularly Champloni, were respectable citizens of reasonably comfortable means and social prestige in their parish. The wedding itself, a costly ceremony because of the fees charged by the Church, demonstrated the freedman's and freedwoman's efforts to obtain respectability – not accommodation – in

---

[24] ACMS, *Casamentos. São Pedro, 1844–1910*, fl. 128v; *Almanak administrativo, mercantil e industrial para o anno de 1859 e 1860* (Bahia: Typographia de Camille Masson, 1861), 380; *Almanak ... de 1873*, 89. Regarding Miguel Champloni, senior, see Ricardo Tadeu C. Silva, "Memórias do tráfico ilegal de escravos nas ações de liberdade: Bahia, 1885–1888," *Afro-Ásia*, no. 35 (2007): 71–80. Regarding Champloni's son of the same name's work as a constable, see *Almanak ... 1863*, 255. The description of the house where Champloni lived is in APEB, *LNT*, vol. 817, fls. 26v–27.

[25] The fact that Antonio and Francisco José Pereira de Albuquerque were siblings and compadres is recorded in ACMS, *Livro de registro de batismos. Freguesia de São Pedro, 1853-1851*, fl. 77v. On June 18, 1855, the subdelegado stood godfather for his two-year-old nephew Arnóbio José Pereira de Albuquerque, and his niece Idemea, age five. Like his uncle, Arnóbio would get a law degree and defended slaves suing for freedom and masters suing to maintain their slaveholding rights in the Bahian courts. Personal communication from Ricardo Tadeu Caires Silva, February 8, 2008. See also Silva, "Memórias do tráfico ilegal," 77.

the white man's world. As yet another evidence of the couple's under-standing of the local norms, their wedding was also associated with more practical issues regarding inheritance rights: the legalization of informal conjugal unions between Africans ensured that both spouses were each other's legal heirs. This may have also been the strongest rea-son for Domingos' *in articulo mortis* marriage to his first wife.[26]

Although he was illiterate and endured the legal limitations set for him as an African freedman, Domingos was a frequent visitor to Salvador's notaries' offices, particularly the one located in his own par-ish. He always took along someone to sign on his behalf, in addition to the two witnesses who were legally required by the bureaucracy, all of whom must have been respectable and trusted associates. I have not found his former master or members of his family among these people, which indicates that, unlike Elias Seixas, for instance, Domingos had somehow managed to escape from the bonds of dependence that fre-quently tied freedpersons to their former masters.[27] This says something about his ability to walk on his own two legs in the urban world he had conquered, despite coming from the world of rural slavery and sugar fields. The ease with which he moved about in Bahian society, particu-larly in the sphere of police stations, notaries' offices and law courts, is expressed in his adoption of the litigious culture that was so common at the time. In fact, a couple of chapters ago, we met two officers of the law who were close friends, and probably clients, of his. In this aspect of his life experience, we can once again see that his circle of acquain-tances was not restricted to Africans like himself but included reputable Brazilian citizens. However, Domingos knew his limits. It seems that he never took whites to court. His adversaries were always Africans like himself. In this aspect, too, he clearly understood the society in which he lived.

DOMINGOS SODRÉ, SLAVE OWNER

While Domingos took part in the freedom business as a diviner-healer and head of a manumission society, he also played a part in the slavery business as a master. There are several records that he owned slaves. I do

---

[26] In this regard, see Jeferson Bacelar, A *hierarquia das raças: negros e brancos em Salvador* (Rio de Janeiro: Pallas, 2001), 31–35. Regarding church fees as a factor in the low rate of official marriages among the poor, see Mattoso, A *família*, 81.

[27] See in this regard Cunha, *Negros, estrangeiros*, 48–53.

not know when he purchased his first, but in the short space of a year, between 1849 and 1850, he acquired at least two slave women, one of them with a son aged about three. In mid-October 1849, Domingos purchased an African woman named Lucrécia, of the Nagô nation, from Emilia Fontes. The slave woman had changed hands "with all her new and old infirmities," according to the deed of sale registered in the notary's office in Conceição da Praia parish. The purchaser therefore knew that the slave was sick – but, alas, Domingos was a "witch doctor"! – and could not return her to the seller for that reason. This may be why he only paid 350,000 reis for Lucrécia, less than the average price for a slave woman at that time, roughly 400,000 reis. And he also got her son in the bargain.[28]

The same slave woman appears in another deed drafted nearly two months later. Without mentioning the first one, this new document was intended to correct legal aspects of the original. First, Lucrécia was sold to Domingos Sodré for the same price, but now the deed stated that she was accompanied by "her minor child of three years, a young creole named Theodoro." Second, the slave woman's previous owner is no longer Emilia Fontes, but her father, Francisco Fontes, as the new deed explains: "whose slave he has registered in the name of his minor child Emilia Fontes." It does not explain why he had not registered Lucrécia in his own name, or why he did not appear as the legal owner in the first transaction, because as a minor, Emilia could not have overseen a deed of sale. That is probably why a new deed was required, and also registered in the Conceição da Praia notary's office in the Lower City. In that same parish, in September of the following year, Domingos had the mother and child baptized. Manoel Pereira, a creole freedman, stood godfather for Lucrécia, and Theodoro's godparents were Gonçalo and Dorotéia, both African freedpersons. With this gesture, the African priest proved a better Catholic than the slaves' former masters, presumably white, who had not had them baptized before selling them. This rite also suggests that Lucrécia was yet another victim of the illegal transatlantic slave trade, as it is very unlikely that she could have arrived in Brazil prior to 1831 and stayed

---

[28] AMS, *Escrituras. Conceição da Praia*, 1849–53, vol. 66.5, fls. 20–20v. On the price of slaves, see Mattoso, *Être esclave au Brésil*, 109, and for manumission prices, Mattoso, Klein, and Engerman, "Notas sobre as tendências e padrões dos preços de alforrias na Bahia, 1819–1888," 66.

a "pagan" for close to twenty years. Clever as he was, Domingos must have known that.[29]

A few months later, Domingos acquired Esperança. According to a deed of sale drawn up in December 1850, he paid 300,000 reis for this slave woman, who was also Nagô, aged thirty-two, and "suffering from an inflammation of the liver." She may have had what we now call hepatitis. As a witness to this purchase, Domingos called in Joaquim Francisco – the officer of the court introduced in Chapter 5 as a witness in his favor against Elias in 1862 – which indicates that the relationship between the two men went back a long way. But the person who signed the document on the African priest's behalf was a twenty-eight-year-old merchant who lived in Santana parish. Domingos' purchase of two slave women in poor health suggests he was looking for slaves on the cheap. He bought Esperança for slightly less than he had paid for Lucrécia two years earlier, although the transatlantic slave trade had been definitively banned that same year, 1850. In both cases, Domingos ended up getting an especially good deal because the price of slaves would skyrocket from that time forward.[30]

Unfortunately, I still do not know how Domingos got the money to buy these two slave women. Could it have been revenue from his ritual services? Could it have been money obtained through the work of other slaves he already owned? Did he inherit money from his first wife, Maria das Mercês, in the case of the purchase of Esperança a few months after her death? Or did the funds come from both sources?

Both Lucrécia and Esperança were probably hire-out slaves who not only paid a weekly sum to their African master but could set aside some money for themselves. Lucrécia put this system to good use. In July 1851, just two years after Domingos purchased her, she bought her manumission from him for 400,000 reis, cash on delivery. It is highly likely that she had saved up part of that sum before she became the freedman's slave, and Domingos, like most urban masters, respected her right to keep her hard-won savings. In addition to citing the amount received,

[29] ACMS, *Escrituras. Conceição da Praia*, 1849–53, vol. 66.5, fls. 53–54; and ACMS, *Livro de registro de batismos. Freguesia da Conceição da Praia*, 1844–1889, fl. 81v.

[30] "Escritura de venda, paga, e quitação que faz Domingos Cardoso a Domingos Sudré, de uma escrava de nome Esperança, Nação Nagô, pela quantia de Réis 300$000," APEB, *LNT*, vol. 295, fls. 134–134v. Francisco Estanislau is listed in AMS, *Livro 30 de Qualificação. Freguesia de Santana*, 1864, fl. 132. Regarding the sharp increase in the prices of slaves after the slave trade ended, see Barickman, *A Bahian Counterpoint*, 139–141.

Domingos wrote in her manumission letter that he was freeing her out of consideration for "the good services she has provided me," without specifying which. Besides using her labor for nearly two years, Domingos added 50,000 reis to the price he had paid for her and her son – and one more thing: he did not free the child along with her.[31]

Theodoro would only receive his manumission four years later, on June 5, 1855, when he was nine years old. His freedom was granted "due to the affection [developed during his] upbringing." It was free of charge, but conditional. Despite his affection, Pai Domingos would only free the young creole "on the express condition that he accompany me, serve me and respect me during my lifetime."[32] The same day he freed Theodoro, the African gave Esperança her own letter of manumission at no charge, "for the good services she has provided me."[33]

In the case of both Esperança and Theodoro, freedom followed a protocol of feelings and expectations that was widespread in Brazil. Domingos was not an original master, white or black, in that regard. Like others, he was grateful to his slaves and emotionally attached to them. The freedman was a paternalistic master, but not an especially benevolent one – quite the contrary: he strove to ensure Theodoro's loyalty, obedience, and good service throughout his own lifetime. As Mattoso aptly puts it, manumission often involved "feelings that were hard to account for," but in this case, Domingos might have been influenced by a sentiment that was common in his native land – a veritable cultural imperative – which was to have children, many children. Having just a few was unfortunate; none at all was catastrophic. Children formed part of the minimum list of gifts requested from the gods. They meant wealth, power and prestige, dependents for labor, and bargaining chips for political status. Polygamy was in large part associated with the production of numerous progeny, but female and child slavery also played a similar role of producing dependents. And Domingos was childless.[34]

---

[31] APEB, *LNT*, vol. 301, fl. 27.
[32] APEB, *LNT*, vol. 320, fl. 72.
[33] APEB, *LNT*, vol. 319, fls. 165v–166.
[34] Mattoso, *Être esclave au Brésil*, 210. Regarding the importance of having children among the Yoruba, see, for example, Peel, *Religious Encounter*, 64, 91–92; Idowu, *Olodumare*, 116; Mann, *Slavery and the Birth of an African City*, 68. Child slavery in Yorubaland is aptly covered by Olatunji Ojo, "Child Slaves in Pre-colonial Nigeria, c. 1725–1860," *Slavery & Abolition*, 33, no. 3 (2012): 417–434. For the complex structure of the Yoruba family, in which children play a central

The diviner had at last three more slaves recorded in manumission documents on different occasions. Regarding one of his slaves, Umbelina, I have not been able to find her deed of sale or letter of manumission. Therefore, I do not know when she was purchased and under what terms she obtained her freedom – whether she paid for it, and if it was conditional or unconditional. I know of Umbelina because her name is listed next to that of her former master, Domingos Sodré, in a brief entry to the index of letters of manumission granted between 1854 and 1858.[35] Therefore, it is likely that Sodré freed her in 1855, the year he emancipated his other two slaves.

In any event, how should we interpret Domingos' lavish gesture in 1855, namely giving three of his slaves their freedom at the same time? Could it have been symptomatic of a crisis of conscience, because he could no longer reconcile his status as slave owner and head of a manumission society? Or was he going through another type of crisis – not moral but spiritual? This last point is worth considering. Domingos was getting on in years at the time – he would have been about sixty – and granting manumission represented a typically Catholic way of preparing for a good death, which included charitable gestures of that kind.[36] I suspect that he dictated the will the police found in his home in 1862 around that time, which would be an even stronger sign that in 1855 he believed his death was nigh. Again, I have been unable to find the original will. One indication that these measures were linked is that the

role as sources of labor and agents of social alliances, see P. C. Lloyd, "The Yoruba Lineage," *Africa*, 25, no 3 (1955): 235–251; and William B. Schwab, "Kinship and Lineage among the Yoruba," *África*, 25, no. 4 (1955): 352–374. The desire for numerous progeny is not specific to the Yoruba. See regarding their Edo neighbors, R. E. Bradbury, *Benin Studies* (London, New York, and Ibadan: International African Institute/Oxford University Press, 1973), 213; and among Dahomeans, Le Herissé, *L'Ancien Royaume du Dahomey*, 224, 225, 226, 228. For African meanings in the formation of slave families in Brazil, see Robert Slenes, *Na senzala uma flor: esperanças e recordações na formação da família escrava – Brasil Sudeste, século XIX* (Rio de Janeiro: Nova Fronteira, 1999), esp. chap. 3; and Florentino and Góes, *A paz nas senzalas*, esp. chap. 7.

35 APEB, *Índice de cartas de liberdade*, maço 2882.
36 For two books on manumission heavily based on wills and testaments, see Roberto Guedes, *Egressos do cativeiro: trabalho, família, aliança e mobilidade social (Porto Feliz, São Paulo, c. 1798 – c. 1850)* (Rio de Janeiro: Mauad X/FAPERJ, 2008); and Márcio de Souza Soares, *A remissão do cativeiro: a dádiva da alforria e o governo dos escravos nos Campos dos Goitacases, c. 1750 – c. 1830* (Rio de Janeiro: Apicuri, 2009).

same notary who registered the three letters of manumission, Manoel Lopes da Costa, also notarized his original will, which is now lost.[37]

Unfortunately, I have not found any trace of Lucrécia, Esperança, Theodoro, and Umbelina after they were freed. Did they all survive the terrible cholera epidemic that ravaged Bahia a few weeks after their manumission? The scourge, which went on for several months until the end of April 1856, struck terror in Salvador and the Recôncavo. There were so many victims that they could not be given a decent burial, whether Bahian or African style, Christian or pagan. The government often collected the corpses, piled them up and buried them in common graves, sometimes burning them beforehand. There were about 10,000 cholera deaths in Salvador alone – possibly 18 percent of its population.[38] I remain extremely curious about what Domingos did during that crisis, because, like other African priests, he must have participated in the efforts to cure the disease and provide spiritual protection. People like Anacleto da Natividade, for example, a Nagô healer and priest of Omolu – the Yoruba god of disease, most notably associated with smallpox – in the Recôncavo town of São Felix. According to oral tradition, he played a leading role in the fight against cholera, protecting and curing people with his alternative medicine – including the family of his master, on whose plantation he was an overseer. In reward, he was allowed to build a Candomblé house on the plantation's grounds, or so goes the oral tradition.[39]

Could Domingos have protected Theodoro during the epidemic? If the boy survived, he may have grown up and, in practice, gained his independence from his former master. Either that, or he somehow managed to negotiate his way out of conditional freedom without fulfilling the terms of his manumission. In any event, he was not a member of the household on Ladeira de Santa Tereza in 1862, when he would have

[37] Regarding attitudes toward death viewed through probate records, see Reis, *A morte é uma festa*, esp. chap. 4, and the bibliography cited therein. Regarding freedpersons in particular, see Oliveira, *Os libertos*, chap. 3; and Mattoso, *Da revolução dos alfaiates à riqueza dos baianos*, 237–244.

[38] Onildo Reis David, *O inimigo invisível: epidemia na Bahia no século XIX* (Salvador: EDUFBa, 1996); Johildo Lopes de Athayde, *Salvador e a grande epidemia de 1855*, Publicações do CEB no. 113 (Salvador: Centro de Estudos Baianos da UFBA, 1985).

[39] See Fayette Wimberley, "The Expansion of Afro-Bahian Religious Practices in Nineteenth-Century Cachoeira," in *Afro-Brazilian Culture and Politics: Bahia, 1790s to 1990s*, ed. Hendrik Kraay (Armonk, NY: M. E. Sharpe, 1998), 82–84.

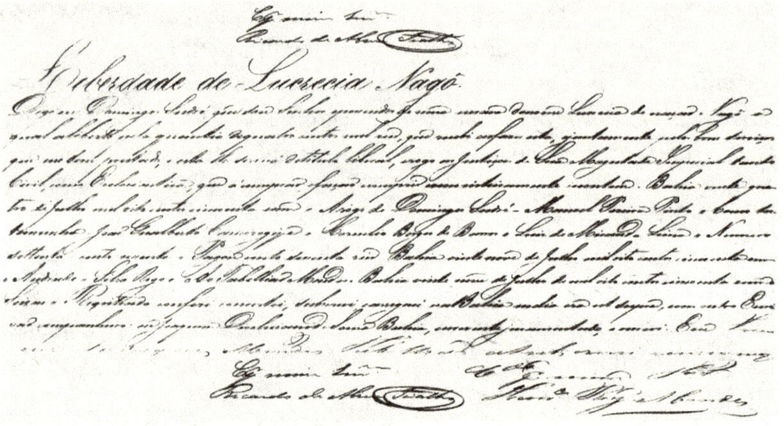

Figure 47. Lucrécia's letter of manumission, 1851.

been sixteen years old. Nor is he mentioned in Domingos' will, drafted in 1882, by which time he would have been thirty-six. If he did stay by his master's side until Domingos' death, he would only have been freed once and for all at the age of forty-one, in 1887, on the eve of the definitive abolition of slavery. It may be that, years before that date, Domingos had already found that he could not control his slaves and dependents because he was getting old, along with the insubordination of slaves and conditional freedpersons that accompanied the rampant breakdown of the institution of slavery in its last decades, particularly in large cities like Salvador.[40] Theodoro's apparent disappearance from Domingos' life suggests that he did not fulfill the plausible role as a surrogate son for the Candomblé priest.

Regardless of the feelings involved, Theodoro's manumission – conditional as it was – signaled that Domingos was still committed to

[40] The slave owners' power went into steep decline when the Free Birth Law of 1871 was enacted for reasons amply explained in Chalhoub, *Visões da liberdade*, esp. 151–161, and, idem, *Machado de Assis, historiador*, chap. 4. See also Hebe M. Mattos de Castro, "Laços de família e direitos no final da escravidão," in *História da vida privada no Brasil. Império: a Corte e a modernidade nacional*, ed. Luiz Felipe de Alencastro (São Paulo: Companhia das Letras, 1997), chap. 7. For the decline of seigniorial authority in Bahia during that period, see Brito, *A abolição na Bahia*, esp. chap. 1; Walter Fraga Filho, *Encruzilhadas da liberdade: histórias de escravos e libertos na Bahia (1870–1910)* (Campinas: Editora Unicamp, 2006), esp. chaps. 1 to 3; and Silva, "Caminhos e descaminhos da abolição," esp. chaps. 4 and 5.

the institution of slavery. It is also possible that Lucrécia, Esperança, Umbelina, and Theodoro were not the only slaves he owned at the time.[41] If they were, he later acquired at least two more slaves. In February 1859, he purchased Maria Ignez or Maria Archanja, another Nagô slave. She was older than forty, and previously owned by Sancho Bittencourt Berenguer Cezar, the scion of an aristocratic family of sugar planters, Commander of the Order of Christ and a colonel in the National Guard, who also lived in São Pedro parish. Domingos paid 800,000 reis for her, 180,000 reis less than the average price that year, most likely because she was past her prime. Maria Ignez, or Maria Archanja, would be arrested along with Domingos and Delfina in 1862, when she pretended to be a freedwoman.[42]

In 1859, Domingos was probably also the master of an African man named Ozório, whose deed of sale I have been unable to find. I have, however, unearthed the record of his manumission. On March 4, 1862, four months before his arrest, Domingos granted Ozório his freedom, "having received from him five hundred and twenty-eight thousand reis," after which "he can from now on enjoy his freedom."[43] Fifteen years later, on May 12, 1877, by which time he was probably no longer the head of the manumission society – possibly because of his age – we find Domingos granting another slave's freedom. This time it was for Maria (most likely the same Maria Ignez mentioned in the previous paragraph), of whom he declared he was the "owner and master." Just as he had done in relation to Ozório, Domingos did not express any gratitude or other sentiments. He tersely observed that Maria Ignez's freedom had been granted, "after receiving from her the amount of five hundred thousand reis."[44] That was all, just business.

According to the accusations of the police and the press, Maria Ignez may have earned a living from Candomblé rituals she helped Domingos perform. But both she and Ozório most certainly also worked for hire.

---

[41] The records show that Domingos Sodré freed a slave named Theodozio between 1854 and 1858, but I believe that he was actually Theodoro, incorrectly registered under that name. APEB, *Índice de cartas de alforria, 1854–1858*, maço 2882, fl. 109v.

[42] AMS, *Escritura de escravos. Freguesia de Conceição da Praia, 1855–1859*, no. 66.7, fls. 105–107. The average price of a slave woman in 1860 is from Mattoso, *Être esclave au Brésil*, 109.

[43] APEB, LNT, vol. 365, fl. 28.

[44] APEB, LNT, vol. 511, fl. 28v.

As a result, they were able to save up enough money to buy their freedom. The prices they paid for it were well below the average market
value for adult slaves. Ozório would have paid as low as less than half his
actual worth as a male adult slave. However, this may not have been a
gracious gesture on their master's part but due to both slaves' advanced
age. In this case, Ozório would actually have paid a bit more than his
market value. As for Maria, by the time of her manumission she must
have been at least sixty, and purchased her freedom for a little less than
her market price after serving Domingos for nearly twenty years. In the
meantime, her master had recouped his initial investment many times
over. To a large extent, he had lived off her earnings.[45]

If readers have attentively followed Domingos' life as a slave owner,
they will have observed that his slave women – I have not managed to
determine Ozório's nation – were all Nagôs, like their master. In Bahia,
the African freedman was not alone in the habit of enslaving his own
people, typically a taboo in Africa.[46] But whom did he consider his people? We cannot know if Domingos enslaved Africans from Lagos, for
instance. We should recall that the concept of Nagô included slaves
from a vast region of Africa populated by diverse Yoruba-speaking
groups that still did not recognize themselves as a single people, and
were always at odds, which included fighting and enslaving each other.
Even so, in Bahia the Nagôs considered each other "kin" – in this
respect Africans belonging to the same nation used the Portuguese term
parente, literally relative – as a result of a complex process of ethnogenesis that I have discussed elsewhere.[47] If I am correct, this means

[45] Mattoso, Klein, and Engerman, "Notas sobre as tendências e padrões dos preços
de alforrias na Bahia," 66 and 71. The comparisons were made for 1859–1860
(Ozório) and 1875–1876 (Maria).
[46] Generally speaking, people of the same lineage were not usually enslaved in
Africa. Those who lost their freedom because they had committed a crime were
sold outside their group. See Claude Meillassoux, Antropologia da escravidão: o
ventre de ferro e dinheiro (Rio de Janeiro: Zahar, 1995).
[47] See Reis, Rebelião escrava no Brasil, esp. chap. 10; and Reis and Mamigonian,
"Nagô and Mina." See also Maria Inês Côrtes de Oliveira, "The Reconstruction
of Ethnicity in Bahia: The Case of the Nagô in the Nineteenth Century,"
and João José Reis, "Ethnic Politics among Africans in Nineteenth-Century
Bahia," both published in Trans-Atlantic Dimension of the African Diaspora, eds.
Paul Lovejoy and David Trotman (London and New York: Continuum, 2003),
158–180 and 240–264, respectively. See also Oliveira, "Viver e morrer no meio
dos seus." Regarding the equivalent phenomenon among Gbe-speaking people,
see Parés, A formação do candomblé, esp. chap. 2.

that the African rules of rightful enslavement were largely cast aside in Bahia. Inês Oliveira even argues that the purchase of slaves of the same nation by African masters could have been a strategy for using their labor immediately after they arrived in Brazil, because their common language would facilitate the newly enslaved Africans' learning process and specifically enable them to understand seigniorial orders of all kinds.[48] But there was more to it than that. It had above all to do with whom the market was offering for sale. As of the 1820s, as I have already discussed, the vast majority of slaves who arrived in Bahia were Yoruba-speaking Nagôs, just as in the middle of the century most freedpersons and potential slave buyers in the African community would also have belonged to that nation. At any rate, Domingos Sodré did not participate actively in the market for newly arrived slaves, his slaves being ladinos, seasoned Africans like him, although older and therefore cheaper. They would, in fact, have been more familiar to him than enslaved folks newly arrived from Africa. But just like them, they were mostly Nagôs. Therefore, similarly to other African freedpersons, Domingos enslaved his Bahian-made ethnic kin.

I have been able to ascertain that Domingos Sodré owned at least six slaves over the years, which does not mean he was the master of that number at any given time. His behavior in this regard, a veritable investment strategy, seems to have been to buy, use, and free his slaves, either free of charge or for a price. I have just called it an investment scheme, but it was also a political strategy for exerting control – his power as a ritual leader not being enough – for his slaves knew that, like other masters, the freedman would be willing to reward them for good service, loyalty, and obedience by granting their manumission on more favorable terms. In 1855, he had at least four slaves, but by 1862, there were just two.

As a slave owner, Domingos was not exceptional among African freedpersons, although he belonged to a minority group in the African community, which included masters who were also enslaved. We have seen that some of his friends and foes with the same social status were also slave owners, such as Manoel Joaquim Ricardo and Elias Seixas. Out of a sample of 395 people whose estates were inventoried after their deaths between 1800 and 1850 in Salvador, twenty-five were Africans. Of these, only four did not own slaves; the others owned

48   Oliveira, "Viver e morrer no meio dos seus," 187–189.

between one and twenty, although the vast majority had just one. Out of a much larger sample Inês Oliveira gathered, of 259 African freedpersons whose estates were posthumously inventoried between 1790 and 1850, 78.4 percent owned slaves. Confirming this result, for the same period Mieko Nishida found that 77.8 percent of 261 freedpersons studied were slave owners.[49]

We know that other leading lights of nineteenth-century Candomblé in Bahia were even more prosperous slave owners than Pai Domingos, and I am not referring to the wealthy Manoel Joaquim Ricardo. The Nagô freedwoman Francisca da Silva, the legendary Iyá Nassô who founded the Casa Branca candomblé – considered the cradle of Afro-Brazilian religion Yoruba style – owned at least fifteen slaves during the brief period between 1832 and 1837. She freed some for money and others without charge. Most of the latter received their manumission on condition that they accompany her on her return voyage to Africa in 1837 to flee the anti-African backlash that followed the 1835 Muslim rebellion in Bahia. Her successor at the head of that venerable institution, who was also a Nagô African woman, Marcelina da Silva, or Obatossi, was the slave of Francisca da Silva and her husband, from whom she purchased her manumission for the high price of 500,000 reis that same year. Once freed, Obatossi became the owner of eighteen slaves between 1844 and 1878.[50] Like Marcelina da Silva's and Francisca da Silva's slave women, it is possible that Domingos' slaves were his initiates in the Oriṣa religion and helped him with his ritual duties. In other words, they may have worked in the secular sphere in the streets and in the sacred sphere at home. This was very likely the case with Maria Ignez.

But how representative of African freedpersons were Francisca da Silva, Marcelina da Silva, Domingos Sodré, and others whose estates were in general inventoried? As for the percentage of African freedpersons who owned slaves in Salvador, a better indicator than probate inventories is the Santana parish census carried out in 1849, near the time when we find Domingos buying slaves and granting manumissions.

---

[49] The data in this paragraph is from Reis, *Rebelião escrava*, 33, 367–370; Oliveira, *O liberto*, 41; Nishida, *Slavery and Identity*, 88.

[50] "Liberdade de Marcelina Nagô," APEB, *LNT*, vol. 255, fl. 65v. The story of Francisca and Marcelina da Silva is recounted in Castillo and Parés, "Marcelina da Silva e seu mundo," 111–150, esp. 149–150 (the list of slaves owned by Francisca da Silva and Marcelina da Silva).

The census lists 304 freedmen and women, the former working for hire in their majority – mainly as porters and sedan chair bearers – and as tradesmen; most of the freedwomen were street vendors and small shopkeepers. In contrast with the data found in probate records, only sixty-seven, or 22 percent, of the freedmen and women in the census owned slaves. Most of them (forty-eight) owned just one or two slaves, and just four had six to eight. Within this world of small slave owners, we could say there was an elite African group internally stratified by the size of its members' slaveholdings. If the data for Santana parish are representative of all African freedpersons in Salvador – and I believe they are – Domingos would have been part of the upper strata of that elite if he had owned all six slaves at once. But he did not. It is possible that he never owned more than four slaves at any given time, perhaps five including Ozório, which would have put him in the roughly 10 percent of slave-owning freedpersons who only had that number of slaves. He was therefore nowhere near as wealthy as the freedwomen who led Casa Branca, or his friend Manoel Joaquim Ricardo, who owned almost thirty slaves at the end of his life and, lest we forget, was also charged with being the head of a Candomblé venue.[51]

Finally, let me introduce you to someone who may have been more typical in economic terms of African freedpersons in nineteenth-century Bahia. Her name was Esperança, which means hope in Portuguese, maybe the same Esperança manumitted by Domingos in 1855. She lived in a tiny room in the basement of a townhouse in Largo Dois de Julho, a square named to celebrate Bahia's independence located not far from Domingos, the independence war veteran's home. When she died in 1872, Esperança had no surname or obligatory heirs, nor did she leave a will bequeathing her estate. For that reason, her earthly goods were auctioned off and the money went to the government. The advertisement for the auction of those goods was published in the press: "The estate of Esperança, who died intestate, containing a box with two packages of cloths, three pieces of chintz, 8 African shawls, 14 strands of red coral beads, and some clothes worn by the dead woman, another box with the same clothing, 2 boxes of ordinary and well-used crockery." The whole lot was sold for 65,000 reis, and probably included merchandise she sold, for she seems to have been a cloth street vendor just like Domingos' wife once was. The value of her assets corresponded

---

[51] APEB, *Relação dos africanos residentes na freguesia de Santana*, maço 2898.

to approximately 10 percent of a bricklayer's yearly salary. Once the costs were paid – the inventory, the auctioneer, the newspaper ad, and so on – all that was left over for the state's coffers was the net sum of 29,484 reis. The objects Esperança left behind included a thick strand of red beads, which probably symbolized her devotion to an African deity and should have been buried with her.[52]

New Investments

When the transatlantic slave trade ended in the early 1850s and slave prices rose sharply, investments in slavery gradually became too rich for small investors, including most freedpersons. Marcelina da Silva and Manoel Joaquim Ricardo were exceptions to the rule. Many small slave owners, black and white, used the change in the market to their advantage, selling their slaves for a hefty profit to meet the demand from the sugar planters in Bahia's Recôncavo, but primarily from coffee producers in southeast Brazil, the main client for the domestic trade in a now booming market. Oliveira observes that, between 1850 and 1890, the rate of slave-owning freedpersons who left probate records fell from nearly 80 percent to 45 percent. Domingos was part of this group, but he also gradually eliminated his slaveholdings, mainly or perhaps exclusively through free and paid manumissions, and not by selling off his slaves. In short, it was only while the transatlantic slave trade lasted that investments in slaves were generally feasible for African freedpersons, and even slaves, some of whom were personally involved in the traffic in human beings in Africa, as we have seen in the case of Manoel Joaquim Ricardo and his business associates. In fact, Ricardo had already been active in the inter-provincial slave trade since at least the mid-1840s.[53]

As for Domingos, he did not just invest in slaves. Three years before he granted Maria's manumission, we find him dealing in real estate, an investment that had become more realistic for people in his income

---

[52] APEB, *Tribunal da Relação. Inventário (arrecadação)*, no. 07/3028/11. For the bricklayer's salary in 1873, see Mattoso, *Bahia: a cidade do Salvador e seu mercado*, 371.

[53] Oliveira, *O liberto*, 41; idem, "Viver e morrer no meio dos seus," 188–189. See also Mattoso, *Da revolução dos alfaiates à riqueza dos baianos*, 249; idem, *Bahia*, 636–638; Barickman, *A Bahian Counterpoint*, 138; Nishida, *Slavery and Identity*, 203–204, n. 57; Reis, "Social Mobility among Slaves."

bracket. At that point, the law that had barred Africans from owning real estate in Bahia was no longer in effect. In September 1874, he and his wife, Delfina, purchased a house with one door and two windows facing the street, a parlor and a dining room, two small bedrooms, and a kitchen, located in Largo Dois de Julho. I have not been able to ascertain how much they paid for the property, but two years later they sold it for 1,850,000 reis. In December of that same year, 1876, Domingos purchased another house on his own (his wife's name was not on the deed) for 1,200,000 reis. It was a more modest property with just one door and one window facing the street, a parlor and dining room, kitchen, attic, and walled patio situated in Sé parish. The deed of sale contains a significant detail: two years before Domingos purchased the house from an African couple. It had belonged to Duarte Santos, the famous priest of Sàngó, better known as Arabonam, whom I introduced in Chapter 3. What a coincidence![54]

The net amount raised by these two transactions totaled 650,000 reis, which Domingos and his wife may have needed to live on or required for other, more urgent expenses. The sale of Maria's manumission a few months later suggests that the couple really needed to beef up their family budget at a time when Domingos was nearly eighty years old and may not have been able to work, not even as the head of the manumission society.

In a study focused on the city of Rio de Janeiro, Zephyr Frank shows that in the first half of the nineteenth century – when the transatlantic slave trade was open, including the illegal phase after 1831 – investments in slaves brought bigger returns for small urban investors. Once the slave trade was definitively banned in 1850, over time nearly the only investors in that market were major players, particularly coffee planters, because of the considerable increase in the price of slave labor. In short, slave ownership became concentrated into fewer hands. After 1850, small and medium-sized investors would start buying real estate, now deriving their income from rentals instead of the earnings of their hire-out slaves. However, this new form of venture was not as lucrative,

---

[54] "Escritura de venda, compra, paga e quitação que fazem Domingos Pereira Sodré e sua mulher Maria Delfina da Conceição a José de Oliveira Castro etc," July 14, 1876; and "Escritura de venda, compra, paga e quitação que fazem Elpidio Lopes da Silva e sua mulher D. Maria do Carmo de Almeida a Domingos Pereira Sodré etc," December 13, 1876, APEB, *LNT*, vol. 479, fls. 30v–31 and 54–54v, respectively.

and resulted in the impoverishment of people who formed what Frank calls "middling groups" in the city of Rio de Janeiro. In other words, the transatlantic trade, one of the cruelest aspects of modern slavery, had fostered a more widely distributive system of slave ownership that benefited slave-owning freedpersons like African barber-surgeon and musician Antonio José Dutra, of the Congo nation, one of the main figures in Frank's book, who owned thirteen slaves when he died in 1849.[55]

The phenomenon Frank studied had already been pointed out in Bahia along general lines by other authors like Kátia Mattoso and Maria Inês Oliveira, but without the formidable statistical apparatus the U.S. historian mobilized. Mattoso's work indicated a process of wealth concentration in general, going beyond slave ownership, between the first and second halves of the nineteenth century. She also observed that in the latter period, among Bahians who were active in urban areas and left probate records, slaves were no longer an important part of their property, and "houses and bank accounts or shares/policies constituted ... the essence of their wealth."[56] This included Domingos. It would be interesting to verify differences in the pace of change in various parts of Brazil. But a macro-historic study would make more sense only if it unveils the micro-historic dynamic of individual lives, which is what most interests us here. I have already observed that, in Bahia, African freedpersons such as Manoel Joaquim Ricardo, Antonio Xavier de Jesus, and Marcelina da Silva continued to be major investors in urban slavery in the second half of the nineteenth century. In fact, when he died in 1865, Ricardo's investments were evenly divided between slaves and real estate, which suggests that death may have surprised him at a time of transition in terms of his investment strategy. Neither he nor (and even more so) Domingos fell into the pattern found in Rio de Janeiro, at least when it comes to the timeline for the process of change. Domingos would only go from slave owner to landlord in the 1870s.

[55] Zephyr L. Frank, *Dutra's World: Wealth and Family in Nineteenth-Century Rio de Janeiro* (Albuquerque: University of New Mexico Press, 2004). See also Silvana Cassab Jeha, "Ganhar a vida: uma história do barbeiro africano José Dutra e sua família: Rio de Janeiro, século XIX," in *Doenças e escravidão: sistema de saúde e práticas terapêuticas*, ed. Ângela Porto (Rio de Janeiro: Casa Oswaldo Cruz/ Fiocruz, 2007), available on CD-ROM.

[56] Mattoso, *Bahia*, 612–616, 634–638. The quotation appears on page 634.

Domingos and Delfina bought the two houses merely as investment. They never lived in the new home purchased in December 1876 or the one they had sold five months earlier. They must have preferred to rent them out, for they continued to live as tenants in the house on Ladeira de Santa Tereza. After so many years of residence in São Pedro parish, Domingos had established an extensive social network there, and Delfina must have too. As we have seen, Domingos' main contacts among Africans and whites were located there. His old associates from the manu-mission society, most of his godchildren, and divination clientele all lived in São Pedro or neighboring parishes. Furthermore, the spacious town-house where they lived was better suited for subletting rooms. Possibly because they had become landlords, the deed for the house on Largo Dois de Julho shows that he and his wife were "making a living from trade." In sum, by the mid-1870s the African couple most probably lived off rents, and perhaps also from Delfina's cloth vending business and Domingos' continuing activities as both a diviner and head of a manumission society. But whatever they did for a living then, their options were dwindling with the coming of age.

By the time the 1880s arrived, the now elderly couple needed enough money to retire on, perhaps because they were both in poor health. They sold the house on Rua da Ordem Terceira sometime between 1882 and 1887. It was probably in 1886, when a serious economic crisis hit the prov-ince. On September 3 of that year, after his wife suffered a stroke that par-alyzed one side of her body and made it difficult for her to walk, Domingos deposited nearly one million reis in her name in Caixa Econômica. As a client of that bank, she appears as Maria da Conceição Sodré Pereira, using her husband's surname for the first time in a document I have located.[57] The money must have come from the sale of the house.

Caixa Econômica, a private financial institution that was then housed in the provincial government palace, was founded in 1834 to serve as a loan bank, among other functions. Many of its clients depos-ited their savings there to keep them safe and earn interest. They could be modestly well off, like Domingos, or very poor – in the second half of the century even slaves entrusted the bank with the money they were saving up to buy their manumission. Black Catholic confraternities,

---

[57] "Autuação do arrolamento dos bens deixados pelo fallecido Africano liberto Domingos Sudré Pereira, Francisco Pinheiro de Souza [inventariante]," APEB, *Judiciária*, 07/3000/08, fls. 2, 13.

including the Rosário Brotherhood of which Pai Domingos was a member, also started using the new banking services, even investing in government bonds.[58]

Caixa Econômica and other savings and loan institutions that were created or grew substantially in the second half of the century would become the competitors of African manumission societies, and may have even led to their extinction. Therefore, it is ironic that, toward the end of his life, Domingos, who had once run one of those societies, should opt for this type of investment. He knew how to mix tradition with innovation. We must also reconsider Nina Rodrigues's peremptory statement that the Africans of his time "tuned the vibrations of their souls to different notes from those of whites."[59] Not always, not always. The problem is that Rodrigues, being a confirmed racialist, chose to isolate Africans from the rest of Bahian society as a method for studying them as a unique, exotic population, a racial "stock" bound for extinction in Bahia.

We can go even further. By investing in Caixa Econômica, Domingos was taking his first steps in the circuit of financial capital fueled by the end of the slave trade. Caixa Econômica and other banks grew when transatlantic human trafficking came to an end, because some of the now idle capital of large and small slave traders migrated to banking. When analyzing the wealth of Bahians, Mattoso has found that the number of people investing in banks grew considerably after 1850.[60] Figures like former slave trader Joaquim Pereira Marinho were among the shareholders of the financial institutions that thrived during that period.[61] The men who had profited from the transatlantic slave trade

[58] See related documents in APEB, *Judiciária*, no. 21/741/02 (1877). Regarding Caixa Econômica da Bahia and other institutions of that period, see Mattoso, *Bahia: Salvador e seu mercado*, 269–271, and, in particular, Waldir Freitas Oliveira, *História de um banco: o Banco Econômico* (Salvador: Museu Eugênio Teixeira Leal, 1993), chap. 1. Reis, "A família negra no tempo da escravidão," 61–74, tells the story of a slave named Augusta whose savings were deposited in Caixa Econômica in 1872 with the approval of her master, Judge João José de Almeida Couto, the future Baron of Desterro, who was the interim president of the province on several occasions between 1870 and 1873. For more information on him, see Wildberger, *Os presidentes da província da Bahia*, 583–588.

[59] *Os africanos no Brasil*, 99.

[60] Mattoso, *Bahia*, 635–636.

[61] For example, Pereira Marinho figured "among the biggest shareholders of Caixa Econômica" (Oliveira, *História de um banco*, 48) and was one of the founders

were now reaping profits from the savings of the people they had sold in Brazil. In addition they were lending former slaves money at interest. We have seen that the freedman Manoel Joaquim Ricardo owed money to the Caixa Econômica and Caixa Comercial banks when he died in 1865.

The new banks were not the only institutions that began to compete with the manumission societies as the depositories of the slaves' life savings. The abolitionist societies formed in the second half of the nineteenth century played the same role, in addition to directly purchasing manumission without cost to the slaves, and lending them interest-free money for the same purpose. Manoel de Abreu Contreiras – the man who in 1862 signed the document on behalf of Domingos in which the African priest undertook to abandon Candomblé – received 300,000 reis for the manumission of his creole slave Izidora from the Seventh of September Liberation Society (Sociedade Libertadora Sete de Setembro), which celebrated in the choice of its name the date when Brazil's independence was proclaimed by its first emperor, Pedro I. The document was drawn up on July 1, 1871, most likely as a way of celebrating the anniversary of Bahia's independence the following day, when Domingos probably joined the parade as a war veteran.[62]

Domingos Sodré's career as a manumission society leader reflects the trajectory of these African institutions, which were formed as an instrument for overcoming slavery and declined along with it. This trend was also associated with the decline of the enslaved African-born population, which was the mainstay of the manumission societies. In this sense, the aging, impoverishment, and death of the African Domingos Sodré could be seen as a metaphor for an entire historic process.

DEATH

Domingos Sodré died on May 3, 1887, eight months after depositing his investment in Caixa Econômica. If he had lived one more year, he would have witnessed abolition, but he had already seen the growing public sentiment against slavery building up in Salvador. Many abolitionist

---

of the Banco da Bahia (Barickman, *A Bahian Counterpoint*, 136, and Lyrio, "Joaquim Pereira Marinho," 7).

[62] "Liberdade de Izidora, creoula," APEB, *LNT*, no. 410, fl. 84. Regarding the work of the abolitionist societies in Bahia, see Brito, *A abolição na Bahia*, 133–151; and Silva, "Caminhos e descaminhos da abolição," 151–157.

rallies with packed audiences took place near the freedman's home in the São João Theater. At the very least, he would have heard from his house the fireworks that accompanied those demonstrations. Could he have converted to abolitionism when he died? If he hadn't, at least he had left his commitment to slavery behind long before.

His death certificate shows that Domingos died at about the age of ninety, of "cerebral apoplexy," now known as a stroke.[63] He was still living in the house the police had raided twenty-five years earlier, for which he now paid 35,000 reis per month in rent to Maria Fernanda Pires de Teive e Argolo, the daughter of a traditional family, one of the oldest, part of Bahia's slave-owning, sugar-planting aristocracy.[64] Domingos' wake was held in his parlor whose walls were covered with pictures of Catholic saints, his body lying at rest in a luxurious coffin set on a table and adorned with four torches that "burned for hours while the body was in the house." The room was decorated for the wake with black fabric and two wreaths. Then, as he had requested, the body was carried in a cortege for burial in the far-off Quinta dos Lázaros cemetery, where fresh funeral decorations had been set up for the ritual of interment in niche no. 22 of his Black Brotherhood of Rosary. Members of that confraternity would certainly have formed part of the cortege, which was Domingos' right, and which he had explicitly requested in his 1882 will and testament. A solemn funeral mass was said for his soul in the Franciscan convent's magnificent church. It was a lavish baroque ceremony, just as his widow had wanted, although the dead man had asked for a funeral "without the slightest ostentation," an expression of Christian humility that was not African in the least.[65]

Unfortunately, I do not know if any African funeral rites were celebrated in his honor. There are, however, accounts in his probate records that lead me to suspect that a certain Leopoldina Sodré overspent on some aspects of the funeral. I have not been able to discover who this

---

[63] Domingos' death certificate is registered in ACMS, *Óbitos. Freguesia de São Pedro, 1880–1911*, fl. 84v.

[64] As I observed in a previous chapter, I suspect that this house had once belonged to the Sodré family. Harding, *A Refuge in Thunder*, 94, states that Domingos owned the townhouse on 7, Ladeira de Santa Tereza, but I have not found any evidence to confirm it.

[65] "Autuação do arrolamento dos bens deixados pelo fallecido Africano liberto Domingos Sudré Pereira," fl. 24.

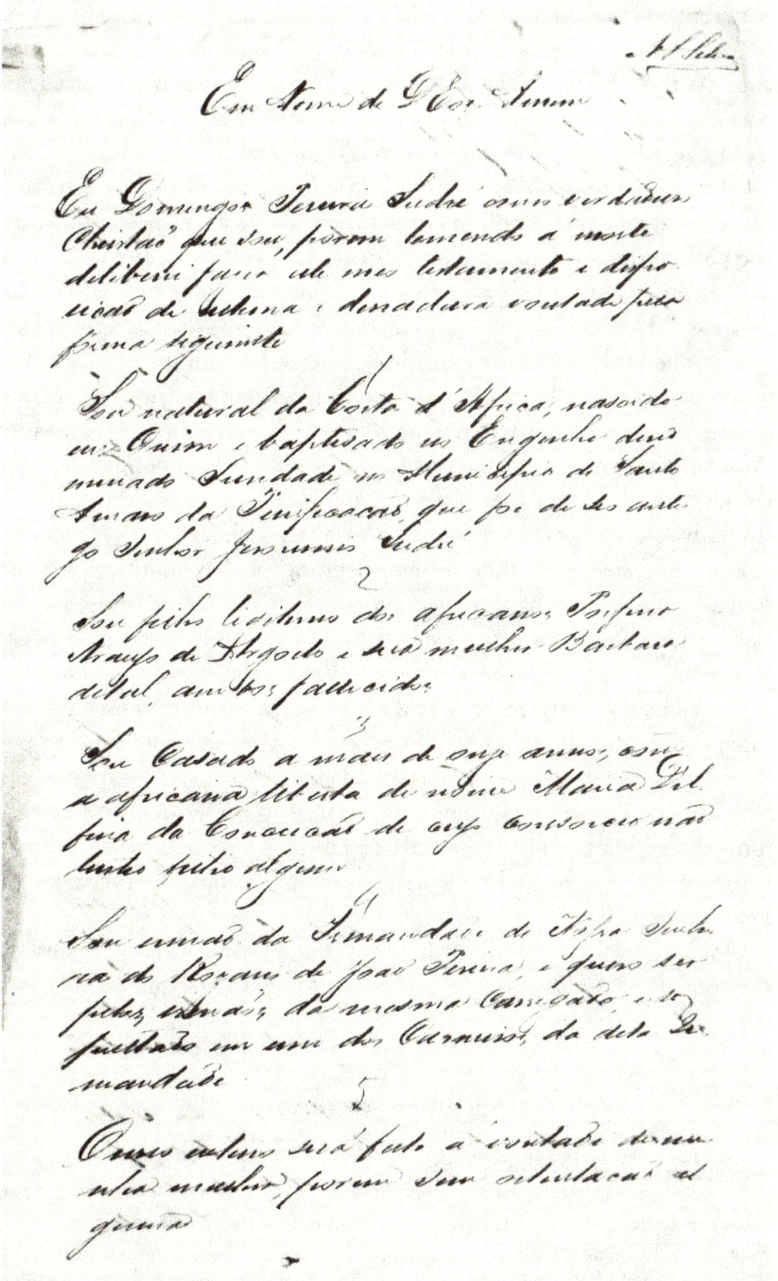

Em Nome de Deos Amem

Eu Domingos Pereira Sodré como verdadeiro Christão que sou, porem temendo a morte deliberei fazer este meu testamento e disposição de ultima e derradeira vontade pela forma seguinte

1

Sou natural da Costa d'Africa, nascido em Onim e baptisado no Engenho denominado Trindade no Municipio de Santo Amaro da Purificação, que foi de meu antigo Senhor Jeronimo Sodré

2

Sou filho legitimo dos africanos Porfirio Araujo de Argolo e sua mulher Barbara de Tal, ambos fallecidos

3

Sou Casado a mais de onze annos, com a africana liberta de nome Maria Delfina da Conceição de cujo consorcio não tenho filho algum

4

Sou irmão da Irmandade de Nossa Senhora do Rozario de João Pereira, e quero ser feito, amortalhado da mesma Irmandade, e sepultado em um dos Carneiros da dita Irmandade

5

O meu enterro será feito a vontade de minha mulher, porem sem ostentação alguma

Figure 48. First page of Domingos Sodré's last will and testament, 1882.

woman was. I believe she was a freedwoman, perhaps an assistant who belonged to the elderly couple's household. The same surname, Sodré, suggests that she had been Domingo's slave – another one – or maybe was the former slave of a member of the African's ex-masters' family. Whatever the case, she was a trusted person of the freed couple. But the trustee responsible for Delfina's inheritance contested the request for reimbursement Leopoldina Sodré submitted for 324,000 reis, which she paid to the undertaker. The trustee thought the price of the coffin, 80,000 reis, was too high, and also questioned the receipts for the decorations in Domingos' home and at the cemetery, 100,000 and 50,000 reis, respectively, which he considered phony. Leopoldina protested but failed to convince him. He only reimbursed her for the price of the coffin.[66] In other cases where Candomblé folk have died, expenses for African ceremonies have also been contested. This happened two years earlier in 1885, upon the death of Candomblé priestess Marcelina da Silva, whose biological daughter, Maria Magdalena da Silva, explicitly accused her stepfather of overspending on her mother's African funeral rites. Similarly, the executor for the Candomblé priest Duarte Soares, also known as Arabonam, would be accused of selling a house belonging to the dead man's estate to cover certain expenses that the deceased had secretly ordered, and I believe they were connected to his funeral.[67] These two examples suggest that when it came time to pay the bills for the inventory, which were legally binding, the expenses did not add up because those that were related to the African side of the funeral could not be clearly stated or backed up with receipts. The same thing could have happened with Pai Domingos' funeral, organized by Leopoldina Sodré.

Aside from the investment in Caixa Econômica, the couple's estate was modest when Domingos died. I have not found Delfina's necklaces,

[66] Domingos Sodré's last will and testament, APEB, *Judiciária. Testamentos*, no. 07/3257/01; "Autuação do arrolamento dos bens deixados pelo fallecido Africano liberto Domingos Sudré Pereira," fls. 15–21. Domingos Sodré left his funeral rites up to his wife. Generally speaking, Africans did not state their desire to be buried according to the precepts of Candomblé or Islam in their wills. See Oliveira, *Os libertos*, chap. 3. For exceptions, see Nishida, *Slavery and Identity*, 115; Mattoso, *Da revolução dos alfaiates*, 243; and regarding the postabolition period in the Brazilian Republic, see Bacelar, *A hierarquia das raças*, 35–36.
[67] Castillo and Parés, "Marcelina da Silva e seu mundo," 142–145; João José Reis, "Arabonam, um sacerdote de Xangô na Bahia oitocentista" (unpublished paper).

jewelry, and balangandãs in the inventory, which means they were probably sold after 1862 if the police ever returned them. The furnishings included a sofa made of good Brazilian rosewood but in poor condition, two tables, two mahogany chests, a wooden water jar holder, two upholstered mahogany armchairs, two covered in canvas, and two "without wooden backing." Everything was well used. The clocks that had attracted such intense interest from the police twenty-five years before were still on the wall, now retired from marking the passage of time. The inventory also included a mirror, three lamps with coverings, a pair of jugs, and a rosewood niche containing carved wooden statues of saints "trimmed with silver." The niche was the most valuable item, priced at 50,000 reis. The value of the other items totaled 70,000 reis. This means that Delfina was left with 1,110,000 reis – 100 times less (I can't resist the comparison) than the amount Jerônimo Sodré had left his heirs six years earlier. As you will recall, Jerônimo was the one who signed the freedman's manumission letter.

The late Domingo's bills included an item that is yet further evidence of his transit between cultures. He had been accused of being a traditional healer, among other things, but used the services of a physician, Dr. Horácio César, who charged 4,000 reis for a visit a few days before he died. Domingos spent another 1,800 reis at the druggist's to purchase the prescribed medicine. It is very likely that he had called in Dr. César after attempting to cure his ills with home remedies, herbs from his garden, and even medicine from other African healers like himself. The fact is that, at least at the end of his life, Domingos turned to conventional medicine, which competed with and now perhaps combined with his own.

Payment of the funeral expenses and a debt, probate fees, including taxes, overdue rent, and water bills, in addition to that doctor's visit and Domingos' medicine, and a medical exam for Delfina, reduced the inheritance to precisely 336,779 reis, less than one-third of the bequest. I do not know why, but as I read the documents I got the distinct impression that the widow was cheated on all sides, with the connivance and perhaps for the benefit of her trustee, Francisco Pinheiro de Souza.[68] Plundering Africans, even posthumously, seems to have been the custom in Bahia. As we can read in a newspaper a few years later, there

[68] "Autuação do arrolamento dos bens deixados pelo fallecido Africano liberto Domingos Sudré Pereira," passim.

were even cunning rascals who mourned their deaths in order to put their hands on the estates they left behind. According to the newspaper *A Coisa*, wills were even drawn up "after the owners were in the other world."[69] I do not mean to say that Delfina's trustee necessarily belonged to that ilk, but it is a possibility.

But why did she have a trustee in the first place? The doctors who examined her for 84,200 reis, a very high fee compared to the amount charged by the doctor who looked after Domingos, had declared Delfina incompetent to preside over her husband's inventory and then declared her mentally unfit. Doctors Paulino Pires da Costa Chastinet and Christovão Francisco de Andrade diagnosed that she was suffering from "incomplete paralysis of the members on the left side due to a cerebral hemorrhage that took place eight years ago," and also showed an "enfeebled memory." It was useless for Delfina to contest this diagnosis in a petition her lawyer submitted to the judge, in which she declared that she was "surprised" to have had a trustee appointed for her. She said she "does not deem herself to be senile" and that "the paralysis on one side had not robbed her of her reason." Delfina requested a hearing with the judge to prove, face to face, that she was not "unwise, stupid or forgetful."[70] But what good was the word of an elderly African woman in the face of the experts of "medical science"? The judge dismissed her petition without even deigning to see her. Domingos was somewhat to blame. After appointing his wife as his first executor, he had made a mistake when appointing his second executor – either that or the person who wrote his will, an eighty-year-old man, erred – and appointed Domingos' long-deceased father instead.[71] That is why the courts appointed Francisco Pinheiro as the executor and Delfina's trustee.

Forced to make do with the little money left over, Delfina was impoverished overnight. Luckily, she had Leopoldina Sodré to take care of her. In addition to organizing Domingos' funeral, Leopoldina submitted receipts for her expenses to the trustee – for doctors, rent, and water supplied by Companhia do Queimado. Afterward, he paid her a monthly stipend of 21,000 reis, withdrawn from the widow's bank account. The

[69] *A Coisa*, June 24, 1900.
[70] "Autuação de petição de Francisco Pinheiro de Souza para nomeação de curador e exame de Sanidade de Maria Delfina da Conceição, viúva do Africano liberto Domingos Sudré," APEB, *Judiciária*, 07/3000/08, fls. 11–11v. See appendix 3.
[71] Domingos dictated his will to Feliciano José Falcão. Regarding Falcão's age, see AMS, *Livro de qualificação de votantes. Freguesia de São Pedro, 1863–1865*, fl. 127.

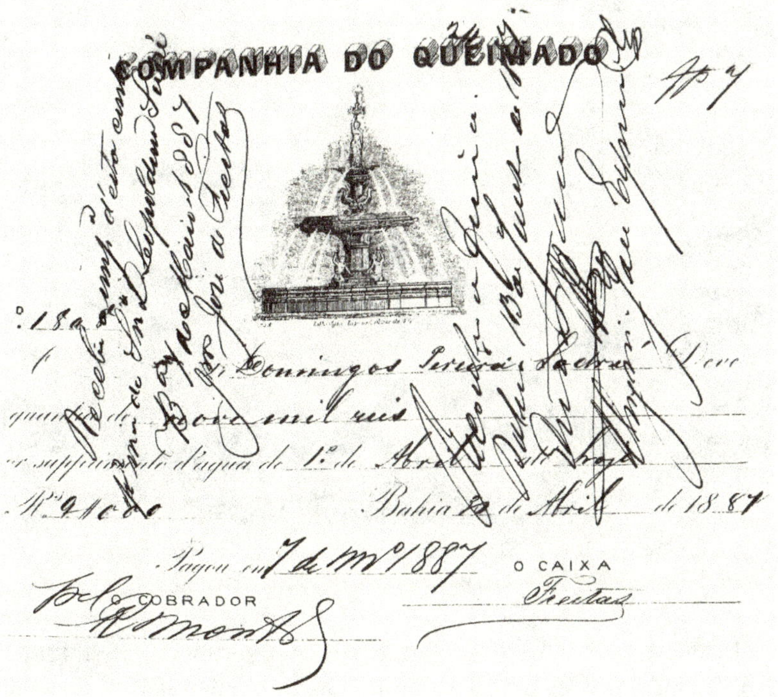

Figure 49. Receipt for 9,000 reis paid to Companhia do Queimado for water supplied to Domingos Sodré's residence in April 1887.

money would only be used to support Delfina, as Leopoldina explained. She made a point of declaring that it did not "take into account her services provided to her [Delfina] because she did it out of charity."[72] If they were sincere, these words suggest that she and the couple enjoyed a very special bond of solidarity.

In September 1887, both women moved to a more modest residence, nearby on Rua do Areal de Cima, rented for 23,000 reis per month – more than the monthly allowance – and the furniture from the old house was sold to help cover the expenses. At some point, Delfina moved again, this time without Leopoldina, and went to live on Rua do Tingui, a narrow street that runs alongside Santana parish church. Far from the neighborhood where she had lived for nearly three decades, at the very least, she was now residing in the home

[72] Petition from Leopoldina Sodré to the Judge of Orphans, October 6, 1887, Idem, fl. 42.

Figures 50 and 51. Rua do Tingui, to the right of Santana parish church, in a photo taken the year of Maria Delfina da Conceição's death, 1888.

of Joana Maria do Amor Divino. I have not yet found any information about this woman. I have located many women named Joana do Amor Divino – particularly in baptismal and manumission records – but it is such a common name that it is no help at all in this sort of investigation.[73]

Maria Delfina da Conceição died in that house on August 20, 1888, a little more than a year after her husband passed away. Nearly three months earlier, the labor system that had caused her and her husband's exile in Brazil had been abolished. The black population in Bahia celebrated the event with tremendous enthusiasm, with drumming, parades, rallies, and solemn masses in Salvador and the Recôncavo, among other places. The celebrations grew so intense that former masters and authorities feared they would turn into a revolution. The Candomblé folk must have joined in the jubilation, as a tradition that is still alive in the Recôncavo city of Santo Amaro, the Bembé festival, suggests.

[73] Idem, passim. In 1872, Rua do Tingui became Rua dos Zuavos, renamed after a black battalion that served in the Paraguay War (1864–1870), the largest armed conflict ever to happen in South America, but the name does not seem to have stuck. See *Almanak . . . 1873*.

Figures 50 and 51. (*continued*)

Meanwhile, according to Silva Campos, the last Africans in Salvador engaged in more muted celebrations of abolition, possibly because they were too old for major festivities, or because, despite abolition, they could not forgive or forget the fact that all the energy of their youth had been consumed by slavery in the white man's land. But in Lagos, Domingos Sodré's home town, the African returnee community's celebrations were as joyous as Bahia's.[74]

By that time, Delfina was probably bedridden. Her illness at the estimated age of eighty-three is vaguely described in her death certificate as "congestion." Unlike her husband, she did not have a luxurious coffin or a solemn funeral mass. She died in poverty, "leaving absolutely nothing," according to her trustee, except for a paltry 9,000 reis deposited in Caixa Econômica. It was not enough to pay a debt for 18,000 reis for six house calls by a doctor. The trustee and Joana do Amor Divino shared

[74] See, among others, Brito, *A abolição na Bahia*, 265–277; Fraga Filho, *Encruzilhadas da liberdade*, chap. 4; Albuquerque, *O jogo da dissimulação*, chap. 2 and 107, regarding the Bembé festival in Santo Amaro; Campos, "Ligeiras notas," 291; on celebrations in Lagos, see Graden, *From Slavery to Freedom*, 195.

those costs and her funeral expenses between them. Delfina was buried in Quinta dos Lázaros cemetery, possibly at Domingos' side.[75]

Maria Delfina da Conceição was Domingos Sodré's partner for much more than twenty years, and during that time she helped him become more than just another African freedman in nineteenth-century Bahia. They were arrested together for practicing Candomblé, officialized their union in a Catholic church, acquired property as a couple, and took care of each other in sickness. He opened a savings account to protect her for the rest of her life, although it failed to do so, and she helped him achieve a good death, this time successfully, and joined him in their brotherhood's cemetery soon afterward. The few traces that she left in the records suggest that she was a decisive woman who may have played a key role in Domingos' life. However, despite the presence of major women leaders of Candomblé at the time, Delfina lived during a period when such leadership was predominantly male, and not just in the art of divination. For now, Delfina only appears as Domingos' assistant in the Afro-religion business, but the archives may still hold secrets that will change this story.

[75] Death certificate dated August 22, 1888, by the vicar of Santana parish, attached to APEB, *Judiciária*, no. 07/3000/08.

EPILOGUE

As a narrative genre, biographical studies of individuals who experienced slavery – even more so those who overcame it – are attracting increasing interest. These studies have so far been particularly focused on the slaveholding complex in the North Atlantic. Biographies of Africans and their descendants enable us to perceive the broad movement of history from a new, more human perspective, including the slave trade, the rise and fall of slavery in the New World, the reshaping of the Old World by colonization and slave labor – in short, the formation of Atlantic societies, economies, and cultures. Telling these personal stories can also serve as a strategy for understanding the historic process that shaped modernity in the broadest sense, particularly societies anchored in the system of slavery that arose from that process.[1]

[1] Old and new examples of this genre include: Douglas Grant, *The Fortunate Slave: An Illustration of African Slavery in the Early Eighteenth Century* (London: Oxford University Press, 1968); Terry Alford, *Prince among Slaves: The True Story of an African Prince Sold into Slavery in the American South* (New York: Oxford University Press, 1977); Melton A. McLaurin, *Celia, a Slave* (New York: Avon Books, 1991); Nell Irvin Painter, *Sojourner Truth: A Life, a Symbol* (New York and London: Norton, 1966); Sparks, *The Two Princes of Calabar*; John Hope Franklin and Loren Schweninger, *In Search of the Promised Land: A Slave Family in the Old South* (New York: Oxford University Press, 2006); Vincent Caretta, *Equiano, the African: Biography of a Self-Made Man* (Athens: University of Georgia Press, 2005); Lindsay and Sweet (eds.), *Biography and the Black Atlantic*. Many of these biographies benefit from the written or dictated narratives of their subjects. Regarding these narratives, see, among numerous studies, introductory essays by Charles T. Davis and Henry Louis Gates (eds.), *The Slave's Narrative* (Oxford and New York: Oxford University Press, 1985); John Blassingame (ed.), *Slave Testimony: Two Centuries of Letters, Speeches, Interviews, and Autobiographies* (Baton Rouge: Louisiana State University Press, 1977),

There is keen interest in biographies of this kind in Brazil as well.
I am not referring to the biographies of major figures, such as black abo-
litionists, but of people who lived in the shadows of anonymity, whose
memory has either been lost or belongs more to the realm of myth and
folklore than history. The subjects of these biographies have multiplied
in Brazilian historiography in recent years, and their names should be
spelled out, such as Rosa Egipcíaca, Dom Obá II d'África, Chica da
Silva, Antônio Dutra, Tito de Camargo, Juca Rosa, Caetana, Liberata,
Rufino José Maria, Domingos Álvares, and others.[2] In some cases,
their lives can be documented from birth to death, but in most, they
can only be seen, sometimes glimpsed, in their "dramatic moments"
before disappearing from the archives without a trace. Aside from the
fact that there are more documents for some than for others, these personal histories are not only significant in their singularity but enable
us better to perceive collective experiences and shed light on broader,
more complex historical contexts and processes. This is what I have

xvii–lxv; and Mahommah G. Baquaqua, *The Biography of Mahommah Gardo Baquaqua: His Passage from Slavery to Freedom in Africa and America*, edited by Robin Law and Paul Lovejoy (Princeton, NJ: Markus Wiener Publishers, 2001), 1–84.

[2] See, among other titles, Luiz Mott, *Rosa Egipcíaca, uma santa africana no Brasil* (Rio de Janeiro: Bertrand Brasil, 1993); Júnia Ferreira Furtado, *Chica da Silva e o contratador de diamantes: o outro lado do mito* (São Paulo: Companhia das Letras, 2003); Sandra Lauderdale Graham, *Caetana Says No: Women Stories from a Brazilian Slave Society* (Cambridge, UK, and New York: Cambridge University Press, 2002); Keila Grinberg, *Liberta, a lei da ambiguidade: as ações de liberdade da Corte de Apelação do Rio de Janeiro no século XIX* (Rio de Janeiro: Relume Dumará, 1994); Silva, *Dom Obá II d'África*; Frank, *Dutra's World*; Xavier, *Religiosidade e escravidão*; Sampaio, *Juca Rosa*; Reis, Gomes and Carvalho, *O alufá Rufino*; and Sweet, *Domingos Álvares*. Other characters can be found in Verger, *Os libertos*; Farias, Eugênio Soares, and Gomes, *No labirinto das nações*, chap. 6; Roberto Guedes, "De ex-escravo a elite escravista: a trajetória de ascensão social do pardo alferes Joaquim Barbosa Neves (Porto Feliz, São Paulo, século XIX)," in *Conquistadores e negociantes: histórias de elites no Antigo Regime nos trópicos*, eds. João Luís R. Fragoso, Carla Maria C. de Almeida, and Antonio Carlos J. de Sampaio (Rio de Janeiro: Civilização Brasileira, 2007), 337–376; the chap-ters by Hebe Mattos, Mariza de Carvalho Soares, Daniela Buono Calainho, and Sheila de Castro Faria in *Retratos do império: trajetórias individuais no mundo por-tuguês nos séculos XVI a XIX*, eds. Ronaldo Vainfas, Georgina S. dos Santos, and Guilherme P. Neves (Rio de Janeiro: EDUFF, 2006). The expression "dramatic moments" used in this paragraph is from the editors of that book (p. 9).

attempted to do in this book by telling the story – or the life and times – of Domingos Sodré.

Many authors would characterize Domingos' life story as a typical process of *creolization*. In this sense, the freedman would be a candidate for the label of "Atlantic Creole," or simply Creole, to employ an expression that is widely used in the specialized literature nowadays. I prefer to call him a *ladino*, and, to stay closer to the subject, to describe his lived experience as a process of *ladinization*. In Brazil in particular, the term "crioulização" (*creolization*) is charged with very strong sociological and demographic meaning because it is associated with locally born *blacks* – and I emphasize dark-skinned persons – whose identification as *crioulos* (or creoles) is found all over the documents to distinguish them from African-born slaves and freedpersons, but also from socially perceived mixed-race people: mulattos, browns, or pardos, and cabras, terms that the reader has come across more than once in this book. In this way I am also keeping to the specific mode of racial classification practiced in Brazil. The social-demographic imperative also has cultural implications because, whether or not they were born into slavery, the creoles – or, for that matter, the mulattos – underwent a thorough process of socialization, including individuals whose parents were born in Africa and those who lived in predominantly African communities in Brazil, which were generally not closed off to the rest of society, as we have seen.

I am not disputing that creoles assimilated a vast amount of African values from their parents and companions in work, play, religion and other customs, but their experience was very different from that of an African ladino, who had once been a *boçal* or "new" African, meaning people who had recently arrived from Africa. But the contrast with Brazilian-born blacks was much more radical than the one between a ladino and a boçal. Emilia Viotti da Costa suggested using the term *ladinização* (*ladinization*) to refer to the Africans' experience after the slave trade was extinguished, which put a definitive end to the ongoing process of cultural re-Africanization that it had engendered by landing wave after wave of slaves in Brazil. But in contrast with Da Costa, I suggest that this expression should be understood practically in its native sense, which is valid for all generations of African-born people who, even when the slave trade was fully active, managed to adapt, reinvent, and recreate their cultural values and practices over time while assimilating many local customs – as well as customs from different parts of Africa other than their own – under the new circumstances and pressure of slavery and racial discrimination on the western side of the Atlantic. However, the ladinos adapted without discarding everything they had learned and experienced on the other side of the ocean. Thus African-born individuals never became crioulos in the sociological, demographic, or cultural sense; they rather became Nagôs, Jejes, Angolas, and so on. Africans who recreated their collective identities in terms of "nations" were ladinos, even if we insist on calling this process one of creolization. But I prefer the term *ladinization* to refer to that cultural dynamic and, more broadly, to the life experience of people like the diviner Domingos Sodré in Bahia.[3]

Although Domingos stood out from most Africans of his time in many ways, he was also representative of his group. He formed part of an elite class of freedpersons who enjoyed a certain amount of prosperity and prestige in nineteenth-century Bahia, along with some of his friends and adversaries, whom we have met in these pages. Toward the end of his life, following a trend among most African freedpersons, his affluence waned, and on his death he left nothing to his wife but poverty. I do not know what happened to his life in Candomblé over the years – whether he remained active or just maintained a private

---

[3] Emilia Viotti da Costa, "Prefácio à segunda edição," in *Da senzala à colônia* (São Paulo: Brasiliense, 1982), 31. The literature on creolization is vast. One of the classic studies in that regard is Sidney Mintz and Richard Price, *An Anthropological Approach to the Afro-American Past: A Caribbean Perspective* (Philadelphia, PA: Institute for the Study of Human Issues, 1976), later published as *The Birth of African-American Culture: An Anthropological Perspective* (Boston, MA: Beacon Press, 1992), an inspiring little book. An update on the debate can be found in Richard Price, "O milagre da crioulização: retrospectiva," *Estudos Afro-Asiáticos*, 24, no. 3 (2003): 383–419. See also Ira Berlin, "From Creole to African: Atlantic Creoles and the Origins of African-American Society in Mainland North America," *William & Mary Quarterly*, 53, no. 2 (1996): 251–288; idem, *Many Thousands Gone: The First Two centuries of Slavery in North America* (Cambridge, MA: The Belknap Press, 1998); and idem, *Generations of Captivity: A History of African-American Studies* (Cambridge: The Belknap Press, 2003). For a good overview of the debate on creolization and Africanization, which generally finds "Americanists" and "Africanists" in opposite camps, see Kristin Mann, "Shifting Paradigms in the Study of the African Diaspora and of the Atlantic History and Culture," in *Rethinking the African Diaspora: The Making of a Black Atlantic World in the Bight of Benin and Brazil* , ed. Kristin Mann and Edna G. Bay (London: Frank Cass, 2001), 3–21. A good collection of essays problematizing the concept of creolization is Charles Stewart (ed.), *Creolization: History, Ethnography, Theory* (Walnut Creek, CA: Left Coast Press, 2007), esp. chap. 1 by the editor.

practice at home without coming into regular contact, or any at all, with a ritual clientele or other African priests and their temples. If he did not abandon his activities in that line altogether, and I believe he did not, it is possible that they, too, decreased at the same rate as he grew older and poorer.

This is not to say that Domingos did not make an impression on the collective memory, as Manuel Querino makes clear when referring, many years later, to the episode of the veteran's uniform, but apparently that memory was short-lived. Perhaps if he had had children or formed a religious community or Candomblé terreiro, his biological or religious descendants might have been able to help us out with some sort of oral tradition today, as is the case with the founders and first high priestesses of traditional Bahian Candomblé temples like Francisca da Silva, or Iyá Nassô, and Marcelina da Silva, or Obatossi, the nineteenth-century leaders of the Casa Branca temple. Domingos, however, may have to be counted among the priests who contributed to the process of establishing Nagô ritual hegemony over the course of the second half of the 1800s.[4] But if that is what really happened, he did not benefit from it. Delfina's destitution at the end of her days suggests that she lacked the care of a Candomblé community of which she and her husband were important members. On the Catholic side, I have also failed to find evidence that Domingos' many godchildren and their parents extended a hand to him or Delfina. There is, however, some question about whether Leopoldina Sodré and Joana do Amor Divino were their ritual kin in Candomblé or the Church. The impression I have is that, if it were not for those two women, Domingos and Delfina would have been all alone in the end, perhaps because most of their friends and coreligionists, elderly Africans like them, had died or gone back to Africa.

At some point in his life, if only for a fleeting moment, Domingos stood out as an important religious leader in Bahia. He was a master diviner, a *Papai*, "number one in the congregation of sortilege and spells," as Subdelegado Pompílio pointed out in 1862. Furthermore, his ability to direct and organize was not limited to the sphere of faith and healing. He was also active as the head of a manumission society for more than a decade. The signs of the connections he made between this activity and his religious practice suggest that he was a sharp and elusive character, capable of shrewdly interpreting the codes of the world he lived in,

---

[4] See Parés, "The 'Nagoization' process," and Matory, *Black Atlantic Religion*.

including its links with the spiritual universe. In the process, he learned
to negotiate positions and cultivate relationships inside and outside the
African community. He was a cultural broker and mediator; a perfect
ladino.

His ritual practices mainly benefited African and Brazilian blacks,
primarily the former, in their day-to-day struggle with their masters.
Although he did not join in a plan for mass rebellion, Domingos worked
toward the individual freedom of slaves by bending the will of their
masters. In this sense, his religion was an instrument for slave resistance. At the same time, also acting as a ritual specialist, he provided
his services to the free white and mixed-race people of Bahia. Many of
them passed through his life in non-ritual circumstances, as we have
seen in the documents from the notaries' offices, courts, and churches
where Domingos was present. As far as his contacts with whites were
concerned, it cannot be said that they engaged in a patron-client relationship in which he was always the dependent. Domingos may have
been the client of one white person or another, but he also had his own
clientele, which included whites. After all, who was the client when
the priest performed divination rites? In his own way, Domingos, too,
was a "big shot," a *figurão*, as the police labeled him in connection to his
wearing of the veteran's uniform.

Domingos showed equal flexibility in both the social and religious
spheres, as he seemed to move between Candomblé and Catholicism
with ease, although he did take care to keep his Catholic saints and
African divinities in separate compartments of his mind and house. He
also moved back and forth between Western and African medicine,
traditional credit institutions, and modern banks. In these respects, he
was no different from many other Africans of his time. He was also like
them, including many members of the Candomblé community, when
he invested in slaves, which was a mark of success in his time. He may
have shown originality when he decided to free some of his slaves – perhaps all – without charge at a time of moral or spiritual crisis. But once
he had recovered, he went back to owning at least two or three slaves at
a time when he was old and needy and could no longer afford to be gen-
erous and free them without pay. This brings to mind the "iron imp" the
police found in his house: it is at the confluence of slavery and freedom
that perhaps lies what best reveals the life experience of this elusive
devotee of the Orișa Eșu, lord of the crossroads, patron of contradiction.

TIMELINE OF DOMINGOS SODRÉ'S LIFE

ca. 1797: Born in Onim (Lagos), a major city in what is now Nigeria, then a Yoruba kingdom and a hub of the transatlantic slave trade.

ca. 1811 – ca. 1823: Succession dispute in Onim between Adele and Oṣinlokun, brothers and members of the ruling family. Domingos was probably made prisoner during this conflict and sold to Brazilian slave traders.

ca. 1815 – ca. 1820: Domingos arrives in Bahia as a slave.

ca. 1816 – ca. 1835: The slave of Colonel Francisco Maria Sodré Pereira, Domingos works on the Trindade plantation in Santo Amaro, in the Bahia Recôncavo region, and possibly on other properties for the same master. Period of intense slave rebellions in the region.

1822: Brazil's independence from Portugal is proclaimed by Portuguese-born Pedro (September 7), who becomes the first emperor of the new country.

1822–1823: War of independence from Portugal in Bahia, Portuguese troops abandon Salvador, and Brazilian troops enter it triumphantly in July 2, 1823.

1824: Revolt of the Periquitos, a black battalion in Salvador with liberal and federalist leanings about to be dismissed from the army.

1831: Emperor Pedro I abdicates (April 7) in favor of his Brazilian-born infant son Pedro II and returns to Portugal, his homeland.

1831: The Regency period begins (June), and lasts until Pedro II, a teenager, is crowned emperor in 1841 at fifteen years of age.

1831: The transatlantic slave trade to Brazil is officially abolished (November 7) but continues, often officially tolerated, until 1850.

1833: Slavery is abolished in British colonies.

1835: The Malê Revolt in Salvador (January 24–25).

1835: Colonel Francisco Maria Sodré Pereira, Domingos' master, dies.

ca. 1835: Fall and abandonment of Ọ̀yọ́ Ile, capital of the Ọ̀yọ́ kingdom, in Yorubaland.

1836: The Cemiterada Revolt against the prohibition of burials inside church buildings (October).

1837–1838: The Sabinada liberal rebellion in Salvador, which is controlled by rebels for five months.

1844: Domingos obtains his manumission paper from Jerônimo Pereira Sodré, eldest son of Colonel Francisco Maria Sodré Pereira and probably the executor of his father's will and testament (October).

1845: Domingos' name appears for the first time in baptismal records as the godfather of twin girls, the daughters of an African slave woman. He would later stand godfather in several other baptisms (November).

1848: Slavery abolished in the French colonies.

1849: Domingos purchases two slaves, Lucrécia and her son Theodoro.

1850: Domingos marries African freedwoman Maria das Mercês Rodrigues de Souza, who dies a few days later (June).

1850: Under strong pressure from Britain, Brazil declares the definitive abolition of the transatlantic slave trade (September 4).

1850: Domingos purchases another slave, Esperança (December).

1851: Domingos issues letter of manumission for Lucrécia (July).

1851: Britain bombards Lagos, deposes and expels oba Kosoko, and installs oba Akitoye as the local ruler.

1852: Domingos sues African freedman Cipriano José Pinto for a debt (February).

1853: Domingos is arrested, but is soon released, amid rumors of an African conspiracy in Salvador (May).

1855: Domingos issues letters of manumission for Esperança, Theodoro, then nine, and probably another slave woman named Umbelina (June).

1855–1856: A cholera epidemic scourges Bahia and other parts of Brazil.

1857: General strike of African street workers, slave and freed, in Salvador, which comes to a halt for at least a week (June).

1859: Domingos purchases a slave, Maria Ignez, also known as Maria Archanja.

1860: Domingos brings a lawsuit against Elias Seixas, the African freedman he accused of murdering a friend and taking money from the manumission society Domingos runs. The lawsuit ends three years later.

1861: Britain occupies Lagos and makes it a British colony.

1862: Domingos issues letter of manumission for a slave named Ozório.

1863: Emancipation Proclamation in the United States amid the Civil War (1860–1865); abolition is ratified by the Thirteenth Amendment in 1865.

1862: Domingos is arrested on charges of fortunetelling, witchcraft, and receiving money and goods that slaves had stolen from their masters (July 25).

1871: Domingos marries Maria Delfina da Conceição.

1871: The "Free-Womb Law" frees all slave children born after that date, but they would have to live under their mothers' masters until the age of twenty-one (September 28).

1876: Domingos sells a house on Largo Dois de Julho (July).

1876: Domingos purchases a house on Rua da Ordem Terceira de São Francisco (December).

1877: Domingos issues letter of manumission for a slave named Maria.

1882: Domingos dictates his last will and testament, leaving his estate to his wife, Maria Delfina da Conceição (May).

1885: The Sexagenarian Law is passed, freeing slaves older than sixty years of age (September 28).

ca. 1886: Domingos sells a house on Rua da Ordem Terceira de São Francisco.

1886: Domingos opens an account in the Caixa Econômica Bank (September).

1887: Domingos dies at the estimated age of ninety (May 3).

1888: Slavery is abolished on May 13.

1888: Maria Delfina da Conceição dies at the estimated age of eighty-three (August 20).

Glossary

Awolorişa – literally "owner of the secret of the Orişa" or "diviner of the Orişa's devotees"

Axé – Yoruba *aşe*, spiritual power

Babalawo – Also *babalaô*. Diviner, usually trained in Africa according to the precepts and lore of Ifá.

Babalorişa – male high priest of a Candomblé community

Balangandã – clusters of charms made of silver, gold, and various materials (such as ivory, horn, tusks, and wood) originally worn by African and creole women in Bahia

Batuque – drumming session, religious or secular

Berimbau – The musical bow that accompanies bouts of *capoeira*. It uses a gourd as a sound box and is played with a coin or stone, long stick, and rattle.

Cabra – dark-skinned mulatto

Cabrinha – *cabra* child

Candomblé (upper case and lower case) – *Candomblé* (upper case) refers to the Afro-Brazilian religion; *candomblé* (lower case) refers to the temples or communities where that religion is practiced.

Cantos – literally corners or songs. Street workers' groups mostly formed by enslaved and freed Africans.

Capoeira – an Afro-Brazilian martial art/dance now widely practiced throughout the world

Crioulo/a – Brazilian term used to denote blacks born in Brazil, often the children of African-born slaves and freedpersons in Domingos Sodré's time

De tal – surname unknown

Delegado – chief constable

Doutor – title of men with law or medical degrees

Engenho – sugar plantation

Eṣuṣu – Yoruba credit institution

Feitiçaria – witchcraft

Feiticeiros – witches or sorcerers

Figurão – big shot

Ganhador – Street worker. Same as *negro de ganho*.

Ifá – divination system and the name of the Yoruba god of divination

Jeje – umbrella term that in Brazil usually refers to the Gbe-speaking groups
    of the Bight of Benin region

Junta de alforria – manumission society

Ladeira – hill, often used as the name for a sloping street

Ladino – Prior to abolition in Brazil, this term identified Africans who were
    familiar with and could decode or adopt the local customs, including
    the language.

Loja – basement, usually of a townhouse, typical housing for slaves and
    freedpersons in nineteenth-century Salvador

Malês – the name given to the Yoruba-speaking Muslims who planned
    and implemented the famous 1835 rebellion known as the Revolt of
    the Malês

Moça – young woman

Moços – youths

Mussulmi – Hausa Muslim

Nagô – Brazilian term for Yoruba-speaking people

Negros de ganho – Slave earners or hired-out slaves, a term also employed
    for non-slave street workers. Same as *ganhador*.

Odù/Odu – verses used in Ifá divination rituals

Òpèlè/ Opele – divining chain used in Ifá divination

Oriṣa – the Yoruba term for divinity

Pai – Literally father. Title of a male Candomblé high priest. Same as *papai*.

Papai – Literally daddy. The expressions *papai* and *mamãe de terreiro* and,
    less frequently, *pai-de-santo* were already used in Bahia in the second
    half of the nineteenth century.

Pardo – brown or light-skinned mulatto

Quilombo – runaway slave community

Recôncavo – Bay area. In Bahia, it specifically refers to the fertile, irri-
    gated region around the Bay of All Saints where numerous sugar and
    tobacco plantations were established.

Roça – small farm, sometimes synonymous with *terreiro*

Rua – street

Saveiro – dhow-like sailboats that ferried merchandise from ships to shore
    and the Recôncavo to Salvador

Senhor – mister or master (slave owner)
Senhor-moço – master's son (literally young master)
Senzala – slave quarters
Subdelegado – deputy chief constable
Tapa – West African ethnic group also known as Nupe
Terreiro – Candomblé community

Domingos Sodré's Last Will and Testament (1882)

In the name of God, Amen

I Domingos Pereira Sudré, as the true Christian I am, but fearing death have decided to make my testament and last will in the following form.

1

I am a native of the Coast of Africa, born in Onim and baptized on the Plantation called Trindade in the Municipality of Santo Amaro da Purificação, whose former Owner was Jerônimo Sudré.

2

I am the legitimate son of the Africans Porfírio Araújo de Argollo and his wife Bárbara [surname unknown], both deceased.

3

I have been married for over eleven years to the African freedwoman by the name of Maria Delfina da Conceição, with whom I have had no children at all.

4

I am a member of the Brotherhood of Nossa Senhora do Rosário of Rua João Pereira, and I would like to be carried by the brothers and buried in one of the said Brotherhood's niches.

5

My funeral will be carried out in accordance with my wife's wishes, but without the slightest ostentation.

6

As my executors I hereby appoint my wife Maria Delfina da Conceição in the first place, and in the second place, Mr. Porfírio Araújo Argollo, whom I ask to please accept this will and testament.

7

I hereby declare that the property I own is a one-story house on Ordem Terceira de São Francisco street, purchased from Elpidio Lopes da Silva and his wife with a deed of sale notarized by the Notary Rodrigues da Costa on December 14, 1876, and the furnishings in my home, including a niche with prepared statues.

8

I declare that I owe nothing to anyone.

9

Seeing as I have no close relatives, I hereby make my wife, Maria Delfina da Conceição, my sole heir.

And in this way I have completed this my testament and last will and want it to have full validity, and if any clause or clauses required by law are missing, I ask the justices of His Imperial Majesty to supply them, and to execute the contents and statements herein.

I have asked Mr. Feliciano José Falcão [to write this] and having done so and finding that it is in all respects as I have dictated, I have signed it with my own hand, Bahia, May 20, I mean, according to what I have said, and as I do not know how to read or write, I have asked the aforesaid gentleman to sign it on my behalf. Bahia May 20, 1882.

At the request of the testator Domingos Pereira Sudré, as he cannot read or write, and as witness that I have made this.

Feliciano José Falcão

APPROVAL

Know all who see this public instrument of approval of this last will and testament, that being the year of the Birth of Our Lord Jesus Christ one thousand eight hundred eighty-two on the thirty-first of May, in this City of Bahia in my notary's office there were present the Testator Domingos Pereira Sodré, recognized by the witnesses named below, and signed by me the Notary Public, as being of sound mind, according to my opinion and the views of those witnesses who gave answers to questions put to him by me and from his hands to mine I received this document written on two pages, which at the end of the process this approval initiates, it is recognized as his testament and last will, which he had written by Mr. Feliciano José Falcão because he does not know how to read or write, and once it was written it was read to him and finding everything according to his will and in the form in which he dictated it, he asked the same [Mr. Falcão] for the same reason to sign it on his behalf, likewise asking me, the Notary, to approve and ratify its validity, which on his part is approved and ratified, and therefore found to be good, strong and valuable, hereby revoking any will or codicil previously made. Then I, the Notary, having received this testament and read it, found it clean and without any bias, and so I have initialed it A. S. Silva and I hereby approve it and find it approved to the extent that my duty and the Law allows, the witnesses thereto being Captain Espiridião Aniceto Gonçalves de Souza Gouvêa, Liberato Barroso de Oliveira, Franquilino Silvério dos Santos, and Feliciano José Falcão, all residents of this City, who signed this approval along with the Testator, on whose behalf, since he declared that he can neither read nor write, it is witnessed by Feliciano José Falcão after this instrument was read before everyone by me, written by Álvaro Lopes da Silva, Notary

> A. L. S.
> Witness
> Álvaro Lopes da Silva
> On behalf of the Testator Domingos
> Pereira Sudré because he cannot read
> or write
> Feliciano José Falcão
> Espiridião Aniceto Gonçalves de Souza
> Luiz Antonio de Souza Gouvêa
> Liberato Barroso de Oliveira
> Franquilino Silvério dos Santos

I have opened it: let it be executed and registered. Bahia, May 10, 1887.

> Vaz Ferreira

OPENING

On the tenth day of May eighteen eighty-seven, in this city of Bahia and the office of Judge, Doctor of Law of the Purveyor's Office, Estevão Vaz Ferreira, acting Notary, and there being present Francisco Pinheiro de Souza, and by him was presented for opening this last will and testament which was sealed, and with which there died on the third day of the current month at his home address

on Ladeira de Santa Teresa the African freedman Domingos Pereira
Sodré. Opened by the judge, it was immediately examined by me,
and not finding in it anything that might cause doubt, I approved it,
and then gave the authorization to have it executed and registered.
And for the record I hereby write this document which is signed by
the Judge and the presenter [of the will]. I Acting Notary Fortunato
Dormud have written this.

Vaz Ferreira
Francisco Pinheiro de Souza

Source: APEBa, *Judiciária. Inventários,* 07/3257/01

Domingos' Manumission and

Manumissions Granted by Him

Domingos

Manumission of Domingos, Nagô

I hereby state [and] undersign that I have today and henceforth freed a slave, of the nagô nation, by name of Domingos, for the amount of five hundred and fifty thousand reis, which I received from the same in the act of making this letter; and this being true, I have had this [document] signed by me drafted so that he can today and henceforth enjoy his freedom. Bahia fifteenth of October eighteen hundred and forty-four. Jeronimo Sodré Pereira as witnesses to what I have written José Martins de Lima e Mello. Agostinho da Silva Paranhos. José Antonio da Silva Serva. I recognize the contents of this letter. Bahia, seventeenth of October eighteen hundred and forty-four. Attesting the truth. Notary's Stamp. Francisco Ribeiro Neves. R. (registry) number fifteen. One hundred and sixty. Paid one hundred and sixty reis. Bahia, seventeenth of October eighteen hundred and forty four. Fernandes Ferreira. To the notary Neves. Bahia, seventeenth of October eighteen hundred and forty-four. Filgueiras. Registered, authenticated and verified in Bahia on the seventeenth of October of eighteen forty-four. Francisco Ribeiro Neves Notary signed by me.

(signed) Francisco Ribeiro Neves

Source: APEB, *LNT*, vol. 282, fl. 19

Esperança

Manumission of the Nagô black woman by the name of Esperança.

I Domingos Sodré am the master and owner of a Nagô slave woman by the name of Esperança, and in consideration for her good service, which she has provided to me, I am freeing her without pay. And in order for her to thus enjoy her freedom, because I cannot read or write, I have asked Mr. Manoel José de Freitas Paço to write this for me and sign it on my behalf, in the presence of the undersigned witnesses. Bahia, fifth of June, eighteen fifty-five. = On behalf of Mr. Domingos Sodré, Manoel José de Freitas Paço = As witnesses Pedro de Salles Ferreira Guimarães = João Gomes de Oliveira. I hereby recognize the above signature. Bahia fifth of June of eighteen fifty-five. In witness of the truth = *Notary's stamp* = Feliciano José Falcão Junior = three hundred and fifty (stamp) one hundred and sixty = Paid one hundred and sixty réis. Bahia fifth of June of eighteen fifty-five = Fernandes Junior = Silva Rego = To the Notary Amado = Bahia twelfth of June in eighteen fifty-five = Seixas = And transcribed from the original I have revised it and signed it along with an associate on the thirteenth of June in eighteen fifty-five. I, Manoel Jorge Ferreira, Acting Notary, have written and signed this.

And on my behalf

As a witness for me ...

Manoel Roque da Costa   Manoel Jorge Ferreira

Source: APEBa, *LNT*, vol. 319, fls. 165v–166

THEODORO

Manumission of the Crioulo boy Theodoro, aged nine.

I Domingos Sudré, am the Master and owner of a Crioulo boy by the name of Theodoro, aged nine, and due to the affection [developed during his] upbringing, I hereby grant him his freedom on the express condition that he accompany me, serve me and respect me during my lifetime. And to register this, and because I cannot read or write, I have asked Mr. Manoel José de Freitas Paço to write this for me and sign it on my behalf, in the presence of the undersigned witnesses. Bahia fifth of June of eighteen fifty-five = On behalf of Mr. Domingos Sodré = Manoel José de Freitas Paço = As witnesses = Pedro de Salles Ferreira Guimarães = João Gomes de Oliveira = I hereby recognize the above signature. Bahia fifth of June of eighteen fifty-five = Seixas = N umber = Three hundred and forty-nine = *Space for the stamp* = One hundred and sixty = one hundred and sixty réis. Bahia fifth of June of

eighteen fifty-five = Fernandes Junior = Silva Rego = And transcribed
from the original = I have written, checked and revised it along with a
fellow official, undersigned and signed in Bahia on the twelfth of June
in eighteen fifty-five. I, Manoel Lopes da Costa Tabelião have written
and signed it.

As a witness   And by me

Manoel Jorge Ferreira   Manoel Roque da Costa

Source: APEBa, *LNT*, vol. 320, fl. 72

LUCRÉCIA

Manumission of Lucrécia, Nagô
  I Domingos Sudré, am the Master and owner of a slave by the name
of Lucrécia of the Nagô Nation, whom I free for the sum of four hundred thousand réis, which I have received in this act, and together with
the good services she has provided me, without encumbrance, and
I beseech the Courts of His Imperial Majesty, both Civil and Religious,
to fulfill it, and fully comply with its contents. Bahia twenty-fourth of
July eighteen fifty-one. On behalf of Domingos Sudré – Manoel Pereira
Pinto = As witnesses – João Gualberto Camorogipe = Cornélio Borges
de Barros = Luis de Miranda Lima = Number seventy one hundred and
sixty = Paid one hundred and sixty réis. Bahia twenty-ninth of July eighteen fifty-one = Andrade = Silva Rego = For the Notary Mendes. Bahia
twenty-ninth of July eighteen fifty-one = Seixas = Registered, I have
conferred and revised, undersigned and signed it in Bahia on the above
date, along with another associated Notary: Joaquim Diocleciano de
Souza. Bahia and sworn clerk has written it. I and Francisco Rodrigues
Mendes Tabelião have undersigned it and . . .

And by me, Mr.   Signed by me

Ricardo de Abreu Fialho   Francisco Roiz Mendes

Source: APEBa, *LNT*, vol. 301, fl. 27

MARIA

Manumission of Maria African woman.
  I the undersigned hereby declare that I am the owner and Master
of the African slave woman of the Nagô nation by the name of Maria,
whose slave through the making of this letter of manumission, having

received from her the sum of five hundred thousand réis, the value
of her freedom which she will enjoy from this day forward as if born
from a free womb, Beseeching the Laws of this Country to give full
effect to this document signed by me. Bahia 11 May 1877. Domingos
Pereira Sodré. As witnesses that I have written this Sidronio Antonio
Galvão = Hermano Alves de Palma. For the Notary Rodrigues da
Costa. Bahia 12 May 1877. Seixas. I recognize the above signatures.
Bahia 12 May 1877. In witness of the truth. *Public stamp*. Frederico
Augusto Rodrigues da Costa. Registered on 12 May 1877.

Source: APEBa, *LNT*, vol. 511, fl. 28v

Ozório

Manumission of Ozório, African man.

I Domingos Sudré declare that the property I own free and clear
includes a slave by the name of Ozório, African, whom I hereby free
and declare freed as if born from a free womb, having received from
him fifteen hundred and twenty-eight thousand réis, and henceforth
he will enjoy his freedom and I ask the Courts of H. I. C. M. (His
Imperial and Constitutional Majesty) to enforce and keep this document. Bahia twenty-fourth March eighteen sixty-two. As I cannot
read or write I have asked Joaquim Manoel da Paixão Ribeiro to write
this and sign this on my behalf. = For Domingos Sudré as he cannot
read or write Joaquim Manoel da Paixão Ribeiro. As witness José
Leocadio Ferreira Mundim = Francisco d'Amorim Falcão = I recognize the above signatures. Bahia twenty-seventh March eighteen
sixty-two (*Public stamp*). In witness to the truth Francisco Rodrigues
Mendes = Number thirty-one = two hundred. Paid two hundred réis.
Bahia twenty-seventh March eighteen sixty-two = Seixas. And transcribed from the original I have checked, undersigned and signed it
in Bahia with an associate on the twenty-seventh of March eighteen sixty-two. And I Manoel Jorge Ferreira Tabelião have myself
undersigned it.

Conceded by me Notary Manoel Jorge Ferreira
And witnessed by me João Antonio Rodrigues.

Source: APEBa, *LNT*, vol. 365, fl. 28

DELFINA'S PETITION GUARANTEEING
HER MENTAL HEALTH

Illustrious Judge of Orphans

Maria Delfina da Conceição Sodré, widow of Domingos Pereira Sodré, was surprised to find that she was considered incompetent by this court for being deemed senile and appointed a trustee for her person and property.

The Supplicant was surprised because she does not deem herself senile, merely ill with a congestion that brought about the paralysis of one side without robbing her of her intellect or affecting her mind. The Supplicant does not require further examination, because from what has been done it is clearly not the case that she is senile, as the seeing that said examination merely states that due to a cerebral hemorrhage the Supplicant's memory was enfeebled.

If the Supplicant is only enfeebled in memory due to an ailment, which mainly affected the lower members and is on the mend, and is not unwise, stupid or forgetful, she cannot be declared incompetent, according to the relevant law, which is Ord. Book 4 tit. 103 p, and the laws of several countries and the opinion of alienists, legislation and authors who provide that a person can only be declared incompetent when he is habitually stupid, insane or furious.

To give proof that she does not find herself in a state that requires a trustee, the Supplicant requests permission to come into Your Excellencies' presence at a time of your choosing.

Accordingly the Supplicant asks Your Excellencies to appoint the place, day and time for her to appear after you lift the interdiction and allow the Supplicant to sign the document naming her executor to continue the inventory of the estate of her late husband, of whom she is the sole heir; a document for which

> We request approval
>
> E. R. M. [Hope to Receive Favor]
>
> Bahia 29 May 1887
> The Attorney
> Antonio Carneiro da Rocha

Source: APEBa, *Judiciária. Inventários*, no. 07/3000/08

Illustration and Map Credits

Every effort was made to identify the origins of the illustrations in this book, but it was not always possible to do so. We will be glad to credit the sources when they are identified by their copyright holders. The reproductions of the images were made by Mariângela de Mattos Nogueira.

1 and 12: Benjamin Mulock/Gilberto Ferrez Collection/Instituto Moreira Salles, Brazil

3 and 44: Fundação Biblioteca Nacional, Brazil

4, 5, 7, 17, 40, 41, 42, 47, 48, and 49: Arquivo Público da Bahia, Brazil

6 and 39: Unknown/Gilberto Ferrez Collection/Instituto Moreira Salles, Brazil

8: Museu Afro Brasil

9, 15, 29, 32, 50, and 51: Ubaldo Sena Repository

10: Victor Frond/Gilberto Ferrez Collection/Instituto Moreira Salles, Brazil

11 and 24 (d): Photographs by Mariângela de Mattos Nogueira

13, 14, and 46: Arquivo Municipal de Salvador, Brazil

16 and 28: Rodolfo Lindemann/Gilberto Ferrez Collection/Instituto Moreira Salles, Brazil

19: Unknown/Gilberto Ferrez Collection/Instituto Moreira Salles, Brazil

20 and 21: João Goston/Instituto Moreira Salles, Brazil

24 (a, b, c): Rodrigues, Os africanos no Brasil

37: Unknown/Tempostal

38: Unknown/Instituto Feminino da Bahia, Brazil

43: Guilherme Gaensly and Rodolfo Lindemann/Gilberto Ferrez Collection/ Instituto Moreira Salles, Brazil

45: Watercolor by Francisco Mangabeira Albernaz

Bibliography

Archives

BAHIA

Arquivo da Cúria Metropolitana de Salvador (ACMS)
Arquivo Municipal de Salvador (AMS)
Arquivo Público do Estado da Bahia (APEB)
Arquivo da Santa Casa da Misericórdia de Salvador (ASCM)

RIO DE JANEIRO

Arquivo do Itamarati (AI)
Arquivo Nacional (AN)
Biblioteca Nacional, Manuscripts Division (BNRJ)

Printed Primary Sources

NEWSPAPERS

O Alabama
O Argos Cachoeirano
A Coisa
Correio Mercantil
Diário da Bahia
O Jornal (RJ)
Jornal da Bahia
O Musaico
O Patriota

OTHER PRINTED PRIMARY SOURCES

Adams, Captain John. *Remarks on the Country Extending from Cape Palmas to the River Congo.* London: Frank Cass, 1966 [orig. 1823].

Allen, William and Thomson, T. R. H. *Narrative of the Expedition Sent by Her Majesty's Government to the River Niger in 1841.* London: Richard Bentley, 1848, 2 vols.

Almanach para o anno de 1845, Bahia: Typ. de M. A. da S. Serva, 1844.

Almanak administrativo, mercantil e industrial para o anno de 1859 e 1860, edited by Camilo de Lelis Masson. Bahia: Typographia de Camille Masson, 1861.

Almanak administrativo, mercantil e industrial da Bahia para o anno de 1863. Bahia: Typographia de Camillo de Lelis Masson e Co., 1863.

Avé-Lallemant, Robert. *Viagens pelas províncias da Bahia, Pernambuco, Alagoas e Sergipe (1859).* Belo Horizonte, Itatiaia/São Paulo: EDUSP, 1980.

Baquaqua, Mahommah Gardo. *The Biography of Mahommah Gardo Baquaqua: His Passage from Slavery to Freedom in Africa and America,* edited by Robin Law and Paul Lovejoy. Princeton, NJ: Markus Wiener Publishers, 2001.

Bowen, Thomas J. *Adventures and Missionary Labours in Several Countries in the Interior of Africa from 1849 to 1856.* London/Edinburgh: Frank Cass, 1968 [orig. 1857].

Burton, Richard F. *Wanderings in West Africa.* New York: Dover, 1991 [orig. 1863].

Candler, John and Burgess, Wilson. *Narrative of a Recent Visit to Brazil.* London: Edward Marsh, Friends' Books, 1853.

Clapperton, Hugh. *Journal of a Second Expedition into the Interior of Africa from the Bight of Benin to Soccatoo,* London: Frank Cass, 1966 [orig. 1829].

Clarke, William W. *Travels and Explorations in Yorubaland, 1854–1858.* Ibadan: Ibadan University Press, 1972.

Código Criminal do Império do Brazil, annotado com os actos dos Poderes Legislativo, Executivo e Judiciário etc por Araújo Filgueiras Junior. Rio de Janeiro: Eduardo & Henrique Laemmert, 1876.

Colleção de leis do Império. Rio de Janeiro: Typ. Nacional, 1876.

Colleção de Leis e Resoluções da Assembléia Legislativa da Bahia sancionadas e publicadas nos annos de 1835 a 1838, Bahia: Typ. de Antonio O. da França Guerra, 1862.

Constituição Política do Império do Brasil. Rio de Janeiro: Typ. de Silva Porto, 1824.

"Devassa do levante de escravos ocorrido em Salvador em 1835." *Anais do Arquivo do Estado da Bahia* 38 (1968): 1–142.

Ferreira, Manoel Jesuíno. *A Província da Bahia: apontamentos.* Rio de Janeiro: Typographia Nacional, 1875.

Filgueiras Junior, Araujo. *Codigo do Processo do Imperio do Brasil.* Rio de Janeiro: Eduardo & Henrique Laemmert, 1874.

Habsburgo, Maximiliano de. *Bahia 1860: esboços de viagem*. Rio de Janeiro: Tempo Brasileiro; Salvador: Fundação Cultural do Estado da Bahia, 1982.

"Inventário do Dr. Antonio José Alves, falecido em 23 de janeiro de 1866." *Anais do APEBA* 30 (1947): 39–202.

Johnson, Samuel. *The History of the Yorubas*. London: Routledge & Kegan Paul, 1966 [orig. 1897].

Lander, Richard and Lander, John. *Journal of an Expedition to Explore the Course and Termination of the Niger*. New York: Harper & Brother, 1837.

Legislação da Província da Bahia sobre o negro, 1835–1888. Salvador: Fundação Cultural do Estado da Bahia/Direção de Bibliotecas Públicas, 1996.

Macedo, Joaquim Manuel de. *As vítimas-algozes*, 3rd ed. Rio de Janeiro: Scipione/ Casa de Rui Barbosa, 1991 [orig. 1869].

Marques, Xavier. *O feiticeiro*. São Paulo: GRD; Brasília: INL, 1975 [orig. 1897].

Oliveira, João José Barbosa de. *As prisões do paiz, o systema penitencial ou hygiene penal. These apresentada e sustentada perante a Faculdade de Medicina da Bahia em dezembro de 1843*. Bahia: Typ. de L. A. Portella e Companhia, 1843.

Ortiz, Fernando. *Los negros brujos*. Havana: Editorial de Ciências Sociales, 1995 [orig. 1906].

Peixoto, Antonio da Costa. *Obra nova da língua geral de mina*. Lisbon: Agência Geral das Colônias, 1943–1944 [orig. 1741].

Posturas da Câmara Municipal da Cidade de S. Salvador, capital da Província da Bahia. Bahia: Typ. de Manoel Agostinho Cruz Mello, 1860.

Querino, Manuel. *A raça africana e os seus costumes*. Salvador: Progresso, 1955.

Relatório apresentado ao excelentíssimo Senhor Conselheiro Joaquim Antão Fernandes Leão, Presidente da Província da Bahia, pelo 4° Vice-Presidente excelentíssimo Senhor Doutor José Augusto Chaves no acto em que passa-lhe a administração da Província da Bahia. Bahia: Typographia Antonio Olavo da França Guerra, 1862.

Repertório de fontes sobre escravidão existentes no Arquivo Municipal de Salvador: as posturas (1631/1889). Salvador: Fundação Gregório de Mattos/Prefeitura Municipal do Salvador, 1988.

Rio, João do. *As religiões no Rio*. Rio de Janeiro: Nova Aguilar, 1976 [orig. 1904].

Rodrigues, Raimundo Nina. *Os africanos no Brasil*. São Paulo: Companhia Editora Nacional, 4th ed., 1976.

O animismo fetichista dos negros bahianos. Rio de Janeiro: Civilização Brasileira, 1935 [orig. 1896].

Silva, Ignácio Accioli de Cerqueira e. *Memórias históricas e políticas da Província da Bahia*, anotadas por Braz do Amaral, 6 vols. Salvador: Imprensa Oficial do Estado, 1931.

Stowe, Harriet Beecher. *A cabana do Pai Thomaz ou a vida dos pretos na America*. Translated by Francisco Ladislau Alvares d'Andrada. Paris: Ray & Belhatte, 1853.

Wetherell, James. *Brazil. Stray Notes from Bahia*. Liverpool: Webb & Hunt, 1860.

Books, Chapters, Articles, Theses, and Dissertations

Abimbola, Wande. "The Bag of Wisdom: Òṣun and the Origins of Ifá Divination." In Joseph M. Murphy and Mei-Mei Sanford (eds.), *Òṣun across the Waters: A Yoruba Goddess in Africa and the Americas*. Bloomington: Indiana University Press, 2001, 141–154.

Ifá: *An Exposition of Ifá Literary Corpus*. Ibadan: Oxford University Press Nigeria, 1976.

Abreu, Frederico José de. *Capoeiras: Bahia, século XIX*. Salvador: Instituto Jair Moura, 2005.

Aderibigbe, A. B. (ed.) *The Development of an African City*. Lagos: Longman Nigeria, 1975.

"Early History of Lagos to about 1850." In A. B. Aderibigbe (ed.) *The Development of an African City*, 1–26.

Albuquerque, Wlamyra R. de. *O jogo da dissimulação: abolição e cidadania negra no Brasil*. São Paulo: Companhia das Letras, 2009.

Alencastro, Luiz Felipe de. *O trato dos viventes: formação do Brasil no Atlântico sul*. São Paulo: Companhia das Letras, 2000.

Alford, Terry. *Prince among Slaves: The True Story of an African Prince Sold into Slavery in the American South*. New York: Oxford University Press, 1977.

Almeida, Katia Lorena Novaes. *Alforrias em Rio de Contas – Bahia, século XIX*. Salvador: EDUFBA, 2012.

Amaral, Braz do. *História da Independência na Bahia*, 2nd ed. Salvador: Progresso, 1957.

Fatos da vida do Brasil. Salvador: Tipografia Naval, 1941.

Amaral, Sharyse P. do. *Um pé calçado, outro no chão: liberdade e escravidão em Sergipe (Cotinguiba, 1860–1900)*. Salvador: EDUFBA; Aracaju: Editora Diário Oficial, 2012.

Amos, Alcione Meira. *Os que voltaram: a história dos retornados afro-brasileiros na África Ocidental no século XIX*. Belo Horizonte: Tradição Planalto, 2007.

Araújo, Ubiratan Castro de. *Sete histórias de negro*. Salvador: EDUFBA, 2006.

"1846: um ano na rota Bahia-Lagos: negócios, negociantes e outros parceiros." *Afro-Ásia*, no. 21/22 (1998–1999): 83–110.

Athayde, Johildo Lopes de. *Salvador e a grande epidemia de 1855*. Salvador: Centro de Estudos Baianos da UFBA, Publicações no. 113, 1985.

Awe, Bolanle. "Iyalode Efusetan Aniwura (Owner of Gold)." In Bolanle Awe (ed.), *Nigerian Women in a Historical Perspective*. Ibadan: Bookcraft, 1992, 55–71.

Azevedo, Esterzilda Berenstein de Azevedo. "Açúcar amargo: a construção de engenhos na Bahia oitocentista." PhD dissertation, Universidade de São Paulo, 1996.

Bacelar, Jefferson. *A hierarquia das raças: negros e brancos em Salvador*. Rio de Janeiro: Pallas, 2001.

Barber, Karin. "How Man Makes God in West Africa: Yoruba Attitudes towards the Orisa." *Africa* 51, no. 3 (1981): 724–745.

Barickman, B. J. *A Bahian Counterpoint: Sugar, Tobacco, Cassava, and Slavery in the Recôncavo, 1780–1860.* Stanford, CA: Stanford University Press, 1998.

Barros, José Flavio Pessoa de and Napoleão, Eduardo. *Ewé Òrìsà: uso litúrgico e terapêutico dos vegetais nas casas de candomblé jêje-nagô*, 3rd ed. Rio de Janeiro: Bertrand Brasil, 2007.

Bascom, William R. *Sixteen Cowries: Yoruba Divination from Africa to the New World.* Bloomington and London: Indiana University Press, 1980.

Ifa Divination: Communication between Gods and Men in West Africa. Bloomington and London: Indiana University Press, 1969.

"The Eṣuṣu: A Credit Institution of the Yoruba". *The Journal of the Royal Anthropological Institute of Great Britain and Ireland*, 82, no. 1 (1952): 63–69.

"The Sanctions of Ifa Divination." *The Journal of the Royal Anthropological Institute of Great Britain and Ireland*, 71, no. 1/2 (1941): 43–54.

Bastide, Roger. *O candomblé da Bahia: rito nagô.* São Paulo: Companhia das Letras, 2001.

As religiões africanas no Brasil, 2 vols. São Paulo: Pioneira/EDUSP, 1971.

and Verger, Pierre. "Contribuição ao estudo da adivinhação em Salvador (Bahia)." In Carlos Eugênio M. de Moura (ed.), *Olóòrìsà: escritos sobre a religião dos orixás.* São Paulo: Ágora, 1981, 57–85.

Berlin, Ira. *Generations of Captivity: A History of African-American Studies.* Cambridge, MA: The Belknap Press, 2003.

Many Thousands Gone: The First Two centuries of Slavery in North America. Cambridge, MA: The Belknap Press, 1998.

"From Creole to African: Atlantic Creoles and the Origins of African-American Society in Mainland North America." *The William and Mary Quarterly* 53, no. 2 (1996): 251–288.

Besmer, Freemont E. *Horses, Musicians, and Gods: The Hausa Cult of Possession Trance.* South Hadley, MA: Bergin & Garvey, 1983.

Bethancourt, Francisco. *O imaginário da magia: feiticeiras, adivinhos e curandeiros em Portugal no século XVI.* São Paulo: Companhia das Letras, 2004.

Blassingame, John W. Blassingame (ed.). *Slave Testimony: Two Centuries of Letters, Speeches, Interviews, and Autobiographies.* Baton Rouge: Louisiana State University Press, 1977.

Blier, Suzanne Preston. *The Royal Arts of Africa: The Majesty of Form.* New York: Harry N. Abrahams, Inc., 1998.

Borges, Dain. *The Family in Bahia, Brazil, 1870–1944.* Stanford, CA: Stanford University Press, 1992.

Bradbury, R. E. *Benin Studies.* London, New York, and Ibadan: International African Institute/Oxford University Press, 1973.

Braga, Julio. *A cadeira de ogã e outros ensaios*. Rio de Janeiro: Pallas, 1999.
  Na gamela do feitiço: repressão e resistência nos candomblés da Bahia. Salvador: CEAO/EDUFBA, 1995.
  . *O jogo de búzios: um estudo da adivinhação no candomblé*. São Paulo: Brasiliense, 1988.
Brito, Jailton Lima. *A abolição na Bahia, 1870–1888*. Salvador: Centro de Estudos Baianos/EDUFBA, 2003.
Brown, Alexandra Kelly. "'On the Vanguard of Civilization': Slavery, the Police, and Conflict between Public and Private Power in Salvador da Bahia, Brazil, 1835–1888." PhD dissertation, University of Texas, 1998.
Calainho, Daniela Buono. *Metrópole das mandingas: religiosidade negra e inquisição portuguesa no antigo regime*. Rio de Janeiro: Garamond/FAPERJ, 2008.
Campos, João da Silva. "Ligeiras notas sobre a vida íntima, costumes e religião dos africanos na Bahia." *Anais do Arquivo do Estado da Bahia*, no. 29 (1943): 289–309.
Cardoso, José Fábio Barreto P. "Modalidades de mão-de-obra escrava na cidade do Salvador (1847–1887)." *Revista de Cultura Vozes* 73, no. 3 (1979): 13–17.
Caretta, Vincent. *Equiano, the African: Biography of a Self-Made Man*. Athens: University of Georgia Press, 2005.
Carneiro, Edison. *Candomblés da Bahia*, 7th ed. Rio de Janeiro: Civilização Brasileira, 1986 [orig. 1948].
Carpentier, Alejo. *Écue-Yamba-Ó*. Madrid: Alianza Editorial, 2002 [orig. 1927].
Carvalho, Marcus J. M. de. "'É fácil serem sujeitos de quem já foram senhores': o ABC do Divino Mestre." *Afro-Ásia*, no. 31 (2004): 327–334.
  "'Que crime é ser cismático?' As transgressões de um pastor negro no Recife patriarcal." *Estudos Afro-Asiáticos*, no. 36 (1999): 97–121.
Castillo, Lisa Earl. "Between Memory, Myth and History: Transatlantic Voyagers of the Casa Branca Temple." In Ana Lúcia Araújo (ed.), *Paths of the Atlantic Slave Trade: Interactions, Identities, and Images*. Amherst, NY: Cambria Press, 2011, 203–238.
  "Vida e viagens de Bamboxê Obitikô." In Air José Souza de Jesus and Vilson Caetano de Souza Jr. (eds.), *Minha vida é orixá*. São Paulo: Editora Ifá, 2011, 55–86.
  Entre a oralidade e a escrita: a etnografia dos candomblés da Bahia. Salvador: EDUFBA, 2010.
Castillo, Lisa Earl and Nicolau Parés, Luis. "Marcelina da Silva: A Nineteenth-Century Candomblé Priestess in Bahia." *Slavery & Abolition* 31 (2010): 1–27.
  "Marcelina da Silva e seu mundo: novos dados para uma historiografia do candomblé ketu." *Afro-Ásia*, no. 36 (2007): 111–150.
Castro, Hebe M. Mattos de. "Laços de família e direitos no final da escravidão." In Fernando Novais (general ed.) and Luiz Felipe de Alencastro (ed.),

História da vida privada no Brasil. Império: a Corte e a modernidade nacional. São Paulo: Companhia das Letras, 1997, vol. 2, chap. 7.

Castro, Yeda Pessoa de. *Falares africanos na Bahia: um vocabulário afro-brasileiro,* 2nd ed. Rio de Janeiro: Topbooks, 2005.

Chalhoub, Sidney. "The Politics of Silence: Race and Citizenship in Nineteenth-Century Brazil." *Slavery & Abolition* 27, no. 1 (2006): 73–87.

Machado de Assis, historiador. São Paulo: Companhia das Letras, 2003.

Visões da liberdade: uma história das últimas décadas da escravidão na corte. São Paulo: Companhia das Letras, 1990.

Cohn, Norman. *Europe's Inner Demons.* Frogmore: Paladin, 1976.

Cole. P. D. "Lagos Society in the Nineteenth Century." In Aderibigbe (ed.), *The Development of an African City,* 27–57.

Costa, Ana de Lourdes. "Ekabó!: Trabalho escravo e condições de moradia e reordenamento urbano em Salvador no século XIX." MA thesis, Universidade Federal da Bahia School of Architecture, 1989.

Costa, Emilia Viotti da. *Da senzala à colônia.* São Paulo: Brasiliense, 1989.

Costa, Luiz Monteiro da. "A devoção de N. S. do Rosário na Cidade do Salvador." *Revista do Instituto Genealógico da Bahia* 11, no. 11 (1959): 155–177.

Couceiro, Luiz Alberto. "Acusações de feitiçaria e insurreições escravas no Sudeste do Império do Brasil." *Afro-Ásia,* no. 38 (2008): 211–244.

Courlander, Harold. *Tales of Yoruba Gods and Heroes.* New York: Crown Publishers, 1973.

Cunha, Manuela Carneiro da. *Negros, estrangeiros: os escravos libertos e sua volta à África.* São Paulo: Brasiliense, 1985.

David, Onildo Reis. *O inimigo invisível: epidemia na Bahia no século XIX.* Salvador: EDUFBA, 1996.

Davis, Charles T. and Gates, Henry Louis (eds.). *The Slave's Narrative.* Oxford and New York: Oxford University Press, 1985.

Davis, Natalie Zemon. *Fiction in the Archives: Pardon Tales and Their Tellers in Sixteenth-Century France.* Stanford, CA: Stanford University Press, 1987.

Drewal, Henry John and Mason, John. *Beads, Body, and Soul: Art and Light in the Yoruba Universe.* Los Angeles, CA: UCLA Fowler Museum of Cultural History, 1998.

Eltis, David. "The Diaspora of Yoruba Speakers, 1650–1865: Dimensions and Implications." In Falola and Childs (eds.), *The Yoruba Diaspora,* 17–39.

Espada Lima, Henrique. "Sob o domínio da precariedade: escravidão e os significados da liberdade de trabalho no século XIX". *Topoi,* 6, no. 11 (2005): 289–326.

Falheiros, Elaine Santos. "Luis e Antonio Xavier de Jesus: Mobilidade social de africanos na Bahia oitocentista." MA thesis, Universidade Federal da Bahia, 2014.

Falola, Toyin. "Slavery and Pawnship in the Yoruba Economy of the Nineteenth Century." *Slavery and Abolition* 15, no. 2 (1994): 221–245.

" 'My Friend the Shylock': Money-Lenders and Their Clients in South-Western Nigeria." *Journal of African History*, no. 34 (1993): 403–423.

Falola, Toyin, and Childs, Matt D. (eds.). *The Yoruba Diaspora in the Atlantic World*. Bloomington and Indianapolis: Indiana University Press, 2004.

Falola, Toyin, and Oguntomisin, G. O. *Yoruba Warlords of the Nineteenth Century*, Trenton, NJ: Africa World Press, 2001.

Faria, Sara Oliveira. "Irmãos de cor, de caridade e de crença: a Irmandade do Rosário do Pelourinho na Bahia do século XIX." MA thesis, Universidade Federal da Bahia, 1997.

Faria, Sheila de Castro. *A colônia em movimento: fortuna e família no cotidiano colonial*. Rio de Janeiro: Nova Fronteira, 1998.

Farias, Juliana B., Gomes, Flávio, and Soares, Carlos Eugênio L. *No labirinto das nações: africanos e identidades no Rio de Janeiro, século XIX*. Rio de Janeiro: Arquivo Nacional, 2005.

Ferreira, Jackson. "'Por hoje acaba a lida': suicídio escravo na Bahia (1850–1888)." *Afro-Ásia*, no. 31 (2004): 197–234.

Ferreti, Mundicarmo (ed.). *Pajelança do Maranhão no século XIX: o processo de Amelia Rosa*. São Luís, CMF/FAPEMA, 2004.

Fett, Sharla M. *Working Cures: Healing, Health, and Power on Southern Slave Plantations*. Chapel Hill and London: University of North Carolina Press, 2002.

Fick, Carolyn. *The Making of Haiti: The Saint Domingue Revolution from Below*. Knoxville: University of Tennessee Press, 1990.

Florence Afonso Bandeira. "Entre o cativeiro e a emancipação: a liberdade dos africanos livres no Brasil (1818–1864)." MA thesis, Universidade Federal da Bahia, 2002.

"Nem escravos, nem libertos: os 'africanos livres' na Bahia." *Cadernos do CEAS*, no. 121 (1989): 58–69.

Florentino, Manolo and Góes, José Roberto. *A paz nas senzalas: famílias escravas e tráfico atlântico, c. 1790 – c. 1850*. Rio de Janeiro: Civilização Brasileira, 1997.

Flory, Thomas. *Judge and Jury in Imperial Brazil, 1808–1871: Social Control and Political Stability in the New State*. Austin: University of Texas Press, 1981.

Fraga Filho, Walter. *Encruzilhadas da liberdade: histórias de escravos e libertos na Bahia (1870–1910)*. Campinas: Editora UNICAMP, 2006.

Mendigos, moleques e vadios na Bahia do século XIX. São Paulo: HUCITEC; Salvador: EDUFBA, 1996.

Frank, Zephyr. *Dutra's World: Wealth and Family in Nineteenth-Century Rio de Janeiro*. Albuquerque: University of New Mexico Press, 2004.

Franklin, John Hope and Schweninger, Loren. *In Search of the Promised Land: A Slave Family in the Old South*. New York: Oxford University Press, 2006.

Frazier, Franklin. "The Negro Family in Bahia, Brazil." *American Sociological Review* 7, no. 4 (1942): 465–478.

Fry, Peter, Carrara, Sérgio, and Martins-Costa, Ana Luiza. "Negros e brancos no Carnaval da Velha República." In João José Reis (ed.), *Escravidão e invenção da liberdade: estudos sobre o negro no Brasil*. São Paulo: Brasiliense, 1988, 232–263.

Furtado, Júnia Ferreira. *Chica da Silva e o contratador de diamantes: o outro lado do mito*. São Paulo: Companhia das Letras, 2003.

Gbadamosi, G. O. "Patterns and Developments in Lagos Religious History." In Aderibigbe (ed.), *The Development of an African City*, 173–196.

Gledhill, Sabrina. "Travessias racialistas no Atlântico Negro: reflexões sobre Booker T. Washington e Manuel R. Querino." PhD dissertation, Universidade Federal da Bahia, 2014.

Gomes, Flávio dos Santos. *Histórias de quilombolas: mocambos e comunidades de senzalas no Rio de Janeiro, século XIX*, 2nd ed. São Paulo: Companhia das Letras, 2006.

A Hidra e os pântanos: mocambos, quilombos e comunidades de fugitivos no Brasil (séculos XVII-XIX). São Paulo: Editora da UNESP, 2005.

Experiências atlânticas: ensaios e pesquisas sobre a escravidão e o pós-emancipação no Brasil. Passo Fundo: Editora da UPF, 2003.

Graden, Dale. "'So Much Superstition among these People!': Candomblé and the Dilemas of Afro-Bahian Intellectuals." In Hendrik Kraay (ed.), *Afro-Brazilian Culture and Politics: Bahia, 1790s to 1990s*. Armonk, NY/London: M. E. Sharpe, 1998, 57–73.

From Slavery to Freedom in Brazil: Bahia, 1835–1900. Albuquerque: University of New Mexico Press, 2006.

Graham, Richard. *Feeding the City: From Street Market to Liberal Reform in Salvador, Brazil, 1780-1860*. Austin: University of Texas Press, 2010.

"Nos tumbeiros mais uma vez? O comércio interprovincial de escravos no Brasil." *Afro-Ásia*, no. 27 (2002): 121–160.

Patronage and Politics in Nineteenth-Century Brazil. Stanford, CA: Stanford University Press, 1990.

Graham, Sandra Lauderdale. *Caetana Says No: Women Stories from a Brazilian Slave Society*. Cambridge, UK, and New York: Cambridge University Press, 2002.

Grant, Douglas. *The Fortunate Slave: An Illustration of African Slavery in the Early Eighteenth Century*. London: Oxford University Press, 1968.

Grinberg, Keila. *Liberata, a lei da ambiqüidade: as ações de liberdade da Corte de Apelação do Rio de Janeiro no século XIX*. Rio de Janeiro: Relume Dumará, 1994.

Gudeman, Stephen and Schwartz, Stuart. "Purgando o pecado original: compadrio e batismo de escravos na Bahia no século XVIII." In João José Reis (ed.), *Escravidão e invenção da liberdade: estudos sobre o negro no Brasil.* São Paulo: Brasiliense, 1988, 33–59.

Guedes, Roberto. *Egressos do cativeiro: trabalho, família, aliança e mobilidade social (Porto Feliz, São Paulo, c. 1798 – c. 1850).* Rio de Janeiro: Mauad X/ FAPERJ, 2008.

"De ex-escravo a elite escravista: a trajetória de ascensão social do pardo alferes Joaquim Barbosa Neves (Porto Feliz, São Paulo, século XIX)." In João Luís R. Fragoso, Carla Maria C. de Almeida, and Antonio Carlos J. de Sampaio (eds.), *Conquistadores e negociantes: histórias de elites no Antigo Regime nos trópicos.* Rio de Janeiro: Civilização Brasileira, 2007, 337–376.

Hall, Robert. "Savoring Africa in the New World." In Herman J. Viola and Carolyn Margolis (eds.), *Seeds of Change.* Washington and London: Smithsonian Institute, 1991, 161–171.

Harding, Rachael E. *A Refuge in Thunder: Candomblé and Alternative Spaces of Blackness.* Bloomington: Indiana University Press, 2000.

Hébrard, Jean. "Esclavage et dénomination: imposition et appropriation d'un nom chez les esclaves de la Bahia au XIXe siècle." *Cahiers du Brésil Contemporain,* nos. 53–54 (2003): 31–92.

Idowu, E. Bolaji. *Olódùmarè: God in Yoruba Belief.* London: Longmans, 1962.

Jeha, Silvana Cassab. "Ganhar a vida: uma história do barbeiro africano José Dutra e sua família: Rio de Janeiro, século XIX." In Ângela Porto (ed.), *Doenças e escravidão: sistema de saúde e práticas terapêuticas.* Rio de Janeiro: Casa Oswaldo Cruz/Fiocruz, available on CD-ROM, 2007.

Johnson, Marion. "The Cowrie Currencies of West Africa," Part I, *The Journal of African History,* 11, no. 1 (1970): 17–49.

"The Cowrie Currencies of West Africa," Part II, 11, no. 3 (1970): 331–353.

July, Robert. *A History of the African People,* 2nd ed. New York: Charles Scribner's Sons, 1974.

Kadra, Haouaria. *Jugurtha, un berbère contre Rome.* Paris: Arléa, 2005.

Klein, Herbert. *The Middle Passage: Comparative Studies in the Atlantic Slave Trade.* Princeton, NJ: Princeton University Press, 1978.

Kraay, Hendrik. "Muralhas da independência e liberdade do Brasil: a participação popular nas lutas políticas (Bahia, 1820–25)." In Jurandir Malerba (ed.), *A Independência brasileira: novas dimensões.* Rio de Janeiro: Editora FGV, 2006, 303–341.

"'Em outra coisa não falavam os pardos, cabras, e crioulos': o recrutamento de escravos na guerra da independência na Bahia." *Revista Brasileira de História* 22, no. 43 (2002): 109–128.

"Entre o Brasil e a Bahia: as comemorações do Dois de Julho em Salvador no século XIX." *Afro-Ásia,* no. 23 (2000): 49–88.

"'Ao abrigo da farda': o exército brasileiro e os escravos fugidos, 1800–1888." *Afro-Ásia,* no. 17 (1996): 29–56.

"'As Terrifying as Unexpected': The Bahian Sabinada, 1837–1838." *The Hispanic American Historical Review,* no. 72 (1992): 501–527.

Lamounier, Maria Lúcia. *Da escravidão ao trabalho livre: a lei de locação de serviços de 1879*. Campinas: Papirus, 1988.

Landes, Ruth. *A cidade das mulheres*. Rio de Janeiro: Civilização Brasileira, 1967.

Lara, Silvia Hunold. "Sedas, panos e balangandãs: o traje de senhoras e escravas nas cidades do Rio de Janeiro e de Salvador (século XVIII)." In Maria Beatriz Nizza da Silva (ed.), *Brasil: colonização e escravidão*. Rio de Janeiro: Nova Fronteira, 2000, 177–191.

Campos da violência escravos e senhores na capitania do Rio de Janeiro. Rio de Janeiro: Paz e Terra, 1988.

Law, Robin. "Francisco Felix de Souza in West Africa, 1820–1849." In José C. Curto and Paul E. Lovejoy (eds). *Enslaving Connections: Changing Cultures of Africa and Brazil during the Era of the Slave Trade*. Amherst, NY: Humanity Books, 2004, 187–211.

"A comunidade brasileira de Uidá e os últimos anos do tráfico atlântico de escravos, 1850–66." *Afro-Ásia*, no. 27 (2002): 41–77.

"Trade and Politics behind the Slave Coast: The Lagoon Traffic and the Rise of Lagos, 1500–1800." *Journal of African History*, no. 24 (1983): 321–348.

"The Career of Adele at Lagos and Badagry, c. 1807 – c. 1837." *Journal of the Historical Society of Nigeria* 9, no. 2 (1978): 35–59.

The Oyo Empire, c. 1600 – c. 1836: A West African Imperialism in the Era of the Atlantic Slave Trade. Oxford: Oxford University Press, 1977.

"The Chronology of the Yoruba Wars of the Early Nineteenth Century: A Reconsideration." *Journal of the Historical Society of Nigeria* 5, no. 2 (1970): 211–222.

and Mann, Kristin. "West Africa and the Atlantic Community: The Case of the Slave Coast." *The William and Mary Quarterly* 56, no. 2 (1999): 307–334.

Leal, Maria das Graças de Andrade. *Manuel Querino entre letras e lutas: Bahia, 1851-1923*. São Paulo: Annablume, 2009.

Le Herrissé, A. *L'Ancien Royaume du Dahomey: moeurs, religion, histoire*. Paris: Émile Larose Libraire-Editeur, 1911.

Leite, Douglas G. *Sabinos e diversos: emergências políticas e projetos de poder na revolta baiana de 1837*. Salvador: EGBA/Fundação Pedro Calmon, 2007.

Lima, Vivaldo da Costa. *A família-de-santo nos candomblés jeje-nagôs da Bahia*. Salvador: Corrupio, 2003.

"O candomblé da Bahia na década de 30." In Waldir Freitas Oliveira and Vivaldo da Costa Lima (eds.), *Cartas de Édison Carneiro a Artur Ramos*. Salvador: Corrupio, 1987, 37–73.

Lloyd, P. C. "The Yoruba Lineage." *Africa* 25, no. 3 (1955): 235–251.

"Osifekunde of Ijebu." In Curtin (ed.), *Africa Remembered*, 217–288.

Lopes, Juliana Sezerdello Crespim. "Identidades políticas e raciais na Sabinada (Bahia, 1837–1838)." MA thesis, Universidade de São Paulo, 2008.

Lovejoy, Paul E. "Biography as Source Material: Towards a Biographical Archive of Enslaved Africans." In Robin Law (ed.), *Source Material for Studying the*

Slave Trade and the African Diaspora. Stirling: Centre of Commonwealth Studies, 1997, 119–140.

"The Central Sudan and the Atlantic Slave Trade." In Robert W. Harms et al. (eds.). *Paths toward the Past: African Historical Essays in Honor of Jan Vansina*. Atlanta, GA: African Studies Association, 1994, 345–370.

Transformations in Slavery: A History of Slavery in Africa. Cambridge, Cambridge University Press, 1983.

Lovejoy, Paul E. and Richardson, David. "The Business of Slaving: Pawnship in Western Africa, c. 1600–1800," *Journal of African History* 42, no. 1 (2001): 67–89.

"Trust, Pawnship, and Atlantic History: The Institutional Foundation of the Old Calabar Slave Trade." *The American Historical Review* 104, no. 2 (1999): 333–355.

Lühning, Angela. "'Acabe com este santo, Pedrito vem aí'..." *Revista USP*, no. 28 (1995–1996): 194–220.

Machado, Maria Helena P. T. *Crime e escravidão: trabalho, luta, resistência nas lavouras paulistas, 1830–1888*. São Paulo: Brasiliense, 1987.

Maestri Filho, Mário José. *Depoimentos de escravos brasileiros*. São Paulo: Ícone, 1988.

Maggie, Yvonne. *Medo do feitiço: relações entre magia e poder no Brasil*. Rio de Janeiro: Arquivo Nacional, 1992.

Maia, Moacir Rodrigo de Castro. "O apadrinhamento de africanos em Minas colonial: o (re)encontro na América (Mariana, 1715–1750)." *Afro-Ásia*, no. 36 (2007): 39–80.

Mamigonian, Beatriz Galotti. "Africanos livres: tráfico, trabalho e direito no Brasil oitocentista" (2014, forthcoming).

"Do que o 'preto mina' é capaz: etnia e resistência entre africanos livres." *Afro-Ásia*, no. 24 (2000): 78–79.

Mann, Kristin. *Slavery and the Birth of an African City: Lagos, 1760–1900*. Bloomington: University of Indiana Press, 2007.

"Shifting Paradigms in the Study of the African Diaspora and of the Atlantic History and Culture." In Kristin Mann and Edna G. Bay (eds.), *Rethinking the African Diáspora: The Making of a Black Atlantic World in the Bight of Benin and Brazil*. London: Frank Cass, 2001, 3–21.

"The World the Slave Traders Made: Lagos, c. 1760–1850," in Paul E. Lovejoy (ed.), *Identifying Enslaved Africans: Proceeding of the UNESCO/ SSHRCC Summer Institute*. Toronto: York University, 1997.

Marquese, Rafael de Bivar. "A dinâmica da escravidão no Brasil: resistência, tráfico negreiro e alforrias." *Novos Estudos*, no. 74 (2006): 107–123.

Matory, J. Lorand. *Black Atlantic Religion: Tradition, Transnationalism, and Matriarchy in the Afro-Brazilian Candomblé*. Princeton, NJ: Princeton University Press, 2003.

Sex and the Empire that Never Was: Gender and the Politics of Metaphor in Ọ̀yọ́ Yoruba Religion. New York and Oxford: Berghahn Books, 1994.

Mattos, Waldemar. "A Bahia de Castro Alves." *Anais do APEBA*, no. 30 (1947): 205–303.

Mattoso, Kátia M. de Queirós. *Família e sociedade na Bahia no século XIX.* Salvador: Corrupio, 1988.

Être esclave au Brésil XVe-XIXe Siècle. Paris: Hachette, 1979.

Testamentos de escravos libertos na Bahia no século XIX: uma fonte para o estudo de mentalidades. Salvador: Centro de Estudos Baianos, 1979.

Bahia: a cidade do Salvador e seu mercado no século XIX. São Paulo: HUCITEC, 1978.

"A Propósito de cartas de alforria." *Anais de História*, no. 4 (1972): 23–52.

Da revolução dos alfaiates à riqueza dos baianos no século XIX. Salvador: Corrupio, 2004.

"The Manumission of Slaves in Brazil in the Eighteenth and Nineteenth Centuries." *Diogenes* 45, no. 179 (1997): 117–138.

Bahia, século XIX: uma província no Império. Rio de Janeiro: Nova Fronteira, 1992.

Mattoso, Kátia M. de Queirós, Herbert S. Klein, and Stanley L. Engerman. "Notas sobre as tendências e padrões dos preços de alforrias na Bahia, 1819–1888." In João José Reis (ed.), *Escravidão e invenção da liberdade: estudos sobre o negro no Brasil.* São Paulo: Brasiliense, 1988, 60–72.

Mclaurin, Melton A. *Celia, a Slave.* New York: Avon Books, 1991.

Mintz, Sidney and Price, Richard. *The Birth of African-American Culture: An Anthropological Perspective.* Boston, MA: Beacon Press, 1992.

An Anthropological Approach to the Afro-American Past: A Caribbean Perspective. Philadelphia, PA: Institute for the Study of Human Issues, 1976.

Monfopuga-Nicolas, Jacqueline. *Ambivalence et Culte de Possession: Contribution à l'Étude du Bori Haoussa.* Paris: Anthropos, 1972.

Moreira, Paulo Roberto Staudt. *Os cativos e os homens de bem: experiências negras no espaço urbano.* Porto Alegre: EST Edições, 2003.

Faces da liberdade, máscaras do cativeiro: experiências de liberdade e escravidão percebidas através das cartas de alforria – Porto Alegre (1858–1888). Porto Alegre: EDIPUCRS, 1996.

Mott, Luiz. *Rosa Egipcíaca, uma santa africana no Brasil.* Rio de Janeiro: Bertrand Brasil, 1993.

Museu AFROBRASIL. *Theodoro Sampaio, o sábio negro entre os brancos.* São Paulo: Museu AfroBrasil, 2008.

Nascimento, Maria Amélia Vieira. *Dez freguesias da cidade do Salvador.* Salvador: Fundação Cultural do Estado da Bahia, 1986.

Nishida, Mieko. *Slavery & Identity: Ethnicity, Gender, and Race in Salvador, Brazil, 1808–1888.* Bloomington and Indianapolis: Indiana University Press, 2003.

"Manumission and Ethnicity in Urban Slavery: Salvador, Brazil, 1808–1888." *The Hispanic American Historical Review* 73, no. 3 (1993): 361–391.

Ogundiran, Akinwumi. "Of Small Things Remembered: Beads, Cowries, and Cultural Translations of the Atlantic Experience in Yorubaland." *International Journal of African Historical Studies* 35, no. 2–3 (2002): 427–457.

Ojo, G. J. Afolabi. *Yoruba Culture: A Geographical Analysis*. Ile Ife and London: University of Ife and University of London Press, 1966.

Ojo, Olatunji. "The Organization of the Atlantic Slave Trade in Yorubaland, ca. 1777 to ca. 1856." *The International Journal of African Historical Studies*, 41, no. 1 (2008): 77–100.

"Child Slaves in Pre-colonial Nigeria, c. 1725–1860." *Slavery & Abolition*, 33, no. 3 (2012): 417–434.

Parés, Luís Nicolau. "Milicianos, barbeiros e traficantes numa irmandade católica de africanos minas e jejes (Bahia, 1770–1830)", *Tempo*, no. 20 (2014): 1-32 <http://www.historia.uff.br/tempo/site/>

"The 'Nagôization' Process in Bahian Candomblé." In Falola and Childs (eds.), *Yoruba Diaspora*, 185–208.

A formação do candomblé: história e ritual da nação jeje na Bahia. Campinas: Editora da UNICAMP, 2006.

Oliveira, Anderson José Machado de. *Devoção negra: santos e catequese no Brasil colonial*. Rio de Janeiro: Quartet/FAPERJ, 2008.

Oliveira, Maria Inês Côrtes de. "The Reconstruction of Ethnicity in Bahia: The Case of the Nagô in the Nineteenth Century." In Paul Lovejoy and David Trotman (eds.), *Trans-Atlantic Dimension of the African Diaspora*. London and New York: Continuum, 2003, 158–180.

"Quem eram os 'negros da Guiné'? A origem dos africanos na Bahia." *Afro-Ásia*, no. 19/20 (1997): 37–73.

"Viver e morrer no meio dos seus: nações e comunidades africanas na Bahia do século XIX." *Revista USP*, no. 28 (1995–1996): 174–193.

"Retrouver une identité: jeux sociaux des africains de Bahia (vers 1750 – vers 1890)." PhD dissertation, Université de Paris IV (Sorbonne), 1992.

O liberto: seu mundo e os outros. São Paulo: Corrupio, 1988.

Oliveira, Waldir Freitas. *História de um banco: o Banco Econômico*. Salvador: Museu Eugênio Teixeira Leal, 1993.

Oroge, E. Adeniyi. "Iwofa: An Historical Survey of the Yoruba Institution of Indenture." *African Economic History*, no. 14 (1985): 75–106.

"The Institution of Slavery in Yorubaland, with Particular Reference to the Nineteenth Century." PhD dissertation, University of Birmingham, 1971.

Ott, Carlos. *Formação étnica da cidade do Salvador*, 2 vols. Salvador: Manú, 1955.

Painter, Nell Irvin. *Sojourner Truth: A Life, a Symbol*. New York and London: Norton, 1996.

Paiva Eduardo França. "Celebrando a alforria: amuletos e práticas culturais entre as mulheres negras e mestiças do Brasil." In Ístvan Jancsó and Íris

Kantor (eds.), *Festa: cultura e sociabilidade na América portuguesa*. São Paulo: Hucitec/Edusp/Imprensa Oficial/Fapesp, 2001, 505–518.

Park, George K. "Divination and Its Social Contexts." *The Journal of the Royal Anthropological Institute of Great Britain and Ireland*, no. 93, part. 2 (1963): 195–209.

Peel, J. D. Y. *Religious Encounter and the Making of the Yoruba*. Bloomington and Indianapolis: Indiana University Press, 2000.

"The Cultural Work of Yoruba Ethnogenesis." In E. Tonkin, E. M. McDonald, and M. Chapman, (eds.), *History and Ethnicity*. London and New York: Routledge & Kegan Paul, 1989, 198–215.

Pesavento, Sandra Jatahy. "Negros feitiços." In Artur César Isaia (ed.), *Orixás e espíritos: o debate interdisciplinar na pesquisa contemporânea*. Uberlândia: EDUFU, 2006, 129–152.

Pierson, Donald. *Brancos e pretos na Bahia*. São Paulo: Companhia Editora Nacional, 1971.

Pinho, Wanderley de. *História de um engenho do Recôncavo*, 2nd ed. São Paulo: Companhia Editora Nacional; Brasília: Instituto Nacional do Livro, 1982.

"Discurso proferido pelo Dr. Wanderley de Araújo Pinho na sessão solemne realizada no Conselho Municipal de Santo Amaro, a 14 de junho de 1922, para solemnisar o início da participação da Villa de S. Amaro na campanha da Independência." *Revista do Instituto Geográfico e Histórico da Bahia*, no. 48 (1923): 1–60.

Pinto, Tânia Maria de Jesus. "Os negros cristãos católicos e o culto aos santos na Bahia colonial." MA thesis, Universidade Federal da Bahia, 2000.

Price, Richard. "O milagre da crioulização: retrospectiva." *Estudos Afro-Asiáticos* 25, no. 3 (2003): 383–419.

Puntoni, Pedro. *Os recenseamentos gerais do Brasil no século XIX: 1872 e 1890*. São Paulo: CEBRAP – Centro Brasileiro de Análise e Planejamento, CD-ROM s/d.

Rediker, Marcus. *The Slave Ship: A Human History*. New York: Viking, 2007.

Reginaldo, Lucilene. *Os Rosários dos angolas: irmandades de africanos e crioulos na Bahia setecentista*. São Paulo: Alameda, 2011.

Reis, Adriana Dantas. *Cora: lições de comportamento feminino na Bahia do século XIX*. Salvador: Centro de Estudos Baianos da UFBA, 2000.

Reis, Isabel Cristina F. dos. "A família negra no tempo da escravidão, 1850–1888." PhD dissertation, UNICAMP, 2007.

Reis, João José. "From Slave to Wealthy Freedman: The Story of Manoel Joaquim Ricardo." In Lisa Lindsay and John Sweet (eds.), *Biography and the Black Atlantic*. Philadelphia: University of Pennsylvania Press, 2014, 131–145.

"Social Mobility among Slaves in Brazil," paper presented at the seminar *Heterodoxies*. University of Vanderbilt, 2013.

"Candomblé and Slave Resistance." In Roger Sansi and Luis Nicolau Parés (eds.), *Witchcraft in the Luso-Atlantic World*. Chicago, IL: University of Chicago Press, 2011, 55–74.

"Arabonam, um sacerdote de Xangô na Bahia oitocentista" (2008, unpublished paper).

"Sacerdotes, devotos e clientes no candomblé da Bahia oitocentista." In Artur César Isaia (ed.). *Orixás e espíritos*. Uberlândia: Editora da Universidade Federal de Uberlândia, 2006, 57–98.

Rebelião escrava no Brasil: a história do levante dos malês em 1835. São Paulo: Companhia das Letras, 2003.

"Ethnic Politics among Africans in Nineteenth-Century Bahia." In Lovejoy and Trotman (eds.), *Trans-Atlantic Dimension*, 240–264.

"Tambores e tremores: a festa negra na Bahia na primeira metade do século XIX." In Maria Clementina Pereira Cunha (ed.), *Carnavais e outras f(r) estas: ensaios de história social da cultura*. Campinas: Editora da UNICAMP, 2002, 101–155.

"De olho no canto: trabalho de rua na Bahia na véspera da Abolição." *Afro-Ásia*, no. 24 (2000): 199–242.

"A greve negra de 1857 na Bahia." *Revista USP*, no. 18 (1993): 6–29.

A morte é uma festa: ritos fúnebres e revolta popular no Brasi do século XIX. São Paulo: Companhia das Letras, 1992.

"Nas malhas do poder escravista: a invasão do candomblé do Accú." In João Reis and Eduardo Silva, *Negociação e conflito: a resistência negra no Brasil escravista*. São Paulo: Companhia das Letras, 1989, 32–61.

"População e rebelião: notas sobre a população escrava na Bahia na primeira metade do século XIX." *Revista das Ciências Humanas*, no. 1 (1980): 148–149.

Reis, João José, and Gomes, Flávio dos Santos. *Liberdade por um fio: história dos quilombos no Brasil*. São Paulo: Companhia das Letras, 1999.

Reis, João José, and Mamigonian, Beatriz. "Nagô and Mina: The Yoruba Diaspora in Brazil." In Toyin Falola and Matt Childs (eds.), *The Yoruba Diaspora in the Atlantic World*. Bloomington and Indianapolis: Indiana University Press, 2004, 77–110.

Reis, João José, and Silveira, Renato da. "Violência repressiva e engenho político na Bahia do tempo dos escravos." *Comunicações do ISER* 5, no. 21 (1986): 61–66.

Reis, João José, Gomes, Flávio, and Carvalho, Marcus. *O alufá Rufino: tráfico, escravidão e liberdade no Atlântico negro (c. 1822 – c. 1853)*. São Paulo: Companhia das Letras, 2010.

Rios, Ana Lugão and Mattos, Hebe. *Memórias do cativeiro: família, trabalho e cidadania no pós-abolição*, Rio de Janeiro: Civilização Brasileira, 2005.

Rios, Venétia Durando Braga. "O Asylo de São João de Deos – as faces da loucura." PhD dissertation, PUC/São Paulo, 2006.

Sachnine, Michka. *Dictionaire usuel yorùbá-français*. Paris/Ibadan: Karthala/ IFRA, 1997.

Sahlins, Marshall. "Two or Three Things that I Know about Culture." *Journal of the Royal Anthropological Institute* 5, no. 3 (1999): 399–421.

Sampaio, Consuelo Novaes. *50 anos de urbanização: Salvador no século XIX*. Rio de Janeiro: Versal, 2005.

Sampaio, Gabriela dos Reis. *Juca Rosa: um pai-de-santo na Corte imperial*. Rio de Janeiro: Arquivo Nacional, 2009.

"Tenebrosos mistérios: Juca Rosa e as relações entre crença e cura no Rio de Janeiro imperial." In Sidney Chalhoub, Vera Regina B. Marques, Gabriela dos Reis Sampaio, and Carlos Roberto Galvão Sobrinho (eds.), *Artes e ofícios de curar no Brasil*. Campinas: Editora Unicamp, 2003, 387–426.

Santos, Jocélio Teles dos. "Candomblés e espaço urbano na Bahia do século XIX." *Estudos Afro-Asiáticos*, 27, nos. 1–3 (2005): 205–226.

Divertimentos estrondosos: batuques e sambas no século XIX." In Livio Sansone and Jocélio T. dos Santos (eds.), *Ritmos em trânsito: socioantropologia da música baiana*. Salvador: Projeto A Cor da Bahia, 1997, 15–38.

Ex-escrava proprietária de escrava (um caso de sevícia na Bahia do século XIX). Salvador: Programa de Estudos do Negro na Bahia – PENBA/FFCH/ UFBA, 1991.

Santos, Ynaê Lopes dos. *Além da senzala: arranjos escravos de moradia no Rio de Janeiro (1808–1850)*. São Paulo: FAPESP/HUCITEC, 2010.

Schwab, William B. "Kinship and Lineage among the Yoruba." *Africa* 25, no. 4 (1955): 352–374.

Schwarcz Lilia Moritz. *Retrato em branco e negro: jornais, escravos e cidadãos em São Paulo no final do século XIX*. São Paulo: Companhia das Letras, 1987.

Schwartz, Stuart. *Slaves, Peasants, and Rebels: Reconsidering Brazilian Slavery*. Urbana and Chicago: Illinois University Press, 1992.

Sugar Plantations in the Formation of Brazilian Society: Bahia, 1535–1835. Cambridge: Cambridge University Press, 1985.

"The Manumission of Slaves in Colonial Brazil: Bahia, 1684–1745." *The Hispanic American Historical Review* 54, no. 4 (1974): 603–635.

Silva, Alberto da Costa e. "Cartas de um embaixador de Onim." *Cadernos do CHDD* 4, no. 6 (2005): 195–205.

Francisco Félix de Souza, mercador de escravos. Rio de Janeiro: Nova Fronteira, 2004.

A manilha e o libambo: a África e a escravidão de 1500 a 1700. Rio de Janeiro: Nova Fronteira, 2002.

Silva, Cândido da Costa e. *Os segadores e a messe: o clero oitocentista na Bahia*. Salvador: EDUFBA, 2000.

Silva, Eduardo. *Dom Oba II d'África, o príncipe do povo: vida, tempo e pensamento de um homem de cor*. São Paulo: Companhia das Letras, 1997.

Silva, Ricardo Tadeu Caires. "Caminhos e descaminhos da abolição: escravos, senhores e direito nas últimas décadas da escravidão (1850–1888)." PhD dissertation, Universidade Federal do Paraná, 2007.

"Memórias do tráfico ilegal de escravos nas ações de liberdade: Bahia, 1885–1888." *Afro-Ásia*, no. 35 (2007): 37–82.

Silva, Simone Trindade. "Referencialidade e representação: um resgate do modo de construção de sentidos nas pencas de balangandãs a partir da coleção do Museu Carlos Costa Pinto." MA thesis, Universidade Federal da Bahia School of Fine Arts, 2005.

Silveira, Renato da. *O candomblé da Barroquinha: processo de constituição do primeiro terreiro baiano de Keto*. Salvador: Maianga, 2006.

Slenes, Robert W. "The Brazilian Internal Slave Trade, 1850–1888: Regional Economies, Slave Experience and the Politics of a Peculiar Market." In Walter Johnson (ed.), *The Chattel Principle: Internal Slave Trades in the Americas*. New Haven, CT: Yale University Press, 2005, 325–370.

Na senzala uma flor: esperanças e recordações na formação da família escrava – Brasil Sudeste, século XIX. Rio de Janeiro: Nova Fronteira, 1999.

"'Malungu n'goma vem!': África coberta e descoberta no Brasil," *Revista USP*, no. 12 (1991–1992): 48–67.

Smith, Robert S. *Kingdoms of the Yoruba*. London: Methuen, 1969.

Soares, Carlos Eugênio Líbano. *Zungú: rumor de muitas vozes*. Rio de Janeiro: Arquivo Público do Estado do Rio de Janeiro, 1998.

Soares, Cecília Moreira. *Mulher negra na Bahia no século XIX*. Salvador: EDUNEB, 2007.

"As ganhadeiras: mulher e resistência negra em Salvador no Século XIX." *Afro-Ásia*, no. 17 (1996): 57–71.

"Resistência negra e religião: a repressão ao candomblé de Paramerim, 1853." *Estudos Afro-Asiáticos*, no. 23 (1992): 133–142.

Soares, Márcio de Souza. *A remissão do cativeiro: a dádiva da alforria e o governo dos escravos nos Campos dos Goitacases, c. 1750 – c. 1830*. Rio de Janeiro: Apicuri, 2009.

Soares, Mariza de Carvalho (ed.) *Rotas atlânticas da diáspora africana: da Baía do Benim ao Rio de Janeiro*. Rio de Janeiro: EDUFF, 2007.

"From Gbe to Yoruba: Ethnic Change in the Mina Nation in Rio de Janeiro." In Falola and Childs (eds.), *The Yoruba Diaspora in the Atlantic World*, 231–247.

Souza, Laura de Mello e. "Revisitando o calundu." In Lina Gorenstein and Maria Luiza Tucci Carneiro (eds.) *Ensaios sobre a intolerância – inquisição, marronismo e anti-semitismo*. São Paulo: Humanitas, 2002, 293–317.

O Diabo e a Terra de Santa Cruz: feitiçaria e religiosidade popular no Brasil colonial, São Paulo: Companhia das Letras, 1986.

Souza, Paulo César. *A Sabinada: a revolta separatista da Bahia*. São Paulo: Brasiliense, 1987.

Sparks, Randy J. *The Two Princes of Calabar: An Eighteenth-Century Odyssey.* Cambridge, MA, and London: Harvard University Press, 2004.

Stewart, Charles (ed.). *Creolization: History, Ethnography, Theory.* Walnut Creek, CA: Left Coast Press, 2007.

Strickrodt, Silke. "'Afro-Brazilians' of the Western Slave Coast in the Nineteenth Century." In José C. Curto and Paul E. Lovejoy (orgs), *Enslaving Connections*, 213–244.

Sweet, James. *Domingos Álvares, African Healing, and the Intellectual History of the Atlantic World.* Chapel Hill: University of North Carolina Press, 2011.

Recreating Africa: Culture, Kinship and Religion in the African-Portuguese World, 1441–1770. Chapel Hill and London: University of North Carolina Press, 2003.

Tavares, Luís Henrique Dias. *Independência do Brasil na Bahia.* Salvador: EDUFBA, 2005.

Thomas, Keith. *Religion and the Decline of Magic.* Harmondsworth: Penguin, 1971.

Torres, Mario. "Os Sodrés." *Revista do Instituto Genealógico da Bahia*, no. 7 (1952): 89–148.

"Os morgados do Sodré." *Revista do Instituto Genealógico da Bahia*, no. 5 (1951): 9–34.

Trindade, Claudia Moraes. "A reforma prisional na Bahia oitocentista". *Revista de História*, n° 158 (2008): 157–198.

Trouillot, Michel-Rolph. *Silencing the Past: Power and the Production of History.* Boston, MA: Beacon Press, 1995.

Vainfas, Ronaldo, Santos, Georgina Silva dos, and Neves, Guilherme Pereira (eds.). *Retratos do império: trajetórias individuais no mundo português nos séculos XVI a XIX.* Rio de Janeiro: EDUFF, 2006.

Vasconcelos, Christiane Silva de. "O circuito social da fotografia da gente negra, Salvador, 1860–1916." MA thesis, Universidade Federal da Bahia, 2006.

Verger, Pierre. *Ewé: o uso das plantas na sociedade iorubá.* São Paulo: Companhia das Letras, 1995.

Os libertos: sete caminhos na liberdade de escravos da Bahia no século XIX. Salvador: Corrupio, 1992.

Flux et reflux de la traite des nègres entre le golfe de Benin et Bahia de Todos os Santos. Paris: Mouton, 1968.

Notes sur le culte des Orisa et Vodun à Bahia, la Baie de Tous les Saints, au Brésil, et l'ancienne Côte des Esclaves en Afrique. Dakar: IFAN, 1957.

"Influence du Brésil au Golfe du Bénin." In *Les Afro-Américains*. Mémoires de l'Institut Français d'Afrique Noire, no. 27. Dakar: IFAN, 1952, 11–104.

Wildberger, Arnold. *Os presidentes da província da Bahia, efectivos e interinos, 1824–1899.* Salvador: Typographia Beneditina, 1949.

Wimberley, Fayette. "The Expansion of Afro-Bahian Religious Practices in Nineteenth-Century Cachoeira." In Hendrik Kraay (ed.), *Afro-Brazilian*

Culture and Politics: Bahia, 1790s to 1990s. Armonk, NY: M. E. Sharpe, 1998, 74–89.

Wissenbach, Maria Cristina. "A mercantilização da magia na urbanização de São Paulo, 1910–1940." *Revista de História*, 150 (2004): 11–39.

Sonhos africanos, vivências ladinas: escravos e forros em São Paulo (1850–1880). São Paulo: Hucitec, 1998.

"Ritos de magia e de sobrevivência. Sociabilidades e práticas mágico-religiosas no Brasil (1890–1940)." PhD dissertation, Universidade de São Paulo, 1997.

Xavier, Regina. *Religiosidade e escravidão, século XIX: mestre Tito.* Porto Alegre: Editora da UFRGS, 2008.

Ximenes, Cristiana F. Lyrio. "Joaquim Pereira Marinho: perfil de um contrabandista de escravos na Bahia, 1828–1887." MA thesis, Universidade Federal da Bahia, 1999.

Acknowledgments

A long list of people and institutions helped me in many ways in the making of this book.

Cândido Domingues, Neuracy de Azevedo Moreira, Carlos Francisco da Silva Junior were crucial as research assistants. Lisa Earl Castillo kindly recommended and copied a large number of the documents used here while she was researching her own study on nineteenth-century Candomblé. I also received other documents and printed materials, as well as bibliographical references and further information, from Wlamyra Albuquerque, Adriana dos Reis Alves, Lizir Arcanjo Alves, Bert Barickman, Argemiro Ribeiro de Souza Filho, Flávio dos Santos Gomes, Dale Graden, Hendrik Kraay, Fábio Batista Lima, Kátia Lorena, Cristiana Lyrio, Paulo Roberto Staudt Moreira, Maria Inês Côrtes de Oliveira, Isabel Cristina Ferreira dos Reis, Carlos Santana, Ligia Santana, Jocélio Teles dos Santos, Ricardo Tadeu Caires Silva, Renato da Silveira, Robert Slenes, Carlos Eugênio Líbano Soares, Claudia Trindade, Christiane Vasconcelos, and Maria Cristina Wissenbach. Renato da Silveira and Luis Nicolau Parés read the near-final draft of this book and made detailed and important observations, most of which have been incorporated here.

Most of the people I have just mentioned, and more besides, get together regularly at meetings of the Slavery and the Invention of Freedom research group of the Universidade Federal da Bahia's Graduate Program in History. The heated debates that took place there regarding a paper that was the original inspiration for this book, as well as other papers that I and others presented, were key to developing and maturing the ideas expressed here. Gabriela Sampaio and Jean Hébrard also commented on that paper. Alberto da Costa e Silva, Karin Barber,

Nikolay Dobronravin, Paulo Farias, and Toyin Falola answered my que-
ries and recommended bibliographic references as specialists in African
history. Kristin Mann provided me what were then manuscript chapters
of her excellent book on the city of Lagos, Nigeria, which has since
been published.

Parts of this book have been presented as lectures and discussed at
the University of Michigan (Ann Arbor), Michigan State University
(Lansing), the twenty-sixth conference of the Latin American Studies
Association (LASA), the Universidade Federal de Pernambuco, and
the Universidade de São Paulo, institutions to which I was invited,
respectively, by Sueann Caulfield, Peter Beattie, Linda Lewin, Marcus
Carvalho, and Rafael de Bivar Marquese. The comments made on those
occasions have been extremely valuable.

I would like to thank the staffs of the libraries and archives where I did
research, especially those at the Arquivo Público do Estado da Bahia,
which contains most of the documents utilized here. At the Eugenio
Veiga Laboratory of the Universidade Católica de Salvador, which
competently and devotedly houses the Archives of the Metropolitan
Curia of Salvador, I received valuable assistance when locating church
records from its director, Venétia Durando Rios, and her right hand,
Renata Oliveira. Some of the records in those archives were damaged
and illegible, but I was able to read them on microfilm, now available
online, at the Family History Center of the Church of Latter Day Saints
in Salvador, Bahia.

Lilia Schwarcz, a friend and the publisher of the Brazilian edition,
read and commented on the entire manuscript and helped improve it
considerably. Marta Garcia and her efficient team were responsible for
the painstaking publication of this book in Brazil.

My colleagues in the Department of History of the Universidade
Federal da Bahia took over my teaching duties on several occasions,
freeing me to invest time in this and other projects. This book is partially the result of a larger research project funded by the Conselho
Nacional de Pesquisa e Desenvolvimento (CNPq), the Brazilian research
council, of which I am a Fellow.

Mariângela de Mattos Nogueira was the most constant presence during the writing of this book from the very start. Her careful reading and
intelligent observations considerably improved the final draft. She is
also responsible for the photographs and reproductions of the images
published here.

For the present edition, some parts have been expanded, and new data and bibliographical references introduced or updated. A semester at the David Rockefeller Center for Latin American Studies – DRCLASS at Harvard University, in 2012, was essential to making the changes and revising the translation. I presented a lecture at the DRCLASS summarizing my findings, and the questions that followed gave me the opportunity to think over, refine, or expand some of my arguments. I thank Sabrina Gledhill for being, besides competent, a good translator to work with. The anonymous readers for Cambridge University Press offered valuable comments and advice that I have tried my best to follow in the pages ahead. I also thank Stuart Schwartz for his suggestions to improve the book and his support to have it published in this series. I should also mention Dain Borges, Bert Barickman, and Hendrik Kraay for their advice, and for helping me choose the title of the book – which is not a literal translation of its original Portuguese title – from a few that I had in mind.

This edition was prepared by a patient, friendly, and careful team of copy-editors under the leadership of Kanimozhi Ramamurthy, and I wish to express my appreciation for their good work.

This English-language edition of *Domingos Sodré* was made possible by Daniela Moreau, whose support for the translation of the book also reflects her strong commitment to the dissemination of African and diasporic studies.

NAME INDEX

Subject Index